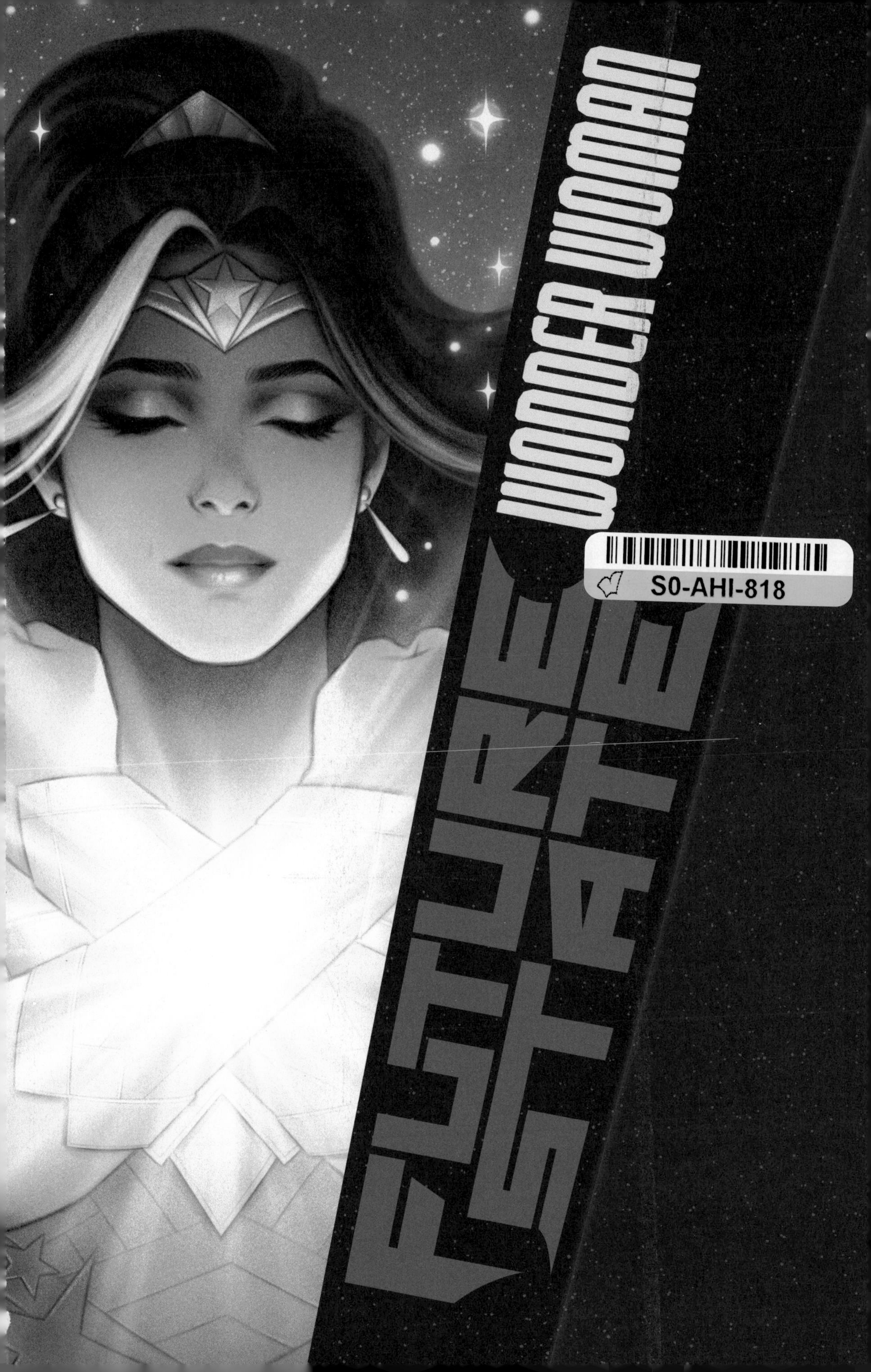
WONDER WOMAN
FUTURE STATE

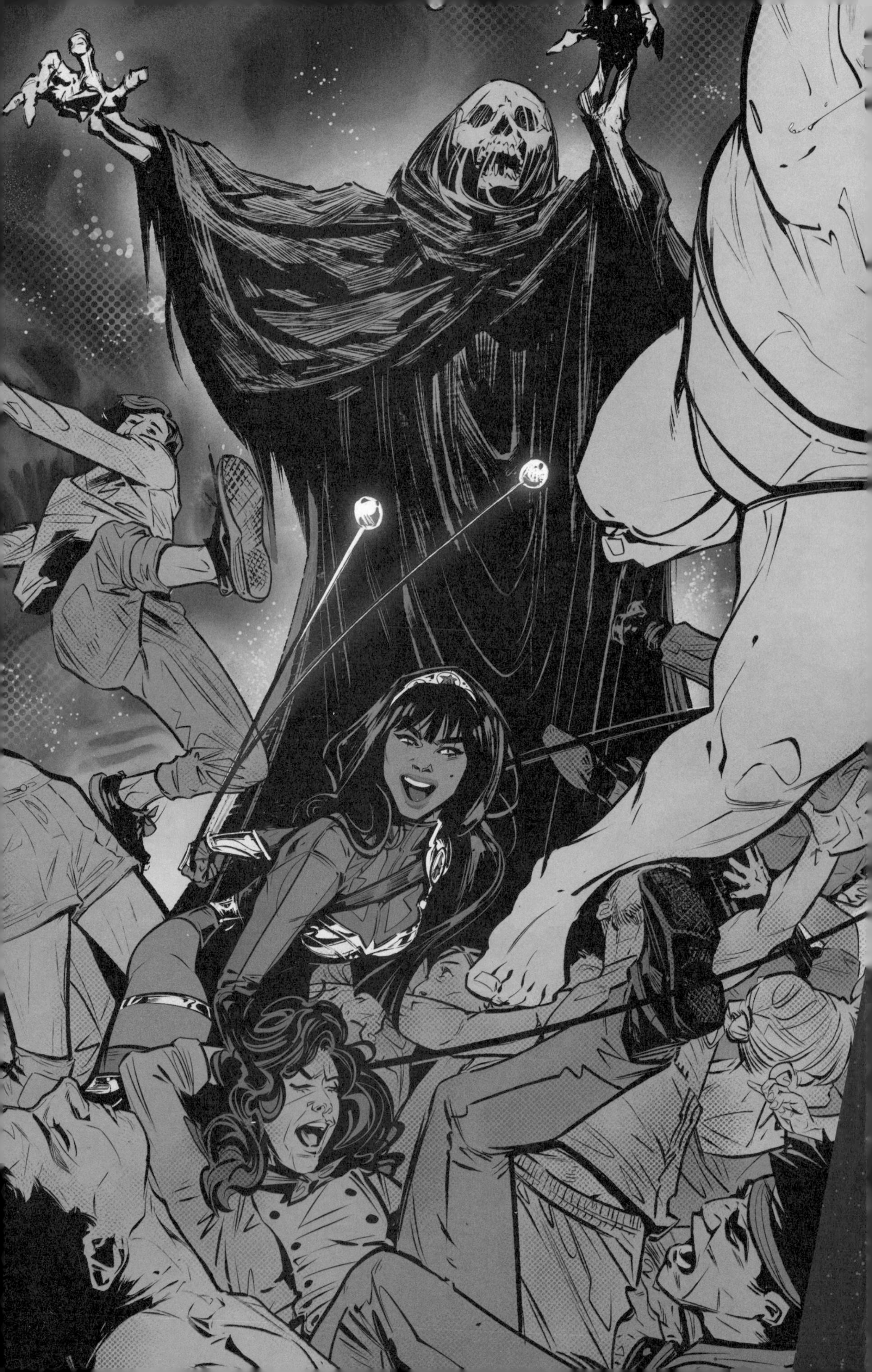

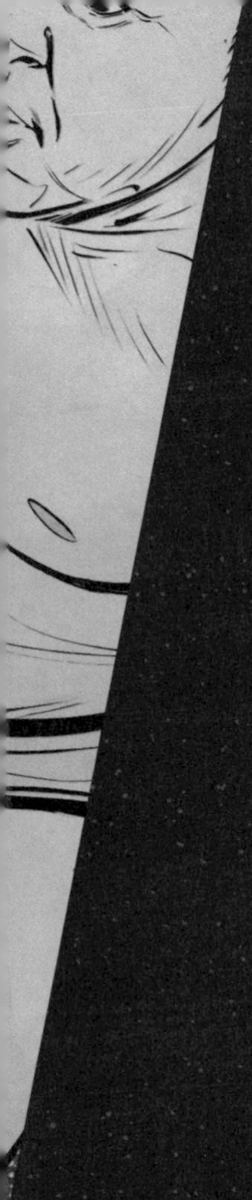

FUTURE STATE
WONDER WOMAN

WRITERS
BECKY CLOONAN
MICHAEL W. CONRAD
JOËLLE JONES
DAN WATTERS
L.L. McKINNEY

PENCILLERS
JEN BARTEL
JOËLLE JONES
LEILA DEL DUCA
ALITHA MARTINEZ

INKERS
JEN BARTEL
JOËLLE JONES
LEILA DEL DUCA
MARK MORALES

COLORISTS
JEN BARTEL
JORDIE BELLAIRE
NICK FILARDI
EMILIO LOPEZ

LETTERERS
PAT BROSSEAU
CLAYTON COWLES
TOM NAPOLITANO
BECCA CAREY

COLLECTION COVER ARTIST
JEN BARTEL

WONDER WOMAN CREATED BY
WILLIAM MOULTON MARSTON

SUPERMAN CREATED BY
JERRY SIEGEL AND JOE SHUSTER.
BY SPECIAL ARRANGEMENT
WITH THE JERRY SIEGEL FAMILY.

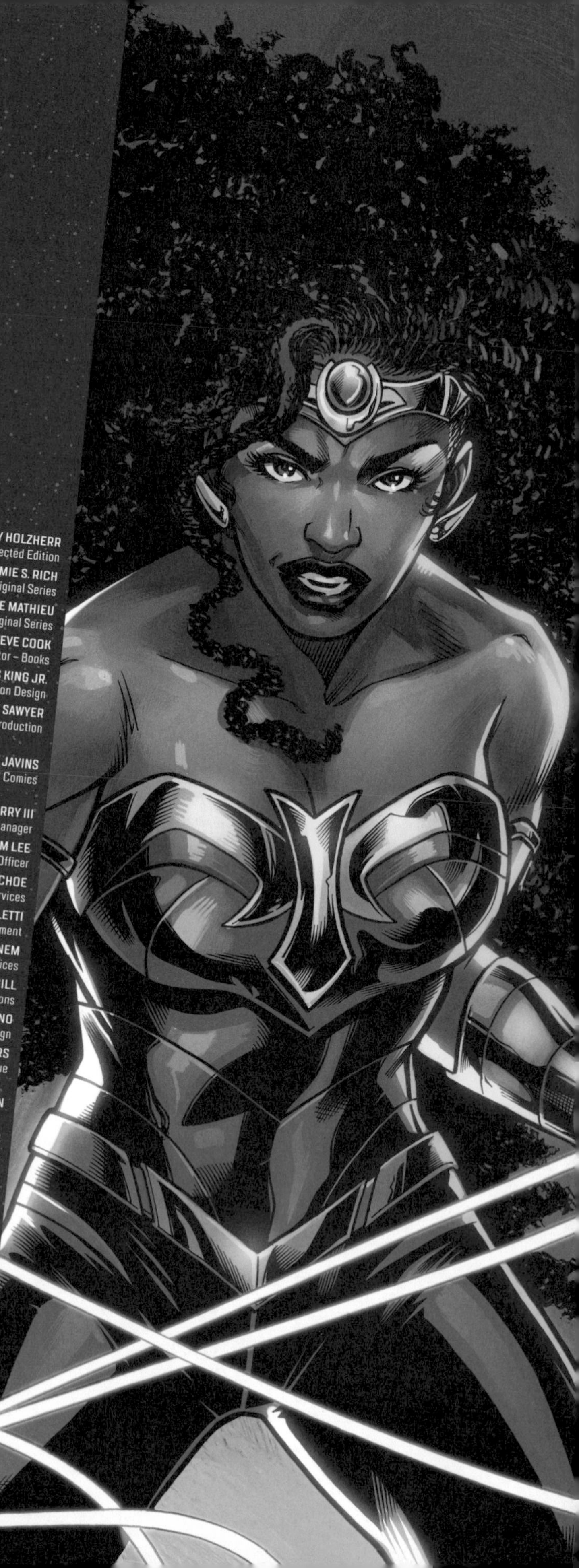

BRITTANY HOLZHERR
Editor – Original Series & Collected Edition
JAMIE S. RICH
Editor – Original Series
BIXIE MATHIEU
Assistant Editor – Original Series
STEVE COOK
Design Director – Books
CURTIS KING JR.
Publication Design
CHRISTY SAWYER
Publication Production

MARIE JAVINS
Editor-in-Chief, DC Comics

DANIEL CHERRY III
Senior VP – General Manager
JIM LEE
Publisher & Chief Creative Officer
JOEN CHOE
VP – Global Brand & Creative Services
DON FALLETTI
VP – Manufacturing Operations & Workflow Management
LAWRENCE GANEM
VP – Talent Services
ALISON GILL
Senior VP – Manufacturing & Operations
NICK J. NAPOLITANO
VP – Manufacturing Administration & Design
NANCY SPEARS
VP – Revenue

FUTURE STATE: WONDER WOMAN

DC Comics, 2900 West Alameda Ave., Burbank, CA 91505
Printed by LSC Communications, Owensville, MO, USA. 6/11/21.
First Printing. ISBN: 978-1-77951-074-7.

Library of Congress Cataloging-in-Publication Data is available.

PEFC Certified
This product is from sustainably managed forests and controlled sources
PEFC
PEFC/29-31-337
www.pefc.org

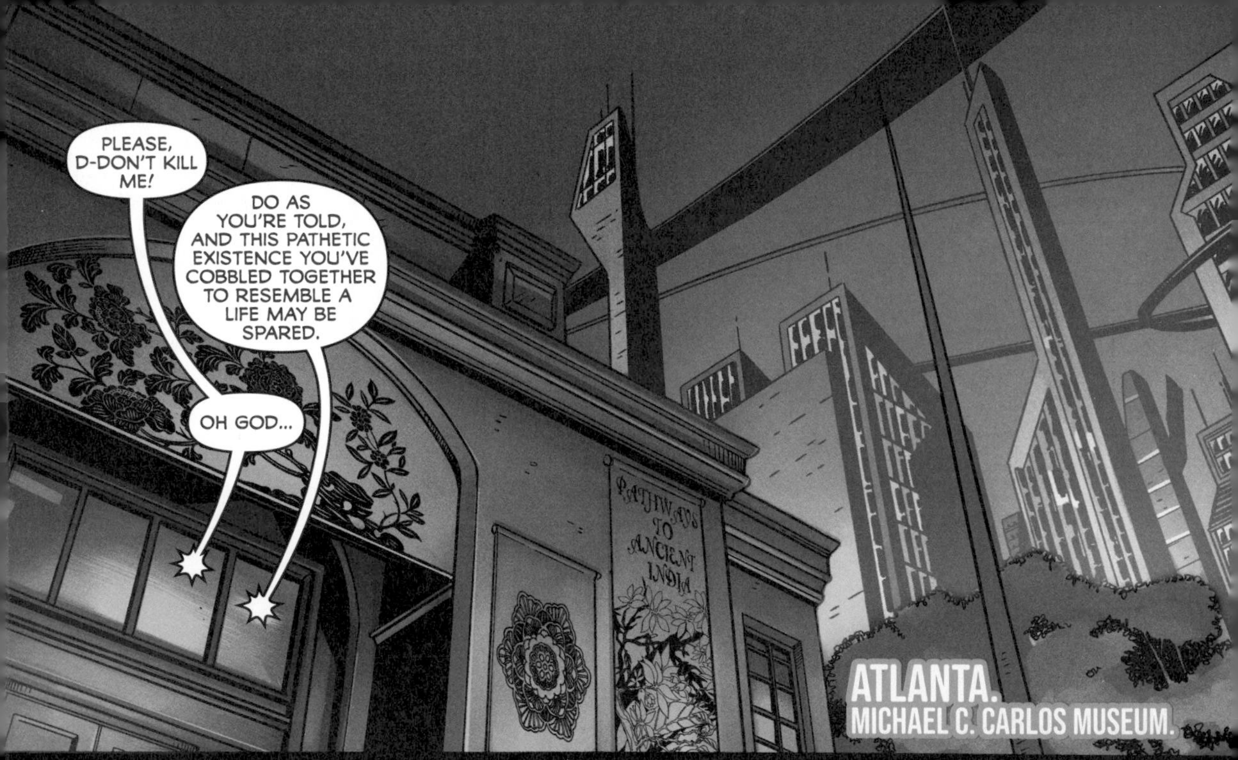
PLEASE, D-DON'T KILL ME!
DO AS YOU'RE TOLD, AND THIS PATHETIC EXISTENCE YOU'VE COBBLED TOGETHER TO RESEMBLE A LIFE MAY BE SPARED.
OH GOD...
PATHWAYS TO ANCIENT INDIA
ATLANTA.
MICHAEL C. CARLOS MUSEUM.

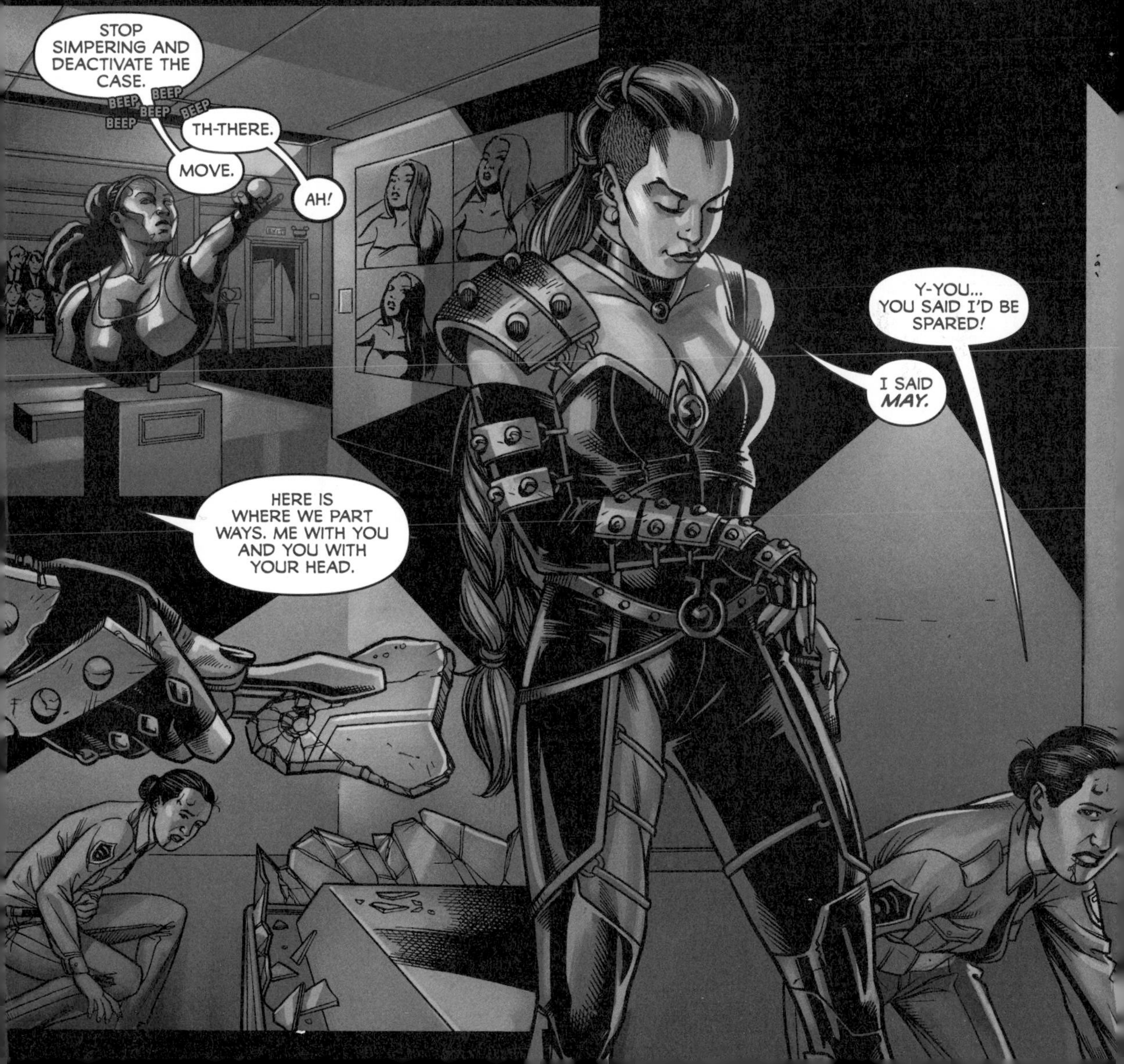
STOP SIMPERING AND DEACTIVATE THE CASE.
BEEP BEEP BEEP BEEP
TH-THERE.
MOVE.
AH!
Y-YOU... YOU SAID I'D BE SPARED!
I SAID *MAY.*
HERE IS WHERE WE PART WAYS. ME WITH YOU AND YOU WITH YOUR HEAD.

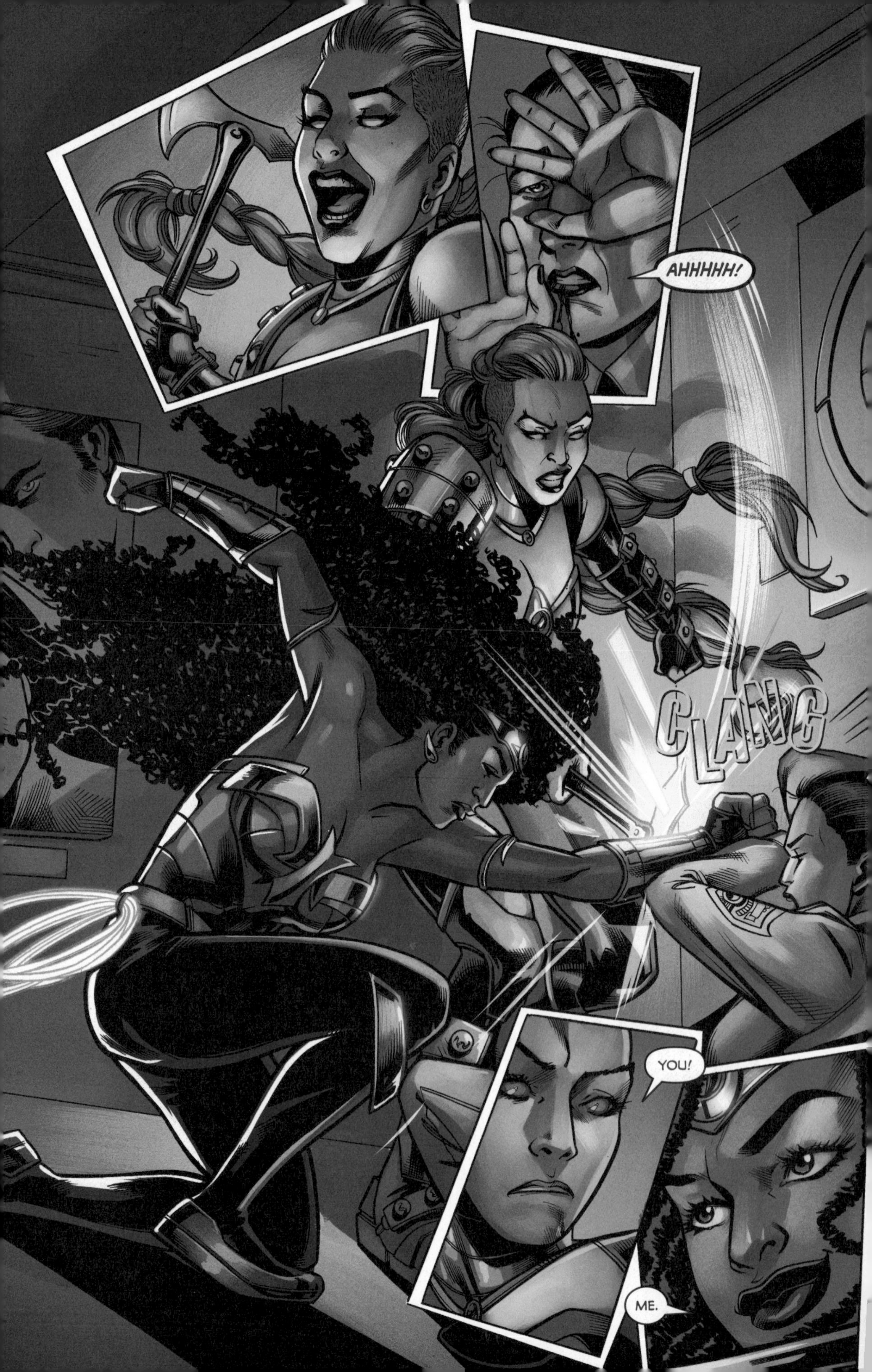
AHHHHH!
CLANG
YOU!
ME.

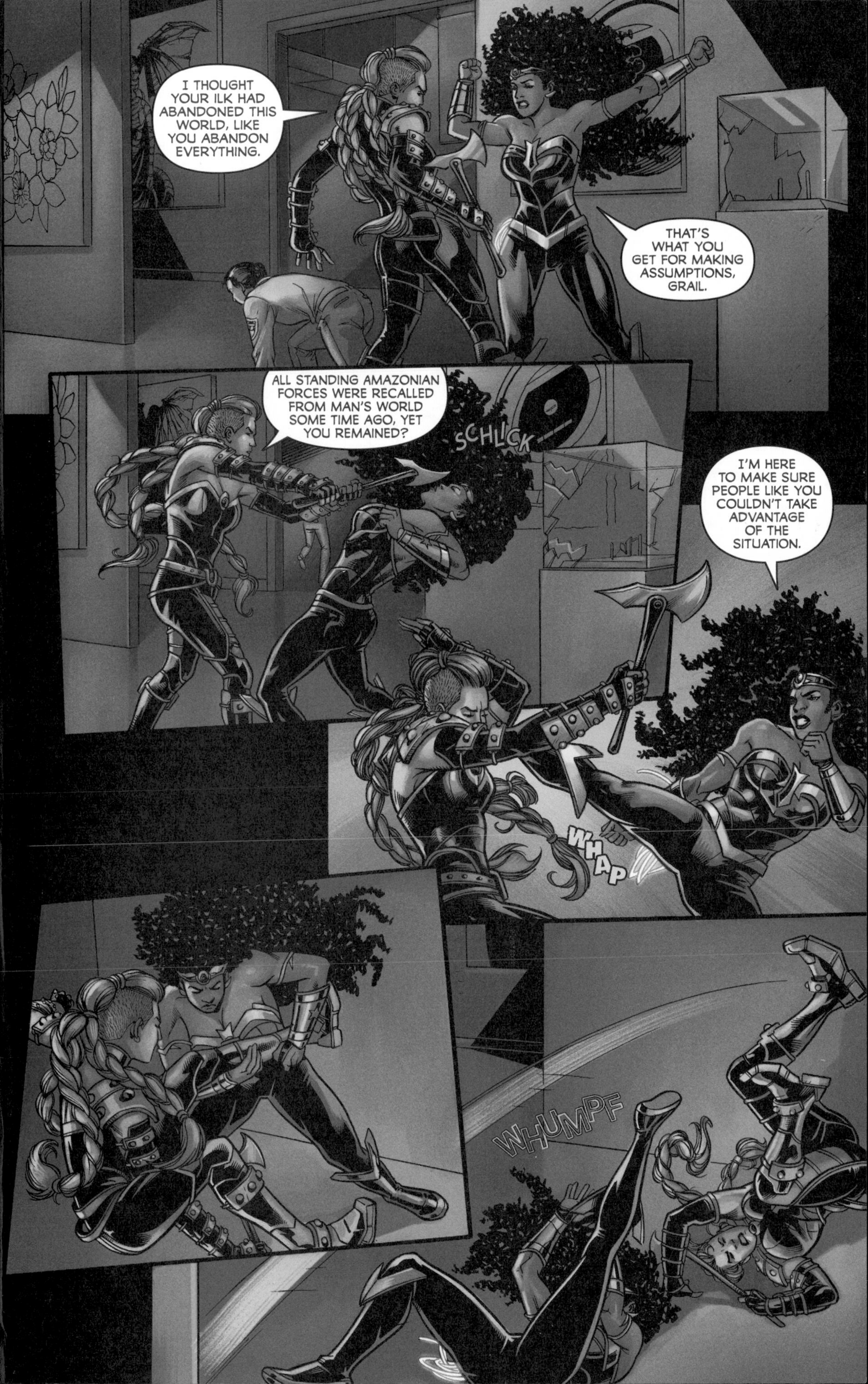
I THOUGHT YOUR ILK HAD ABANDONED THIS WORLD, LIKE YOU ABANDON EVERYTHING.
THAT'S WHAT YOU GET FOR MAKING ASSUMPTIONS, GRAIL.
ALL STANDING AMAZONIAN FORCES WERE RECALLED FROM MAN'S WORLD SOME TIME AGO, YET YOU REMAINED?
SCHLICK
I'M HERE TO MAKE SURE PEOPLE LIKE YOU COULDN'T TAKE ADVANTAGE OF THE SITUATION.
WHAP
WHUMPF

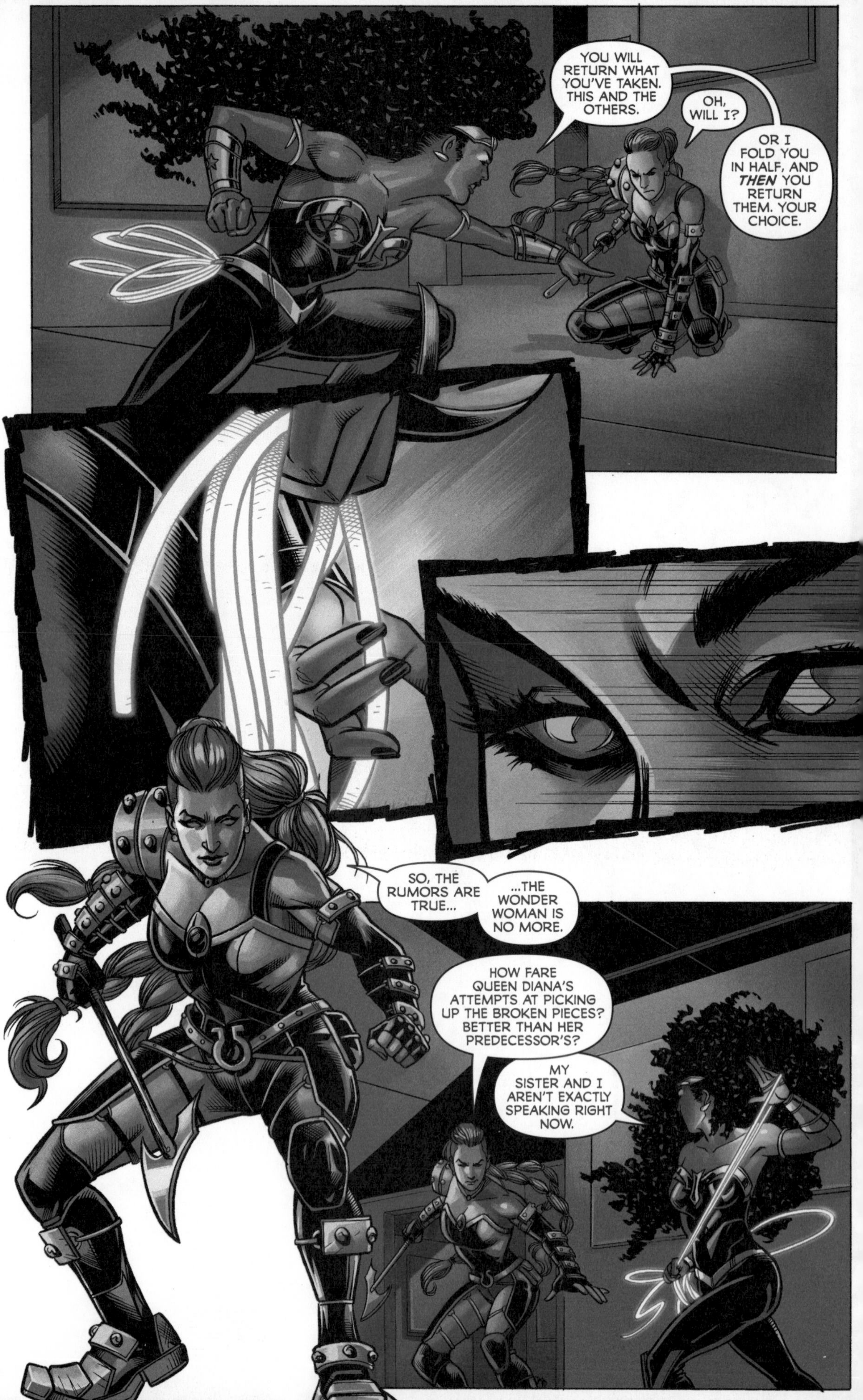
YOU WILL RETURN WHAT YOU'VE TAKEN. THIS AND THE OTHERS.
OH, WILL I?
OR I FOLD YOU IN HALF, AND ***THEN*** YOU RETURN THEM. YOUR CHOICE.
SO, THE RUMORS ARE TRUE...
...THE WONDER WOMAN IS NO MORE.
HOW FARE QUEEN DIANA'S ATTEMPTS AT PICKING UP THE BROKEN PIECES? BETTER THAN HER PREDECESSOR'S?
MY SISTER AND I AREN'T EXACTLY SPEAKING RIGHT NOW.

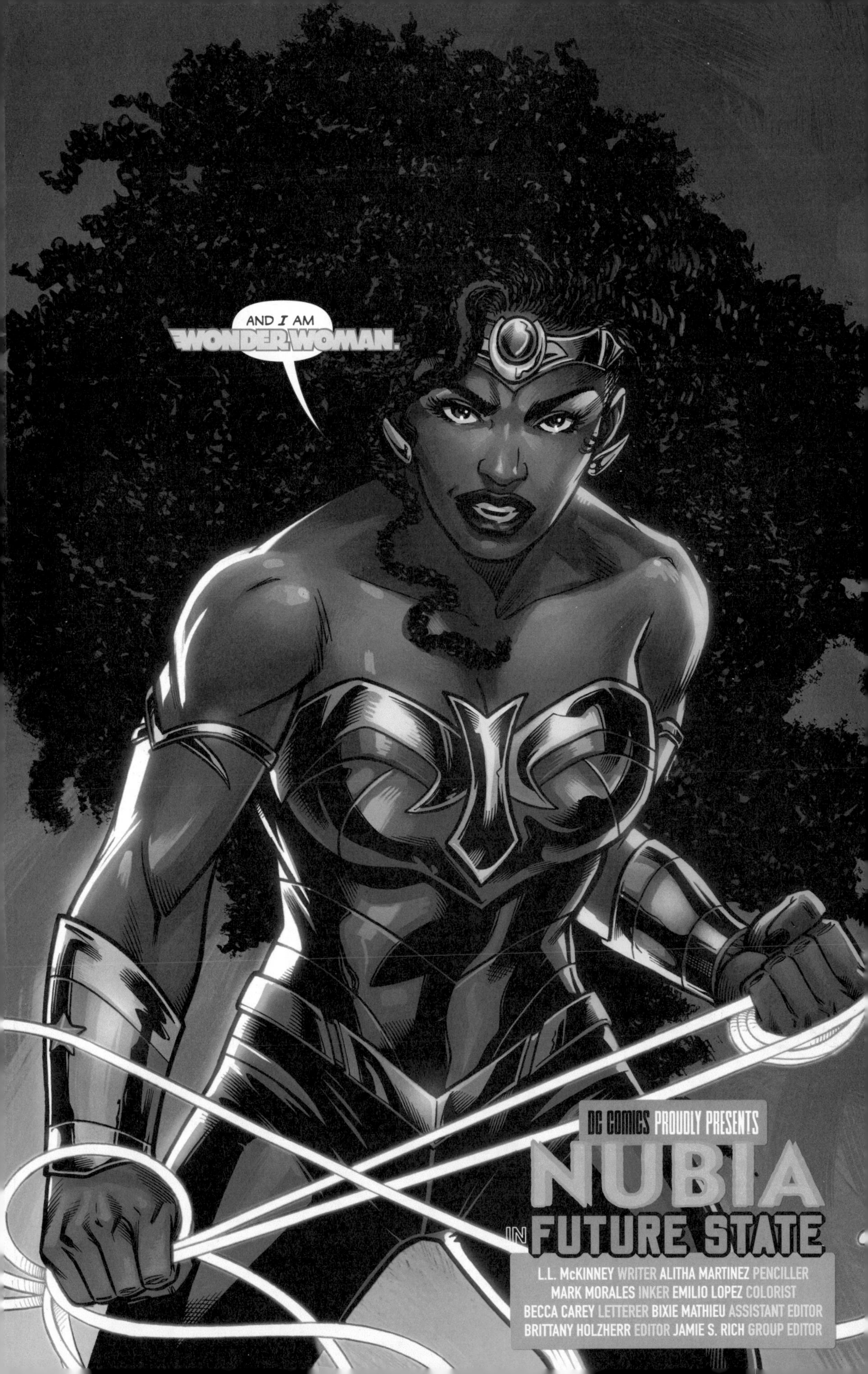
AND I AM
WONDER WOMAN.
DC COMICS PROUDLY PRESENTS
NUBIA
IN FUTURE STATE
L.L. McKINNEY WRITER ALITHA MARTINEZ PENCILLER
MARK MORALES INKER EMILIO LOPEZ COLORIST
BECCA CAREY LETTERER BIXIE MATHIEU ASSISTANT EDITOR
BRITTANY HOLZHERR EDITOR JAMIE S. RICH GROUP EDITOR

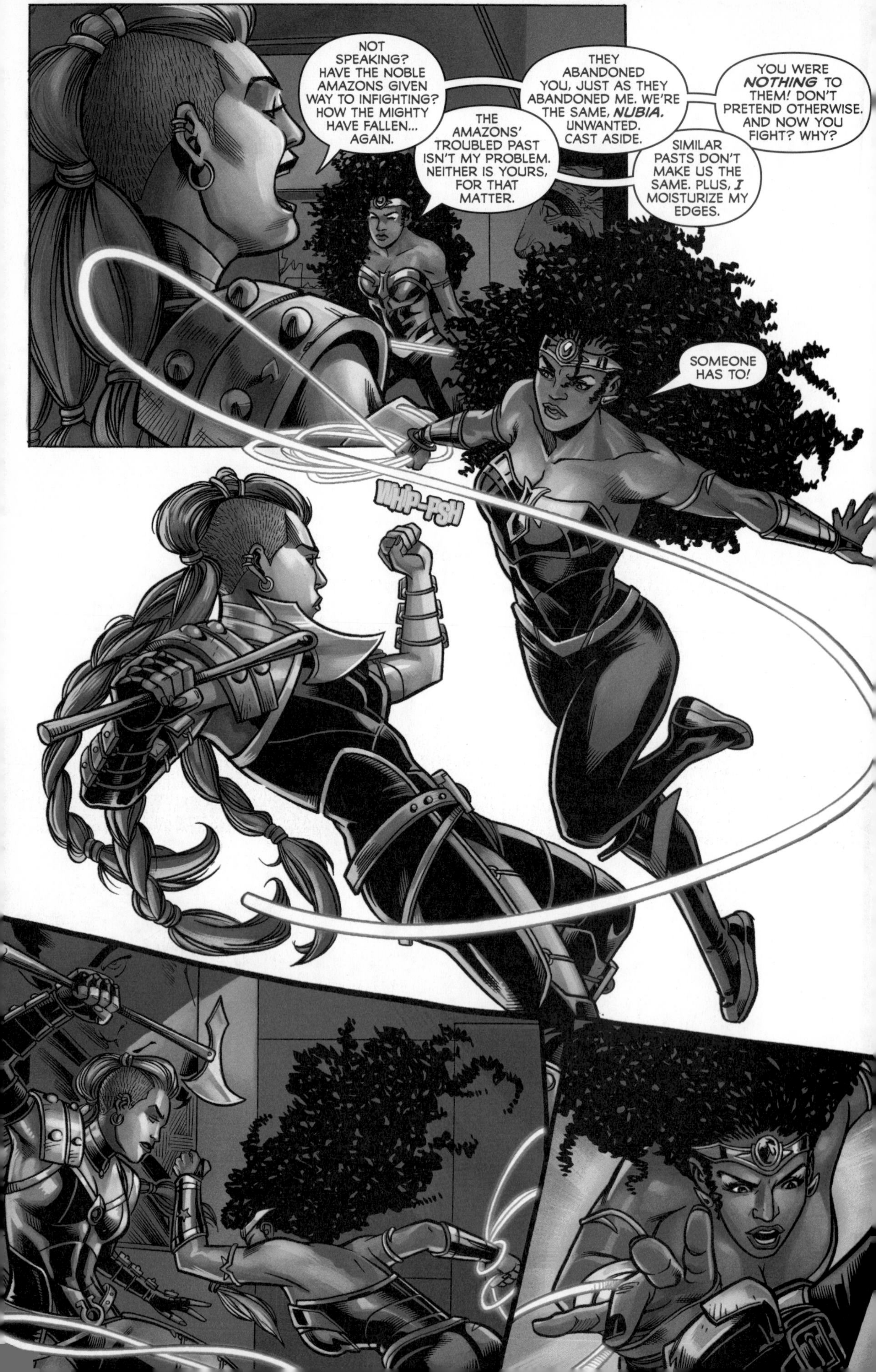

NOT SPEAKING? HAVE THE NOBLE AMAZONS GIVEN WAY TO INFIGHTING? HOW THE MIGHTY HAVE FALLEN... AGAIN.
THE AMAZONS' TROUBLED PAST ISN'T MY PROBLEM. NEITHER IS YOURS, FOR THAT MATTER.
THEY ABANDONED YOU, JUST AS THEY ABANDONED ME. WE'RE THE SAME, *NUBIA.* UNWANTED. CAST ASIDE.
SIMILAR PASTS DON'T MAKE US THE SAME. PLUS, *I* MOISTURIZE MY EDGES.
YOU WERE *NOTHING* TO THEM! DON'T PRETEND OTHERWISE. AND NOW YOU FIGHT? WHY?
SOMEONE HAS TO!
WHIP-PSH

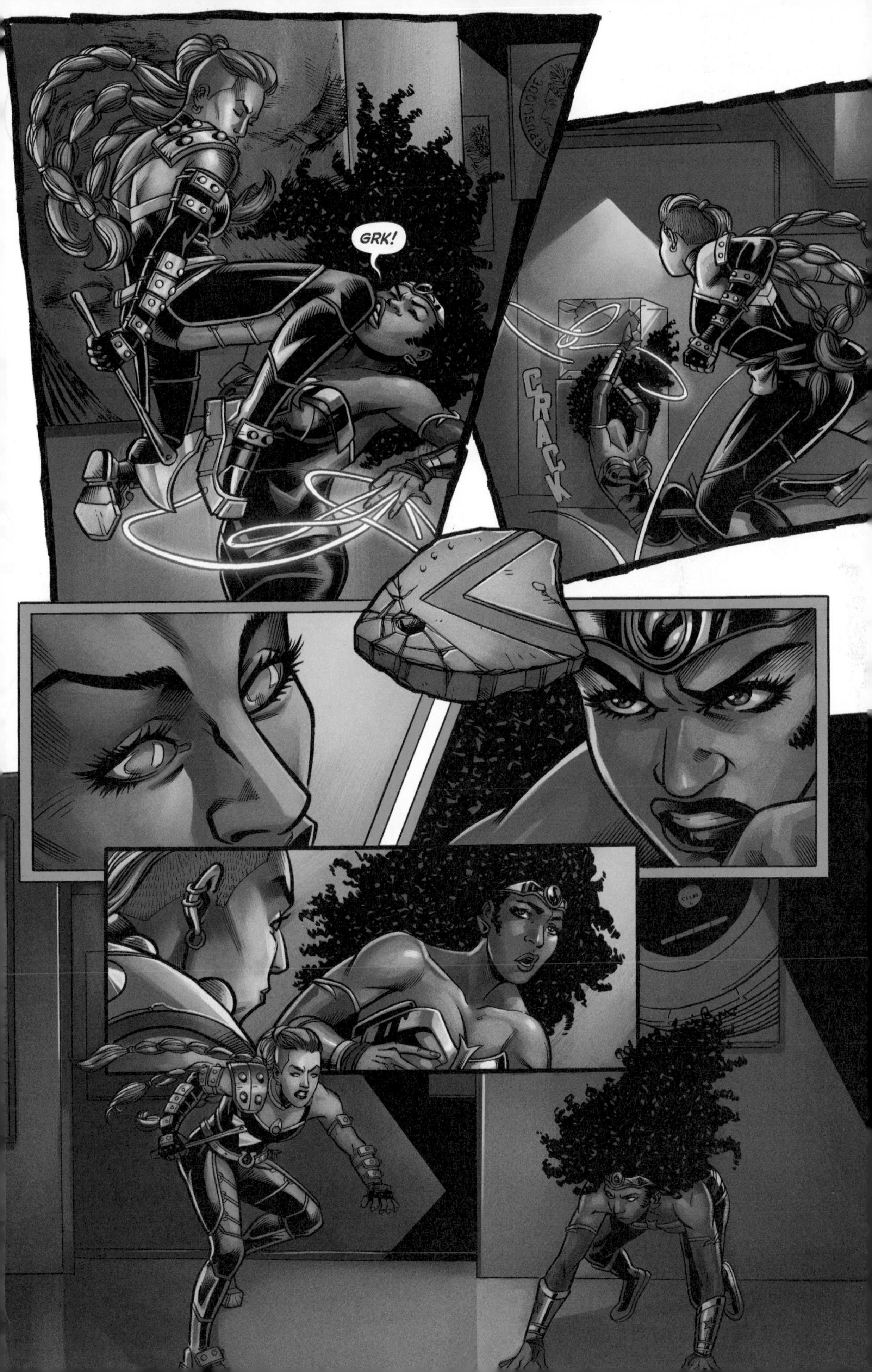
GRK!
CRACK

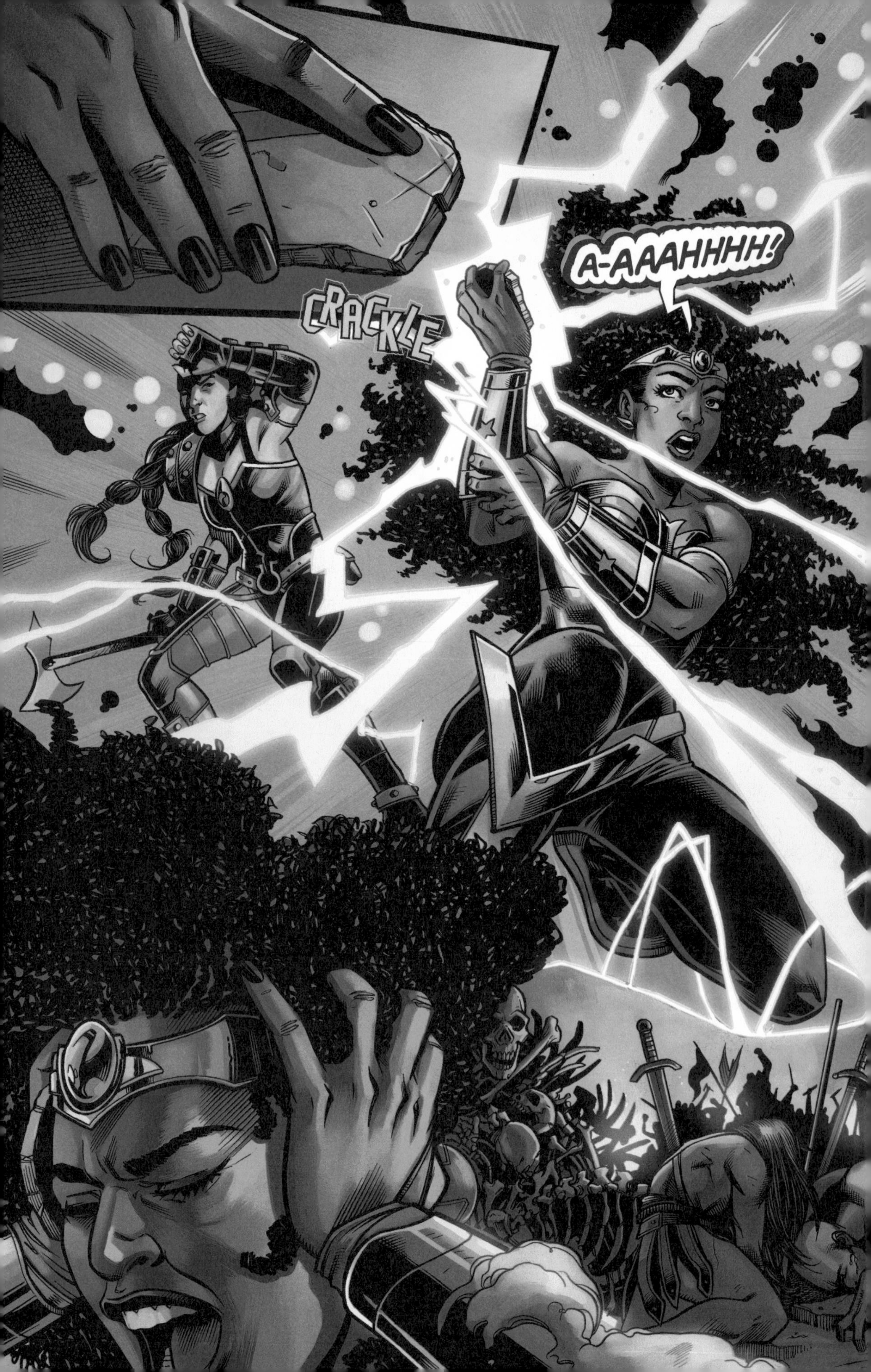
CRACKLE
A-AAAHHHH!

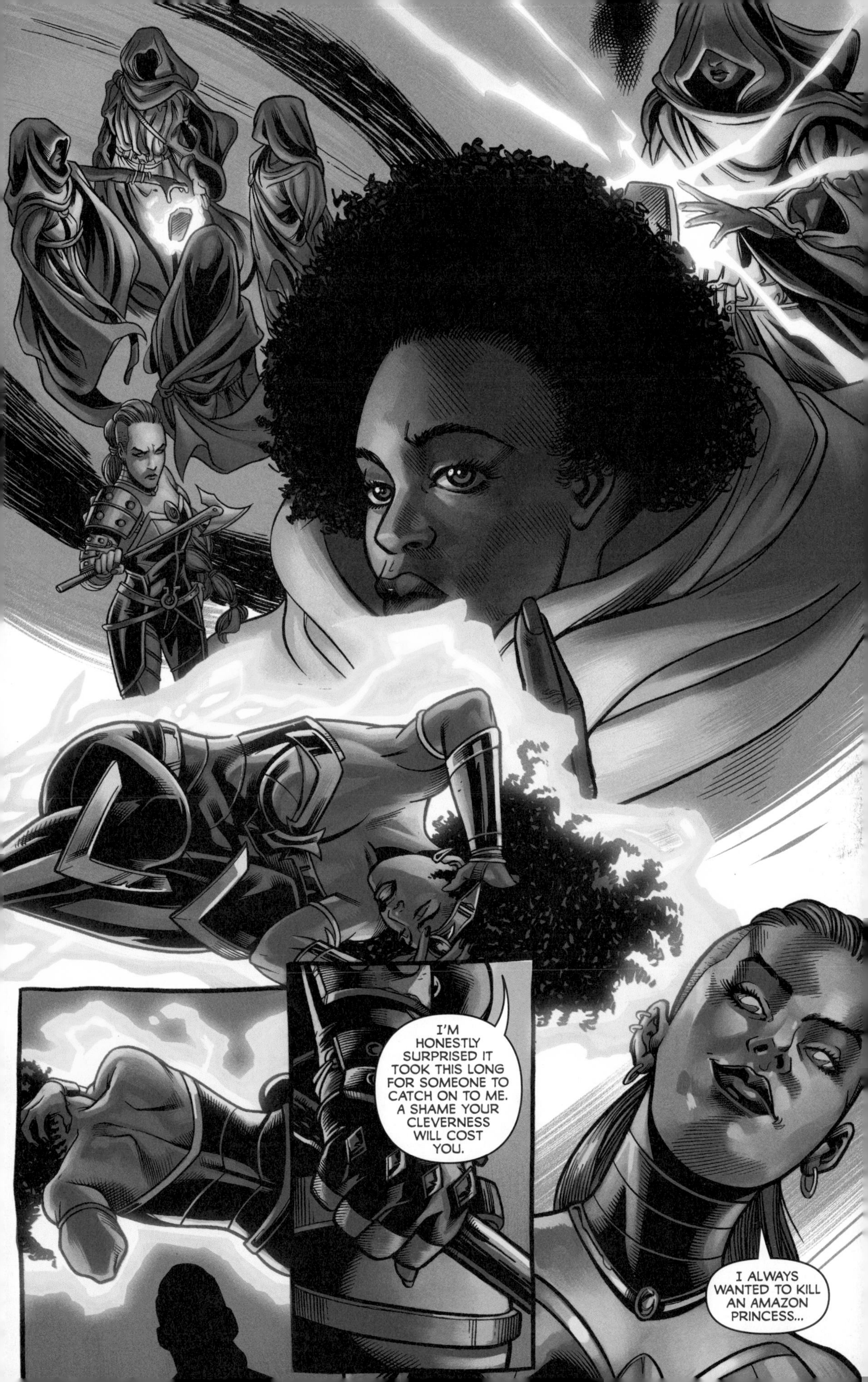
I'M HONESTLY SURPRISED IT TOOK THIS LONG FOR SOMEONE TO CATCH ON TO ME. A SHAME YOUR CLEVERNESS WILL COST YOU.
I ALWAYS WANTED TO KILL AN AMAZON PRINCESS...

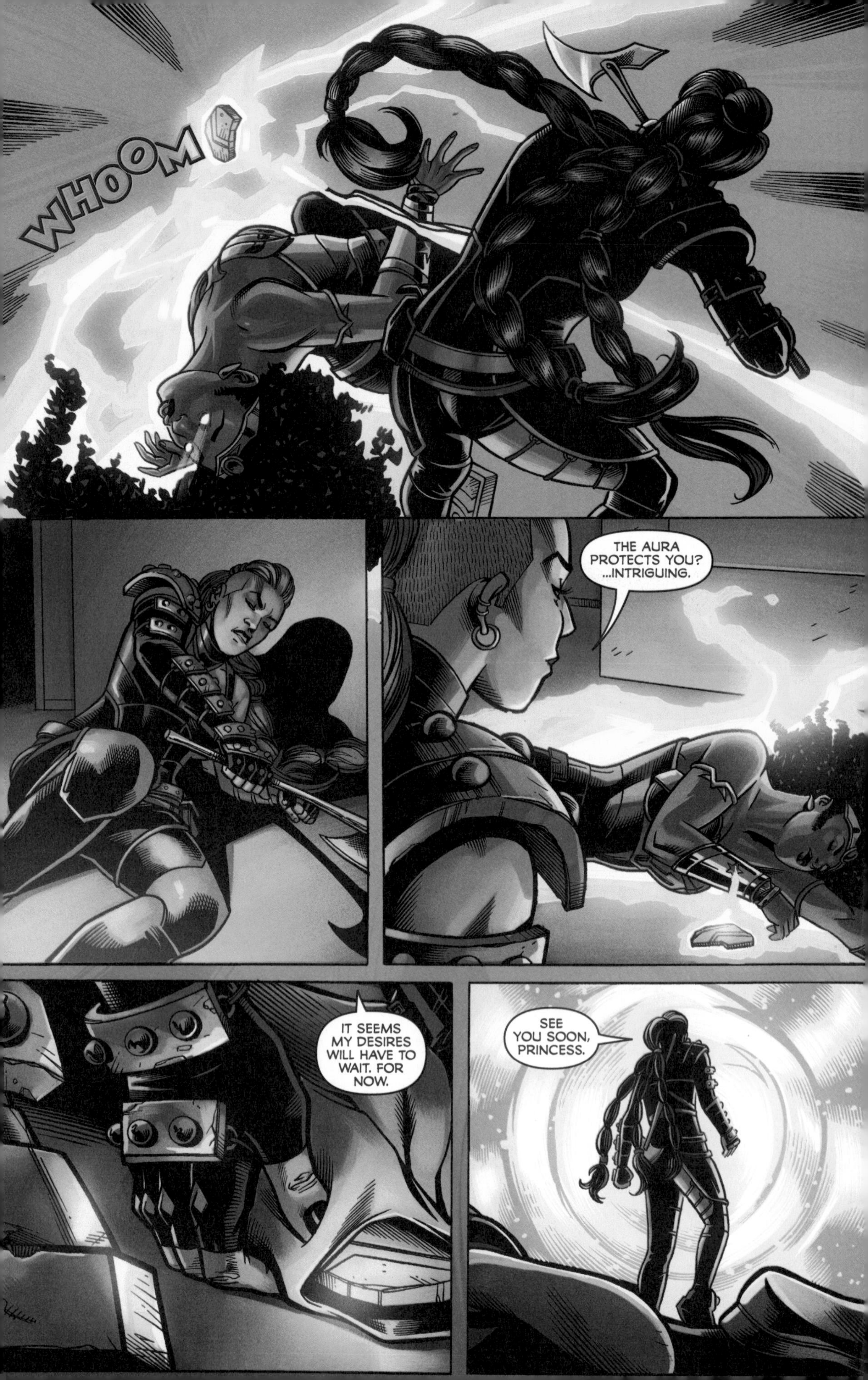
WHOOM
THE AURA PROTECTS YOU? ...INTRIGUING.
IT SEEMS MY DESIRES WILL HAVE TO WAIT. FOR NOW.
SEE YOU SOON, PRINCESS.

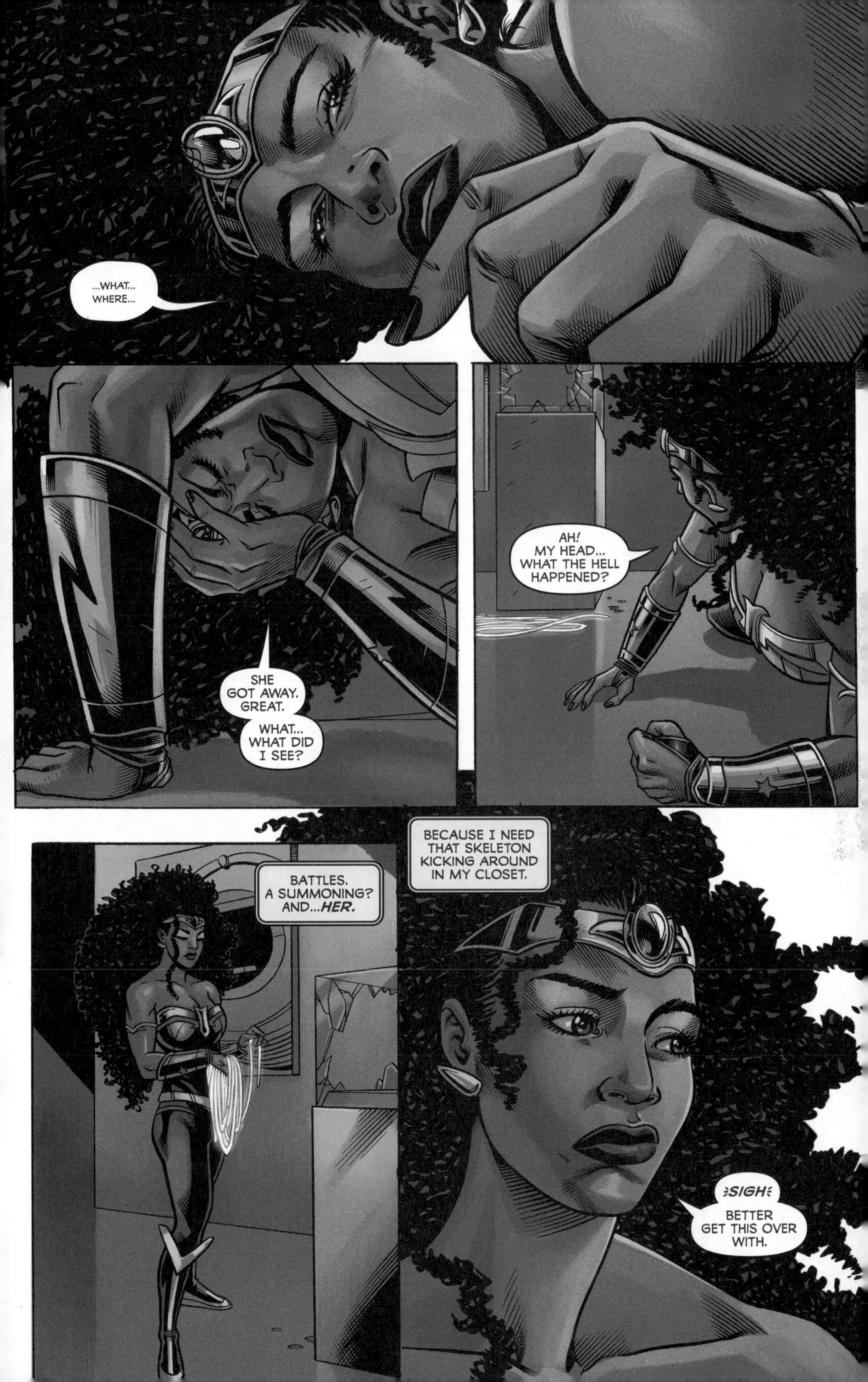
...WHAT...
WHERE...
SHE GOT AWAY. GREAT.
WHAT... WHAT DID I SEE?
AH! MY HEAD... WHAT THE HELL HAPPENED?
BATTLES. A SUMMONING? AND...*HER.*
BECAUSE I NEED THAT SKELETON KICKING AROUND IN MY CLOSET.
SIGH
BETTER GET THIS OVER WITH.

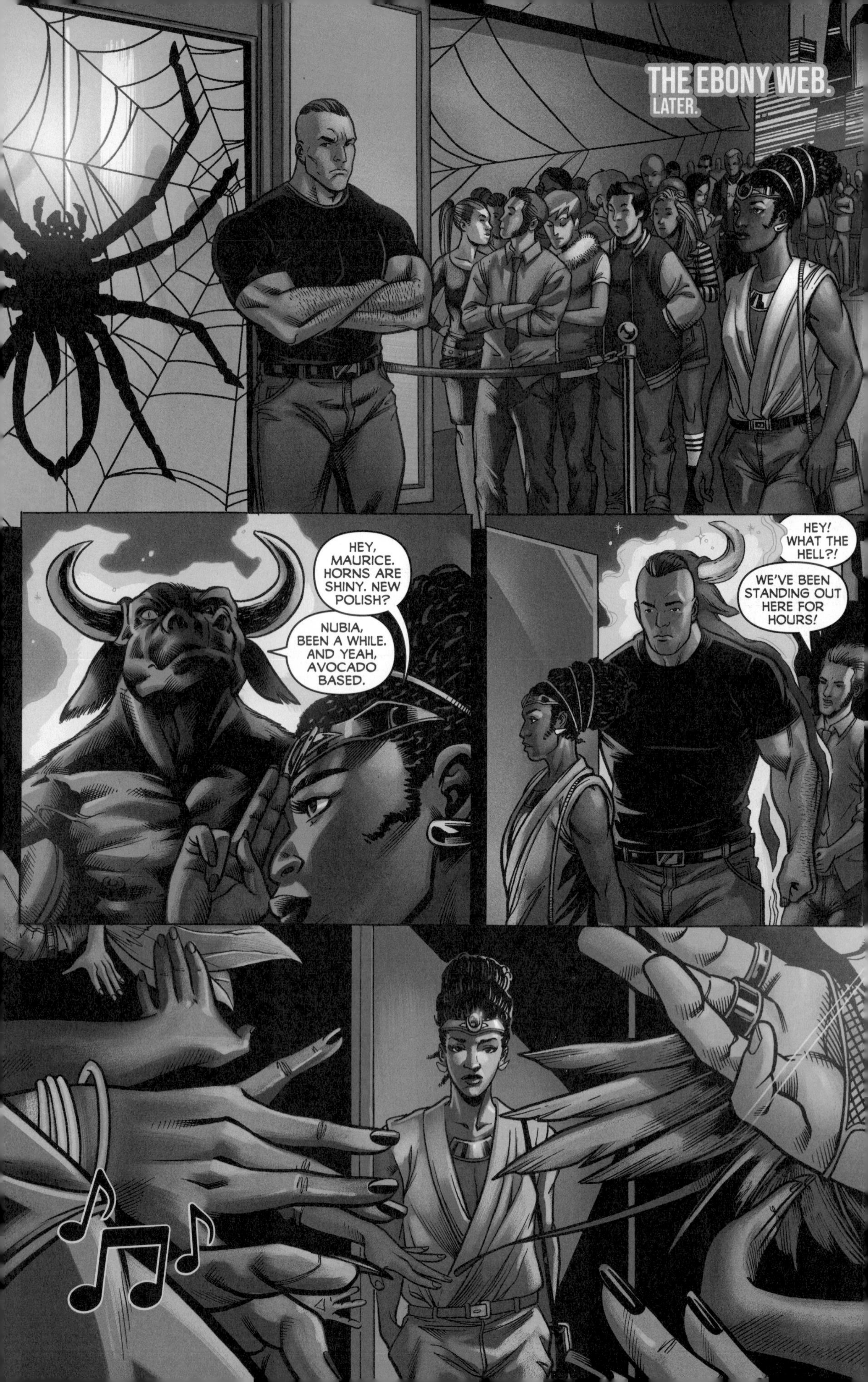
THE EBONY WEB.
LATER.
HEY, MAURICE. HORNS ARE SHINY. NEW POLISH?
NUBIA, BEEN A WHILE. AND YEAH, AVOCADO BASED.
HEY! WHAT THE HELL?!
WE'VE BEEN STANDING OUT HERE FOR HOURS!

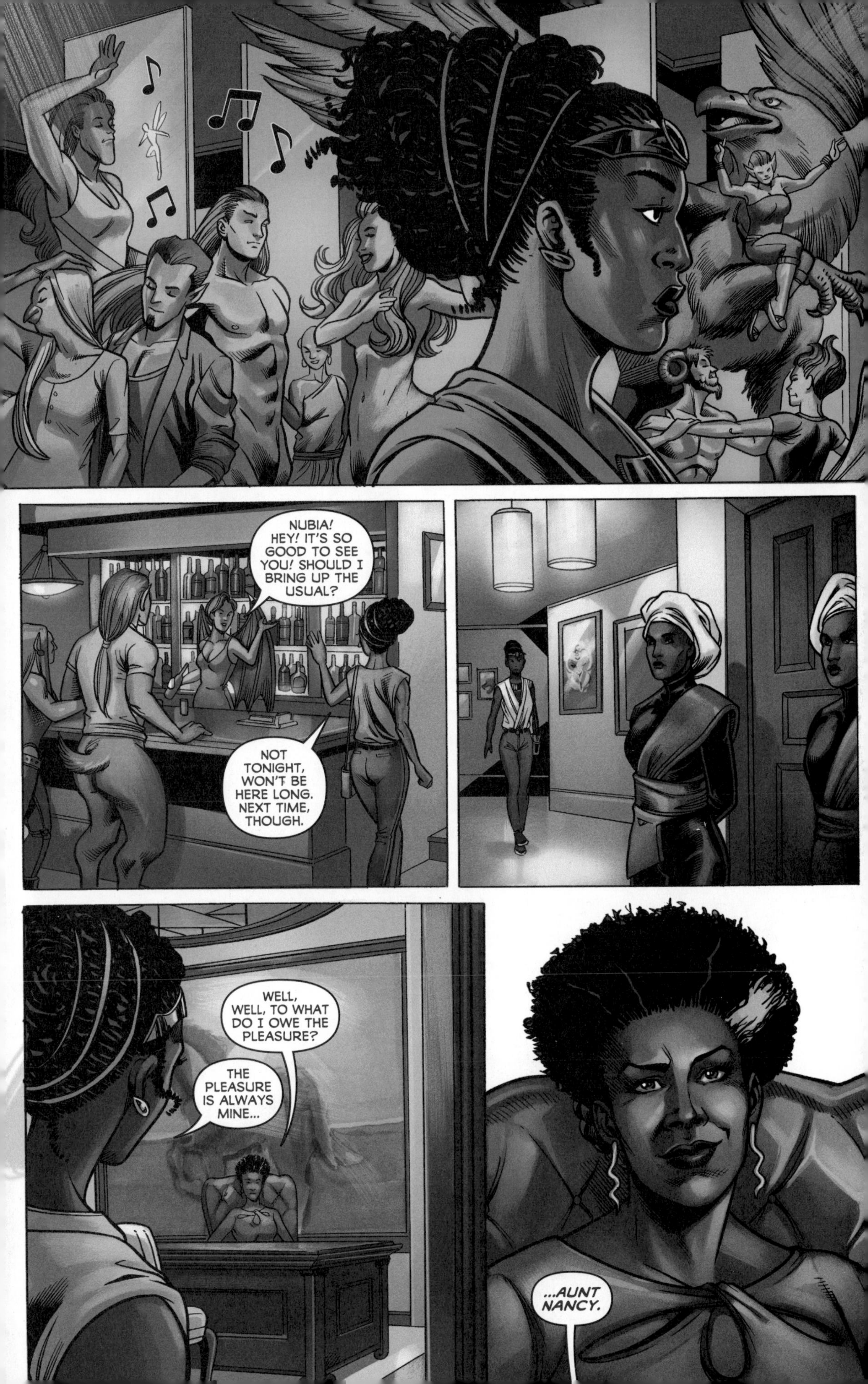
NUBIA! HEY! IT'S SO GOOD TO SEE YOU! SHOULD I BRING UP THE USUAL?
NOT TONIGHT, WON'T BE HERE LONG. NEXT TIME, THOUGH.
WELL, WELL, TO WHAT DO I OWE THE PLEASURE?
THE PLEASURE IS ALWAYS MINE...
...AUNT NANCY.

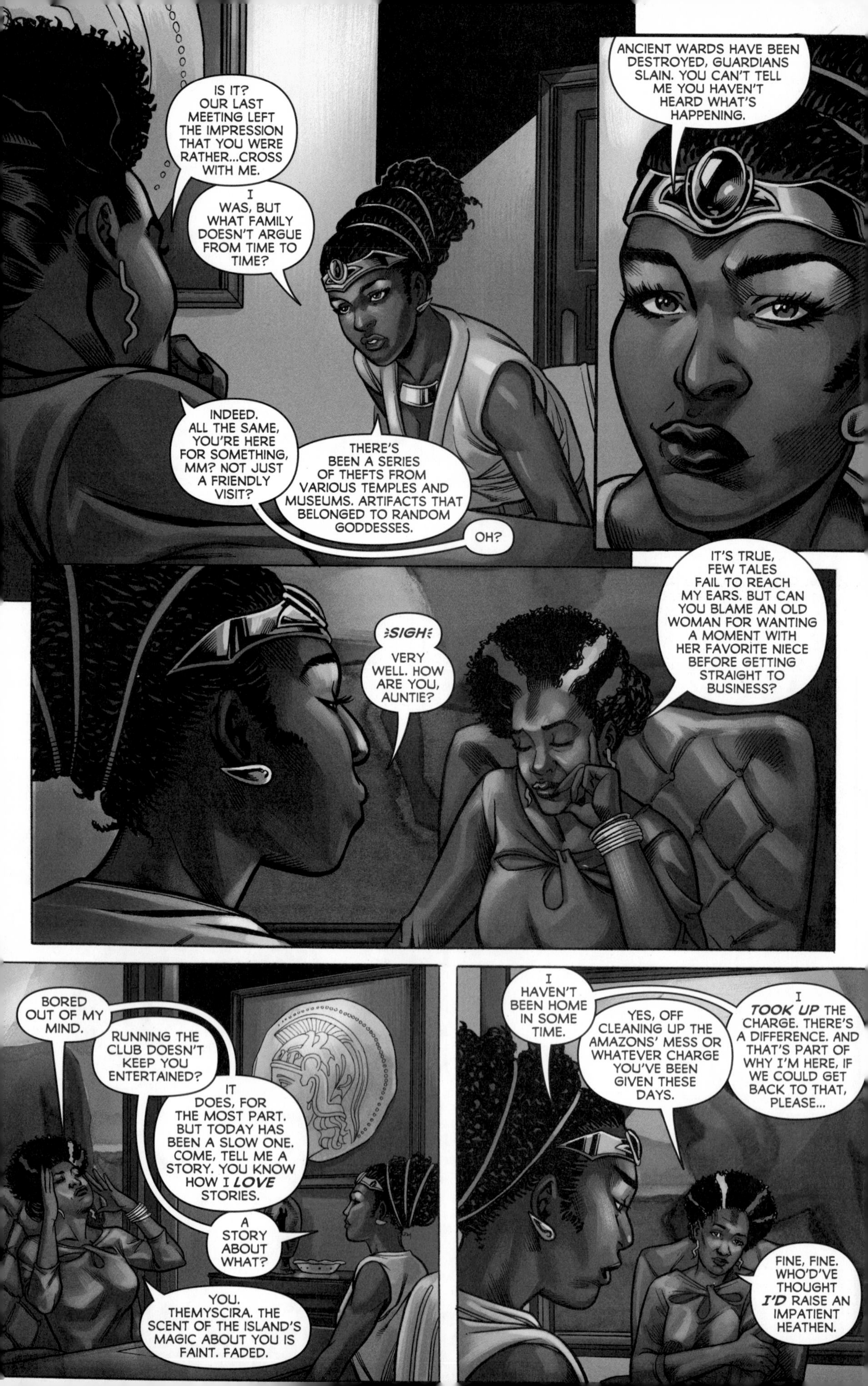
IS IT? OUR LAST MEETING LEFT THE IMPRESSION THAT YOU WERE RATHER...CROSS WITH ME.
I WAS, BUT WHAT FAMILY DOESN'T ARGUE FROM TIME TO TIME?
ANCIENT WARDS HAVE BEEN DESTROYED, GUARDIANS SLAIN. YOU CAN'T TELL ME YOU HAVEN'T HEARD WHAT'S HAPPENING.
INDEED. ALL THE SAME, YOU'RE HERE FOR SOMETHING, MM? NOT JUST A FRIENDLY VISIT?
THERE'S BEEN A SERIES OF THEFTS FROM VARIOUS TEMPLES AND MUSEUMS. ARTIFACTS THAT BELONGED TO RANDOM GODDESSES.
OH?
SIGH
VERY WELL. HOW ARE YOU, AUNTIE?
IT'S TRUE, FEW TALES FAIL TO REACH MY EARS. BUT CAN YOU BLAME AN OLD WOMAN FOR WANTING A MOMENT WITH HER FAVORITE NIECE BEFORE GETTING STRAIGHT TO BUSINESS?
BORED OUT OF MY MIND.
RUNNING THE CLUB DOESN'T KEEP YOU ENTERTAINED?
IT DOES, FOR THE MOST PART. BUT TODAY HAS BEEN A SLOW ONE. COME, TELL ME A STORY. YOU KNOW HOW I ***LOVE*** STORIES.
A STORY ABOUT WHAT?
YOU. THEMYSCIRA. THE SCENT OF THE ISLAND'S MAGIC ABOUT YOU IS FAINT. FADED.
I HAVEN'T BEEN HOME IN SOME TIME.
YES, OFF CLEANING UP THE AMAZONS' MESS OR WHATEVER CHARGE YOU'VE BEEN GIVEN THESE DAYS.
I ***TOOK UP*** THE CHARGE. THERE'S A DIFFERENCE. AND THAT'S PART OF WHY I'M HERE, IF WE COULD GET BACK TO THAT, PLEASE...
FINE, FINE. WHO'D'VE THOUGHT ***I'D*** RAISE AN IMPATIENT HEATHEN.

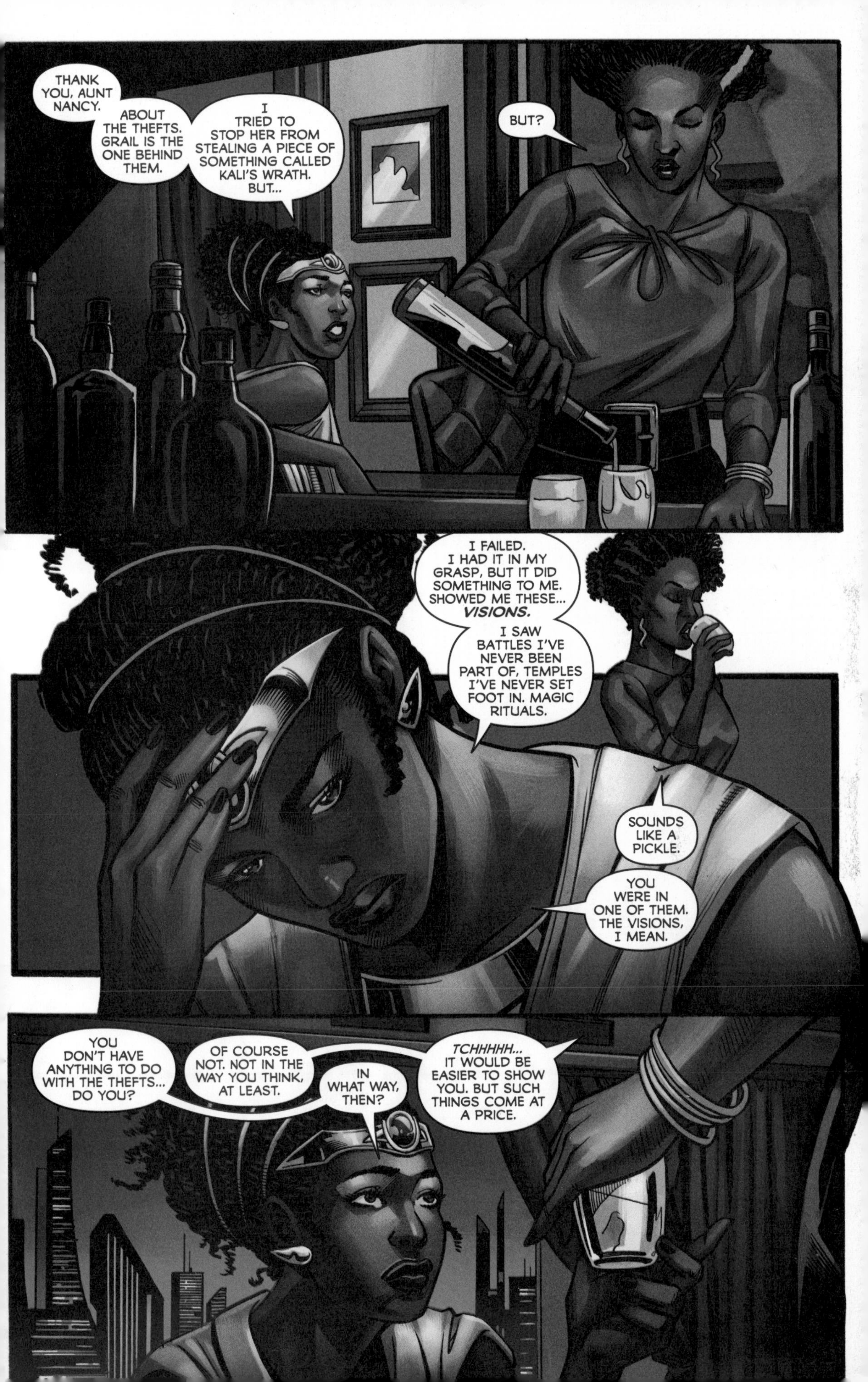
THANK YOU, AUNT NANCY.
ABOUT THE THEFTS. GRAIL IS THE ONE BEHIND THEM.
I TRIED TO STOP HER FROM STEALING A PIECE OF SOMETHING CALLED KALI'S WRATH. BUT...
BUT?
I FAILED. I HAD IT IN MY GRASP, BUT IT DID SOMETHING TO ME. SHOWED ME THESE... *VISIONS.*
I SAW BATTLES I'VE NEVER BEEN PART OF, TEMPLES I'VE NEVER SET FOOT IN. MAGIC RITUALS.
SOUNDS LIKE A PICKLE.
YOU WERE IN ONE OF THEM. THE VISIONS, I MEAN.
YOU DON'T HAVE ANYTHING TO DO WITH THE THEFTS... DO YOU?
OF COURSE NOT. NOT IN THE WAY YOU THINK, AT LEAST.
IN WHAT WAY, THEN?
TCHHHHH... IT WOULD BE EASIER TO SHOW YOU. BUT SUCH THINGS COME AT A PRICE.

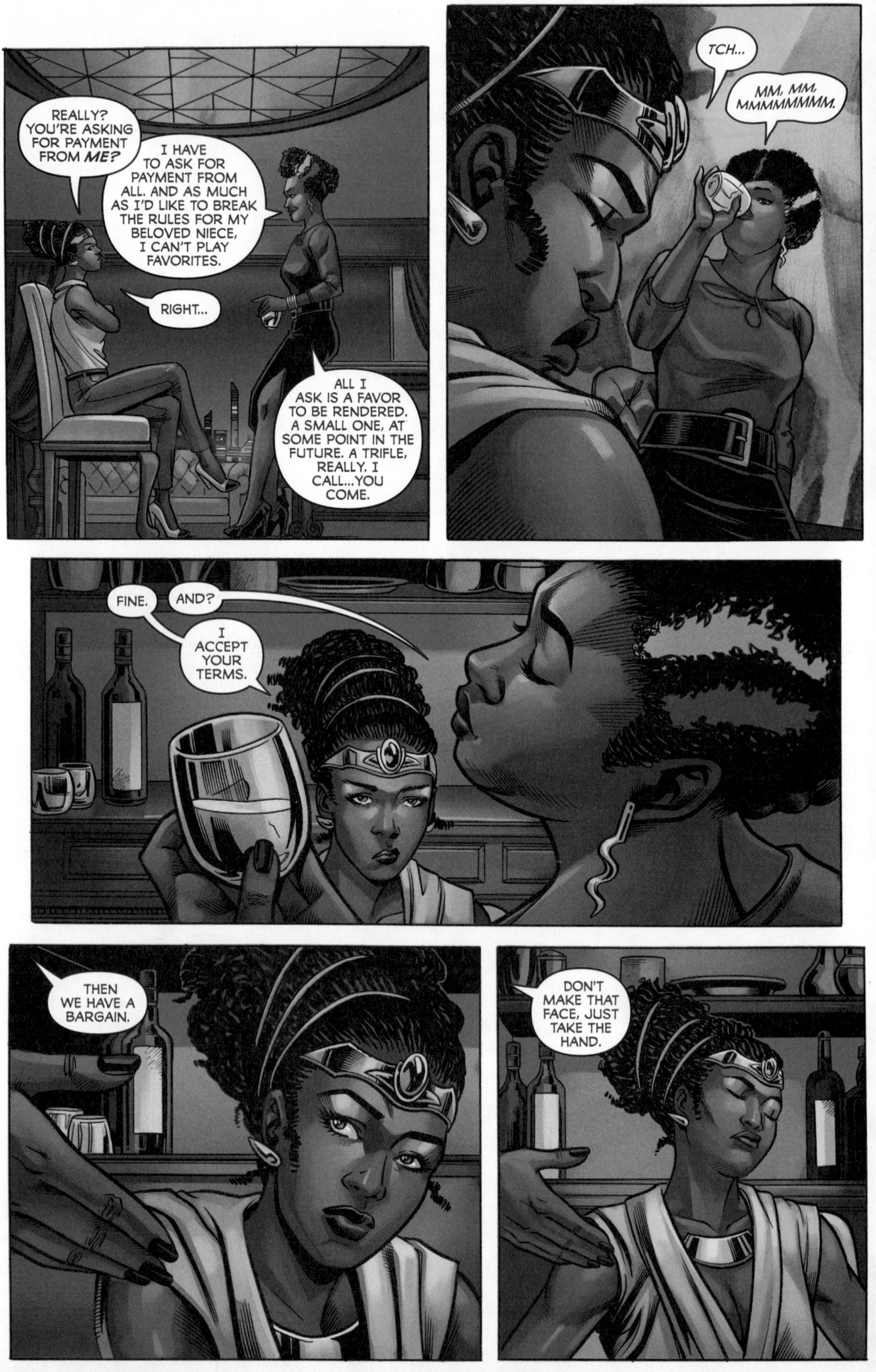
REALLY? YOU'RE ASKING FOR PAYMENT FROM ME?
I HAVE TO ASK FOR PAYMENT FROM ALL. AND AS MUCH AS I'D LIKE TO BREAK THE RULES FOR MY BELOVED NIECE, I CAN'T PLAY FAVORITES.
RIGHT...
ALL I ASK IS A FAVOR TO BE RENDERED. A SMALL ONE, AT SOME POINT IN THE FUTURE. A TRIFLE, REALLY. I CALL...YOU COME.
TCH...
MM, MM, MMMMMMMM.
FINE.
AND?
I ACCEPT YOUR TERMS.
THEN WE HAVE A BARGAIN.
DON'T MAKE THAT FACE, JUST TAKE THE HAND.

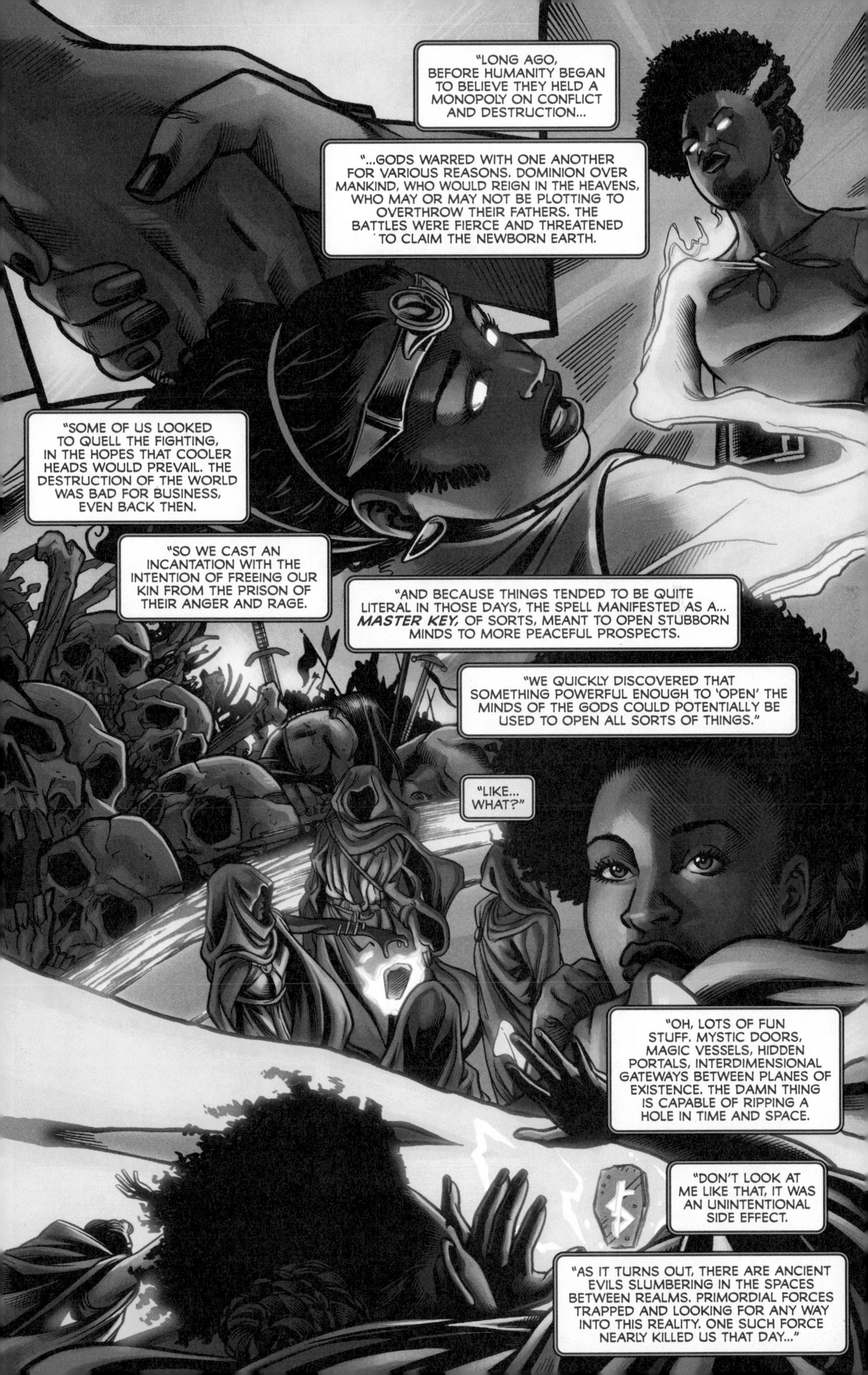
"LONG AGO, BEFORE HUMANITY BEGAN TO BELIEVE THEY HELD A MONOPOLY ON CONFLICT AND DESTRUCTION...
"...GODS WARRED WITH ONE ANOTHER FOR VARIOUS REASONS. DOMINION OVER MANKIND, WHO WOULD REIGN IN THE HEAVENS, WHO MAY OR MAY NOT BE PLOTTING TO OVERTHROW THEIR FATHERS. THE BATTLES WERE FIERCE AND THREATENED TO CLAIM THE NEWBORN EARTH.
"SOME OF US LOOKED TO QUELL THE FIGHTING, IN THE HOPES THAT COOLER HEADS WOULD PREVAIL. THE DESTRUCTION OF THE WORLD WAS BAD FOR BUSINESS, EVEN BACK THEN.
"SO WE CAST AN INCANTATION WITH THE INTENTION OF FREEING OUR KIN FROM THE PRISON OF THEIR ANGER AND RAGE.
"AND BECAUSE THINGS TENDED TO BE QUITE LITERAL IN THOSE DAYS, THE SPELL MANIFESTED AS A... *MASTER KEY,* OF SORTS, MEANT TO OPEN STUBBORN MINDS TO MORE PEACEFUL PROSPECTS.
"WE QUICKLY DISCOVERED THAT SOMETHING POWERFUL ENOUGH TO 'OPEN' THE MINDS OF THE GODS COULD POTENTIALLY BE USED TO OPEN ALL SORTS OF THINGS."
"LIKE... WHAT?"
"OH, LOTS OF FUN STUFF. MYSTIC DOORS, MAGIC VESSELS, HIDDEN PORTALS, INTERDIMENSIONAL GATEWAYS BETWEEN PLANES OF EXISTENCE. THE DAMN THING IS CAPABLE OF RIPPING A HOLE IN TIME AND SPACE.
"DON'T LOOK AT ME LIKE THAT, IT WAS AN UNINTENTIONAL SIDE EFFECT.
"AS IT TURNS OUT, THERE ARE ANCIENT EVILS SLUMBERING IN THE SPACES BETWEEN REALMS. PRIMORDIAL FORCES TRAPPED AND LOOKING FOR ANY WAY INTO THIS REALITY. ONE SUCH FORCE NEARLY KILLED US THAT DAY..."

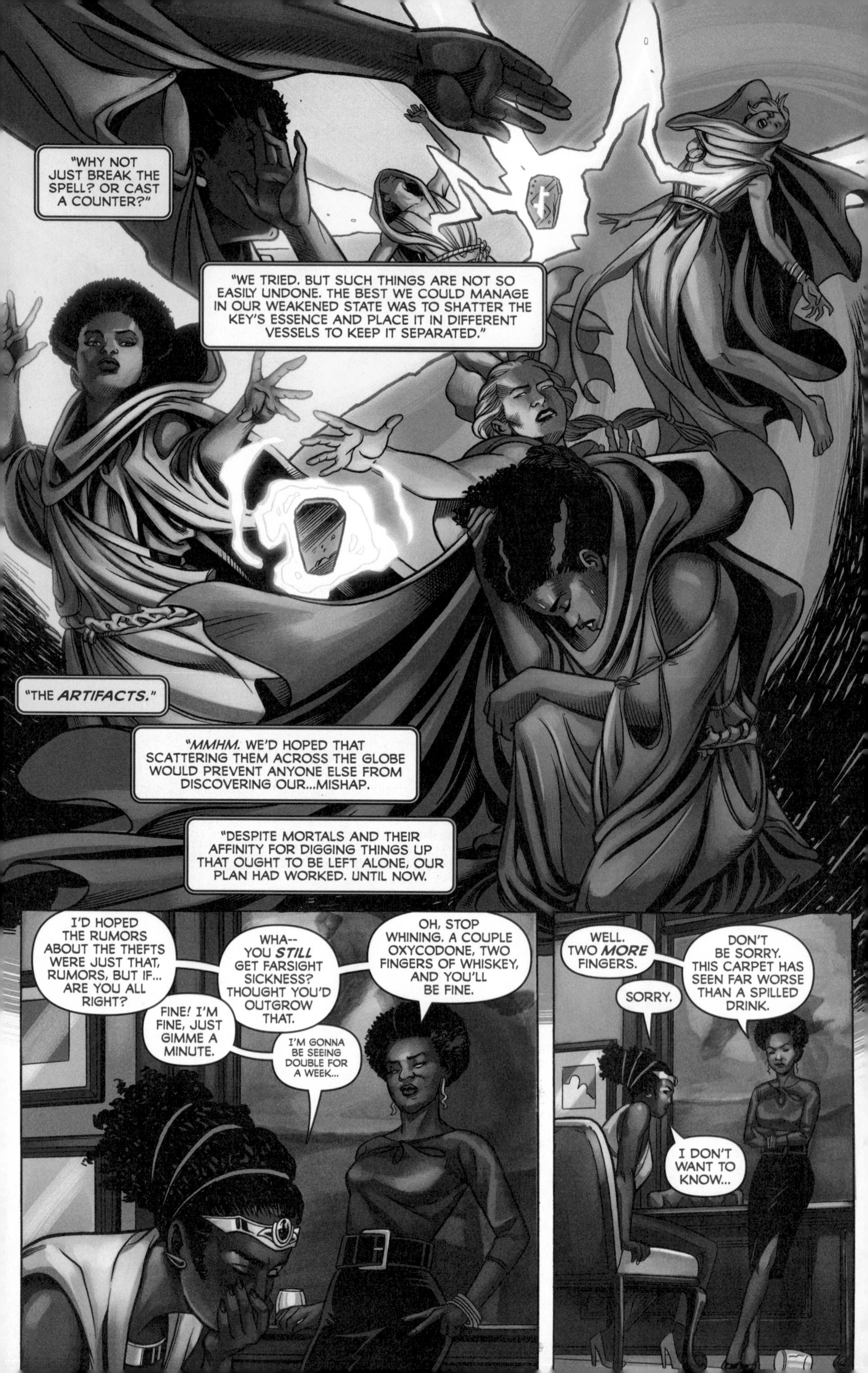
"WHY NOT JUST BREAK THE SPELL? OR CAST A COUNTER?"
"WE TRIED. BUT SUCH THINGS ARE NOT SO EASILY UNDONE. THE BEST WE COULD MANAGE IN OUR WEAKENED STATE WAS TO SHATTER THE KEY'S ESSENCE AND PLACE IT IN DIFFERENT VESSELS TO KEEP IT SEPARATED."
"THE *ARTIFACTS.*"
"*MMHM.* WE'D HOPED THAT SCATTERING THEM ACROSS THE GLOBE WOULD PREVENT ANYONE ELSE FROM DISCOVERING OUR...MISHAP.
"DESPITE MORTALS AND THEIR AFFINITY FOR DIGGING THINGS UP THAT OUGHT TO BE LEFT ALONE, OUR PLAN HAD WORKED. UNTIL NOW.
I'D HOPED THE RUMORS ABOUT THE THEFTS WERE JUST THAT, RUMORS, BUT IF... ARE YOU ALL RIGHT?
WHA-- YOU ***STILL*** GET FARSIGHT SICKNESS? THOUGHT YOU'D OUTGROW THAT.
FINE! I'M FINE, JUST GIMME A MINUTE.
I'M GONNA BE SEEING DOUBLE FOR A WEEK...
OH, STOP WHINING. A COUPLE OXYCODONE, TWO FINGERS OF WHISKEY, AND YOU'LL BE FINE.
WELL. TWO ***MORE*** FINGERS.
SORRY.
DON'T BE SORRY. THIS CARPET HAS SEEN FAR WORSE THAN A SPILLED DRINK.
I DON'T WANT TO KNOW...

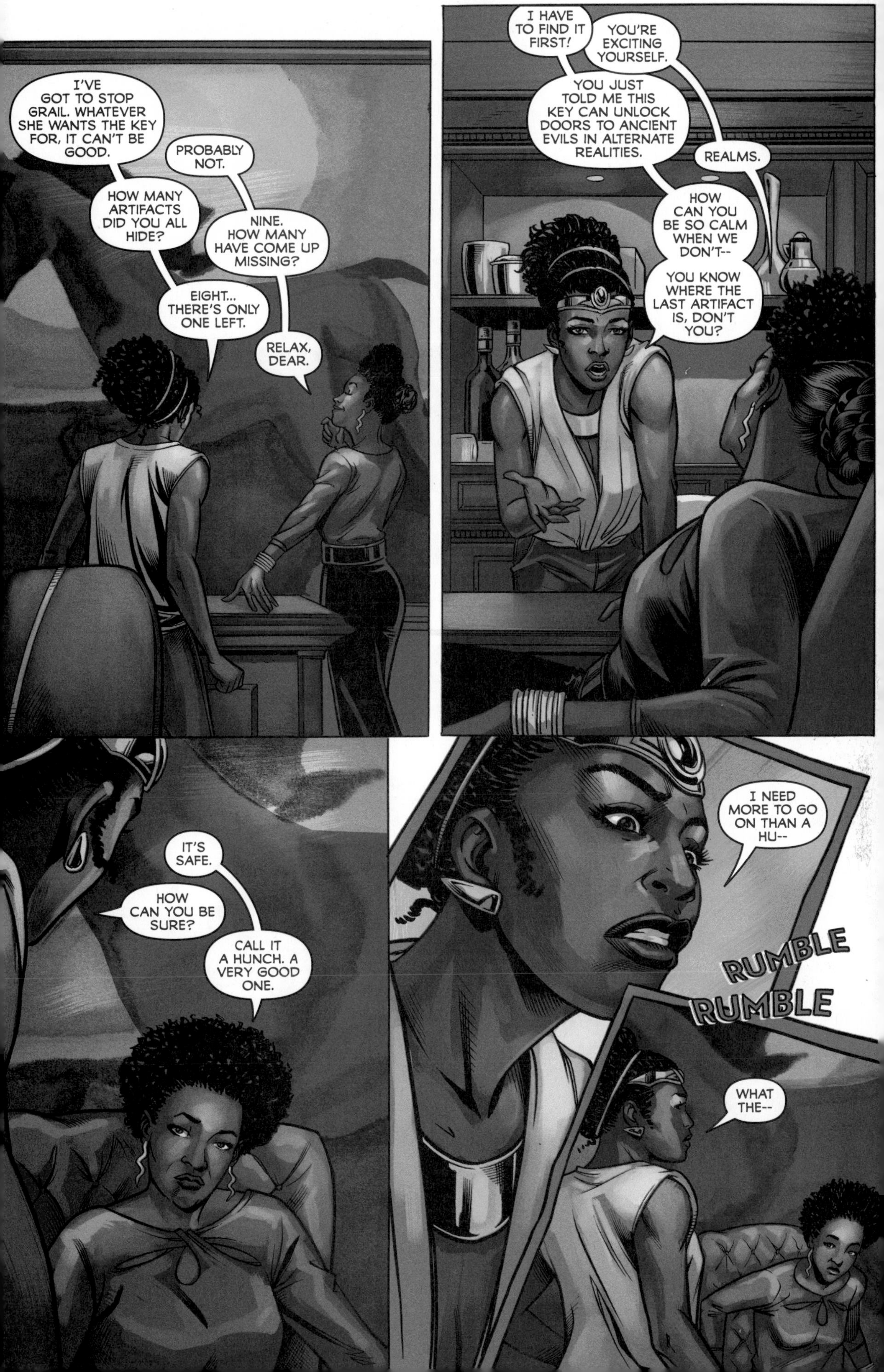
I'VE GOT TO STOP GRAIL. WHATEVER SHE WANTS THE KEY FOR, IT CAN'T BE GOOD.
PROBABLY NOT.
HOW MANY ARTIFACTS DID YOU ALL HIDE?
NINE. HOW MANY HAVE COME UP MISSING?
EIGHT... THERE'S ONLY ONE LEFT.
RELAX, DEAR.
I HAVE TO FIND IT FIRST!
YOU'RE EXCITING YOURSELF.
YOU JUST TOLD ME THIS KEY CAN UNLOCK DOORS TO ANCIENT EVILS IN ALTERNATE REALITIES.
REALMS.
HOW CAN YOU BE SO CALM WHEN WE DON'T--
YOU KNOW WHERE THE LAST ARTIFACT IS, DON'T YOU?
IT'S SAFE.
HOW CAN YOU BE SURE?
CALL IT A HUNCH. A VERY GOOD ONE.
I NEED MORE TO GO ON THAN A HU--
RUMBLE
RUMBLE
WHAT THE--

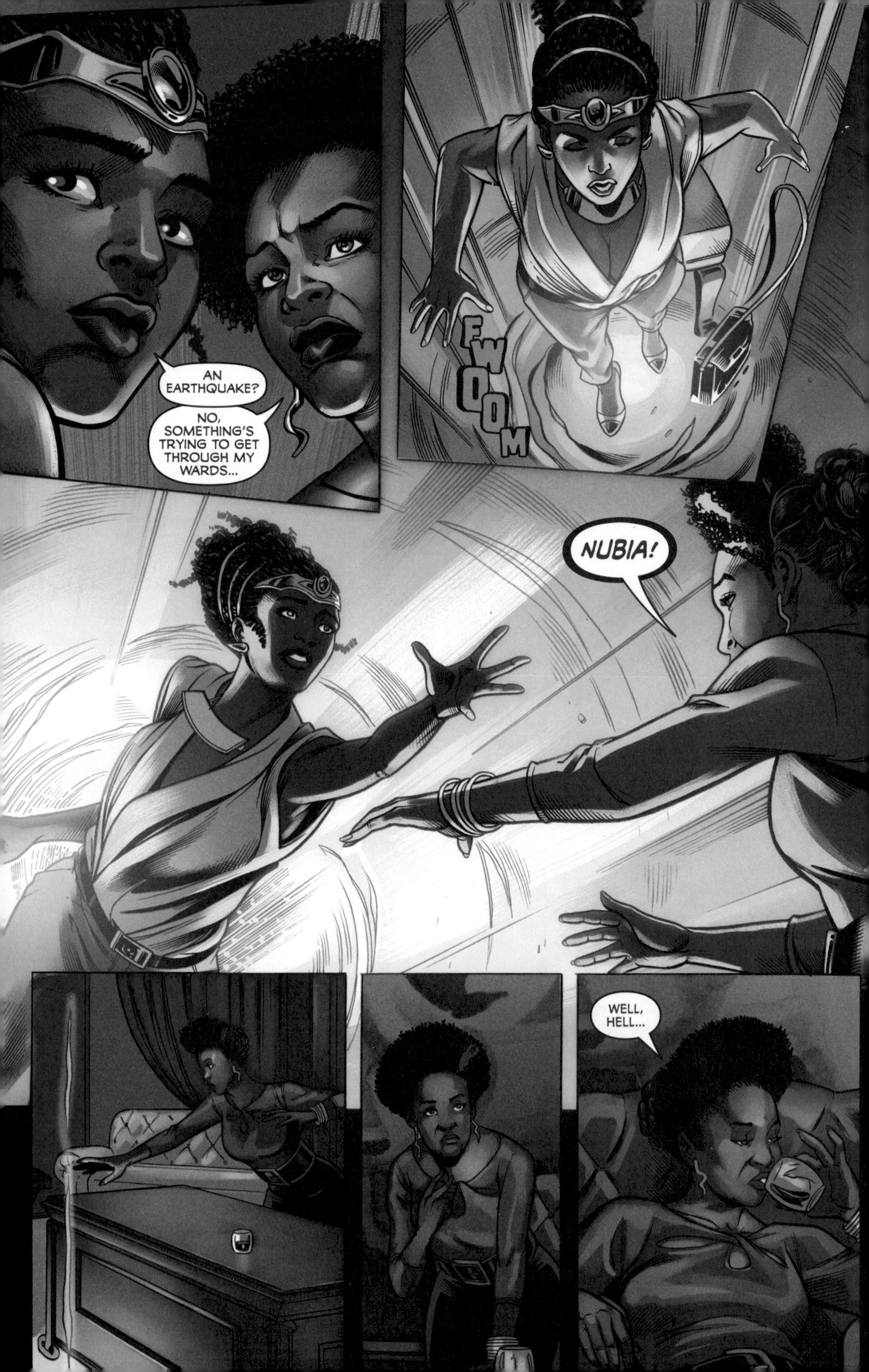
AN EARTHQUAKE?
NO, SOMETHING'S TRYING TO GET THROUGH MY WARDS...
FWOOOM
NUBIA!
WELL, HELL...

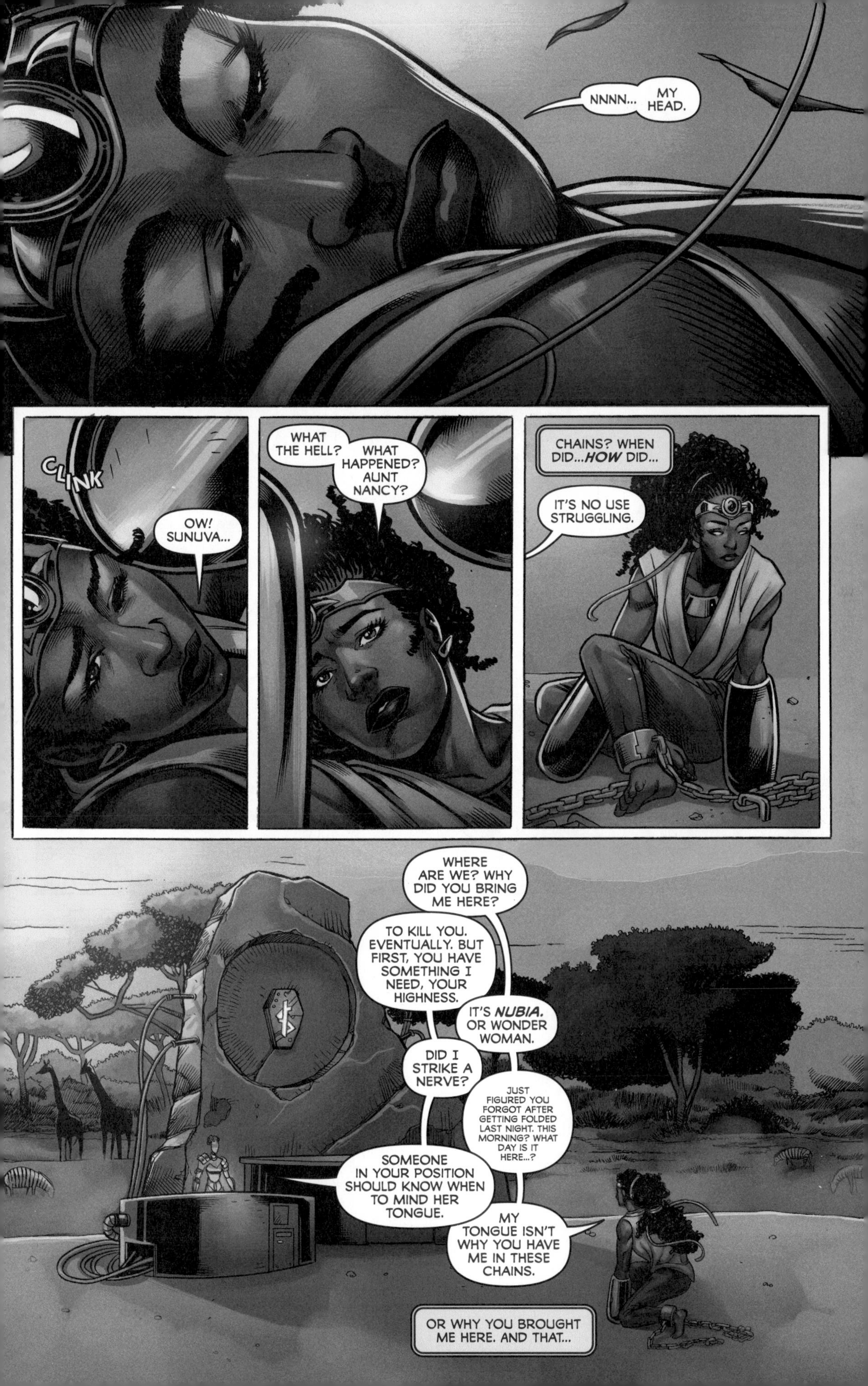
NNNN... MY HEAD.
CLINK
OW! SUNUVA...
WHAT THE HELL?
WHAT HAPPENED? AUNT NANCY?
CHAINS? WHEN DID...*HOW* DID...
IT'S NO USE STRUGGLING.
WHERE ARE WE? WHY DID YOU BRING ME HERE?
TO KILL YOU. EVENTUALLY. BUT FIRST, YOU HAVE SOMETHING I NEED, YOUR HIGHNESS.
IT'S *NUBIA.* OR WONDER WOMAN.
DID I STRIKE A NERVE?
JUST FIGURED YOU FORGOT AFTER GETTING FOLDED LAST NIGHT. THIS MORNING? WHAT DAY IS IT HERE...?
SOMEONE IN YOUR POSITION SHOULD KNOW WHEN TO MIND HER TONGUE.
MY TONGUE ISN'T WHY YOU HAVE ME IN THESE CHAINS.
OR WHY YOU BROUGHT ME HERE. AND THAT...

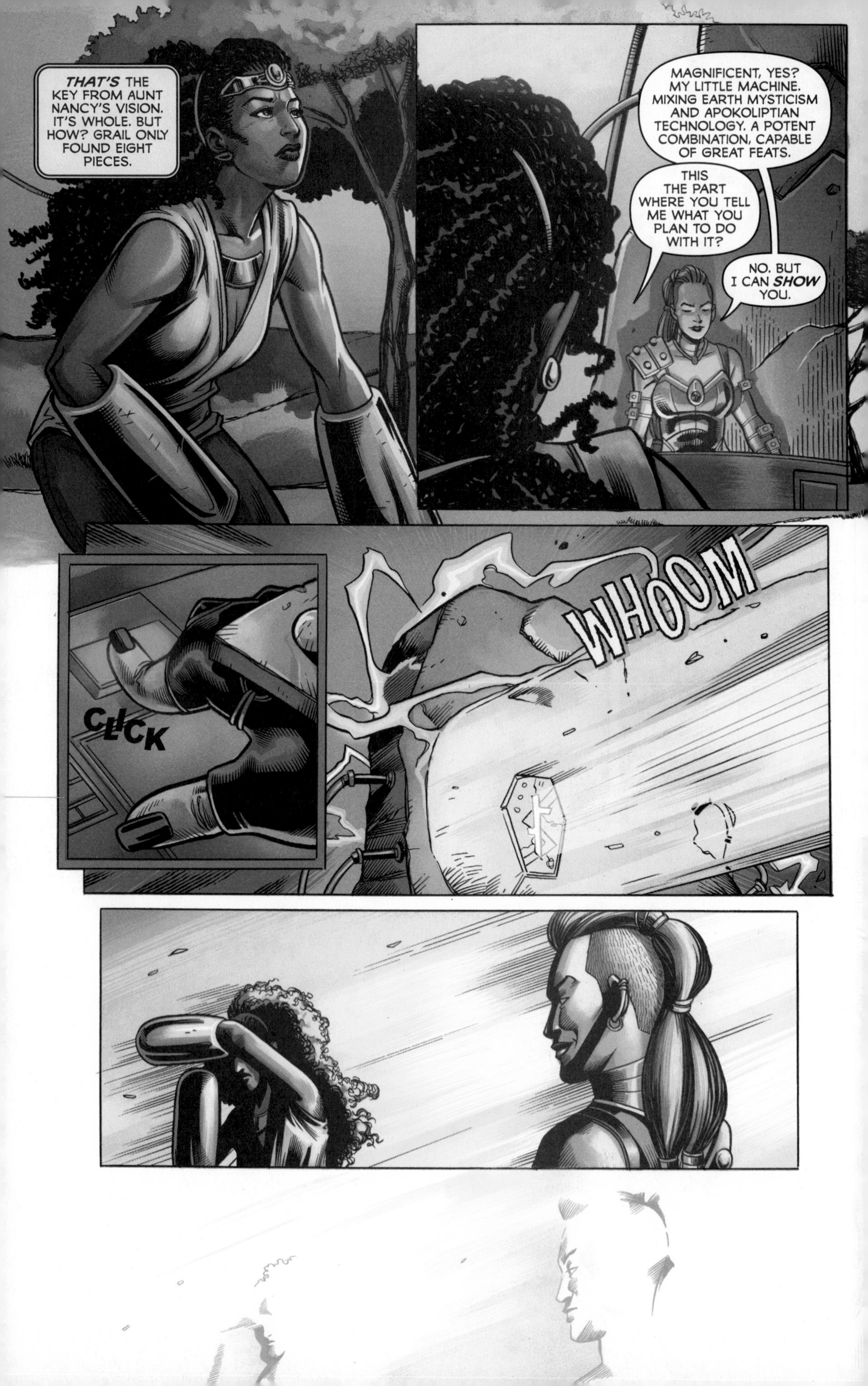
THAT'S THE KEY FROM AUNT NANCY'S VISION. IT'S WHOLE. BUT HOW? GRAIL ONLY FOUND EIGHT PIECES.
MAGNIFICENT, YES? MY LITTLE MACHINE. MIXING EARTH MYSTICISM AND APOKOLIPTIAN TECHNOLOGY. A POTENT COMBINATION, CAPABLE OF GREAT FEATS.
THIS THE PART WHERE YOU TELL ME WHAT YOU PLAN TO DO WITH IT?
NO. BUT I CAN SHOW YOU.
CLICK
WHOOM

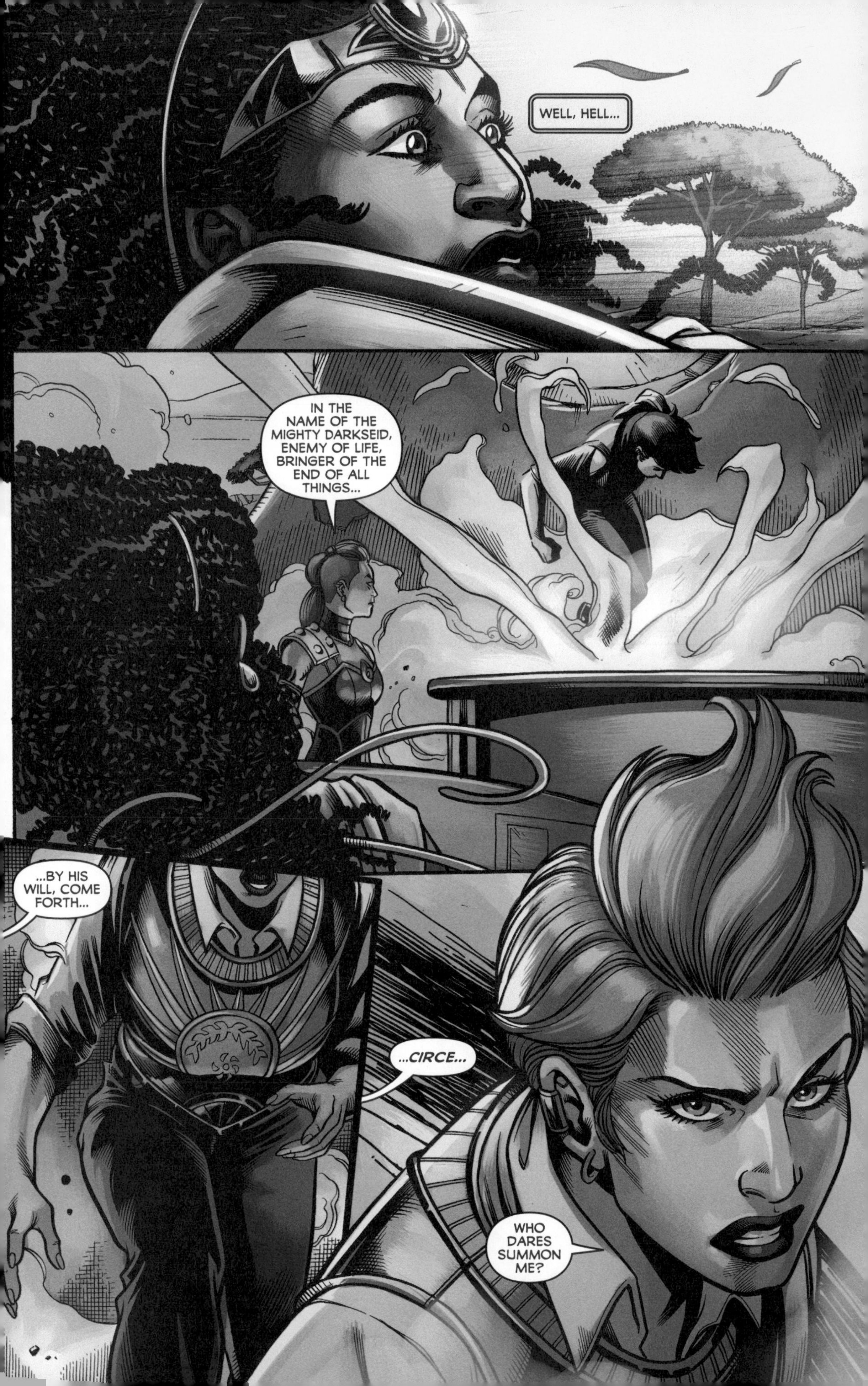
WELL, HELL...
IN THE NAME OF THE MIGHTY DARKSEID, ENEMY OF LIFE, BRINGER OF THE END OF ALL THINGS...
...BY HIS WILL, COME FORTH...
...CIRCE...
WHO DARES SUMMON ME?

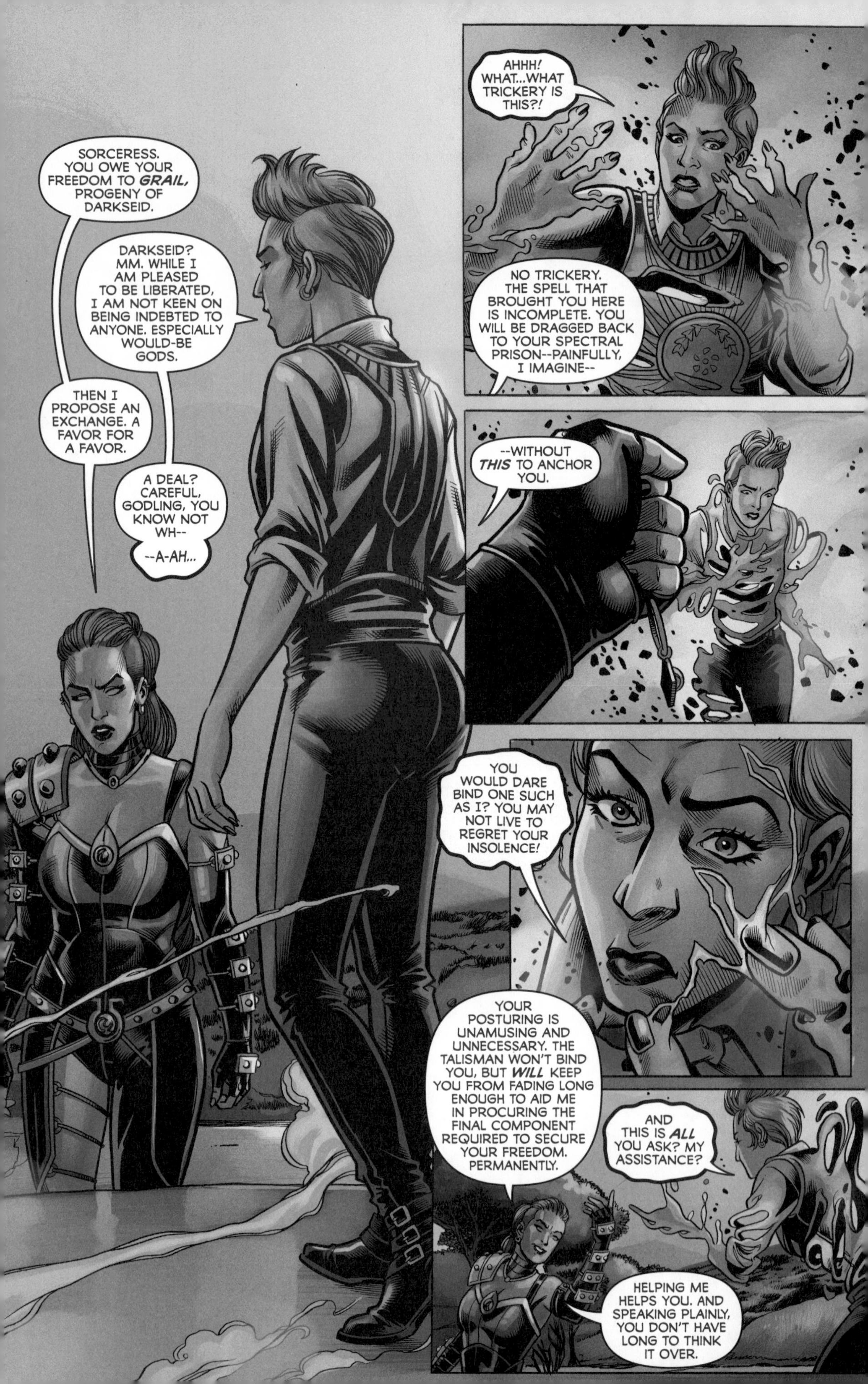

SORCERESS. YOU OWE YOUR FREEDOM TO GRAIL, PROGENY OF DARKSEID.
DARKSEID? MM. WHILE I AM PLEASED TO BE LIBERATED, I AM NOT KEEN ON BEING INDEBTED TO ANYONE. ESPECIALLY WOULD-BE GODS.
THEN I PROPOSE AN EXCHANGE. A FAVOR FOR A FAVOR.
A DEAL? CAREFUL, GODLING, YOU KNOW NOT WH--
--A-AH...
AHHH! WHAT...WHAT TRICKERY IS THIS?!
NO TRICKERY. THE SPELL THAT BROUGHT YOU HERE IS INCOMPLETE. YOU WILL BE DRAGGED BACK TO YOUR SPECTRAL PRISON--PAINFULLY, I IMAGINE--
--WITHOUT THIS TO ANCHOR YOU.
YOU WOULD DARE BIND ONE SUCH AS I? YOU MAY NOT LIVE TO REGRET YOUR INSOLENCE!
YOUR POSTURING IS UNAMUSING AND UNNECESSARY. THE TALISMAN WON'T BIND YOU, BUT WILL KEEP YOU FROM FADING LONG ENOUGH TO AID ME IN PROCURING THE FINAL COMPONENT REQUIRED TO SECURE YOUR FREEDOM. PERMANENTLY.
AND THIS IS ALL YOU ASK? MY ASSISTANCE?
HELPING ME HELPS YOU. AND SPEAKING PLAINLY, YOU DON'T HAVE LONG TO THINK IT OVER.

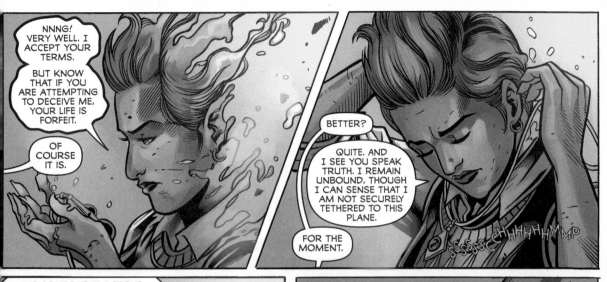

NNNG! VERY WELL. I ACCEPT YOUR TERMS.

BUT KNOW THAT IF YOU ARE ATTEMPTING TO DECEIVE ME, YOUR LIFE IS FORFEIT.

OF COURSE IT IS.

BETTER?

QUITE. AND I SEE YOU SPEAK TRUTH. I REMAIN UNBOUND, THOUGH I CAN SENSE THAT I AM NOT SECURELY TETHERED TO THIS PLANE.

FOR THE MOMENT.

THE COMPONENT I SPOKE OF IS PROTECTED BY POWERFUL SPELLWORK NATIVE TO THIS WORLD. I AM NOT A PRACTITIONER, AND WHILE THE TECHNOLOGY AT MY DISPOSAL IS ADVANCED ENOUGH TO RESEMBLE WHAT MORTALS CALL SORCERY--

IT'S STILL TECHNOLOGY, AND MAGIC MUST DEFEAT MAGIC.

SO I HAVE EXPERIENCED.

FINE. WHERE IS IT?

THERE.

THAT LOOK CAN'T BE GOOD.

THE AMAZON? INTERESTING...

YOU CAN TELL SHE IS OF THEMYSCIRA?

I DETECT THE ISLAND'S MAGIC ALL ABOUT HER. THE SCENT IS FAINT, BUT STILL MARKS HER AS ONE OF ITS CHILDREN.

MMM...

IN FACT, I DARE SAY I SENSE THE SAME OF YOU.

MIND YOURSELF, WITCH.

WORRY NOT, GODLING. YOUR ANCESTRY MATTERS LITTLE TO ME. THOUGH I AM CURIOUS WHAT LED YOU TO OFFER UP ONE OF YOUR OWN.

I REQUIRE HER TIARA. I TRUST YOUR MAGICS--UNTETHERED AS YOU ARE--REMAIN UP TO THE TASK.

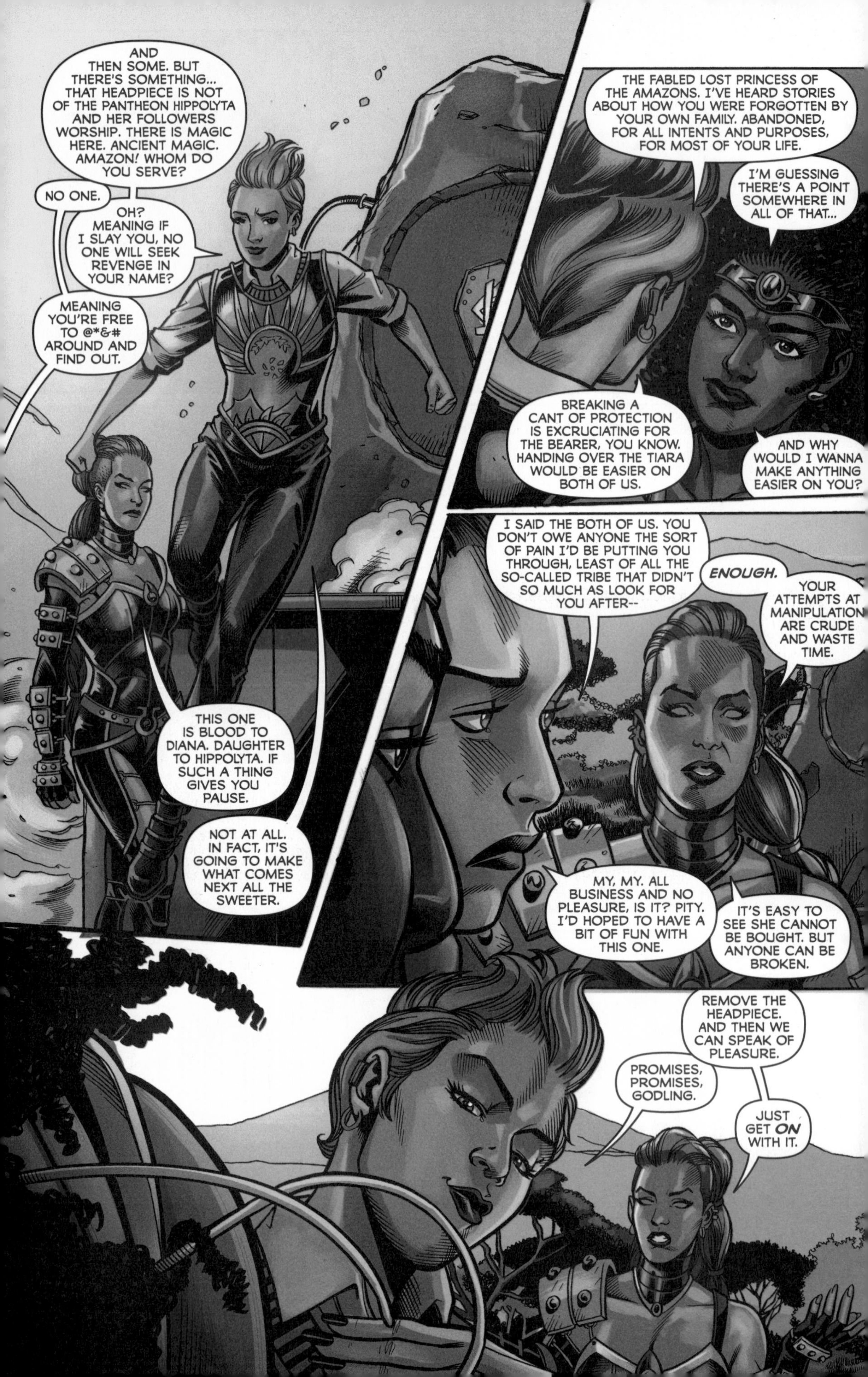
AND THEN SOME. BUT THERE'S SOMETHING... THAT HEADPIECE IS NOT OF THE PANTHEON HIPPOLYTA AND HER FOLLOWERS WORSHIP. THERE IS MAGIC HERE. ANCIENT MAGIC. AMAZON! WHOM DO YOU SERVE?
NO ONE.
OH? MEANING IF I SLAY YOU, NO ONE WILL SEEK REVENGE IN YOUR NAME?
MEANING YOU'RE FREE TO @*&# AROUND AND FIND OUT.
THIS ONE IS BLOOD TO DIANA. DAUGHTER TO HIPPOLYTA. IF SUCH A THING GIVES YOU PAUSE.
NOT AT ALL. IN FACT, IT'S GOING TO MAKE WHAT COMES NEXT ALL THE SWEETER.
THE FABLED LOST PRINCESS OF THE AMAZONS. I'VE HEARD STORIES ABOUT HOW YOU WERE FORGOTTEN BY YOUR OWN FAMILY. ABANDONED, FOR ALL INTENTS AND PURPOSES, FOR MOST OF YOUR LIFE.
I'M GUESSING THERE'S A POINT SOMEWHERE IN ALL OF THAT...
BREAKING A CANT OF PROTECTION IS EXCRUCIATING FOR THE BEARER, YOU KNOW. HANDING OVER THE TIARA WOULD BE EASIER ON BOTH OF US.
AND WHY WOULD I WANNA MAKE ANYTHING EASIER ON YOU?
I SAID THE BOTH OF US. YOU DON'T OWE ANYONE THE SORT OF PAIN I'D BE PUTTING YOU THROUGH, LEAST OF ALL THE SO-CALLED TRIBE THAT DIDN'T SO MUCH AS LOOK FOR YOU AFTER--
ENOUGH.
YOUR ATTEMPTS AT MANIPULATION ARE CRUDE AND WASTE TIME.
MY, MY. ALL BUSINESS AND NO PLEASURE, IS IT? PITY. I'D HOPED TO HAVE A BIT OF FUN WITH THIS ONE.
IT'S EASY TO SEE SHE CANNOT BE BOUGHT. BUT ANYONE CAN BE BROKEN.
REMOVE THE HEADPIECE. AND THEN WE CAN SPEAK OF PLEASURE.
PROMISES, PROMISES, GODLING.
JUST GET ON WITH IT.

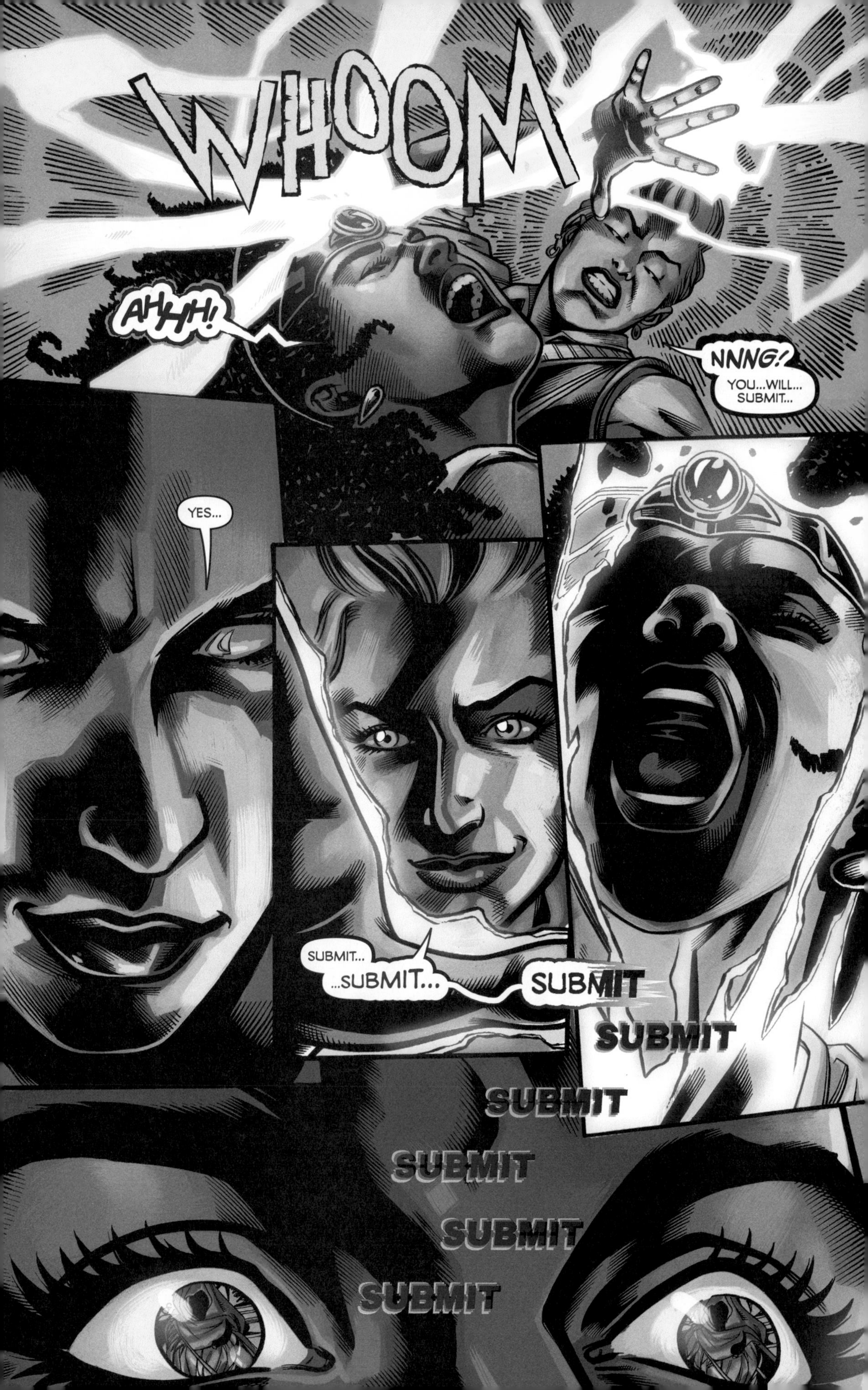
WHOOM
AHHH!
NNNG! YOU...WILL... SUBMIT...
YES...
SUBMIT...
...SUBMIT...
SUBMIT
SUBMIT
SUBMIT
SUBMIT
SUBMIT
SUBMIT

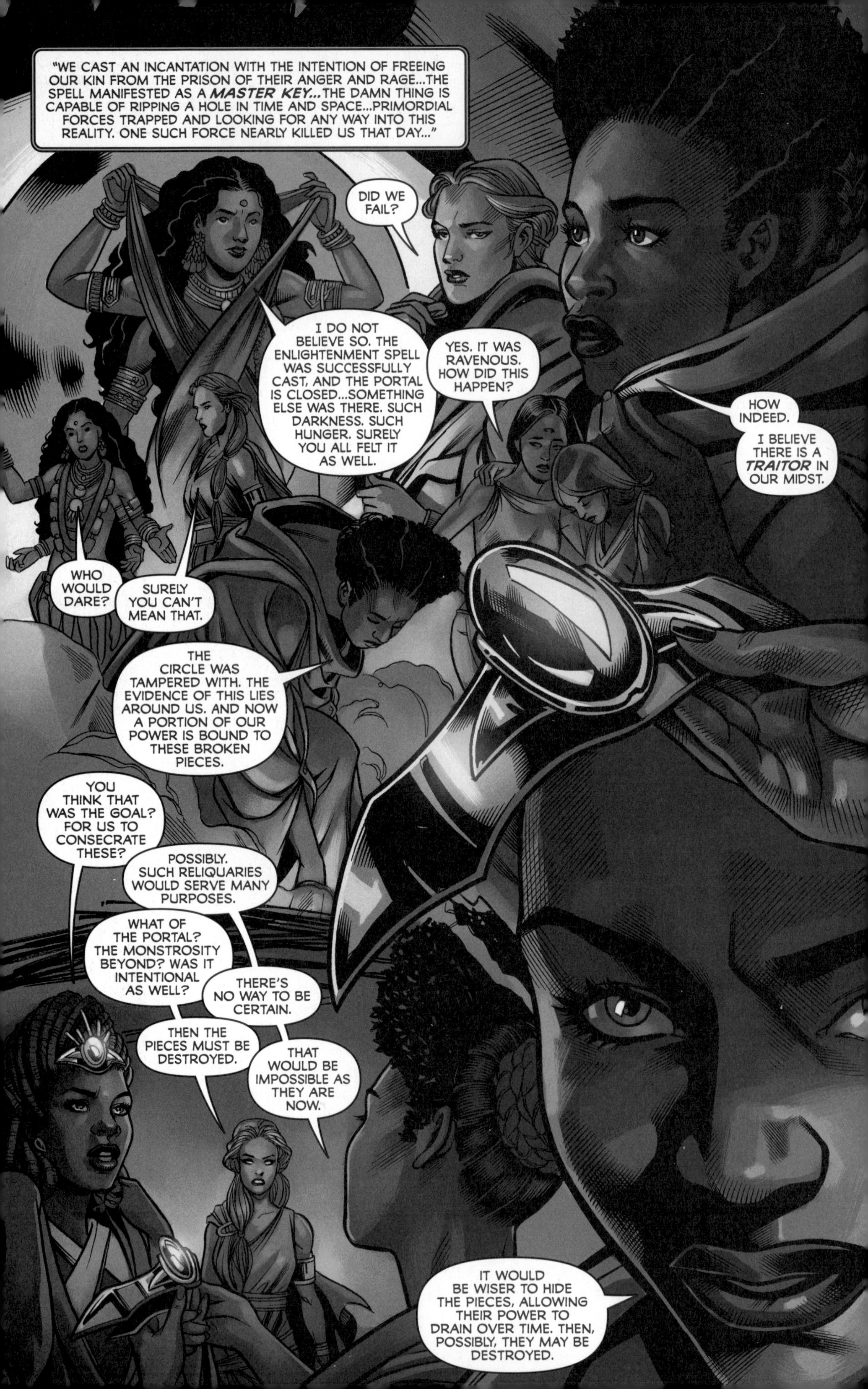
"WE CAST AN INCANTATION WITH THE INTENTION OF FREEING OUR KIN FROM THE PRISON OF THEIR ANGER AND RAGE...THE SPELL MANIFESTED AS A MASTER KEY...THE DAMN THING IS CAPABLE OF RIPPING A HOLE IN TIME AND SPACE...PRIMORDIAL FORCES TRAPPED AND LOOKING FOR ANY WAY INTO THIS REALITY. ONE SUCH FORCE NEARLY KILLED US THAT DAY..."
DID WE FAIL?
I DO NOT BELIEVE SO. THE ENLIGHTENMENT SPELL WAS SUCCESSFULLY CAST, AND THE PORTAL IS CLOSED...SOMETHING ELSE WAS THERE. SUCH DARKNESS. SUCH HUNGER. SURELY YOU ALL FELT IT AS WELL.
YES. IT WAS RAVENOUS. HOW DID THIS HAPPEN?
HOW INDEED.
I BELIEVE THERE IS A TRAITOR IN OUR MIDST.
WHO WOULD DARE?
SURELY YOU CAN'T MEAN THAT.
THE CIRCLE WAS TAMPERED WITH. THE EVIDENCE OF THIS LIES AROUND US. AND NOW A PORTION OF OUR POWER IS BOUND TO THESE BROKEN PIECES.
YOU THINK THAT WAS THE GOAL? FOR US TO CONSECRATE THESE?
POSSIBLY. SUCH RELIQUARIES WOULD SERVE MANY PURPOSES.
WHAT OF THE PORTAL? THE MONSTROSITY BEYOND? WAS IT INTENTIONAL AS WELL?
THERE'S NO WAY TO BE CERTAIN.
THEN THE PIECES MUST BE DESTROYED.
THAT WOULD BE IMPOSSIBLE AS THEY ARE NOW.
IT WOULD BE WISER TO HIDE THE PIECES, ALLOWING THEIR POWER TO DRAIN OVER TIME. THEN, POSSIBLY, THEY MAY BE DESTROYED.

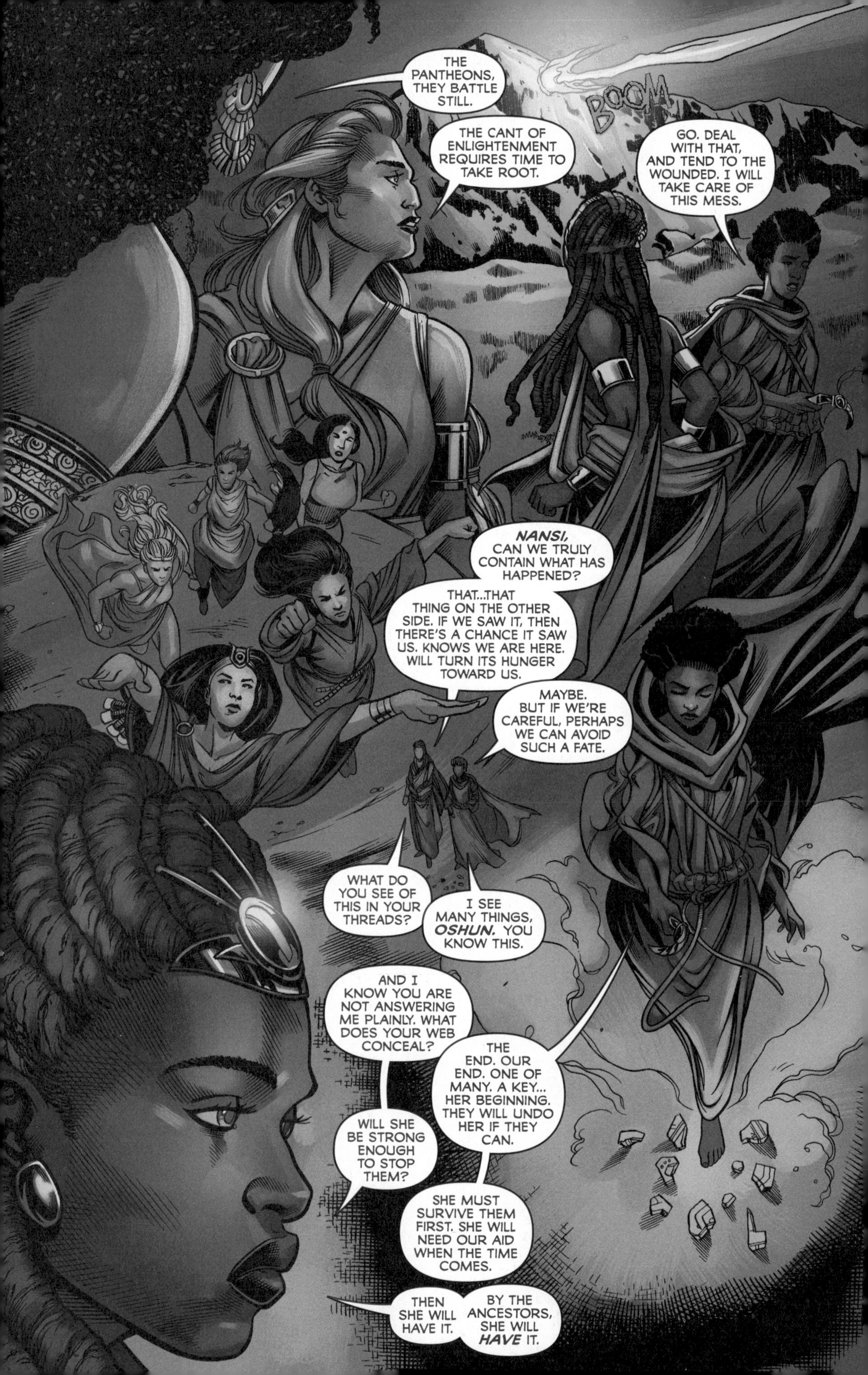

THE PANTHEONS, THEY BATTLE STILL.
BOOM
THE CANT OF ENLIGHTENMENT REQUIRES TIME TO TAKE ROOT.
GO. DEAL WITH THAT, AND TEND TO THE WOUNDED. I WILL TAKE CARE OF THIS MESS.
NANSI, CAN WE TRULY CONTAIN WHAT HAS HAPPENED?
THAT...THAT THING ON THE OTHER SIDE. IF WE SAW IT, THEN THERE'S A CHANCE IT SAW US. KNOWS WE ARE HERE. WILL TURN ITS HUNGER TOWARD US.
MAYBE. BUT IF WE'RE CAREFUL, PERHAPS WE CAN AVOID SUCH A FATE.
WHAT DO YOU SEE OF THIS IN YOUR THREADS?
I SEE MANY THINGS, OSHUN. YOU KNOW THIS.
AND I KNOW YOU ARE NOT ANSWERING ME PLAINLY. WHAT DOES YOUR WEB CONCEAL?
THE END. OUR END. ONE OF MANY. A KEY... HER BEGINNING. THEY WILL UNDO HER IF THEY CAN.
WILL SHE BE STRONG ENOUGH TO STOP THEM?
SHE MUST SURVIVE THEM FIRST. SHE WILL NEED OUR AID WHEN THE TIME COMES.
THEN SHE WILL HAVE IT.
BY THE ANCESTORS, SHE WILL HAVE IT.

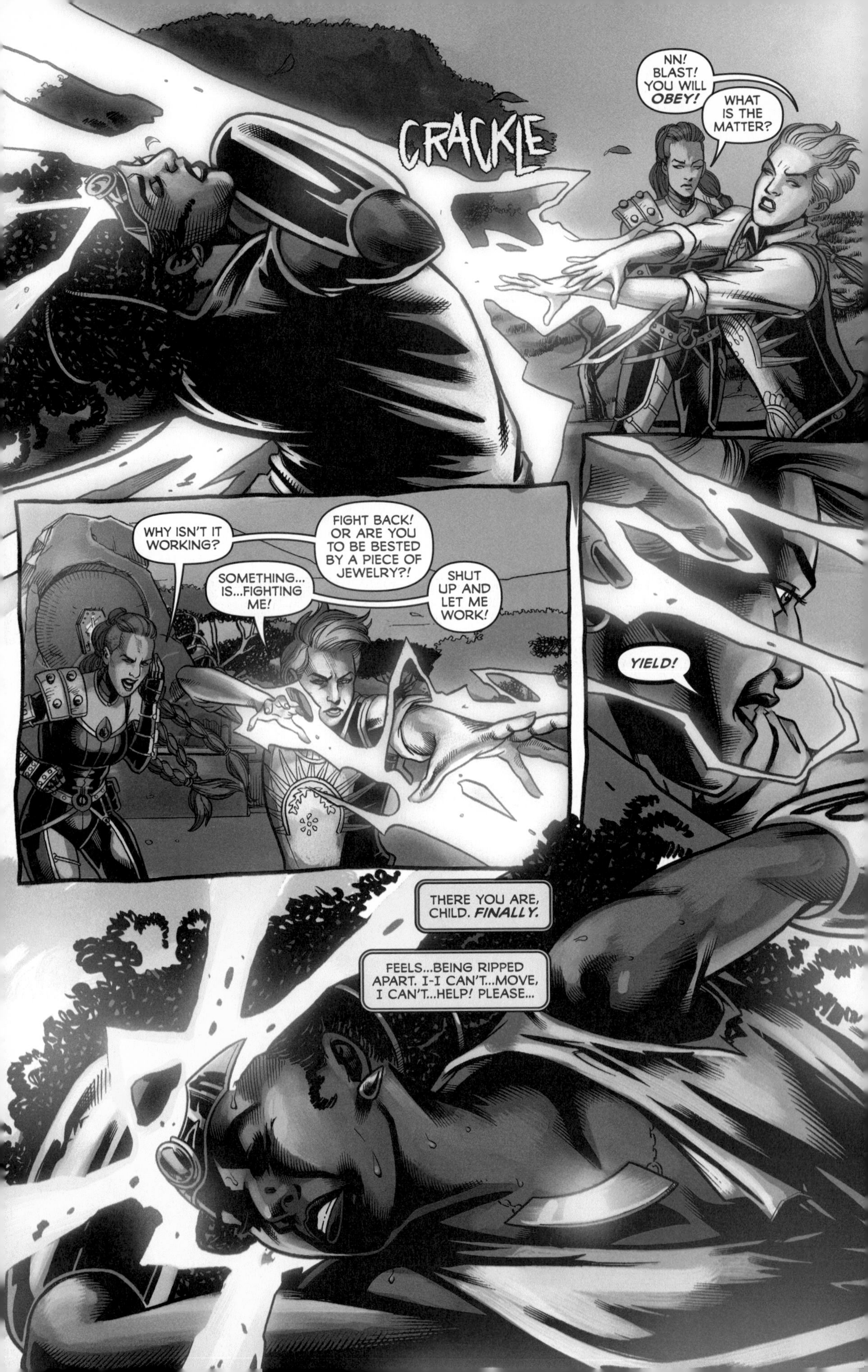
CRACKLE
NN! BLAST! YOU WILL *OBEY!*
WHAT IS THE MATTER?
WHY ISN'T IT WORKING?
FIGHT BACK! OR ARE YOU TO BE BESTED BY A PIECE OF JEWELRY?!
SOMETHING... IS...FIGHTING ME!
SHUT UP AND LET ME WORK!
YIELD!
THERE YOU ARE, CHILD. *FINALLY.*
FEELS...BEING RIPPED APART. I-I CAN'T...MOVE, I CAN'T...HELP! PLEASE...

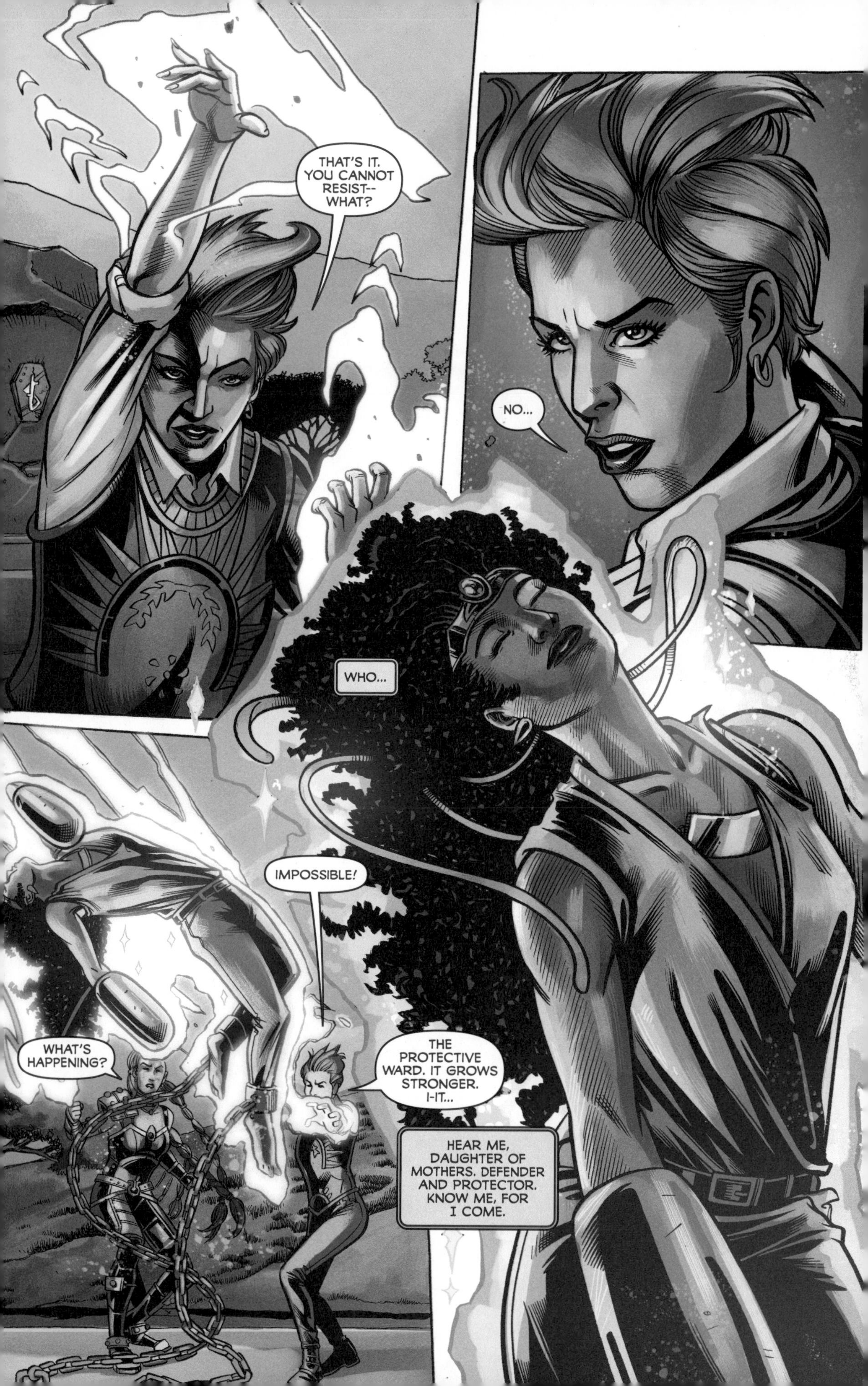
THAT'S IT. YOU CANNOT RESIST-- WHAT?
NO...
WHO...
IMPOSSIBLE!
WHAT'S HAPPENING?
THE PROTECTIVE WARD. IT GROWS STRONGER. I-IT...
HEAR ME, DAUGHTER OF MOTHERS. DEFENDER AND PROTECTOR. KNOW ME, FOR I COME.

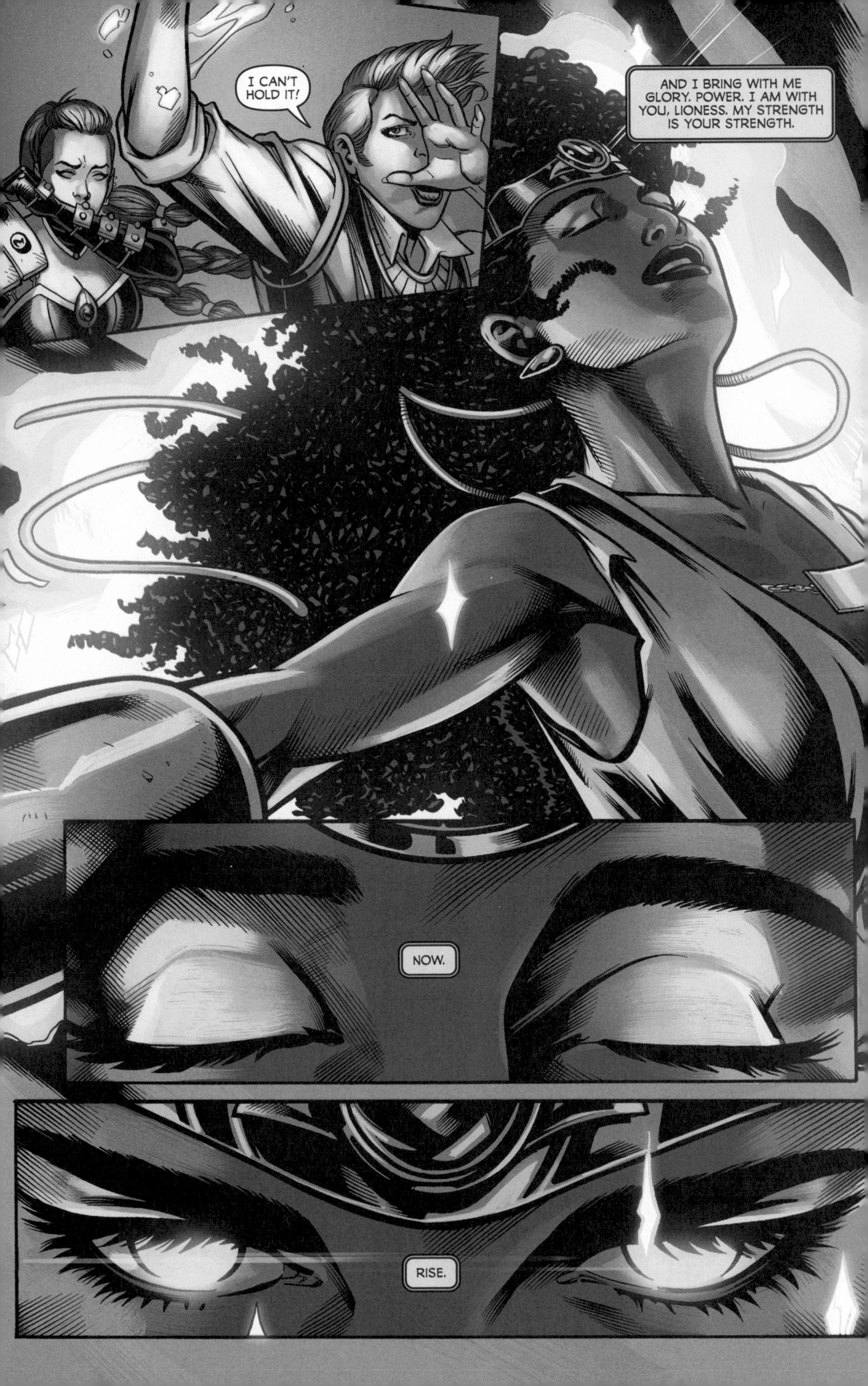
I CAN'T HOLD IT!
AND I BRING WITH ME GLORY. POWER. I AM WITH YOU, LIONESS. MY STRENGTH IS YOUR STRENGTH.
NOW.
RISE.

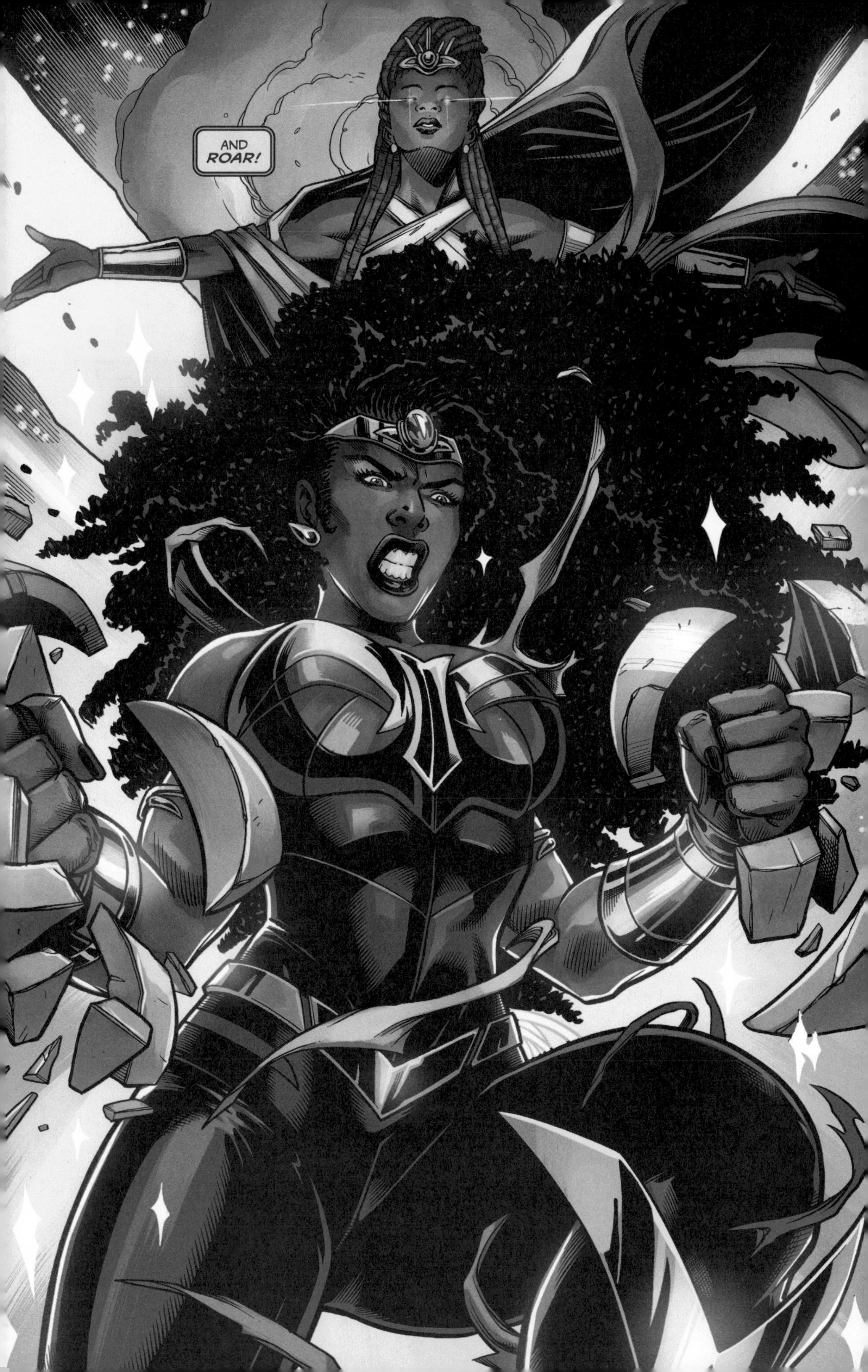
AND ROAR!

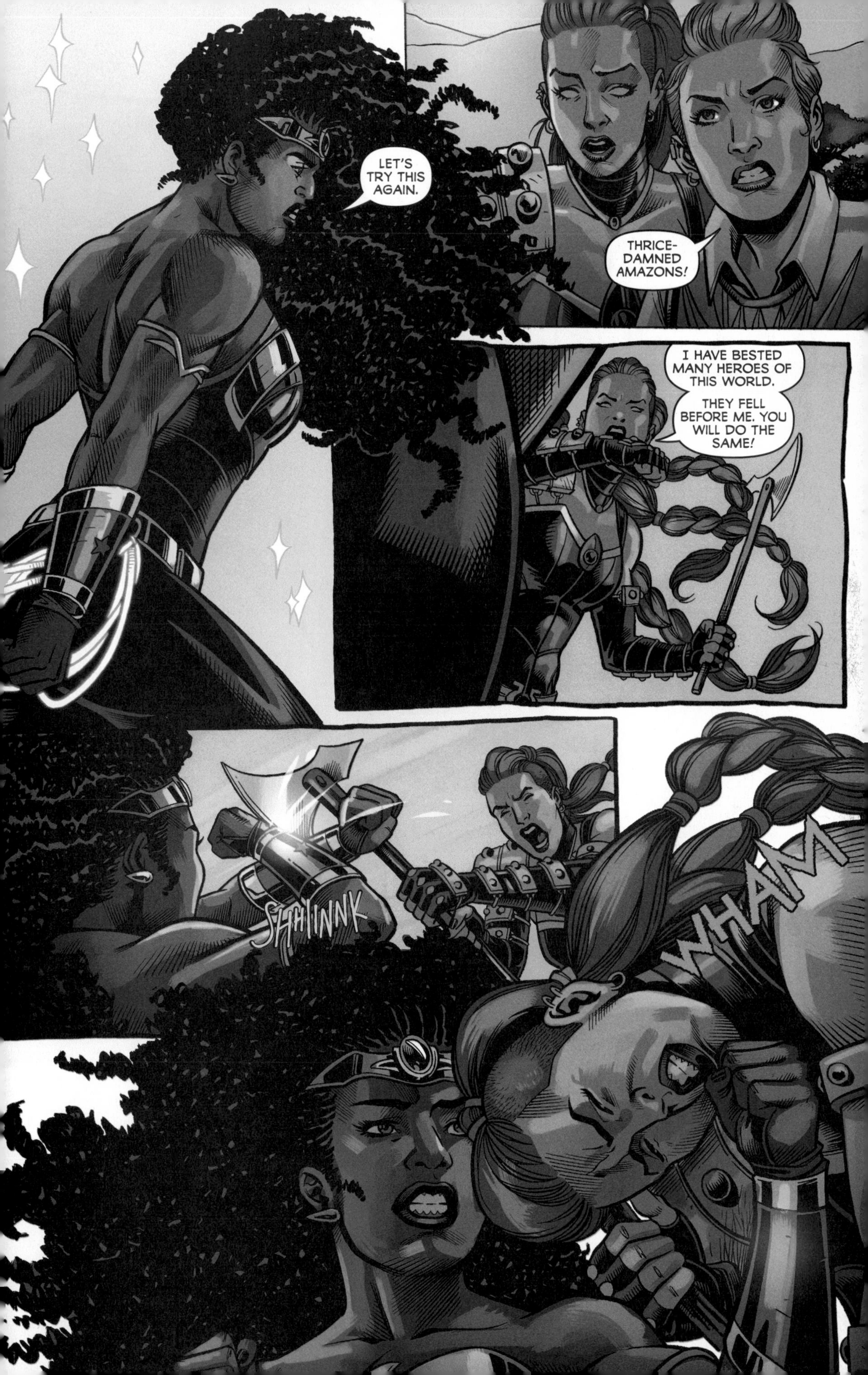
LET'S TRY THIS AGAIN.
THRICE-DAMNED AMAZONS!
I HAVE BESTED MANY HEROES OF THIS WORLD.
THEY FELL BEFORE ME. YOU WILL DO THE SAME!
SHHIINNK
WHAM

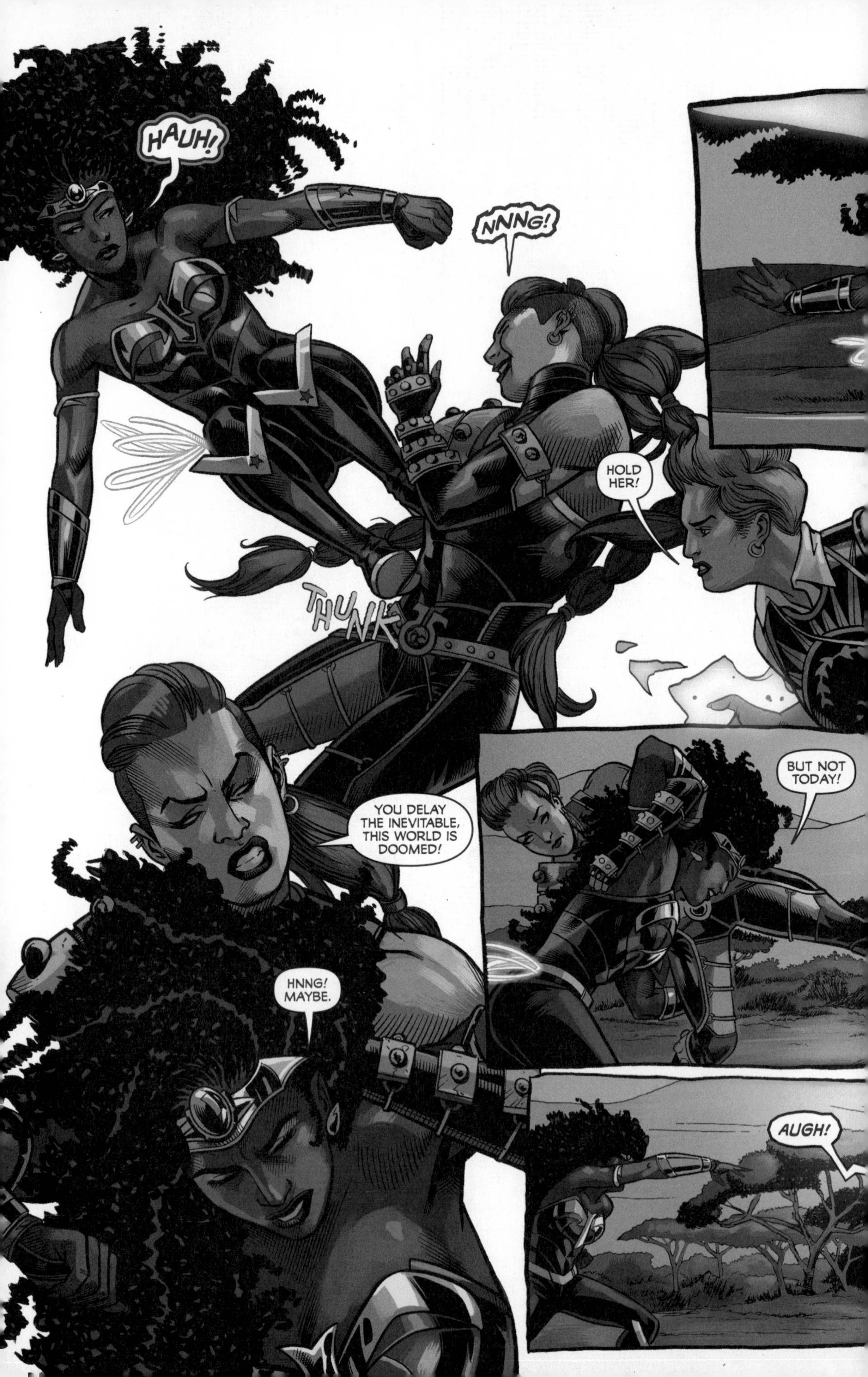
HAUH!
NNNG!
THUNK
HOLD HER!
YOU DELAY THE INEVITABLE, THIS WORLD IS DOOMED!
HNNG! MAYBE.
BUT NOT TODAY!
AUGH!

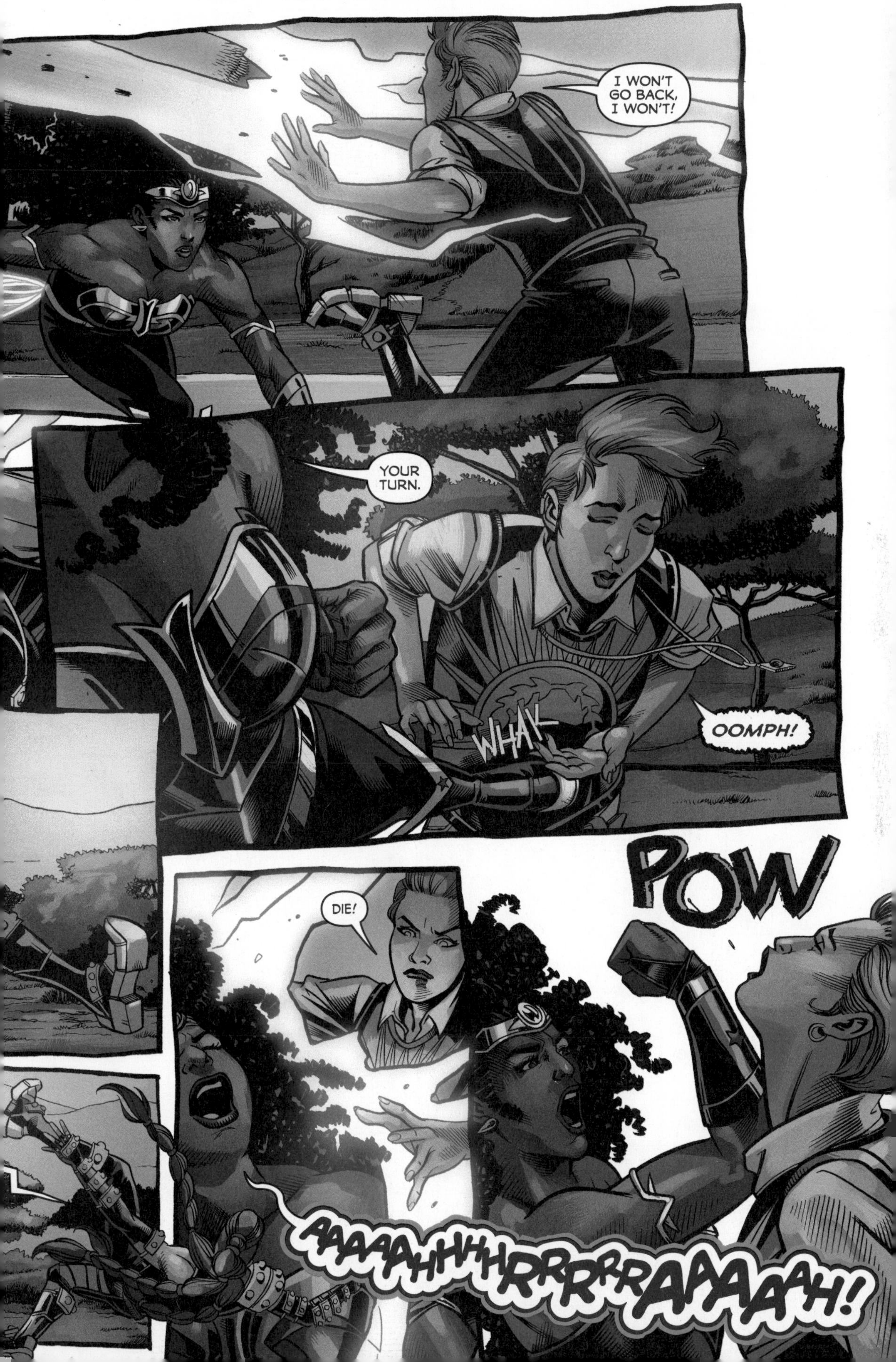
I WON'T GO BACK, I WON'T!
YOUR TURN.
WHAK
OOMPH!
POW
DIE!
AAAAAHHHHRRRRRRAAAAAAH!

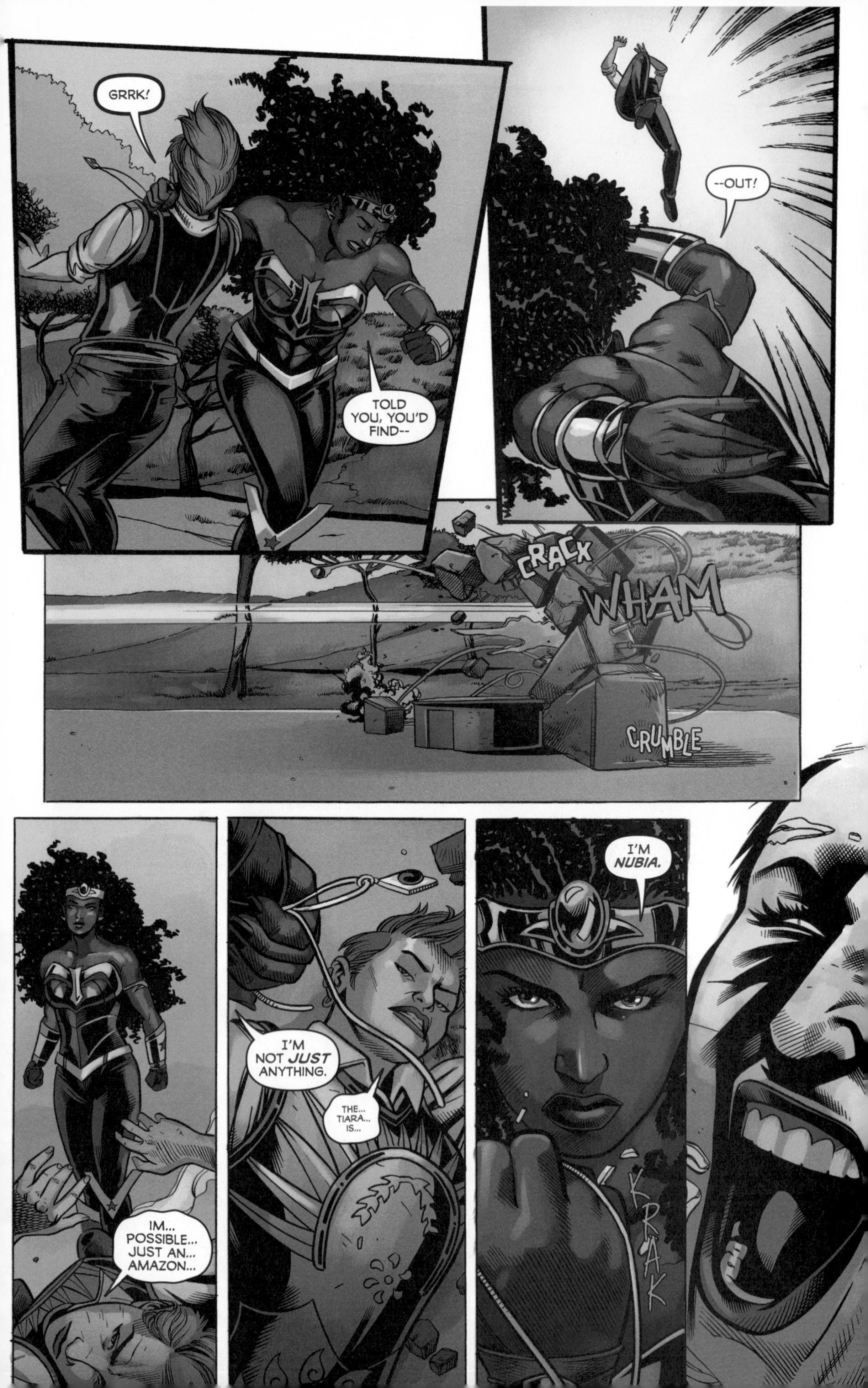
GRRK!
TOLD YOU, YOU'D FIND--
--OUT!
CRACK
WHAM
CRUMBLE
IM... POSSIBLE... JUST AN... AMAZON...
I'M NOT *JUST* ANYTHING.
THE... TIARA... IS...
I'M *NUBIA.*
KRAK

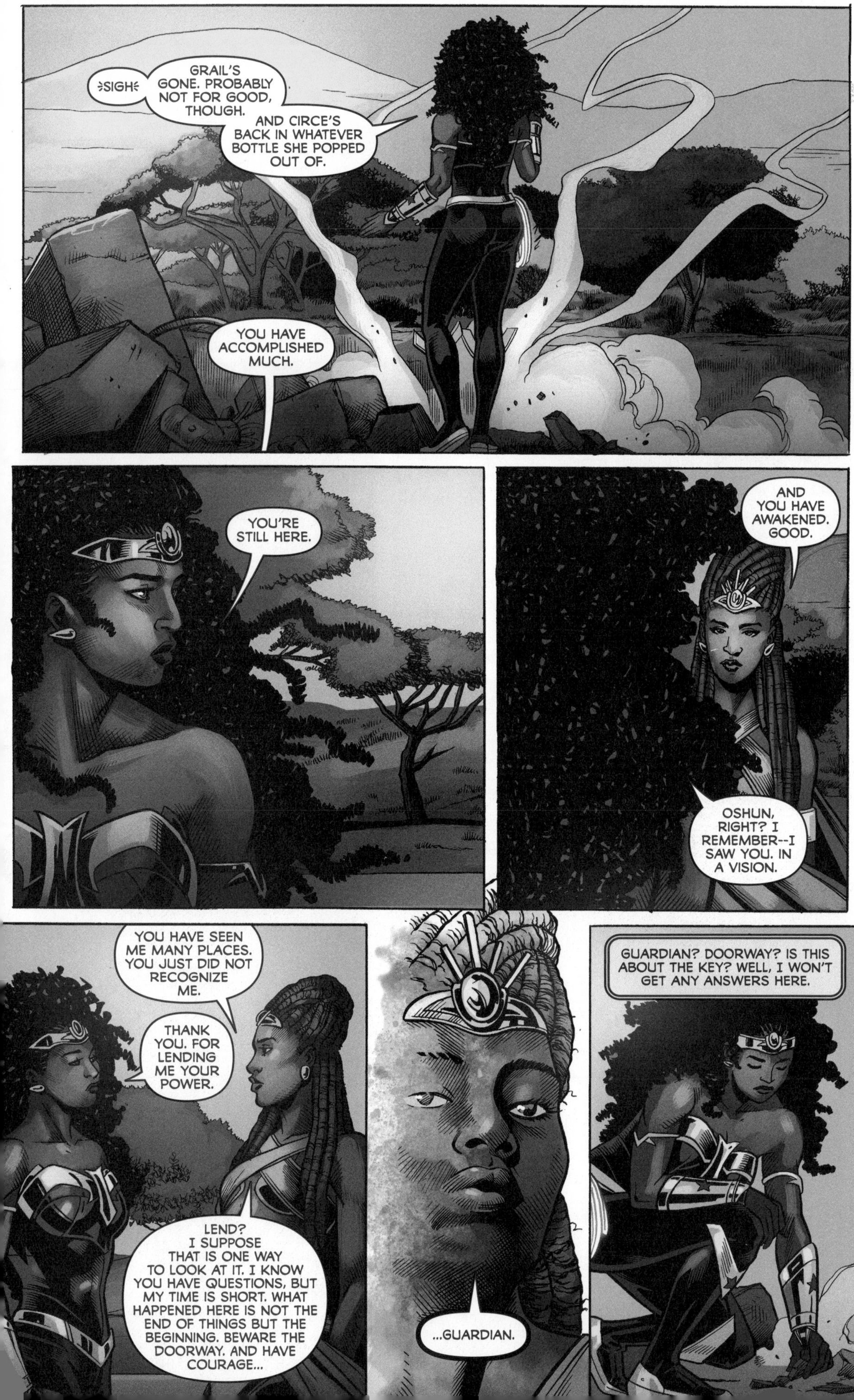

SIGH
GRAIL'S GONE. PROBABLY NOT FOR GOOD, THOUGH.
AND CIRCE'S BACK IN WHATEVER BOTTLE SHE POPPED OUT OF.
YOU HAVE ACCOMPLISHED MUCH.
YOU'RE STILL HERE.
AND YOU HAVE AWAKENED. GOOD.
OSHUN, RIGHT? I REMEMBER--I SAW YOU. IN A VISION.
YOU HAVE SEEN ME MANY PLACES. YOU JUST DID NOT RECOGNIZE ME.
THANK YOU. FOR LENDING ME YOUR POWER.
LEND? I SUPPOSE THAT IS ONE WAY TO LOOK AT IT. I KNOW YOU HAVE QUESTIONS, BUT MY TIME IS SHORT. WHAT HAPPENED HERE IS NOT THE END OF THINGS BUT THE BEGINNING. BEWARE THE DOORWAY. AND HAVE COURAGE...
...GUARDIAN.
GUARDIAN? DOORWAY? IS THIS ABOUT THE KEY? WELL, I WON'T GET ANY ANSWERS HERE.

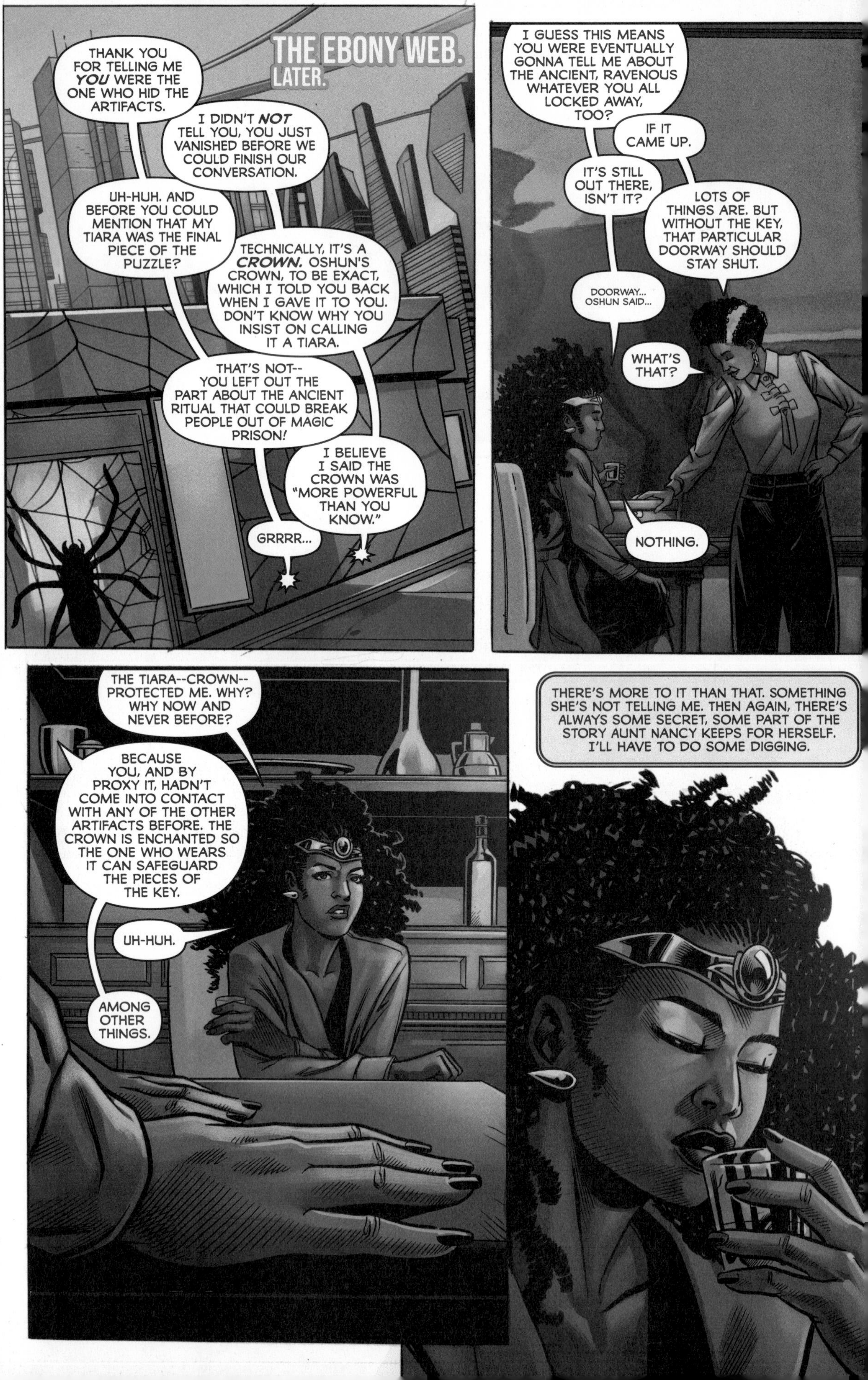
THE EBONY WEB. LATER.
THANK YOU FOR TELLING ME *YOU* WERE THE ONE WHO HID THE ARTIFACTS.
I DIDN'T *NOT* TELL YOU, YOU JUST VANISHED BEFORE WE COULD FINISH OUR CONVERSATION.
UH-HUH. AND BEFORE YOU COULD MENTION THAT MY TIARA WAS THE FINAL PIECE OF THE PUZZLE?
TECHNICALLY, IT'S A *CROWN.* OSHUN'S CROWN, TO BE EXACT, WHICH I TOLD YOU BACK WHEN I GAVE IT TO YOU. DON'T KNOW WHY YOU INSIST ON CALLING IT A TIARA.
THAT'S NOT-- YOU LEFT OUT THE PART ABOUT THE ANCIENT RITUAL THAT COULD BREAK PEOPLE OUT OF MAGIC PRISON!
I BELIEVE I SAID THE CROWN WAS "MORE POWERFUL THAN YOU KNOW."
GRRRR...
I GUESS THIS MEANS YOU WERE EVENTUALLY GONNA TELL ME ABOUT THE ANCIENT, RAVENOUS WHATEVER YOU ALL LOCKED AWAY, TOO?
IF IT CAME UP.
IT'S STILL OUT THERE, ISN'T IT?
LOTS OF THINGS ARE. BUT WITHOUT THE KEY, THAT PARTICULAR DOORWAY SHOULD STAY SHUT.
DOORWAY... OSHUN SAID...
WHAT'S THAT?
NOTHING.
THE TIARA--CROWN-- PROTECTED ME. WHY? WHY NOW AND NEVER BEFORE?
BECAUSE YOU, AND BY PROXY IT, HADN'T COME INTO CONTACT WITH ANY OF THE OTHER ARTIFACTS BEFORE. THE CROWN IS ENCHANTED SO THE ONE WHO WEARS IT CAN SAFEGUARD THE PIECES OF THE KEY.
UH-HUH.
AMONG OTHER THINGS.
THERE'S MORE TO IT THAN THAT. SOMETHING SHE'S NOT TELLING ME. THEN AGAIN, THERE'S ALWAYS SOME SECRET, SOME PART OF THE STORY AUNT NANCY KEEPS FOR HERSELF. I'LL HAVE TO DO SOME DIGGING.

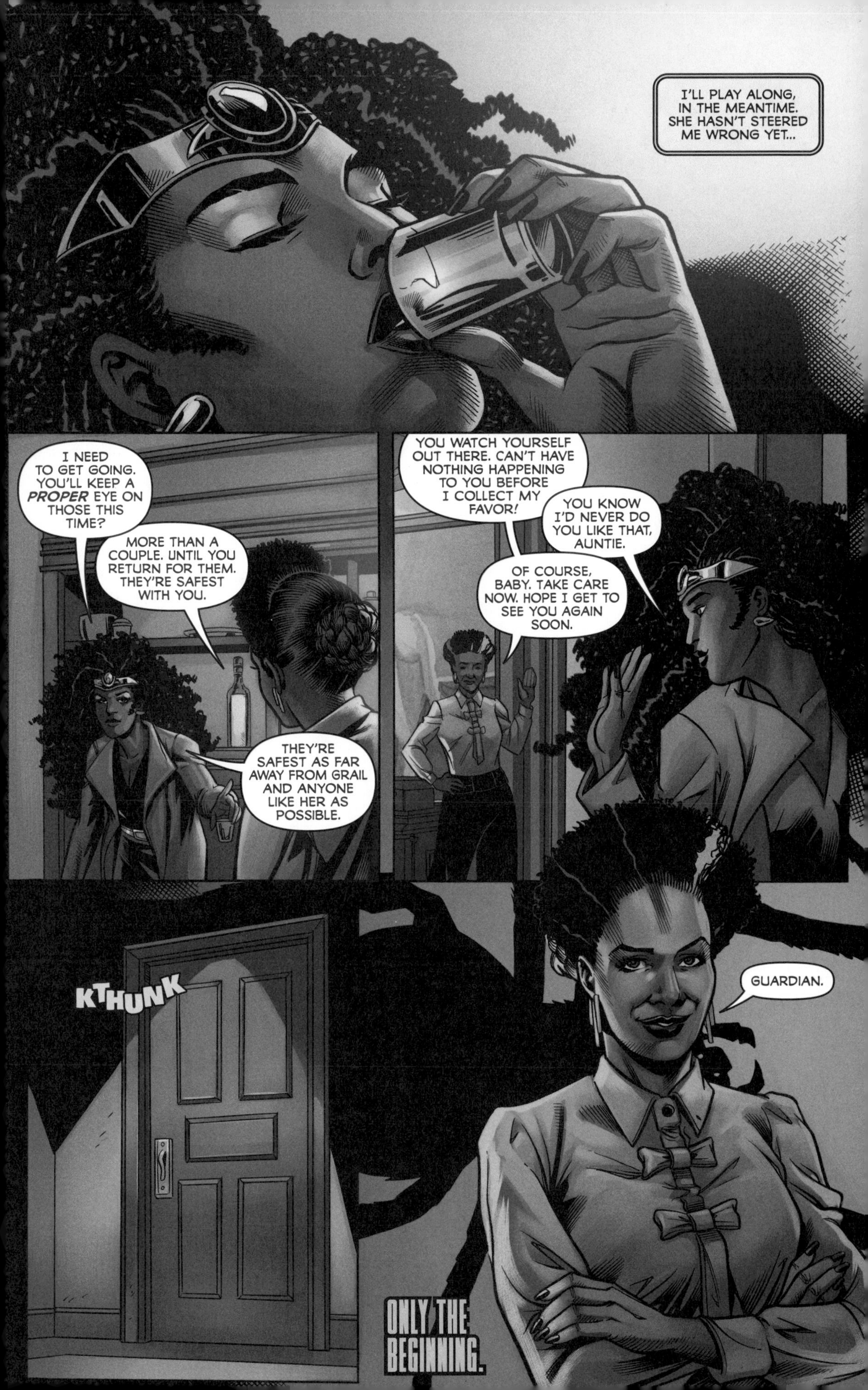
I'LL PLAY ALONG, IN THE MEANTIME. SHE HASN'T STEERED ME WRONG YET...
I NEED TO GET GOING. YOU'LL KEEP A *PROPER* EYE ON THOSE THIS TIME?
MORE THAN A COUPLE. UNTIL YOU RETURN FOR THEM. THEY'RE SAFEST WITH YOU.
THEY'RE SAFEST AS FAR AWAY FROM GRAIL AND ANYONE LIKE HER AS POSSIBLE.
YOU WATCH YOURSELF OUT THERE. CAN'T HAVE NOTHING HAPPENING TO YOU BEFORE I COLLECT MY FAVOR!
YOU KNOW I'D NEVER DO YOU LIKE THAT, AUNTIE.
OF COURSE, BABY. TAKE CARE NOW. HOPE I GET TO SEE YOU AGAIN SOON.
KTHUNK
GUARDIAN.
ONLY THE BEGINNING.

FUTURE STATE

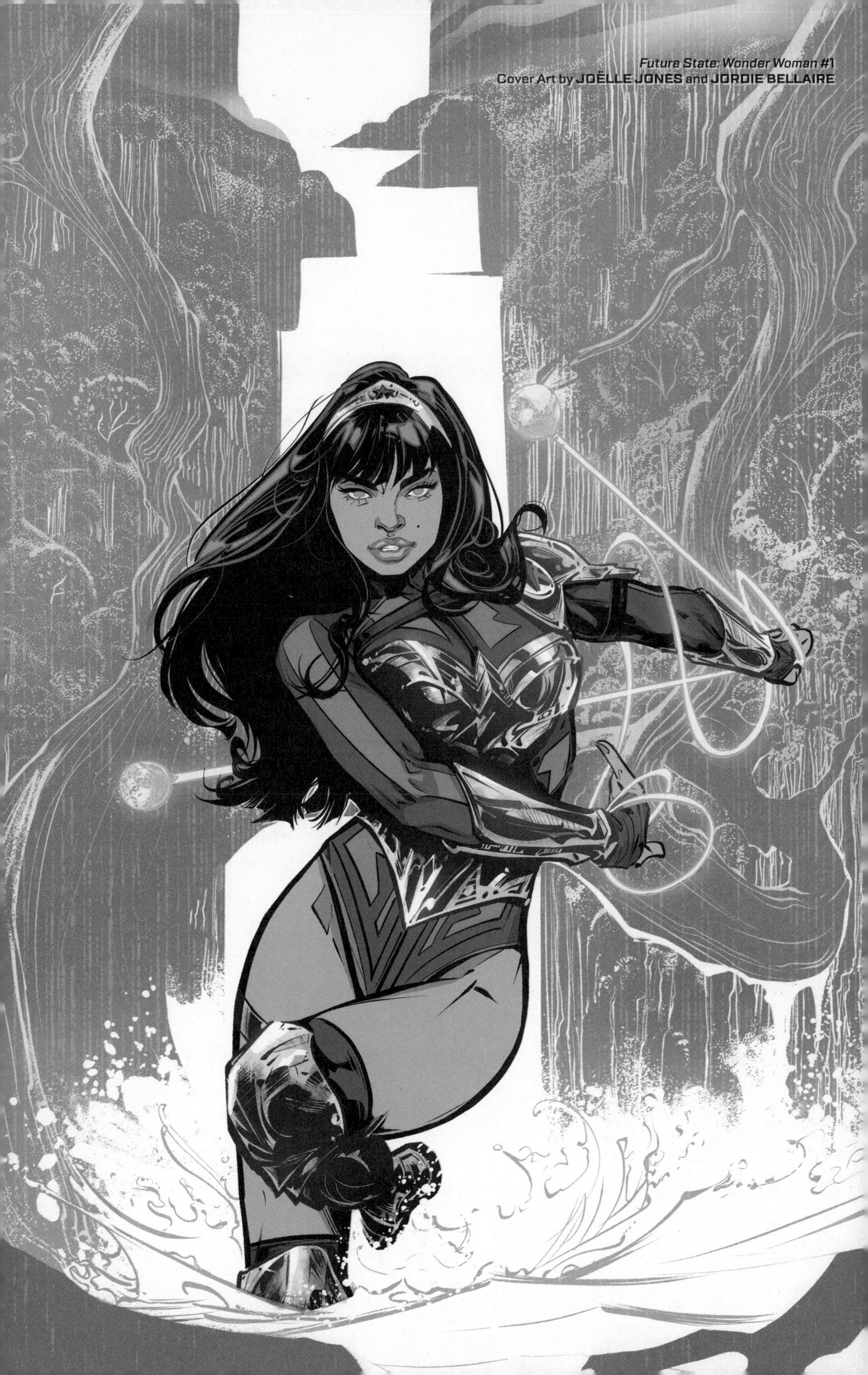

Future State: Wonder Woman #1
Cover Art by **JOËLLE JONES** and **JORDIE BELLAIRE**

FUTURE STATE

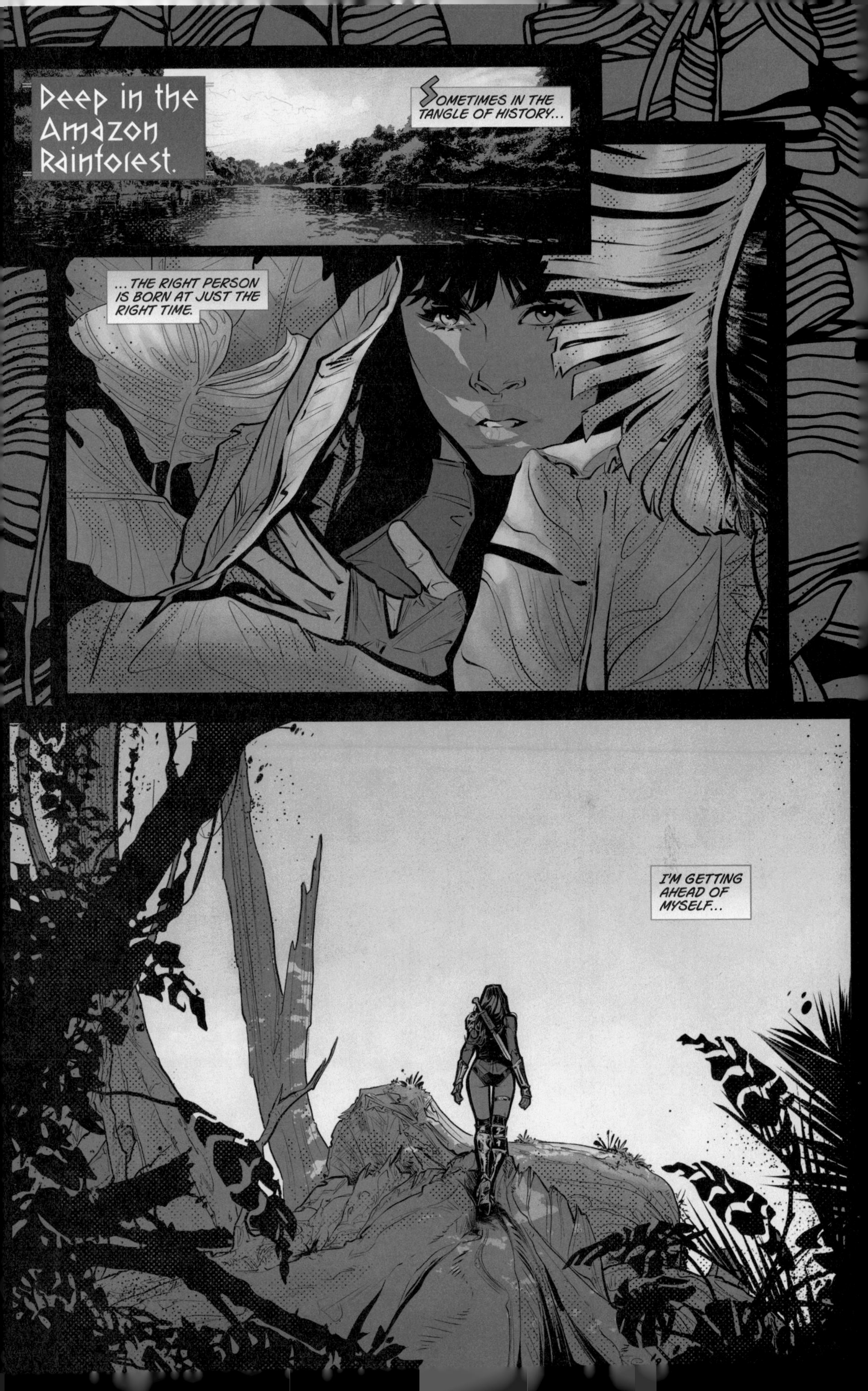
Deep in the Amazon Rainforest.
SOMETIMES IN THE TANGLE OF HISTORY...
...THE RIGHT PERSON IS BORN AT JUST THE RIGHT TIME.
I'M GETTING AHEAD OF MYSELF...

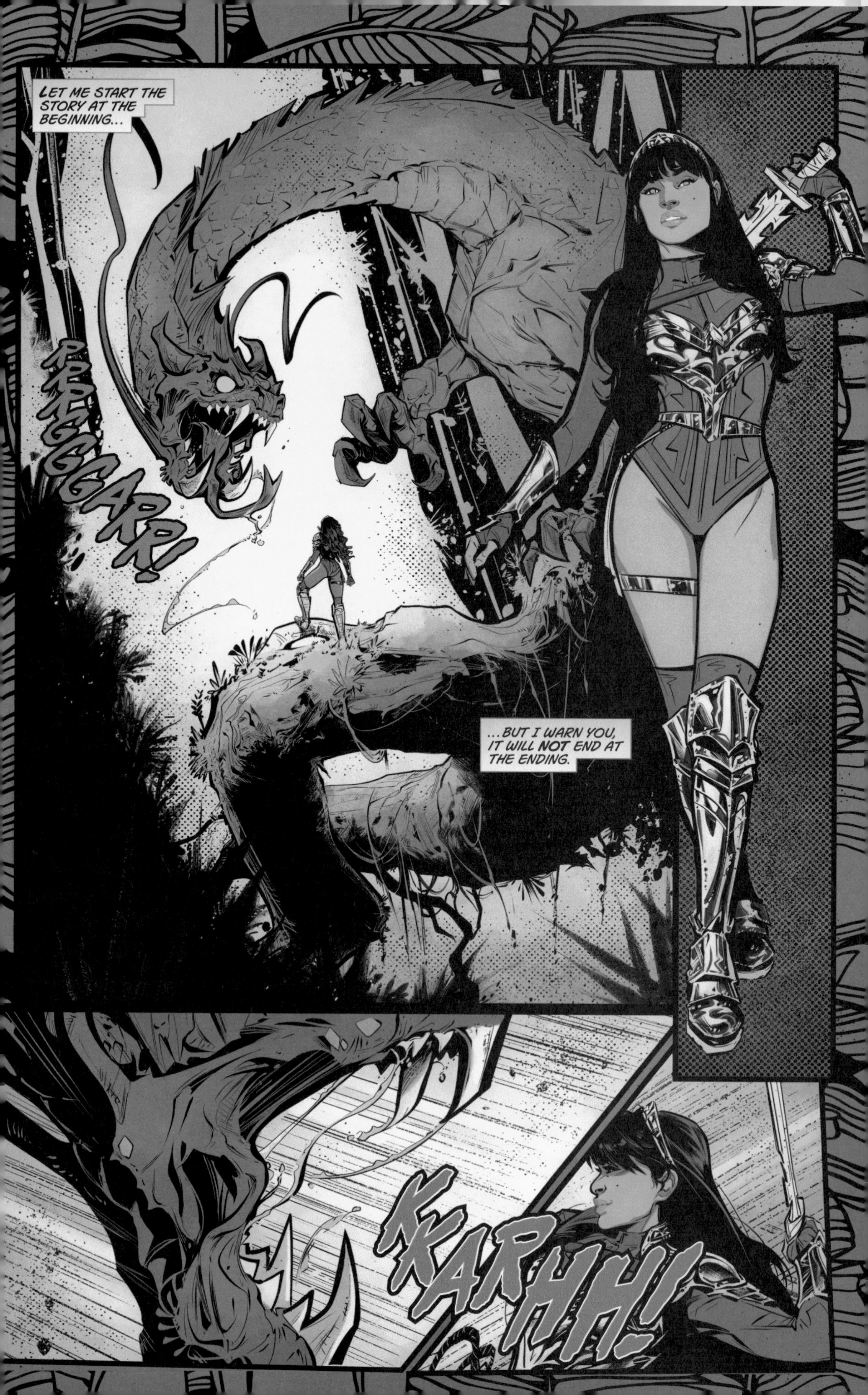
LET ME START THE STORY AT THE BEGINNING...
RRRGGARR!
...BUT I WARN YOU, IT WILL NOT END AT THE ENDING.
KKARHH!

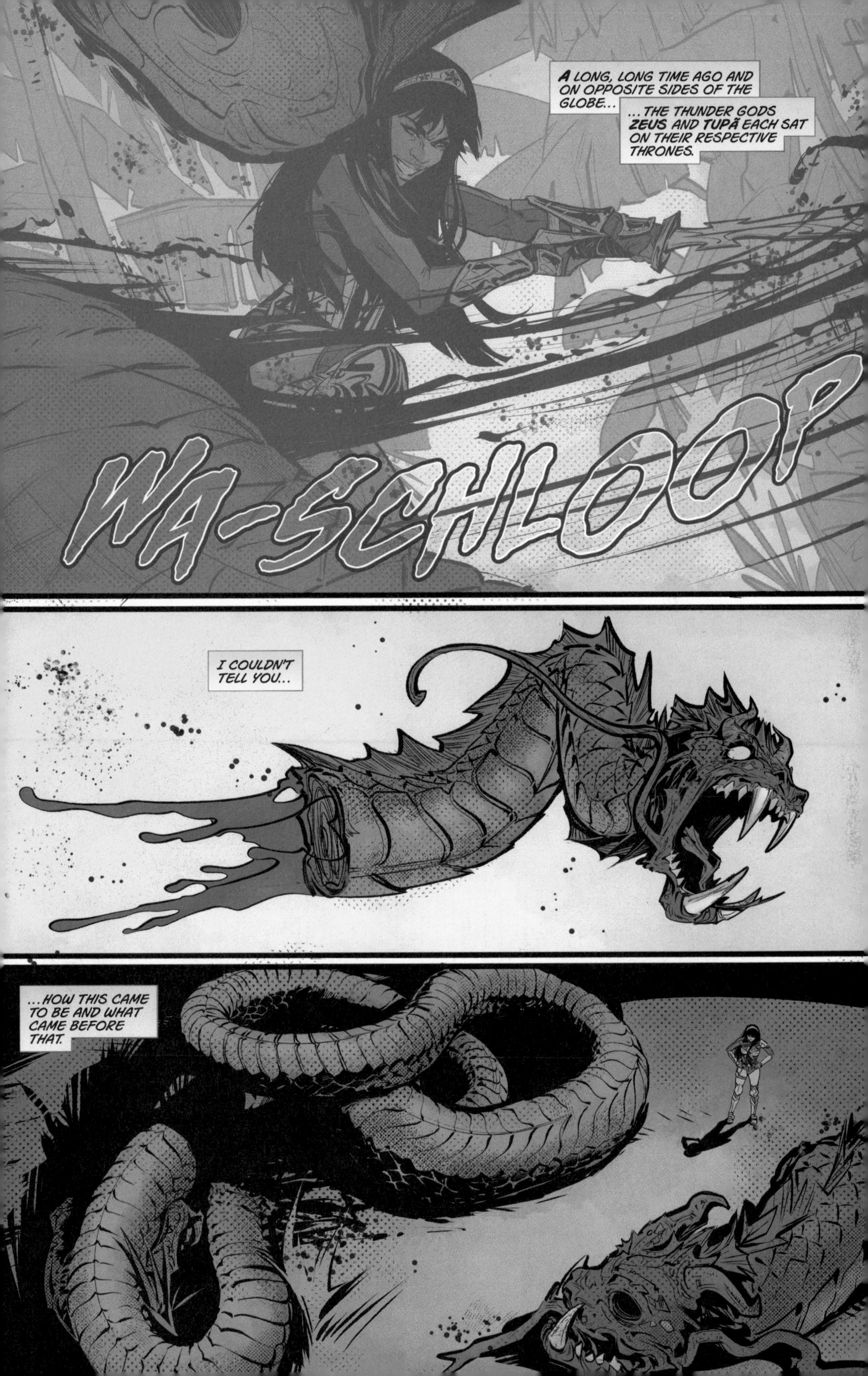
A LONG, LONG TIME AGO AND ON OPPOSITE SIDES OF THE GLOBE...
...THE THUNDER GODS ZEUS AND TUPÃ EACH SAT ON THEIR RESPECTIVE THRONES.
WA-SCHLOOP
I COULDN'T TELL YOU...
...HOW THIS CAME TO BE AND WHAT CAME BEFORE THAT.

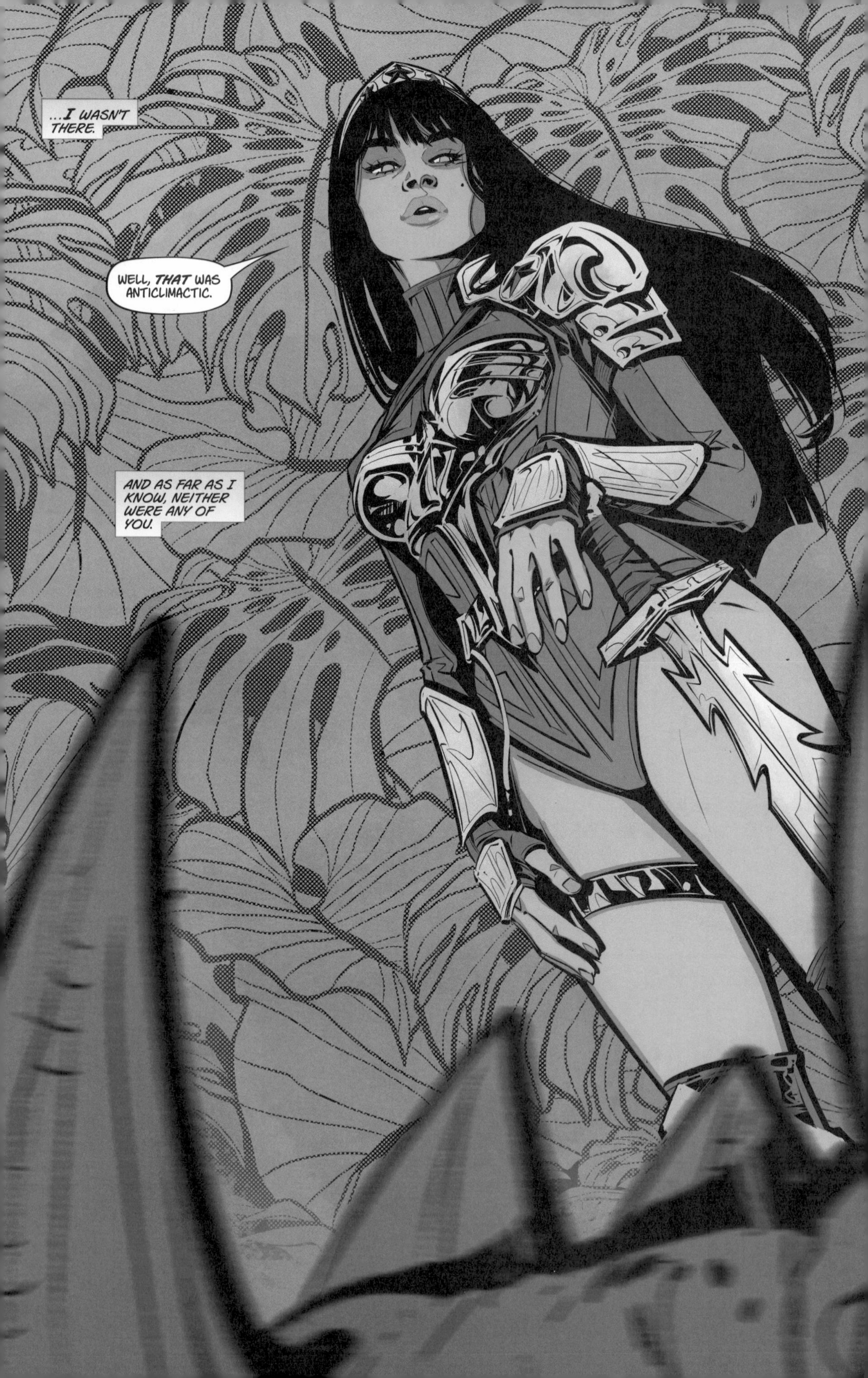
...I WASN'T THERE.
WELL, THAT WAS ANTICLIMACTIC.
AND AS FAR AS I KNOW, NEITHER WERE ANY OF YOU.

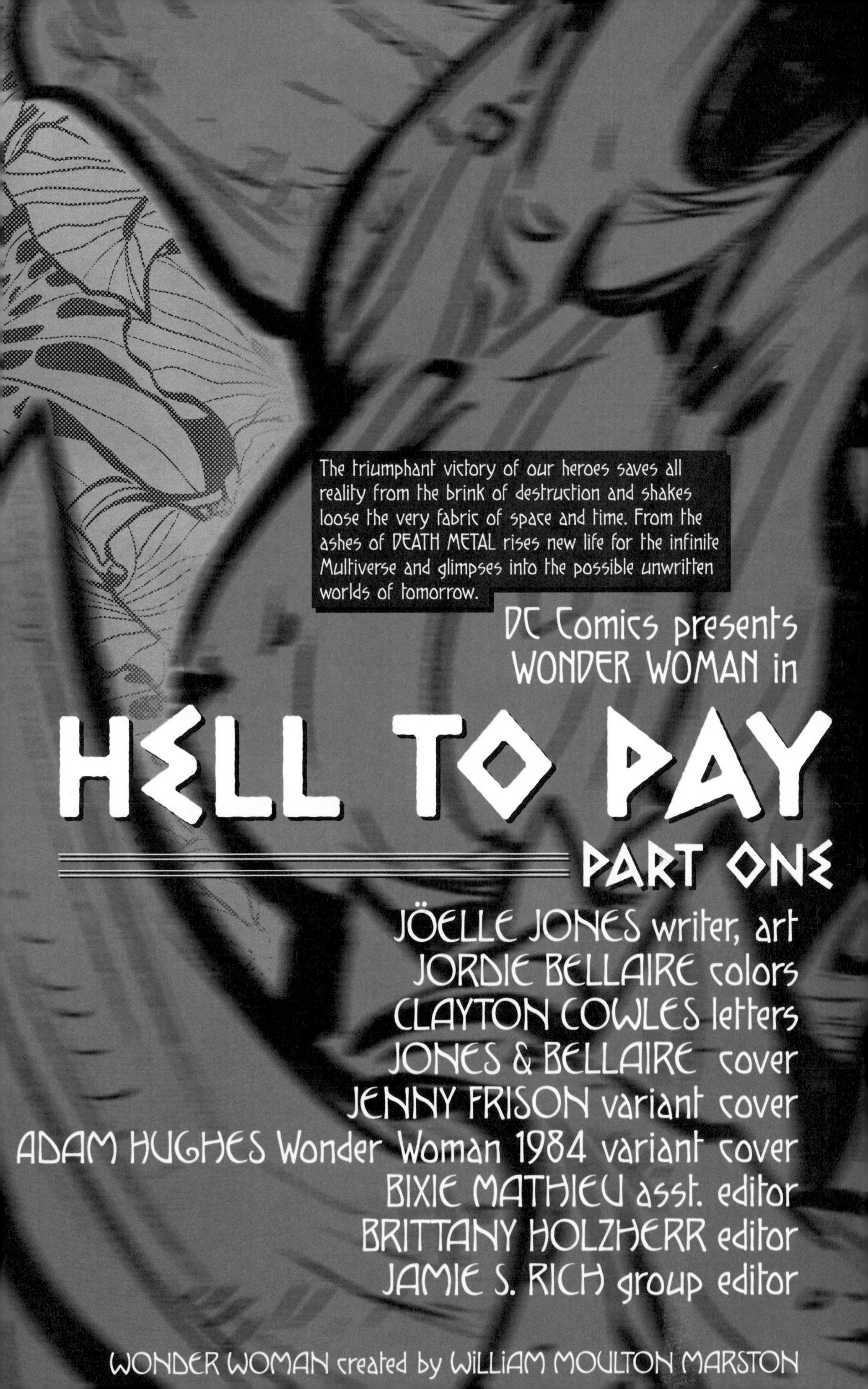
The triumphant victory of our heroes saves all reality from the brink of destruction and shakes loose the very fabric of space and time. From the ashes of DEATH METAL rises new life for the infinite Multiverse and glimpses into the possible unwritten worlds of tomorrow.
DC Comics presents
WONDER WOMAN in
HELL TO PAY
PART ONE
JÖELLE JONES writer, art
JORDIE BELLAIRE colors
CLAYTON COWLES letters
JONES & BELLAIRE cover
JENNY FRISON variant cover
ADAM HUGHES Wonder Woman 1984 variant cover
BIXIE MATHIEU asst. editor
BRITTANY HOLZHERR editor
JAMIE S. RICH group editor
WONDER WOMAN created by WILLIAM MOULTON MARSTON

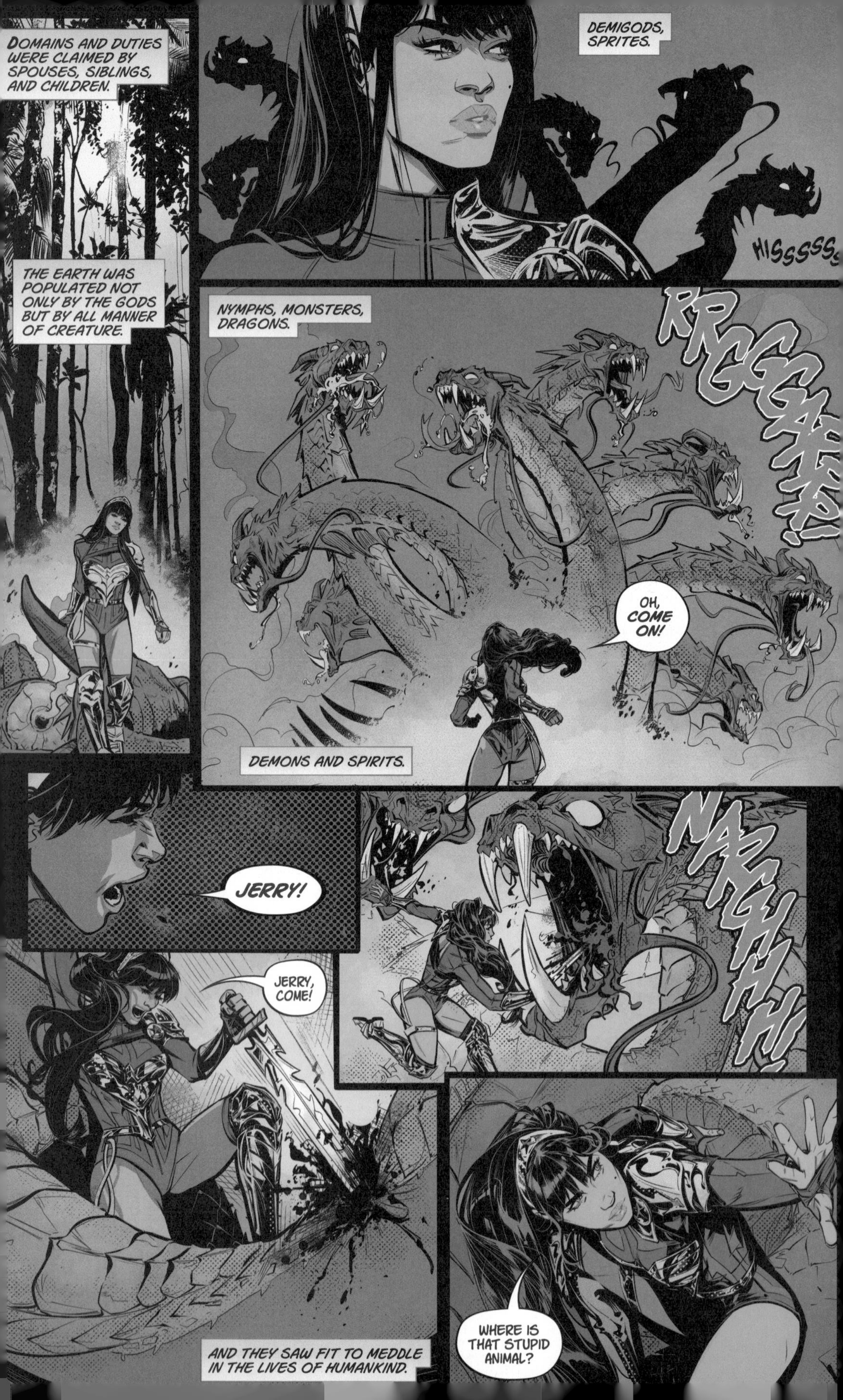

DOMAINS AND DUTIES WERE CLAIMED BY SPOUSES, SIBLINGS, AND CHILDREN.
THE EARTH WAS POPULATED NOT ONLY BY THE GODS BUT BY ALL MANNER OF CREATURE.
DEMIGODS, SPRITES.
HISSSSSS
NYMPHS, MONSTERS, DRAGONS.
RRGGGAAAHH!!
OH, COME ON!
DEMONS AND SPIRITS.
JERRY!
NARGHHH!!
JERRY, COME!
AND THEY SAW FIT TO MEDDLE IN THE LIVES OF HUMANKIND.
WHERE IS THAT STUPID ANIMAL?

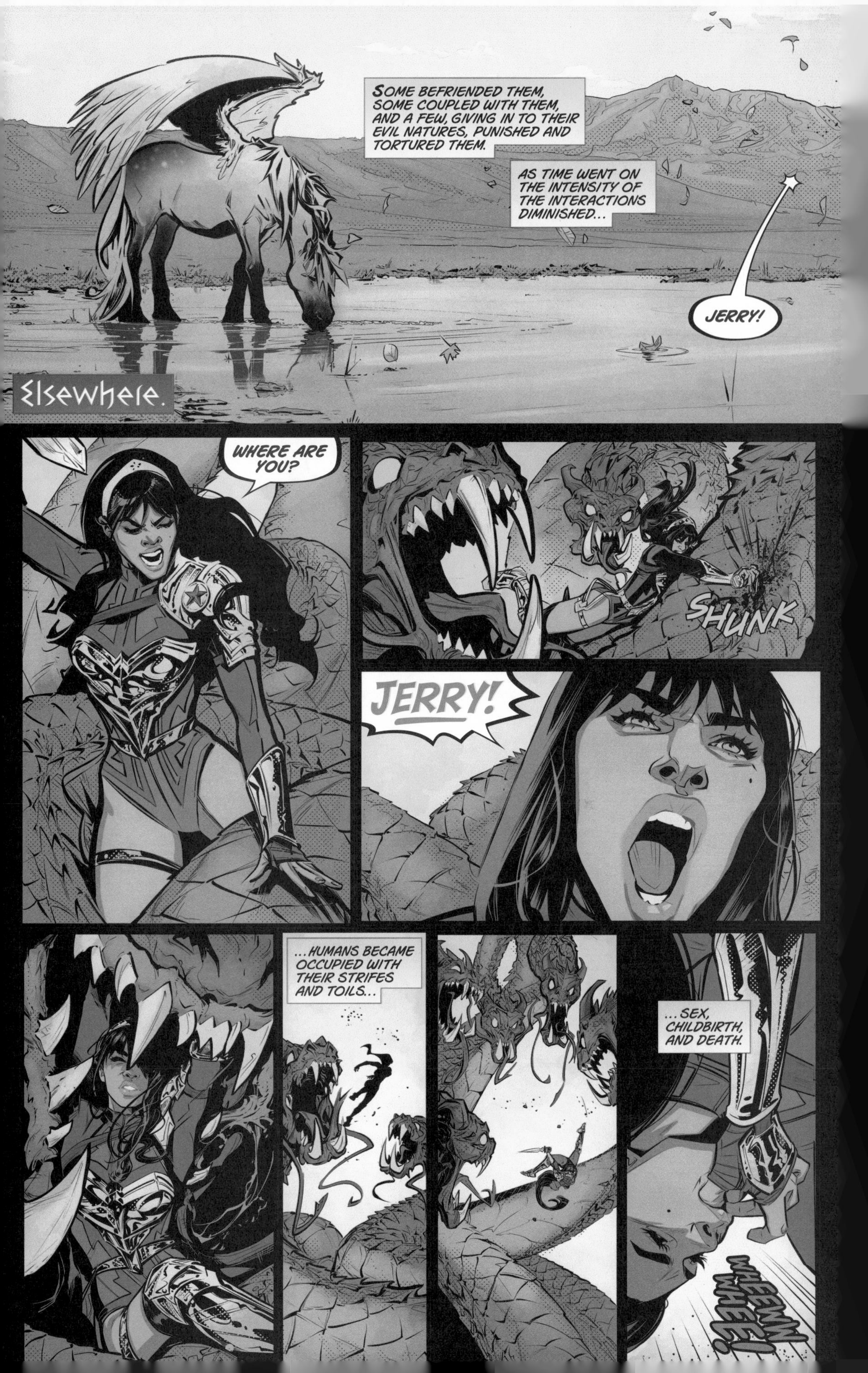
SOME BEFRIENDED THEM, SOME COUPLED WITH THEM, AND A FEW, GIVING IN TO THEIR EVIL NATURES, PUNISHED AND TORTURED THEM.
AS TIME WENT ON THE INTENSITY OF THE INTERACTIONS DIMINISHED...
JERRY!
Elsewhere.
WHERE ARE YOU?
SHUNK
JERRY!
...HUMANS BECAME OCCUPIED WITH THEIR STRIFES AND TOILS...
...SEX, CHILDBIRTH, AND DEATH.
WHEEWW WHEE!

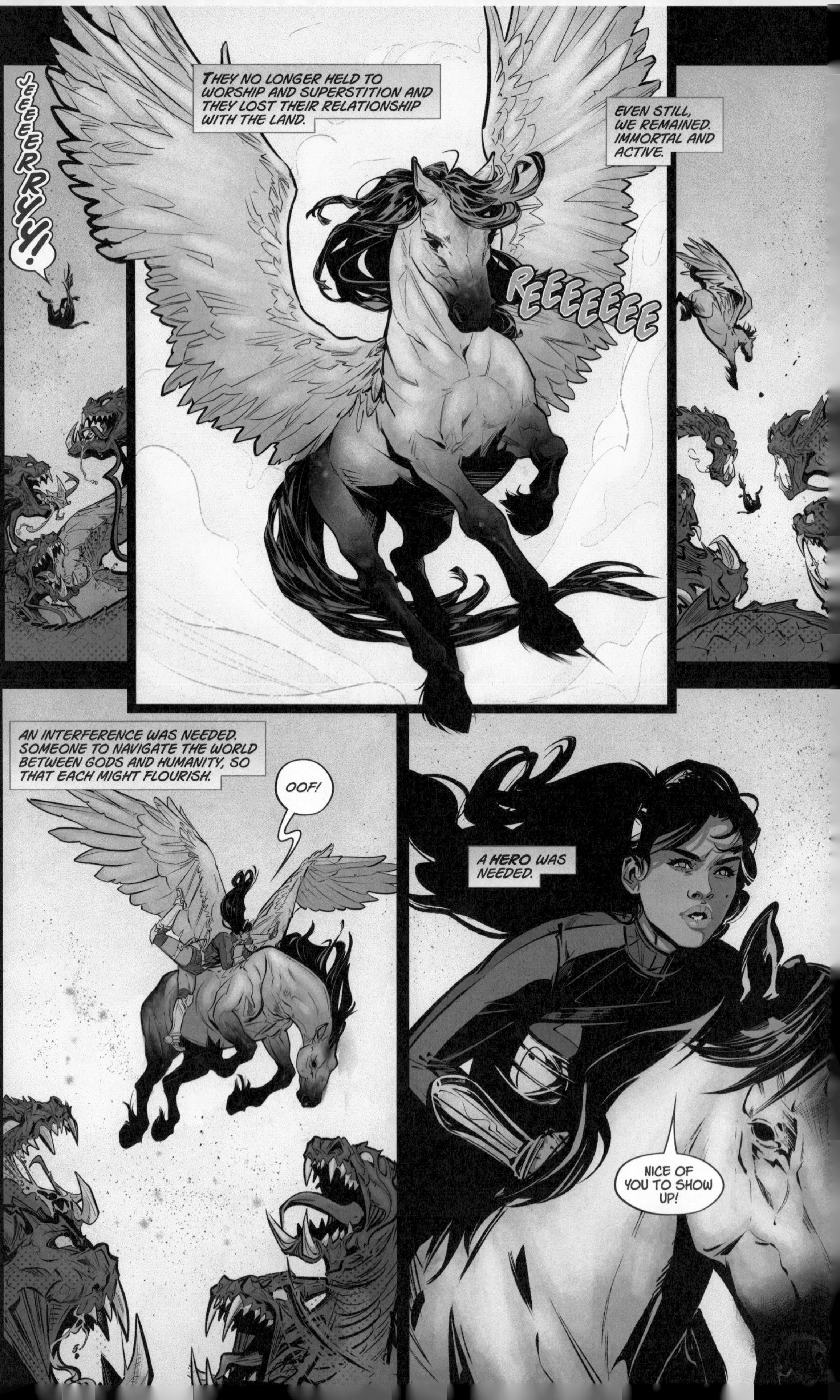
JEEEERRYYY!
THEY NO LONGER HELD TO WORSHIP AND SUPERSTITION AND THEY LOST THEIR RELATIONSHIP WITH THE LAND.
EVEN STILL, WE REMAINED. IMMORTAL AND ACTIVE.
REEEEEEE
AN INTERFERENCE WAS NEEDED. SOMEONE TO NAVIGATE THE WORLD BETWEEN GODS AND HUMANITY, SO THAT EACH MIGHT FLOURISH.
OOF!
A HERO WAS NEEDED.
NICE OF YOU TO SHOW UP!

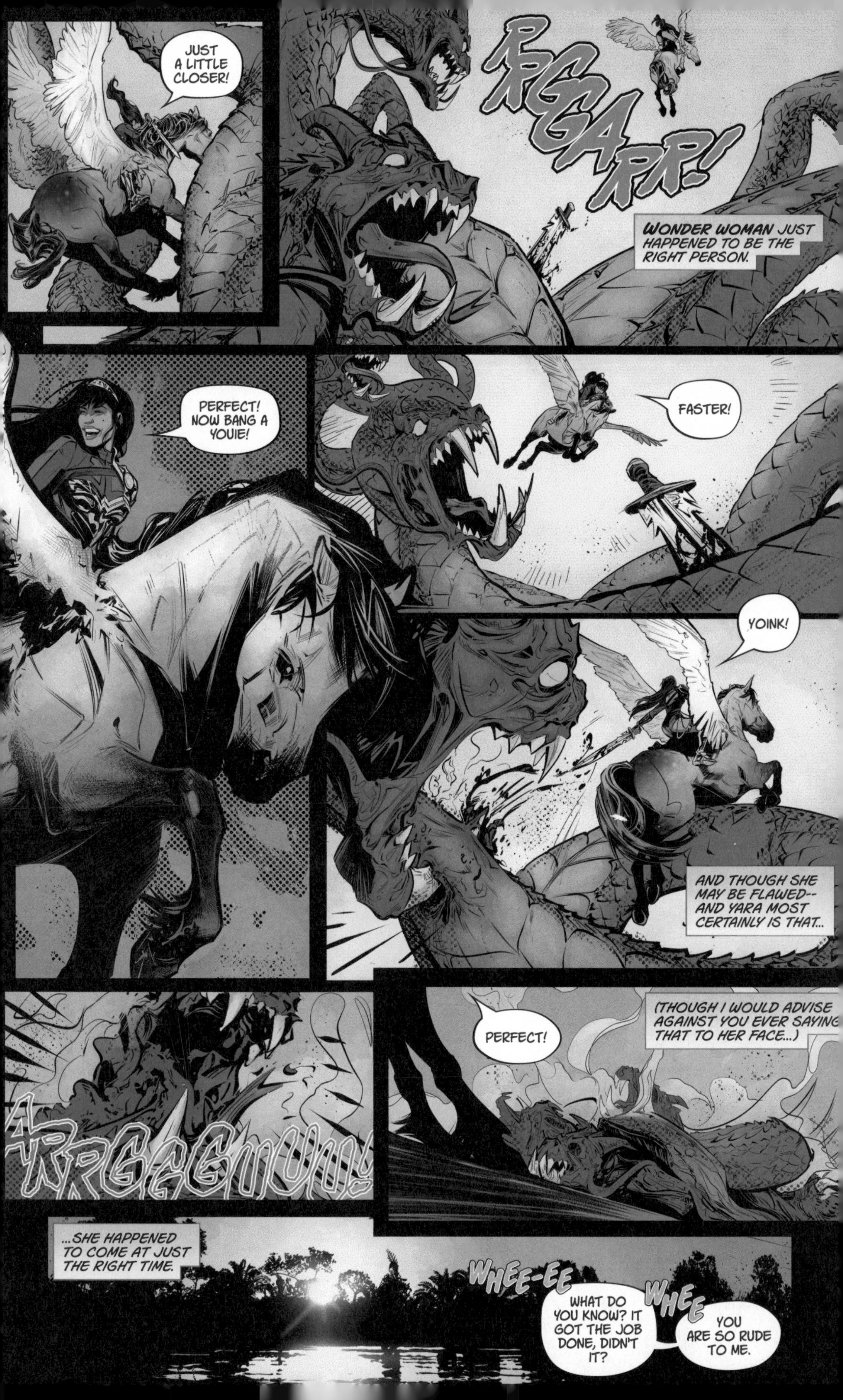
JUST A LITTLE CLOSER!
RRGARR!
WONDER WOMAN JUST HAPPENED TO BE THE RIGHT PERSON.
PERFECT! NOW BANG A YOUIE!
FASTER!
YOINK!
AND THOUGH SHE MAY BE FLAWED-- AND YARA MOST CERTAINLY IS THAT...
PERFECT!
(THOUGH I WOULD ADVISE AGAINST YOU EVER SAYING THAT TO HER FACE...)
...SHE HAPPENED TO COME AT JUST THE RIGHT TIME.
WHEE-EE
WHAT DO YOU KNOW? IT GOT THE JOB DONE, DIDN'T IT?
WHEE
YOU ARE SO RUDE TO ME.

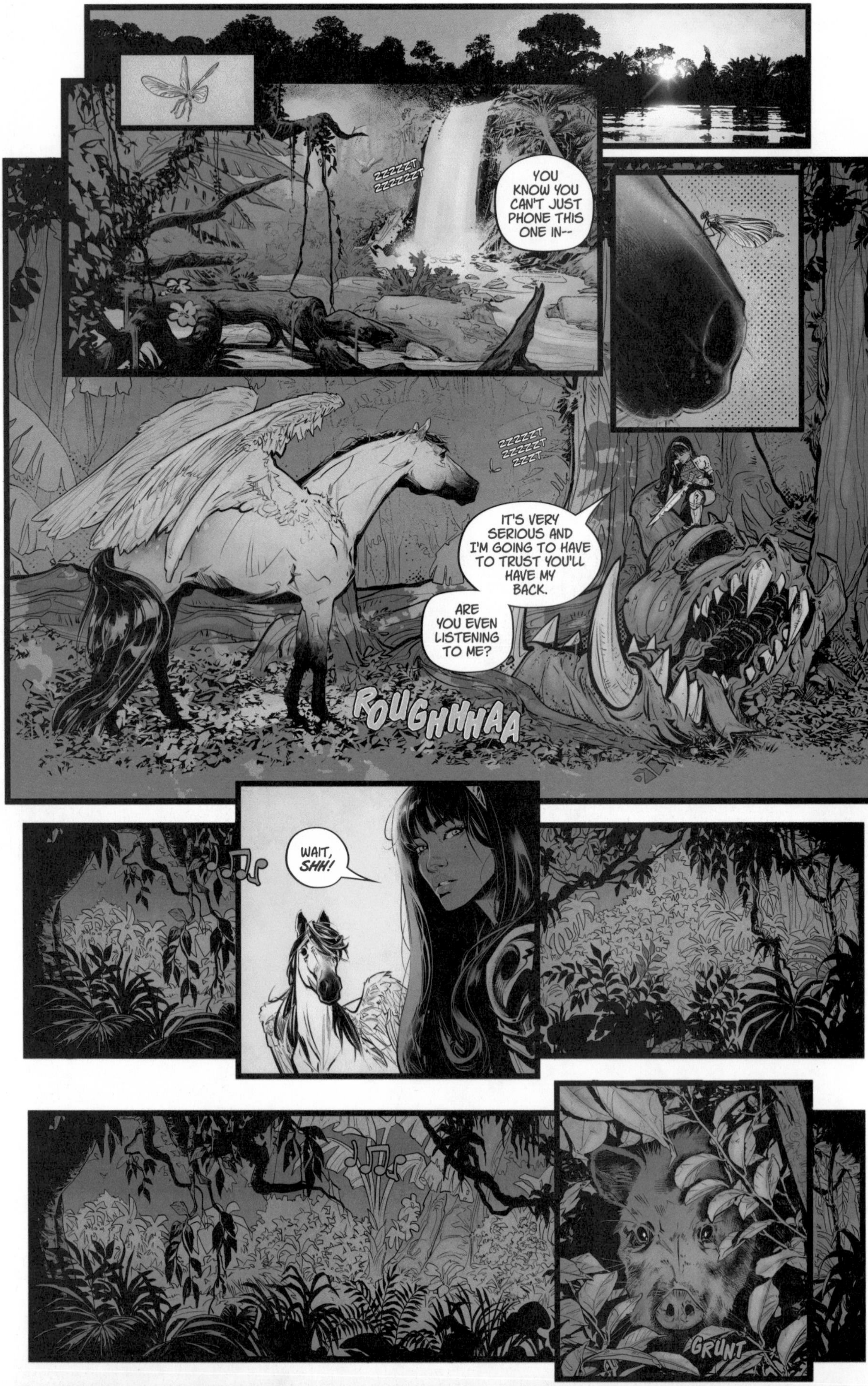
ZZZZZZT ZZZZZZT
YOU KNOW YOU CAN'T JUST PHONE THIS ONE IN--
ZZZZZT ZZZZZT ZZZT
IT'S VERY SERIOUS AND I'M GOING TO HAVE TO TRUST YOU'LL HAVE MY BACK.
ARE YOU EVEN LISTENING TO ME?
ROUGHHHAA
WAIT, SHH!
GRUNT

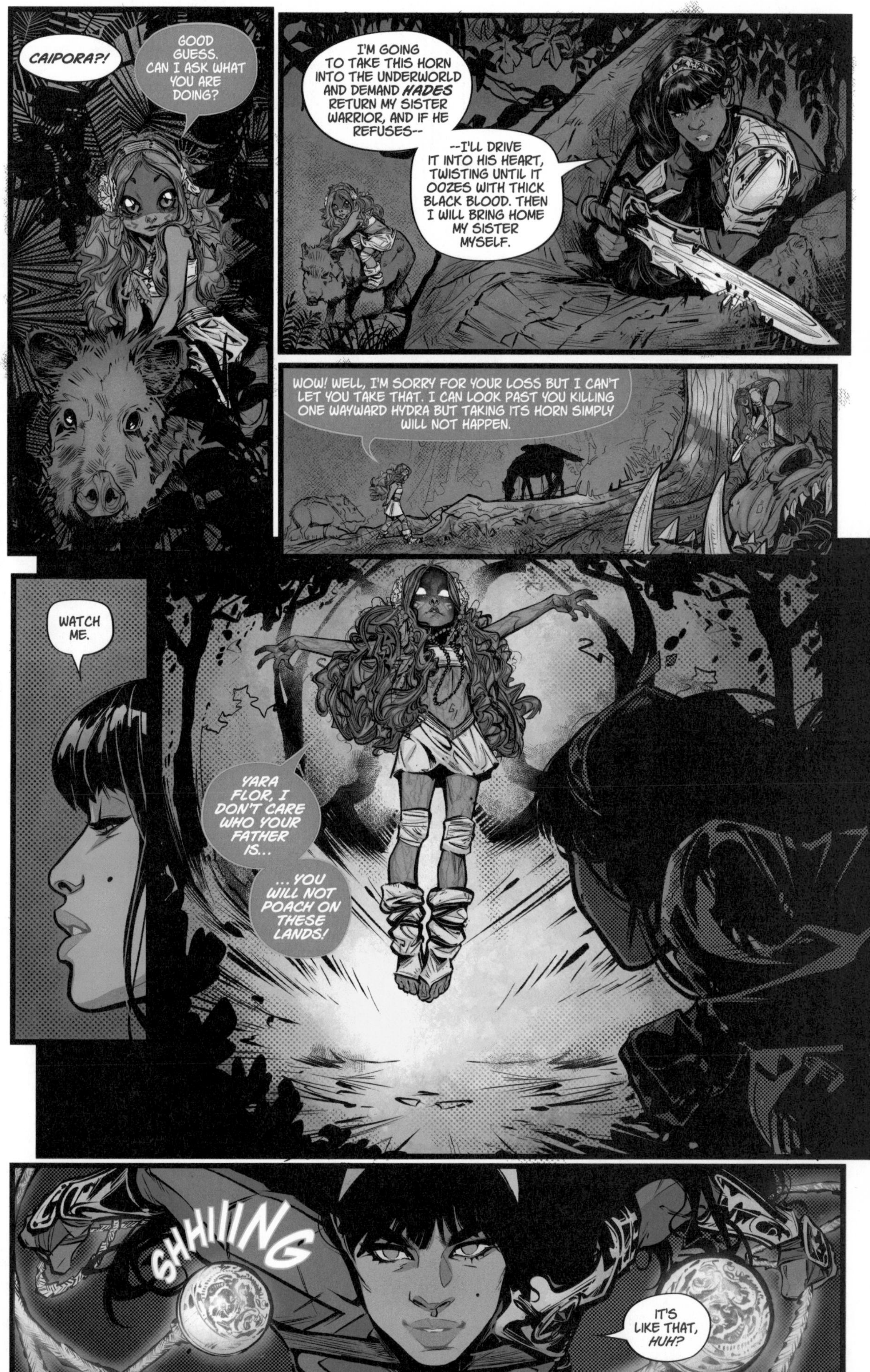
CAIPORA?!
GOOD GUESS. CAN I ASK WHAT YOU ARE DOING?
I'M GOING TO TAKE THIS HORN INTO THE UNDERWORLD AND DEMAND HADES RETURN MY SISTER WARRIOR, AND IF HE REFUSES--
--I'LL DRIVE IT INTO HIS HEART, TWISTING UNTIL IT OOZES WITH THICK BLACK BLOOD. THEN I WILL BRING HOME MY SISTER MYSELF.
WOW! WELL, I'M SORRY FOR YOUR LOSS BUT I CAN'T LET YOU TAKE THAT. I CAN LOOK PAST YOU KILLING ONE WAYWARD HYDRA BUT TAKING ITS HORN SIMPLY WILL NOT HAPPEN.
WATCH ME.
YARA FLOR, I DON'T CARE WHO YOUR FATHER IS...
...YOU WILL NOT POACH ON THESE LANDS!
SHHIIING
IT'S LIKE THAT, HUH?

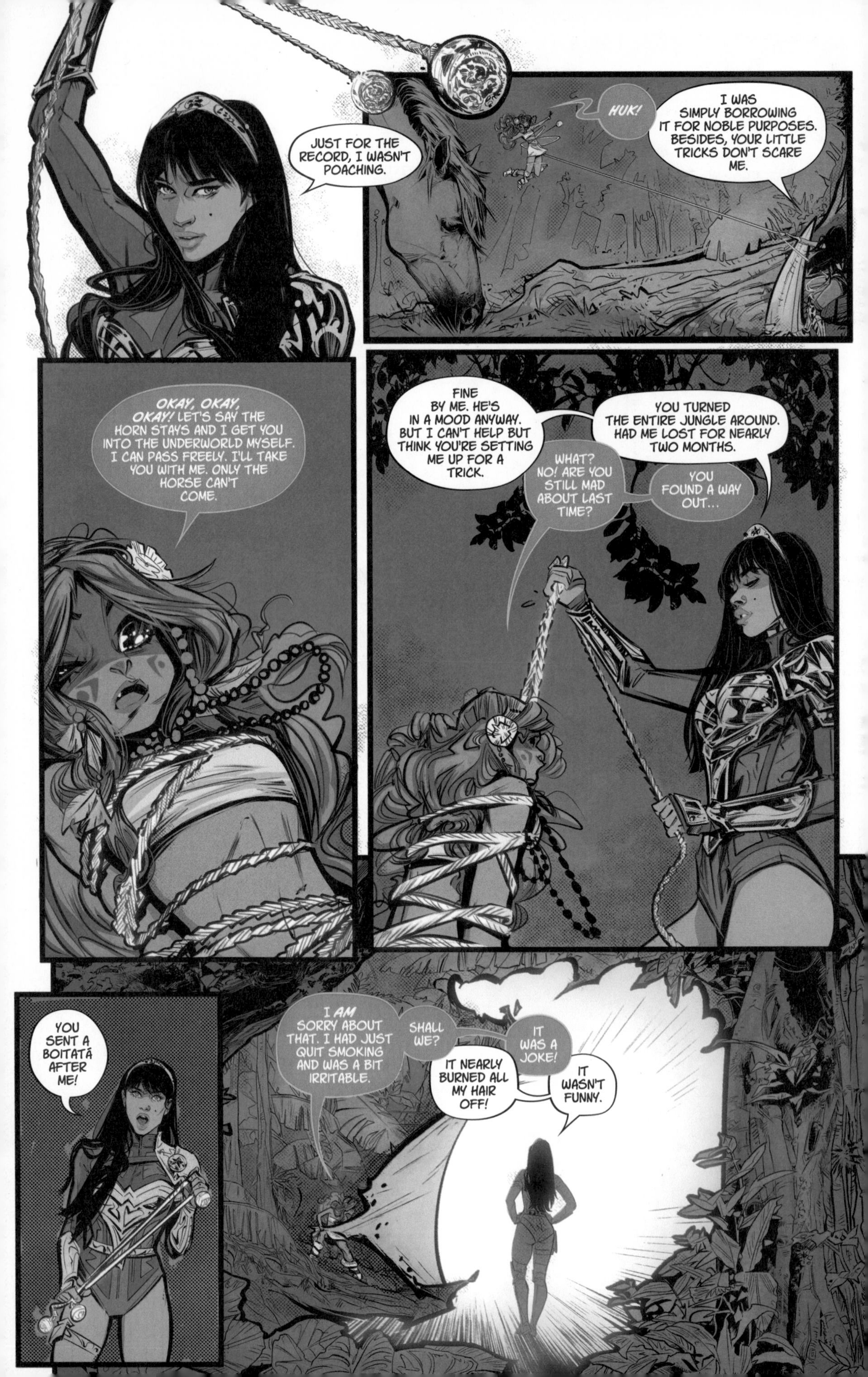
JUST FOR THE RECORD, I WASN'T POACHING.
HUK!
I WAS SIMPLY BORROWING IT FOR NOBLE PURPOSES. BESIDES, YOUR LITTLE TRICKS DON'T SCARE ME.
OKAY, OKAY, OKAY! LET'S SAY THE HORN STAYS AND I GET YOU INTO THE UNDERWORLD MYSELF. I CAN PASS FREELY. I'LL TAKE YOU WITH ME. ONLY THE HORSE CAN'T COME.
FINE BY ME. HE'S IN A MOOD ANYWAY. BUT I CAN'T HELP BUT THINK YOU'RE SETTING ME UP FOR A TRICK.
WHAT? NO! ARE YOU STILL MAD ABOUT LAST TIME?
YOU TURNED THE ENTIRE JUNGLE AROUND. HAD ME LOST FOR NEARLY TWO MONTHS.
YOU FOUND A WAY OUT...
YOU SENT A BOITATÁ AFTER ME!
I AM SORRY ABOUT THAT. I HAD JUST QUIT SMOKING AND WAS A BIT IRRITABLE.
SHALL WE?
IT WAS A JOKE!
IT NEARLY BURNED ALL MY HAIR OFF!
IT WASN'T FUNNY.

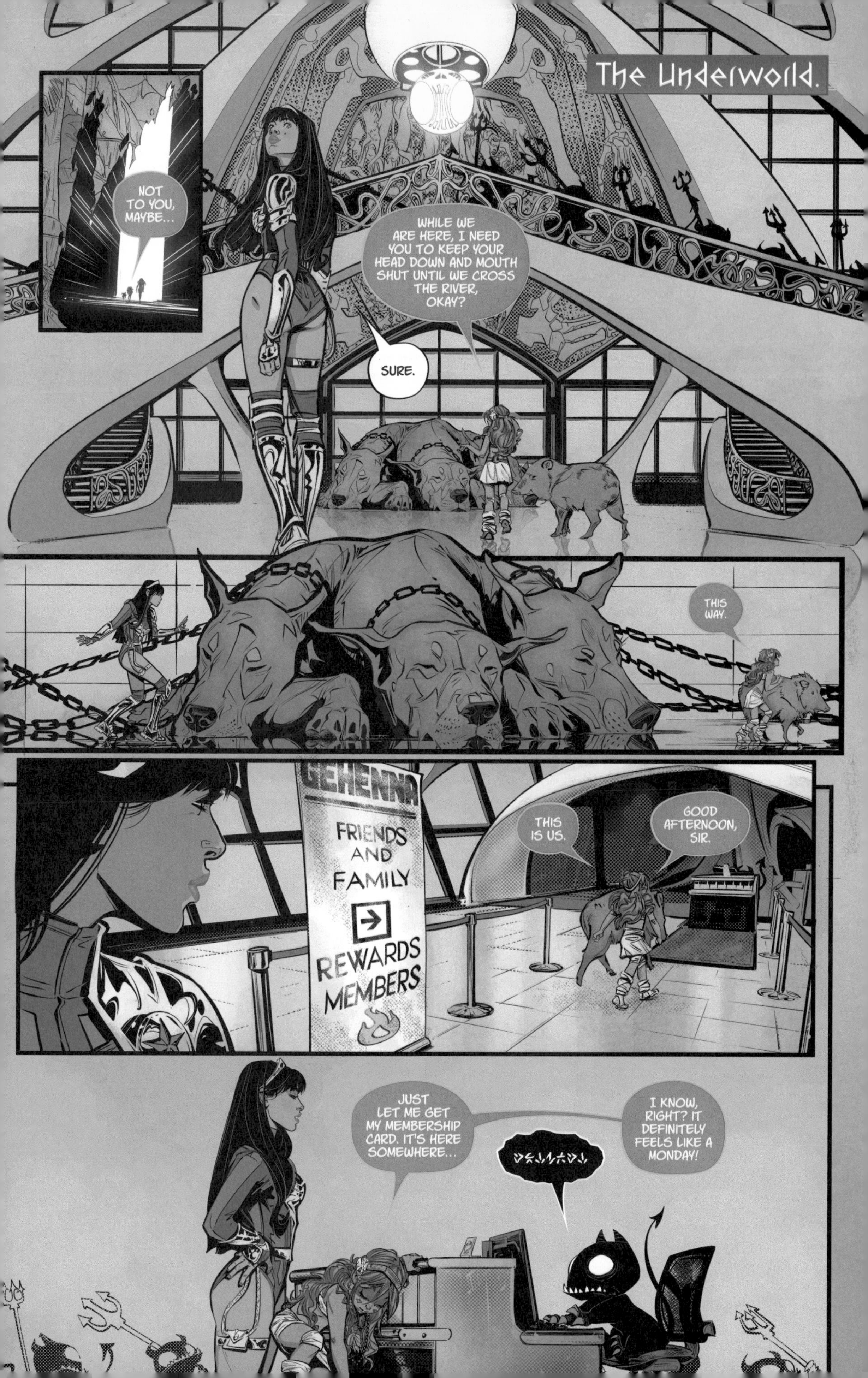
The Underworld.
NOT TO YOU, MAYBE...
WHILE WE ARE HERE, I NEED YOU TO KEEP YOUR HEAD DOWN AND MOUTH SHUT UNTIL WE CROSS THE RIVER, OKAY?
SURE.
THIS WAY.
GEHENNA
FRIENDS AND FAMILY
REWARDS MEMBERS
THIS IS US.
GOOD AFTERNOON, SIR.
JUST LET ME GET MY MEMBERSHIP CARD. IT'S HERE SOMEWHERE...
I KNOW, RIGHT? IT DEFINITELY FEELS LIKE A MONDAY!

HEY, WHILE I'VE GOT YOU HERE, CAN I ASK A QUICK QUESTION?

ᐱᏨᏚᏯᏤᏨᏚ

HA HA, OKAY, ANOTHER ONE THEN! IF I WERE TO UPGRADE MY STATUS, WHAT IS THE DIFFERENCE BETWEEN THE GOLD AND THE PLATINUM TIER?

ᏚᐱᏨᏚᏯᐱ ᐱᏨᏚᏨᏱᏨᏨᏯ ᏨᏱᏯᏯᏨᏱᏱ ᏨᏱ

ᐱᏨᏚᏨᏱᏨᏱ ᏯᏯᏨᏱᏱᏱᏱ ᏨᏚᏨᏚᏨᏱ

UH-HUH, AND WHAT DOES THAT ENTAIL?

ᏤᏱᏨᏱᏱᏨ ᏨᏱ ᏯᏨᏚᏨᏱ ᏱᏱ Ꮸ

CLICK

CLICK

EH?

SURE, SURE.

ᏨᏱᏱᏚᏯᏚᏨᏱᏱᏨᏱ ᏱᏱ ᏯᏨᏨᏱᏨᏚᏯᏚᏨᏱ ᏚᏚᏱᏯᏱ ᏨᏨᏱᏱ

ARE THERE ANY BLACKOUT DATES?

ᏯᏚᏯᏯᏨᏱ ᏨᏚᏯᏱᏯᏨᏯᏨᏚᏱ ᏚᏨᏯᏨᏚᏱ

CLICK

CLICK CLICK

OKAY.

ᐱᏯᏨᏚ ᏯᏨᏨᏱᏨᏚᏯᏚ ᏨᏨ ᏨᏯᏯ

UH-HUH.

ᏨᏯᏨᏱ ᏯᏱᏯᏱᏨᏱ Ꮿ ᏱᏯᏱ

ONE LAST QUESTION--YOU'RE NOT STILL GIVING OUT THOSE DELICIOUS OATMEAL COOKIES, ARE YOU?

CLICK

CLICK CLICK

CLICK CLICK

WRRRNNG

CLICK CLICK CLICK

ENOUGH!

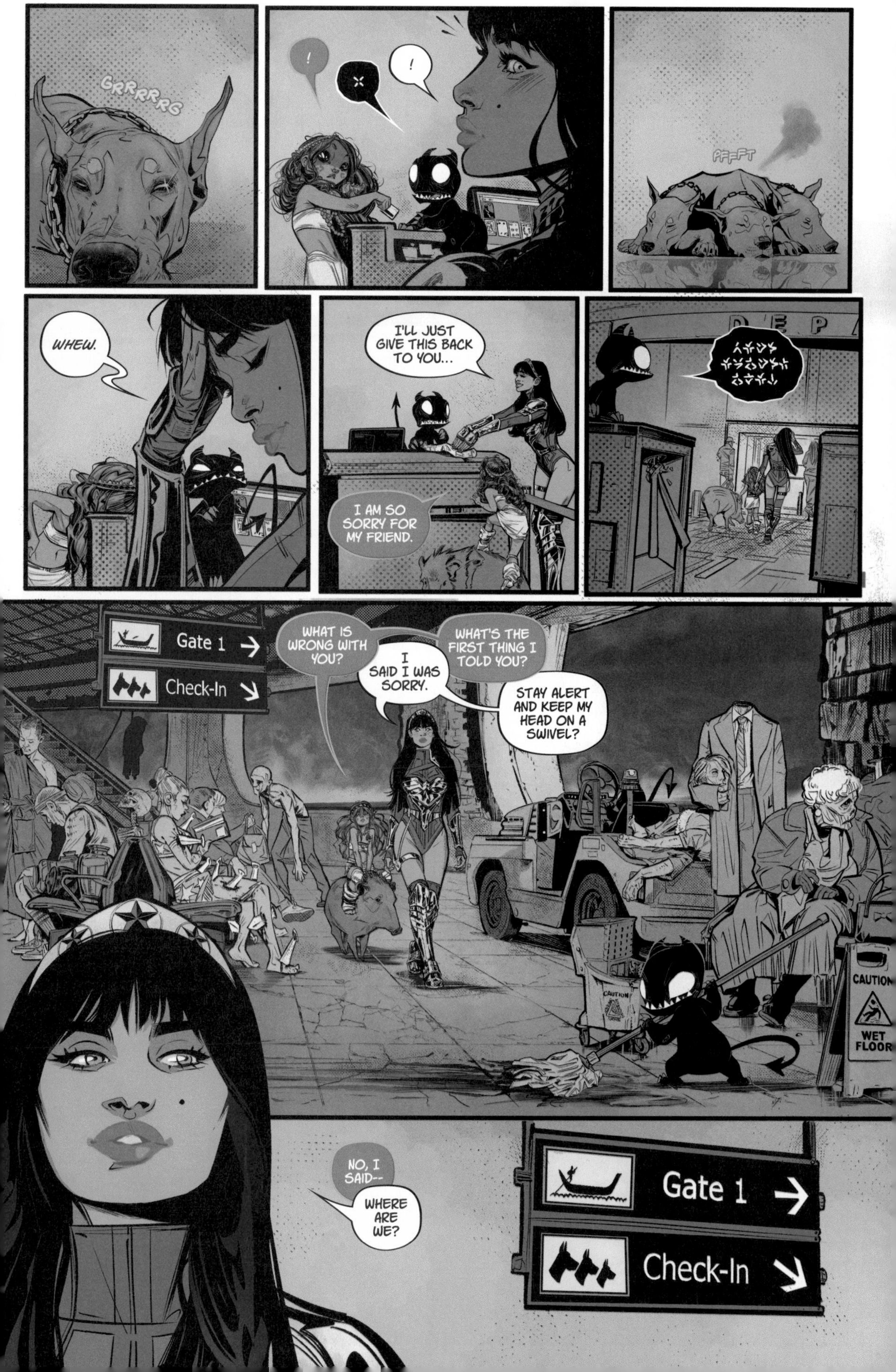
GRRRRRG
!
!
!
PFFFT
WHEW.
I'LL JUST GIVE THIS BACK TO YOU...
I AM SO SORRY FOR MY FRIEND.
DEPA
Gate 1
Check-In
WHAT IS WRONG WITH YOU?
I SAID I WAS SORRY.
WHAT'S THE FIRST THING I TOLD YOU?
STAY ALERT AND KEEP MY HEAD ON A SWIVEL?
CAUTION
CAUTION
WET FLOOR
NO, I SAID--
WHERE ARE WE?
Gate 1
Check-In

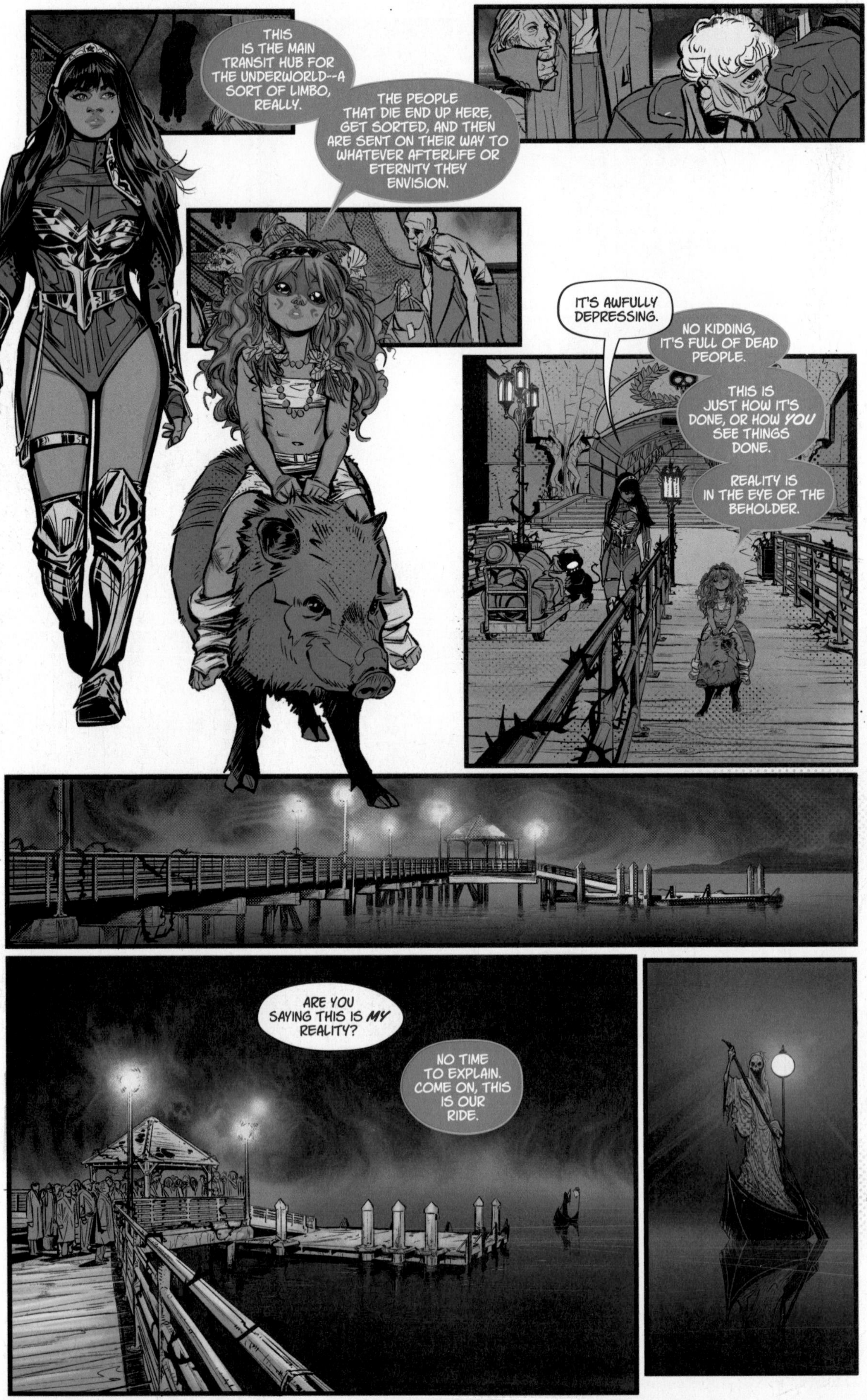
THIS IS THE MAIN TRANSIT HUB FOR THE UNDERWORLD--A SORT OF LIMBO, REALLY.
THE PEOPLE THAT DIE END UP HERE, GET SORTED, AND THEN ARE SENT ON THEIR WAY TO WHATEVER AFTERLIFE OR ETERNITY THEY ENVISION.
IT'S AWFULLY DEPRESSING.
NO KIDDING, IT'S FULL OF DEAD PEOPLE.
THIS IS JUST HOW IT'S DONE, OR HOW YOU SEE THINGS DONE.
REALITY IS IN THE EYE OF THE BEHOLDER.
ARE YOU SAYING THIS IS MY REALITY?
NO TIME TO EXPLAIN. COME ON, THIS IS OUR RIDE.

SHOULDN'T HAVE COME THIS TIME OF DAY. IT'S ALWAYS SUPER BUSY.

WHAT'S GOING ON UP THERE? I CAN'T SEE.

STOP FIDGETING.

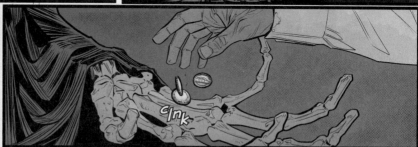

C1nk

YOU HAVE THE PATIENCE OF A FLOOD, YOU KNOW THAT?

DID YOU KNOW WE HAD TO PAY?

OF COURSE, DIDN'T YOU?

NO I-- AH!

OH... UH...

...I... UM...

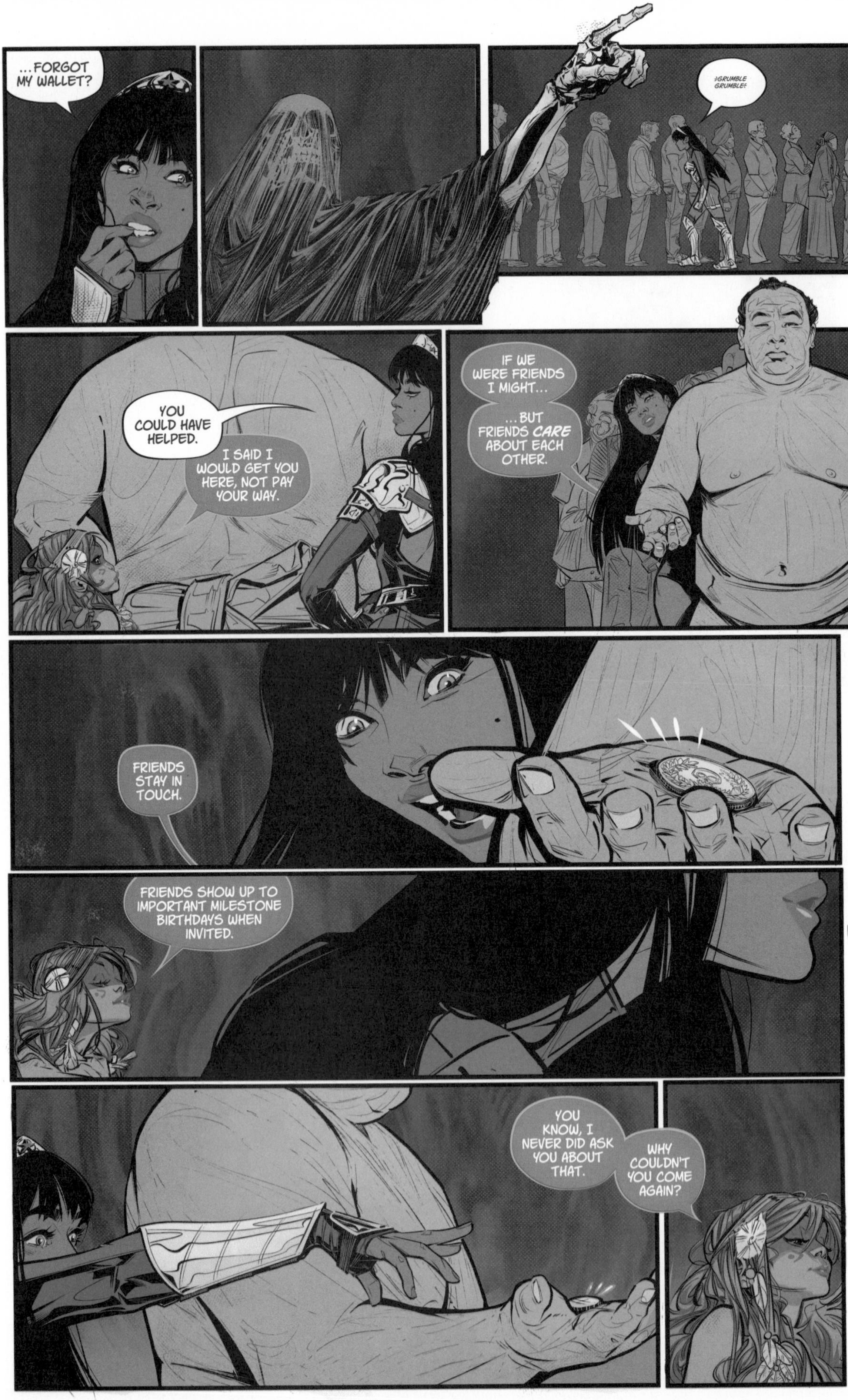
...FORGOT MY WALLET?
GRUMBLE GRUMBLE
YOU COULD HAVE HELPED.
I SAID I WOULD GET YOU HERE, NOT PAY YOUR WAY.
IF WE WERE FRIENDS I MIGHT...
...BUT FRIENDS CARE ABOUT EACH OTHER.
FRIENDS STAY IN TOUCH.
FRIENDS SHOW UP TO IMPORTANT MILESTONE BIRTHDAYS WHEN INVITED.
YOU KNOW, I NEVER DID ASK YOU ABOUT THAT.
WHY COULDN'T YOU COME AGAIN?

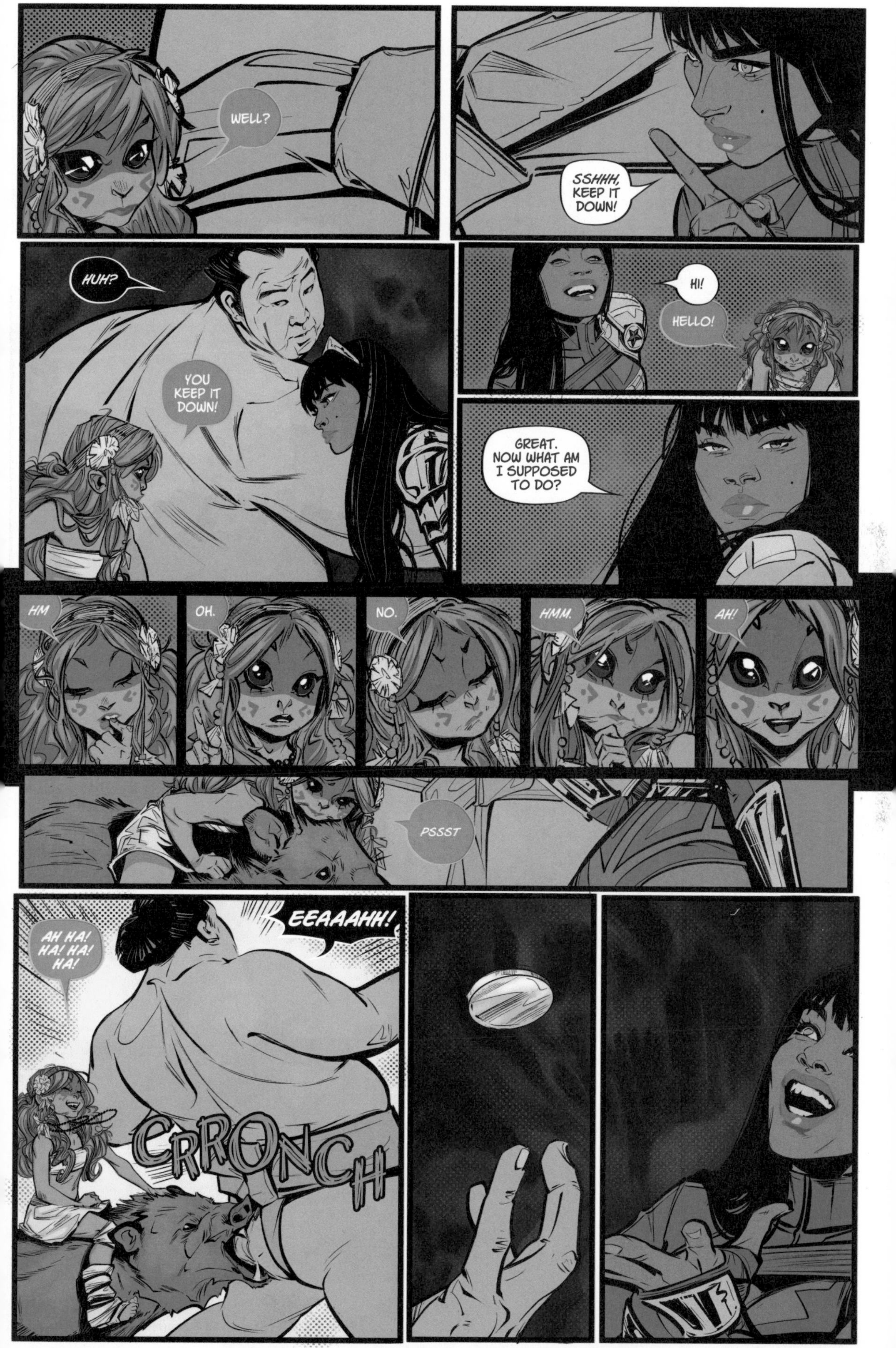
WELL?
SSHHH, KEEP IT DOWN!
HUH?
YOU KEEP IT DOWN!
HI!
HELLO!
GREAT. NOW WHAT AM I SUPPOSED TO DO?
HM
OH.
NO.
HMM.
AH!
PSSST
EEAAAAHH!
AH HA! HA! HA! HA!
CRRONCH

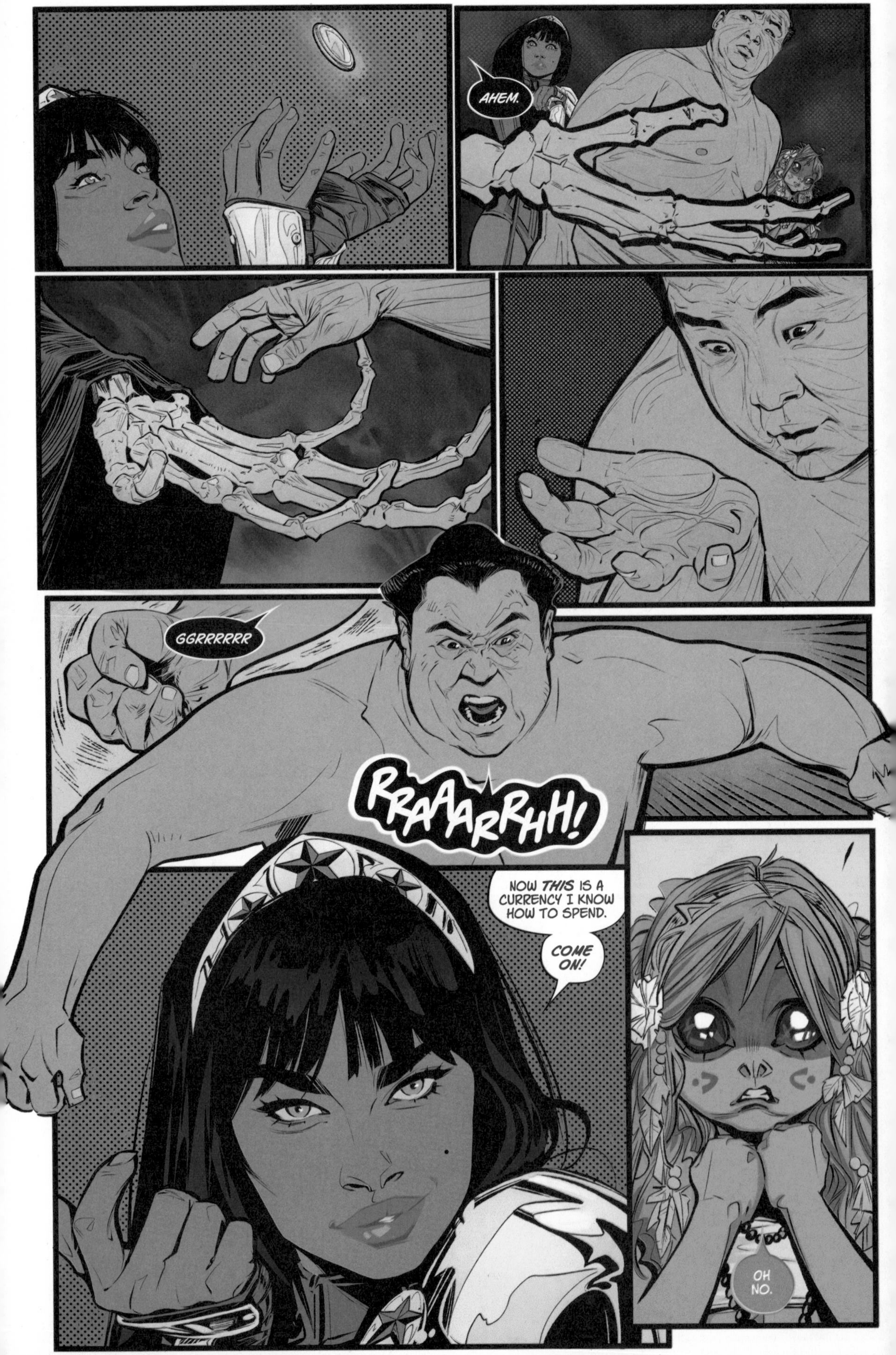
AHEM.
GGRRRRRR
RRAAARRHH!
NOW *THIS* IS A CURRENCY I KNOW HOW TO SPEND.
COME ON!
OH NO.

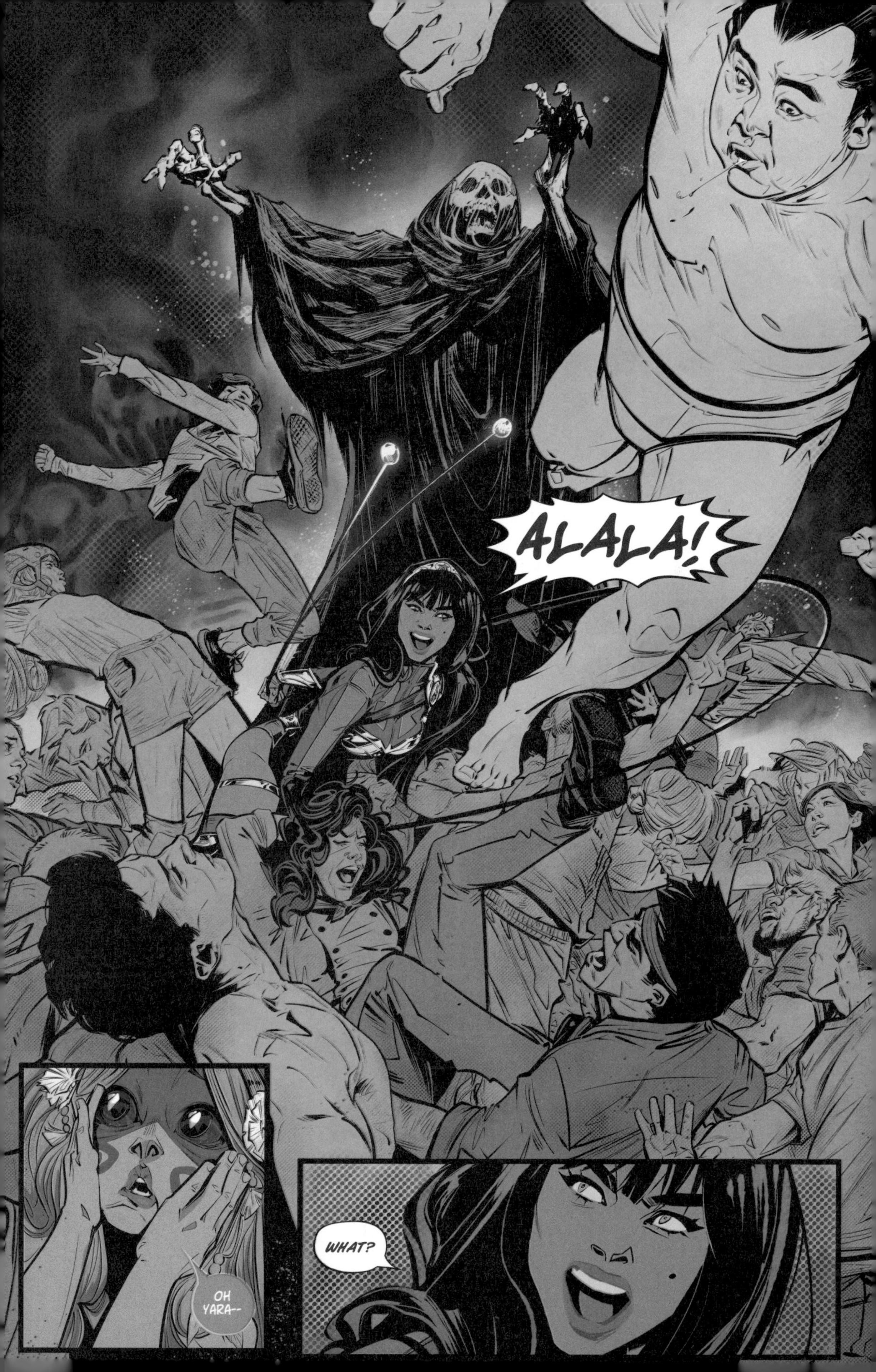
ALALA!
OH YARA--
WHAT?

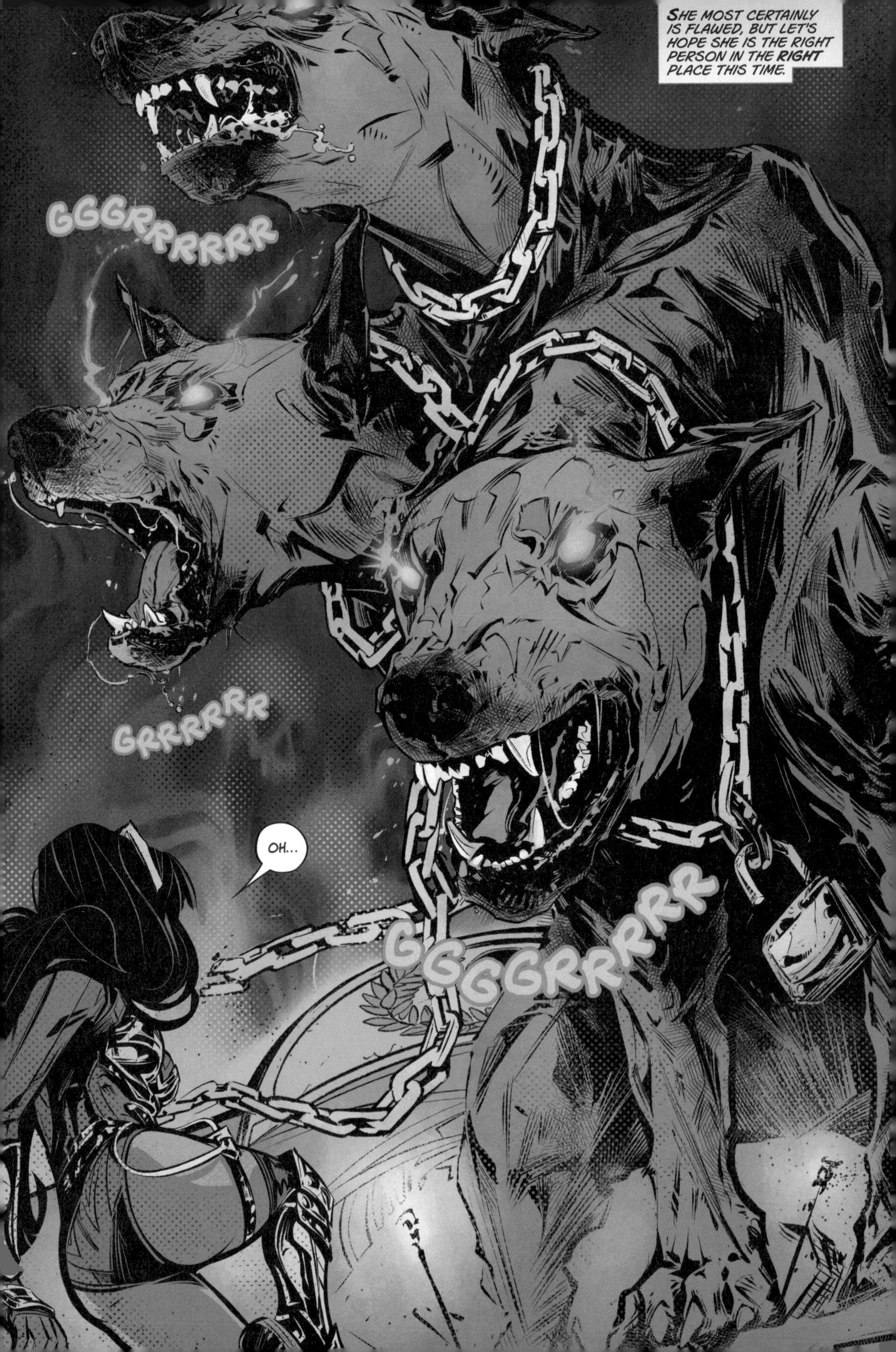
SHE MOST CERTAINLY IS FLAWED, BUT LET'S HOPE SHE IS THE RIGHT PERSON IN THE RIGHT PLACE THIS TIME.
GGGRRRRRRR
GRRRRRR
OH...
GGGGRRRRRR

Future State: Wonder Woman #2
Cover Art by **JOËLLE JONES** and **JORDIE BELLAIRE**

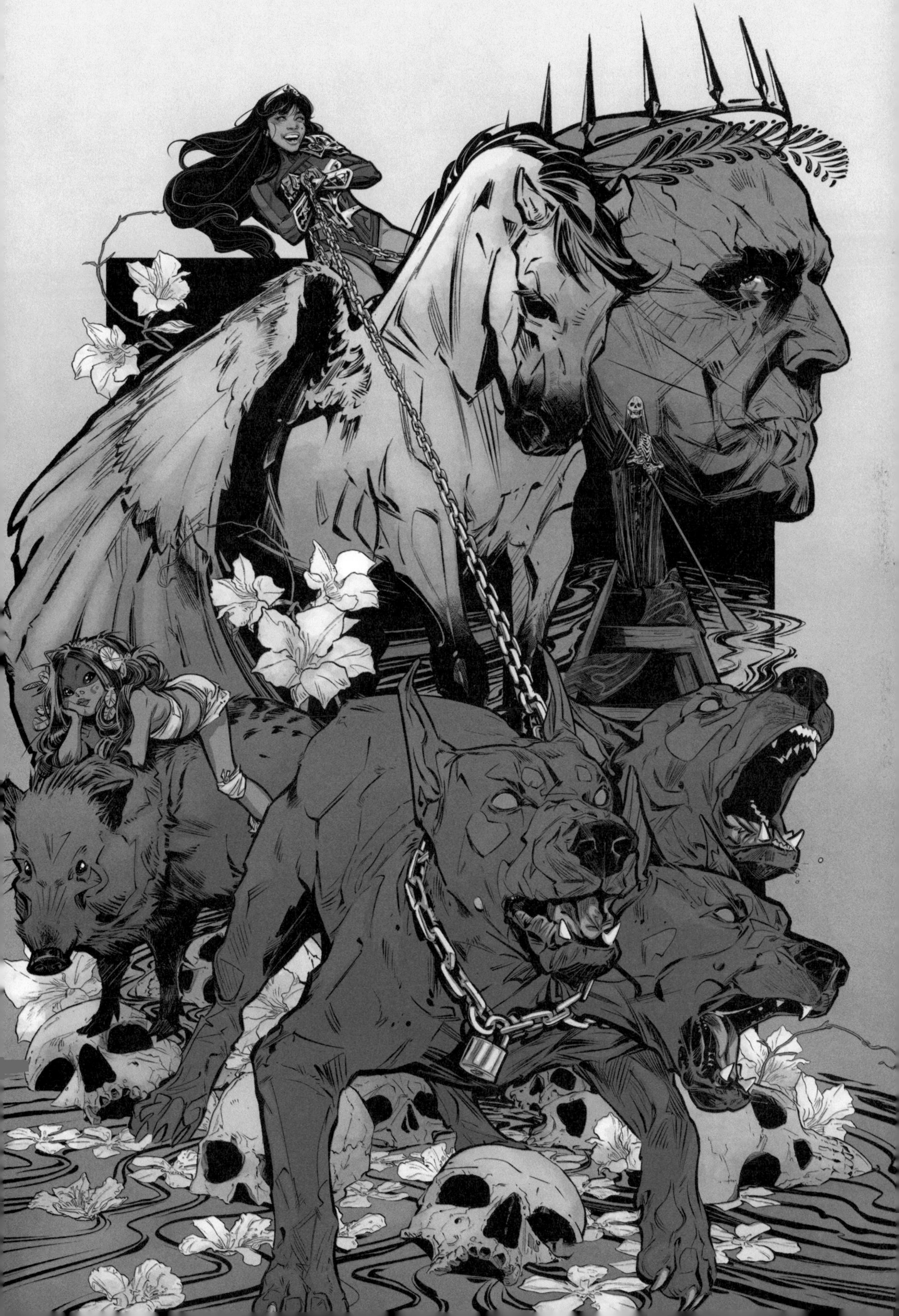

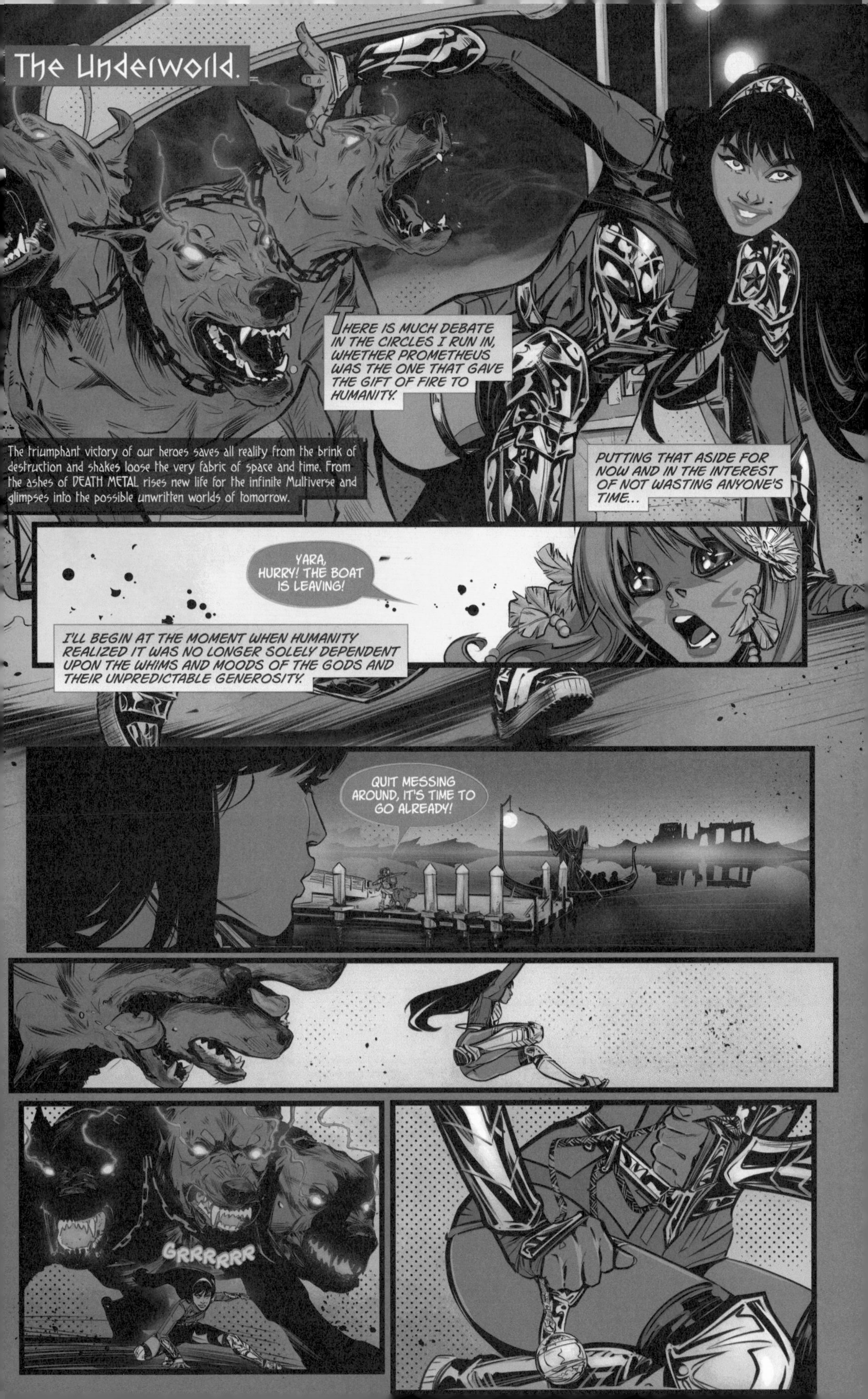
The Underworld.
THERE IS MUCH DEBATE IN THE CIRCLES I RUN IN, WHETHER PROMETHEUS WAS THE ONE THAT GAVE THE GIFT OF FIRE TO HUMANITY.
The triumphant victory of our heroes saves all reality from the brink of destruction and shakes loose the very fabric of space and time. From the ashes of DEATH METAL rises new life for the infinite Multiverse and glimpses into the possible unwritten worlds of tomorrow.
PUTTING THAT ASIDE FOR NOW AND IN THE INTEREST OF NOT WASTING ANYONE'S TIME...
YARA, HURRY! THE BOAT IS LEAVING!
I'LL BEGIN AT THE MOMENT WHEN HUMANITY REALIZED IT WAS NO LONGER SOLELY DEPENDENT UPON THE WHIMS AND MOODS OF THE GODS AND THEIR UNPREDICTABLE GENEROSITY.
QUIT MESSING AROUND, IT'S TIME TO GO ALREADY!
GRRRRRR

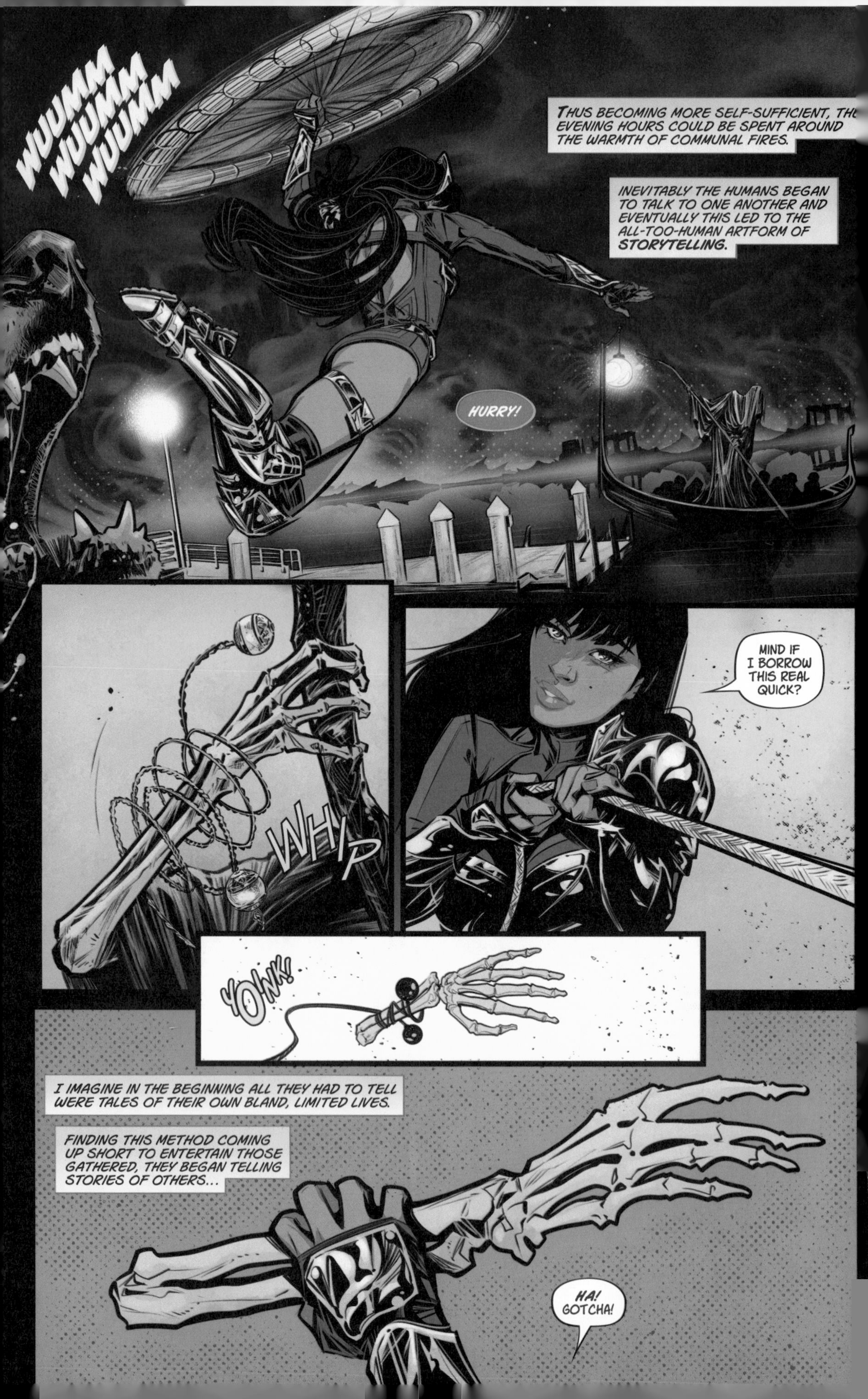
WUUMM WUUMM WUUMM
THUS BECOMING MORE SELF-SUFFICIENT, THE EVENING HOURS COULD BE SPENT AROUND THE WARMTH OF COMMUNAL FIRES.
INEVITABLY THE HUMANS BEGAN TO TALK TO ONE ANOTHER AND EVENTUALLY THIS LED TO THE ALL-TOO-HUMAN ARTFORM OF STORYTELLING.
HURRY!
WHIP
MIND IF I BORROW THIS REAL QUICK?
YOINK!
I IMAGINE IN THE BEGINNING ALL THEY HAD TO TELL WERE TALES OF THEIR OWN BLAND, LIMITED LIVES.
FINDING THIS METHOD COMING UP SHORT TO ENTERTAIN THOSE GATHERED, THEY BEGAN TELLING STORIES OF OTHERS...
HA! GOTCHA!

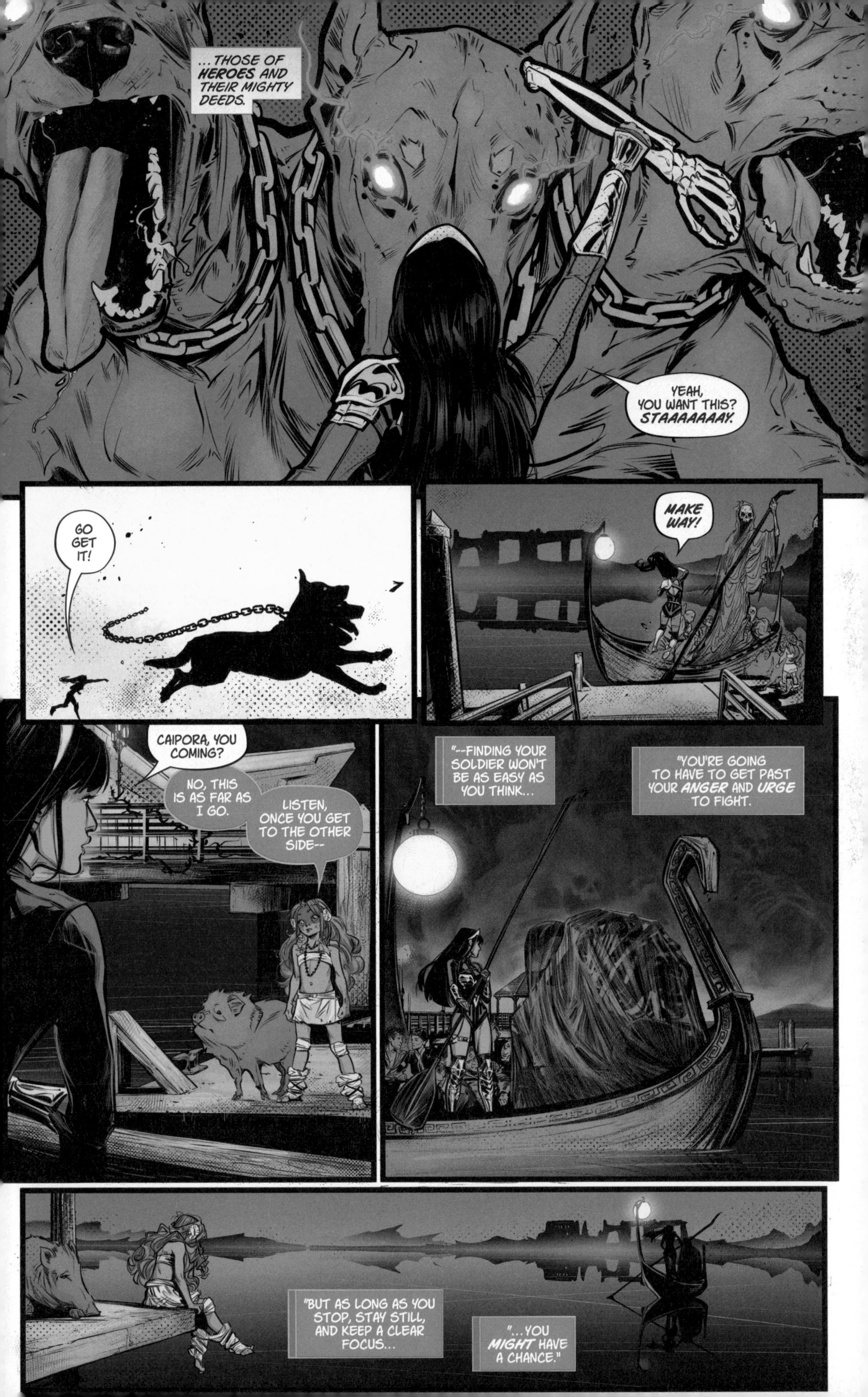

...THOSE OF HEROES AND THEIR MIGHTY DEEDS.
YEAH, YOU WANT THIS? STAAAAAAAY.
GO GET IT!
MAKE WAY!
CAIPORA, YOU COMING?
NO, THIS IS AS FAR AS I GO.
LISTEN, ONCE YOU GET TO THE OTHER SIDE--
"--FINDING YOUR SOLDIER WON'T BE AS EASY AS YOU THINK...
"YOU'RE GOING TO HAVE TO GET PAST YOUR ANGER AND URGE TO FIGHT.
"BUT AS LONG AS YOU STOP, STAY STILL, AND KEEP A CLEAR FOCUS...
"...YOU MIGHT HAVE A CHANCE."

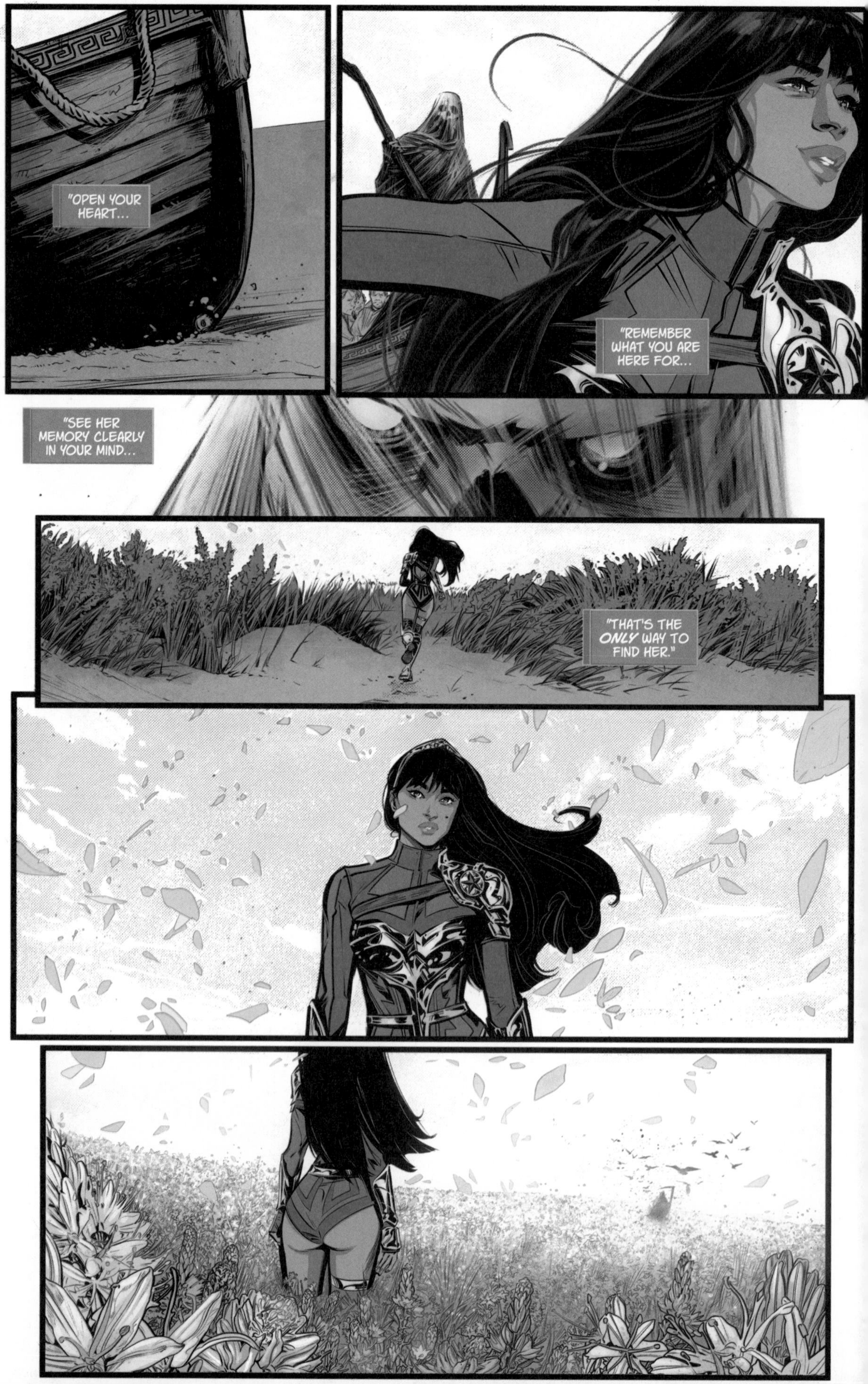
"OPEN YOUR HEART...
"REMEMBER WHAT YOU ARE HERE FOR...
"SEE HER MEMORY CLEARLY IN YOUR MIND...
"THAT'S THE *ONLY* WAY TO FIND HER."

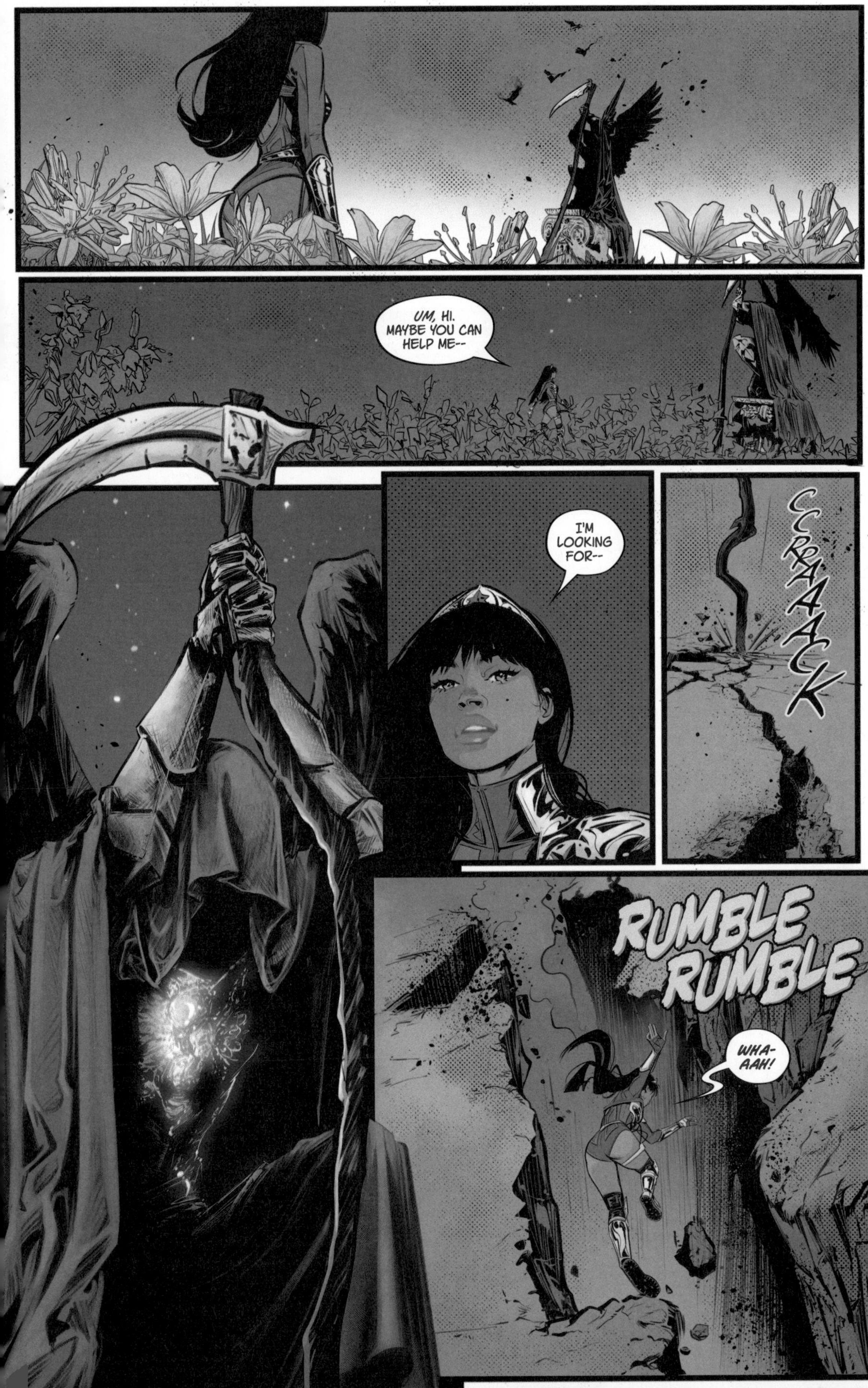
UM, HI. MAYBE YOU CAN HELP ME--
I'M LOOKING FOR--
CCRRAAACK
RUMBLE RUMBLE
WHA-AAH!

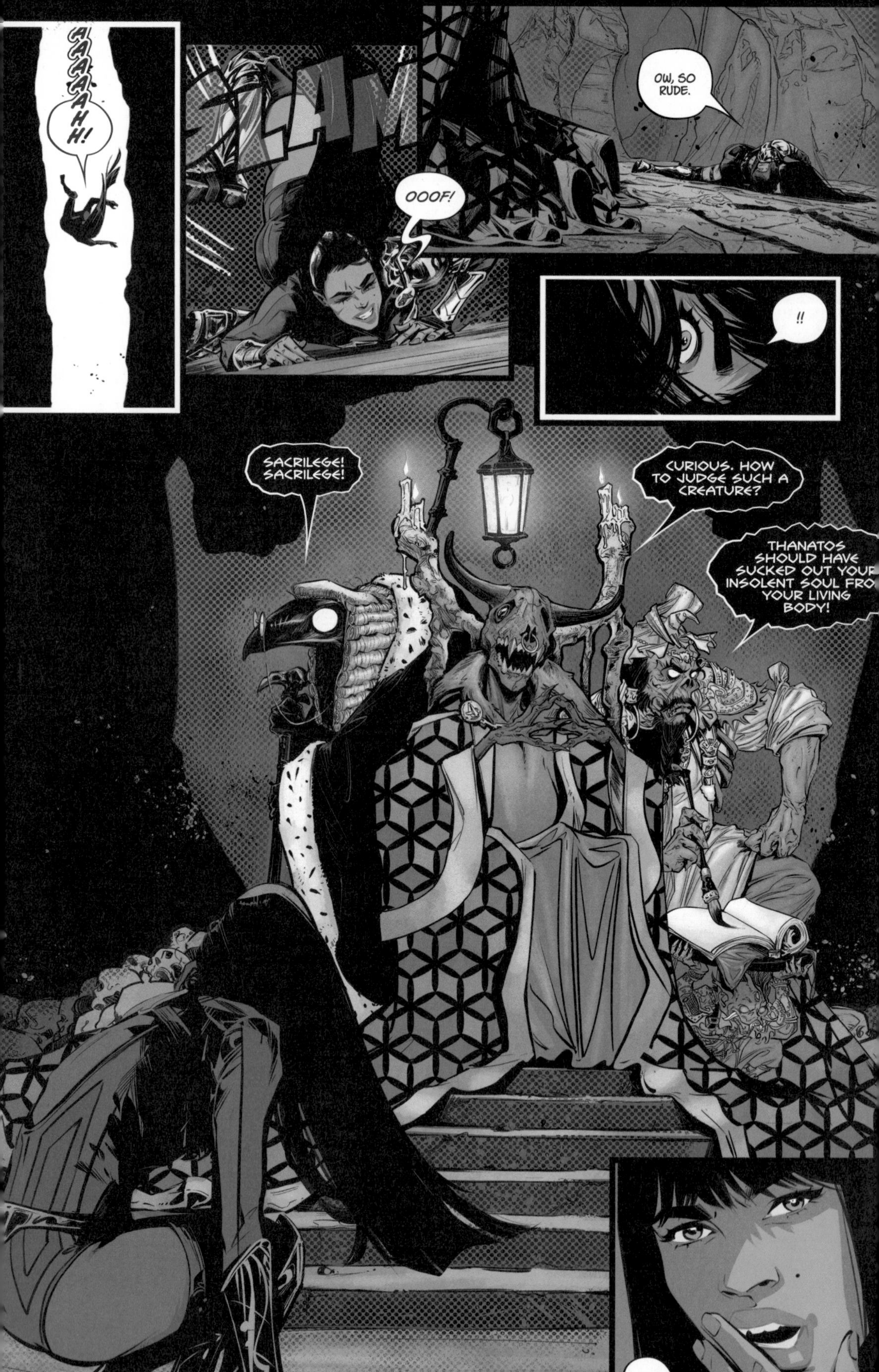
AAAAAAAHH!
SLAM
OOOF!
OW, SO RUDE.
!!
SACRILEGE! SACRILEGE!
CURIOUS. HOW TO JUDGE SUCH A CREATURE?
THANATOS SHOULD HAVE SUCKED OUT YOUR INSOLENT SOUL FRO YOUR LIVING BODY!
UH...

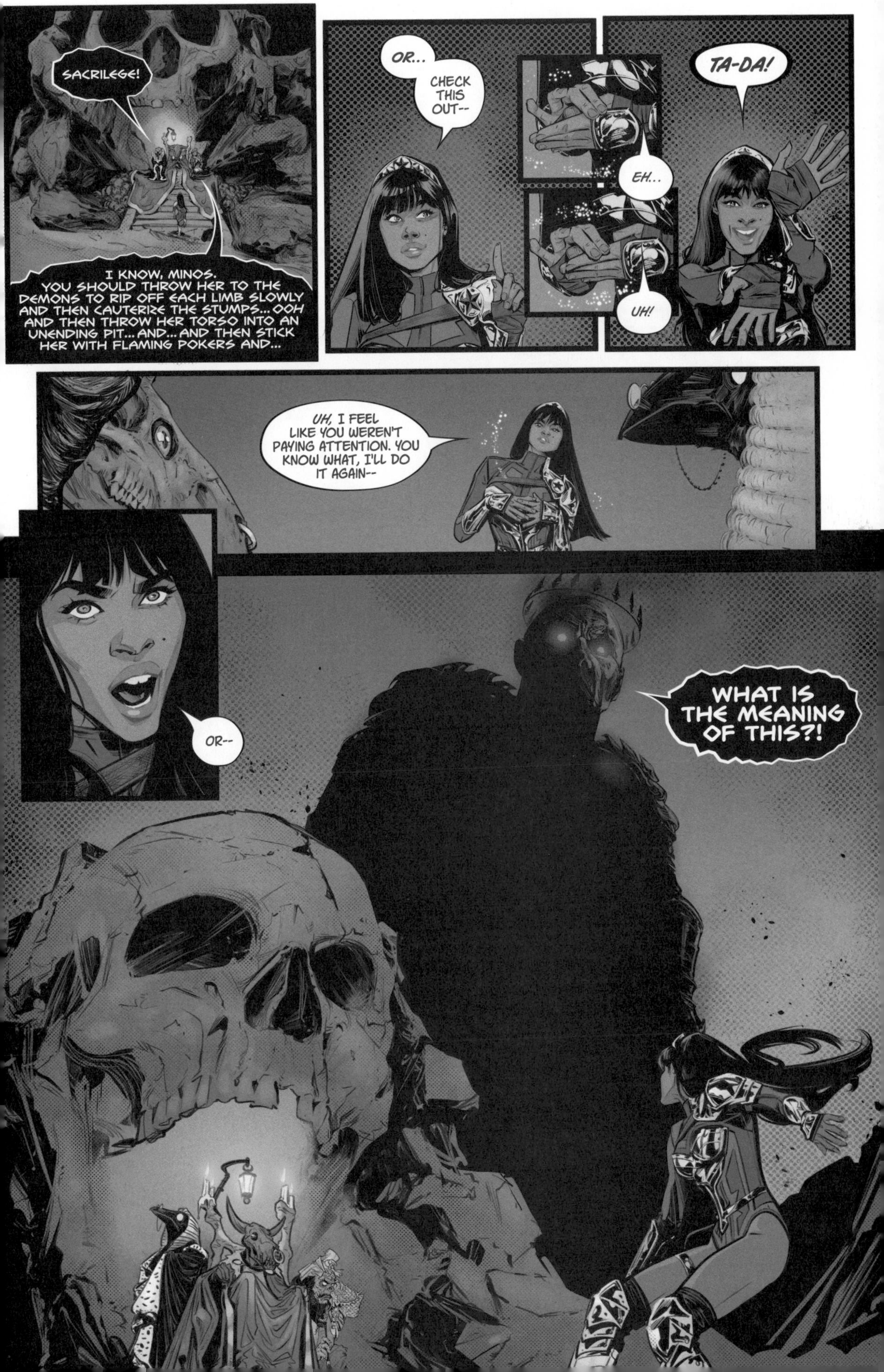
SACRILEGE!
I KNOW, MINOS. YOU SHOULD THROW HER TO THE DEMONS TO RIP OFF EACH LIMB SLOWLY AND THEN CAUTERIZE THE STUMPS... OOH AND THEN THROW HER TORSO INTO AN UNENDING PIT... AND... AND THEN STICK HER WITH FLAMING POKERS AND...
OR...
CHECK THIS OUT--
EH...
UH!
TA-DA!
UH, I FEEL LIKE YOU WEREN'T PAYING ATTENTION. YOU KNOW WHAT, I'LL DO IT AGAIN--
OR--
WHAT IS THE MEANING OF THIS?!

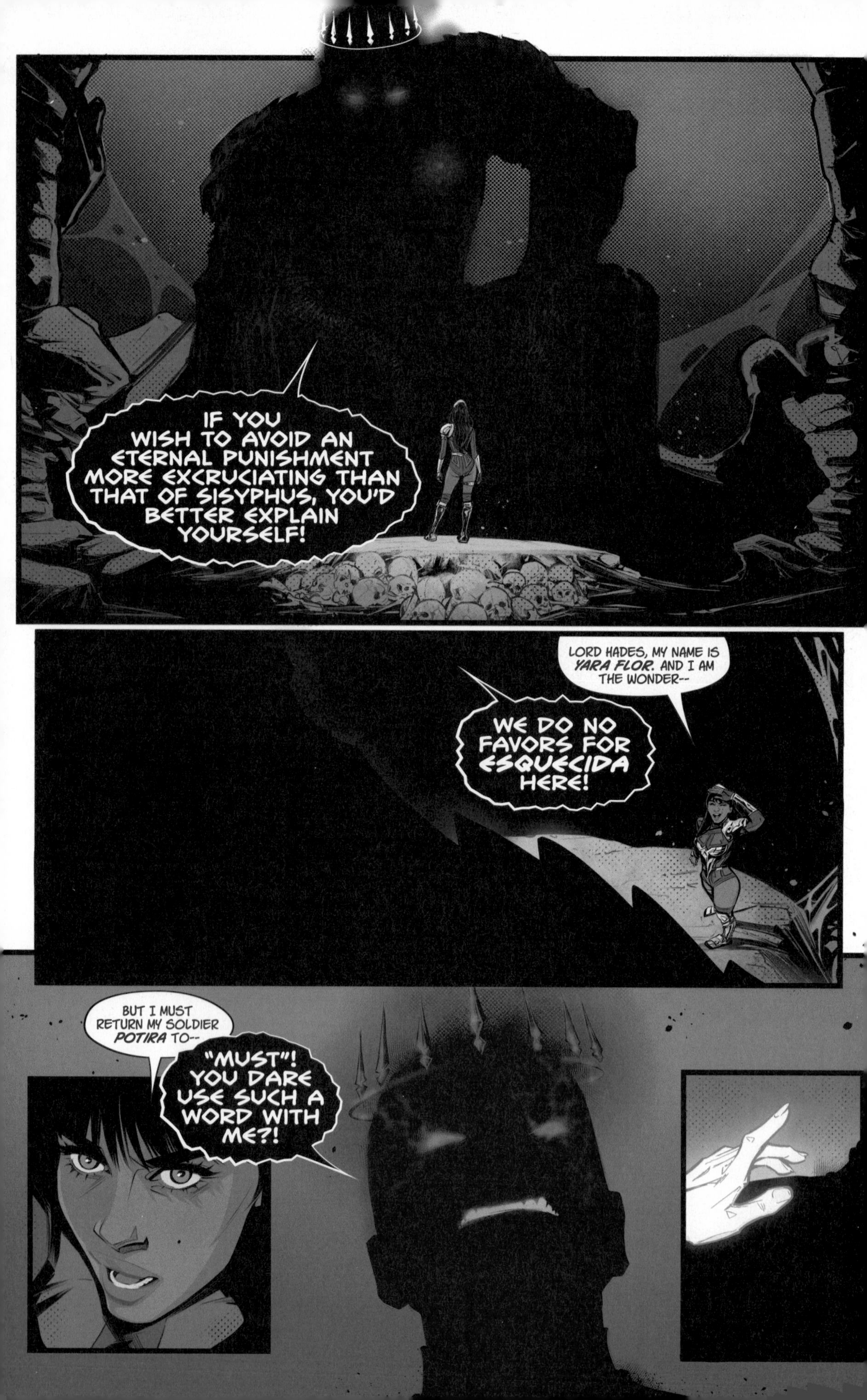
IF YOU WISH TO AVOID AN ETERNAL PUNISHMENT MORE EXCRUCIATING THAN THAT OF SISYPHUS, YOU'D BETTER EXPLAIN YOURSELF!
LORD HADES, MY NAME IS YARA FLOR. AND I AM THE WONDER--
WE DO NO FAVORS FOR ESQUECIDA HERE!
BUT I MUST RETURN MY SOLDIER POTIRA TO--
"MUST"! YOU DARE USE SUCH A WORD WITH ME?!

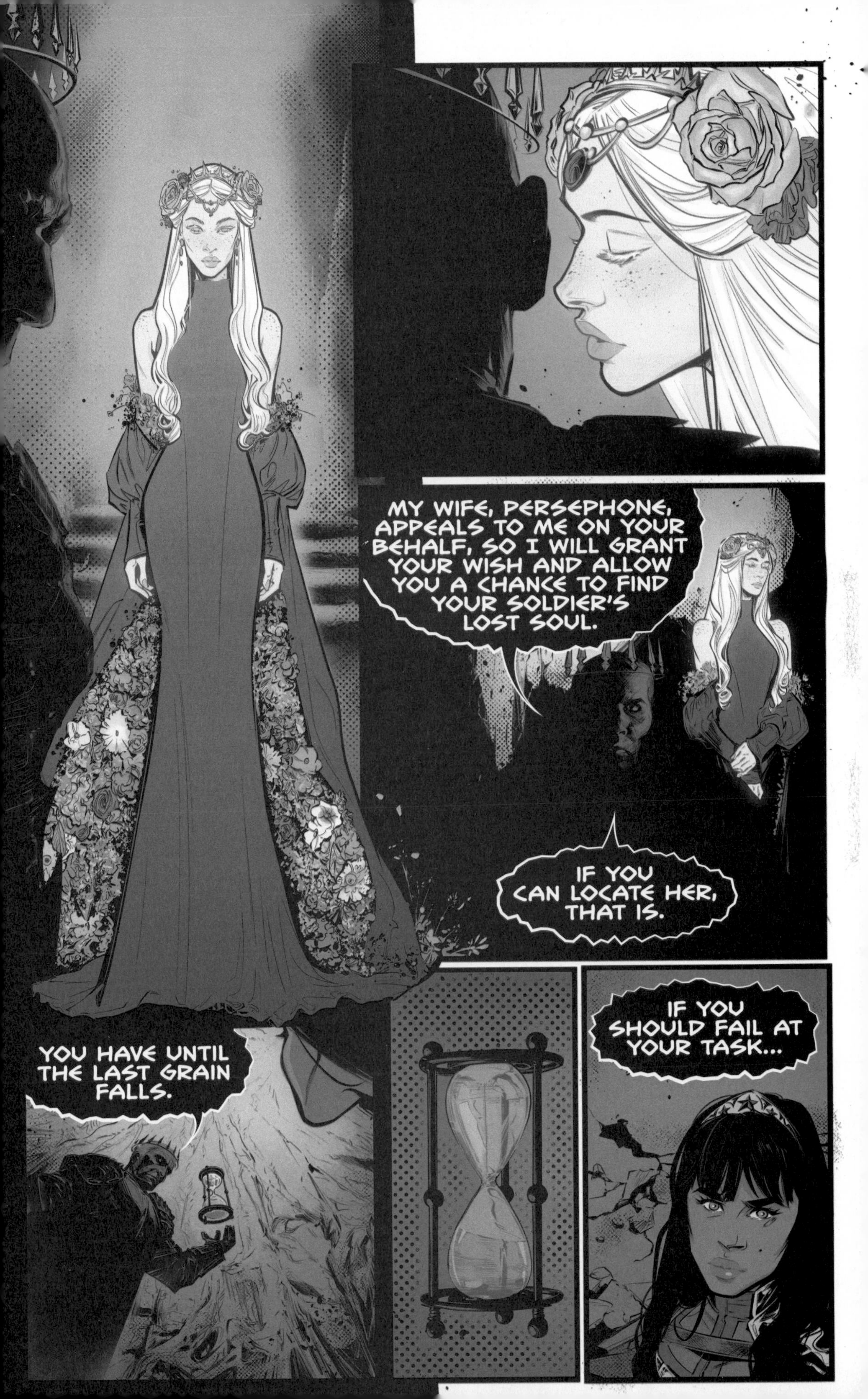
MY WIFE, PERSEPHONE, APPEALS TO ME ON YOUR BEHALF, SO I WILL GRANT YOUR WISH AND ALLOW YOU A CHANCE TO FIND YOUR SOLDIER'S LOST SOUL.
IF YOU CAN LOCATE HER, THAT IS.
YOU HAVE UNTIL THE LAST GRAIN FALLS.
IF YOU SHOULD FAIL AT YOUR TASK...

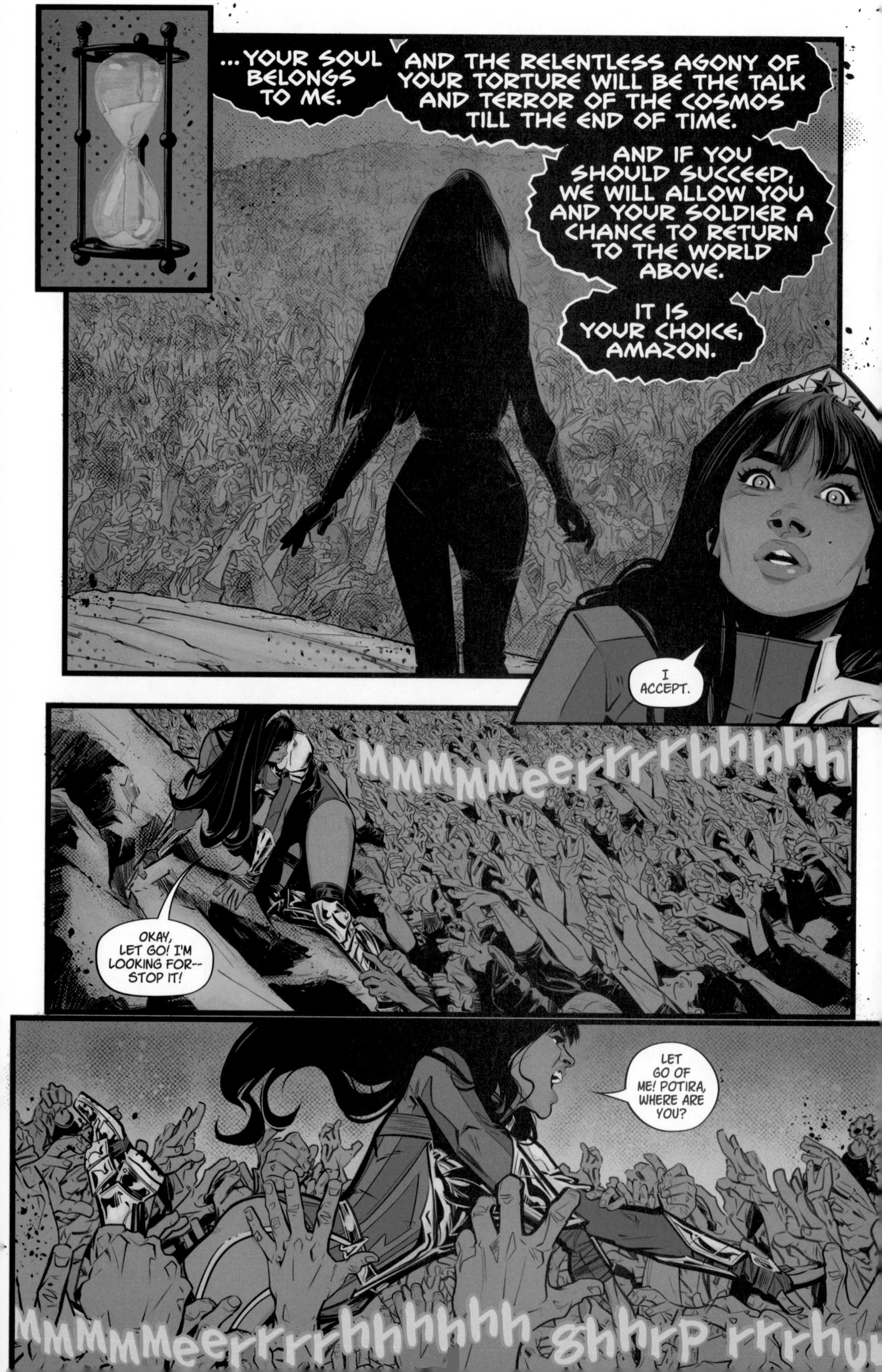
...YOUR SOUL BELONGS TO ME.
AND THE RELENTLESS AGONY OF YOUR TORTURE WILL BE THE TALK AND TERROR OF THE COSMOS TILL THE END OF TIME.
AND IF YOU SHOULD SUCCEED, WE WILL ALLOW YOU AND YOUR SOLDIER A CHANCE TO RETURN TO THE WORLD ABOVE.
IT IS YOUR CHOICE, AMAZON.
I ACCEPT.
MMMMMeerrrrhhhhh
OKAY, LET GO! I'M LOOKING FOR-- STOP IT!
LET GO OF ME! POTIRA, WHERE ARE YOU?
MMMMMeerrrrhhhhhhh
shhrp
rrrhu

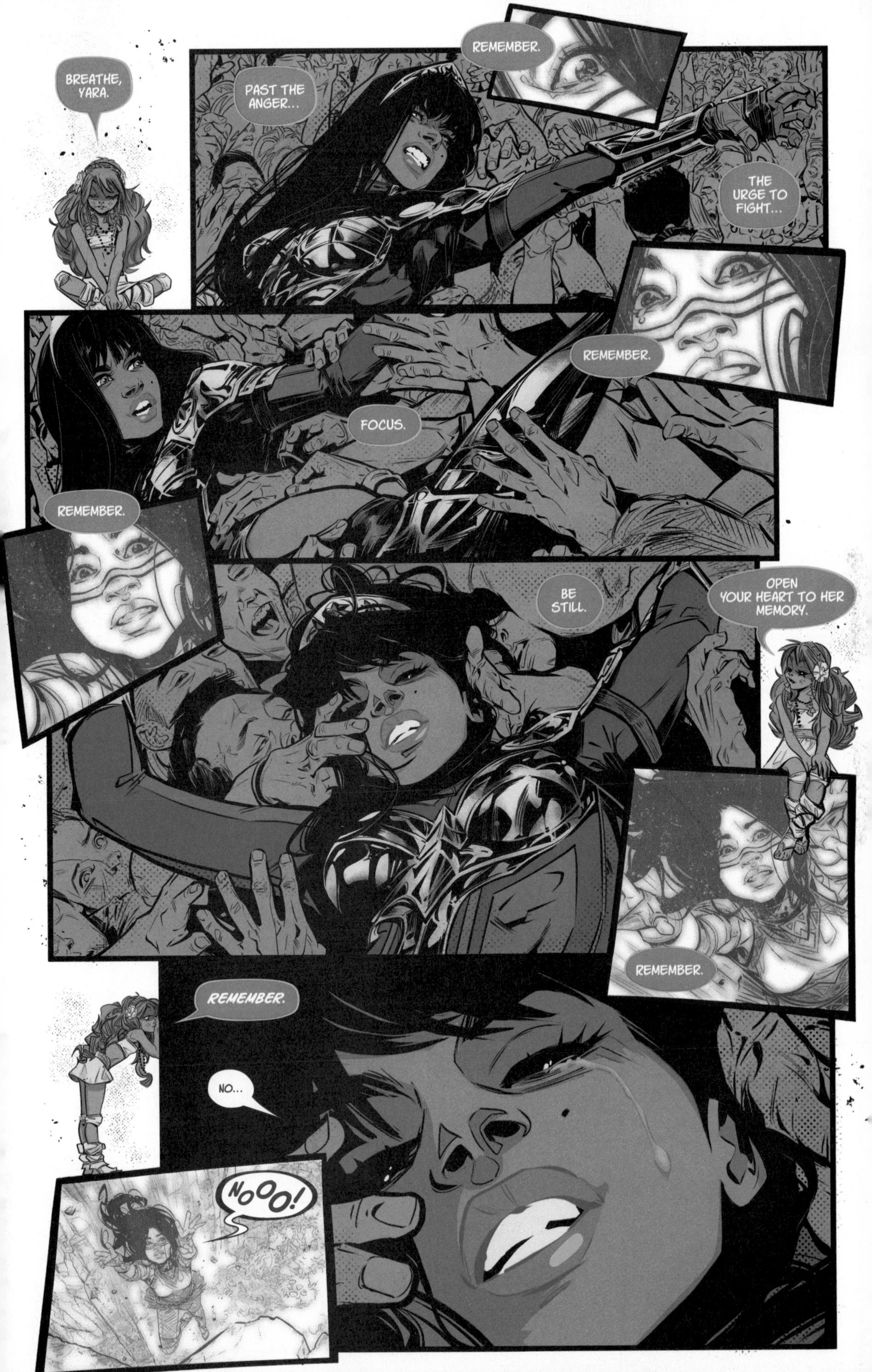
BREATHE, YARA.
PAST THE ANGER...
REMEMBER.
THE URGE TO FIGHT...
REMEMBER.
FOCUS.
REMEMBER.
BE STILL.
OPEN YOUR HEART TO HER MEMORY.
REMEMBER.
REMEMBER.
NO...
NOOO!

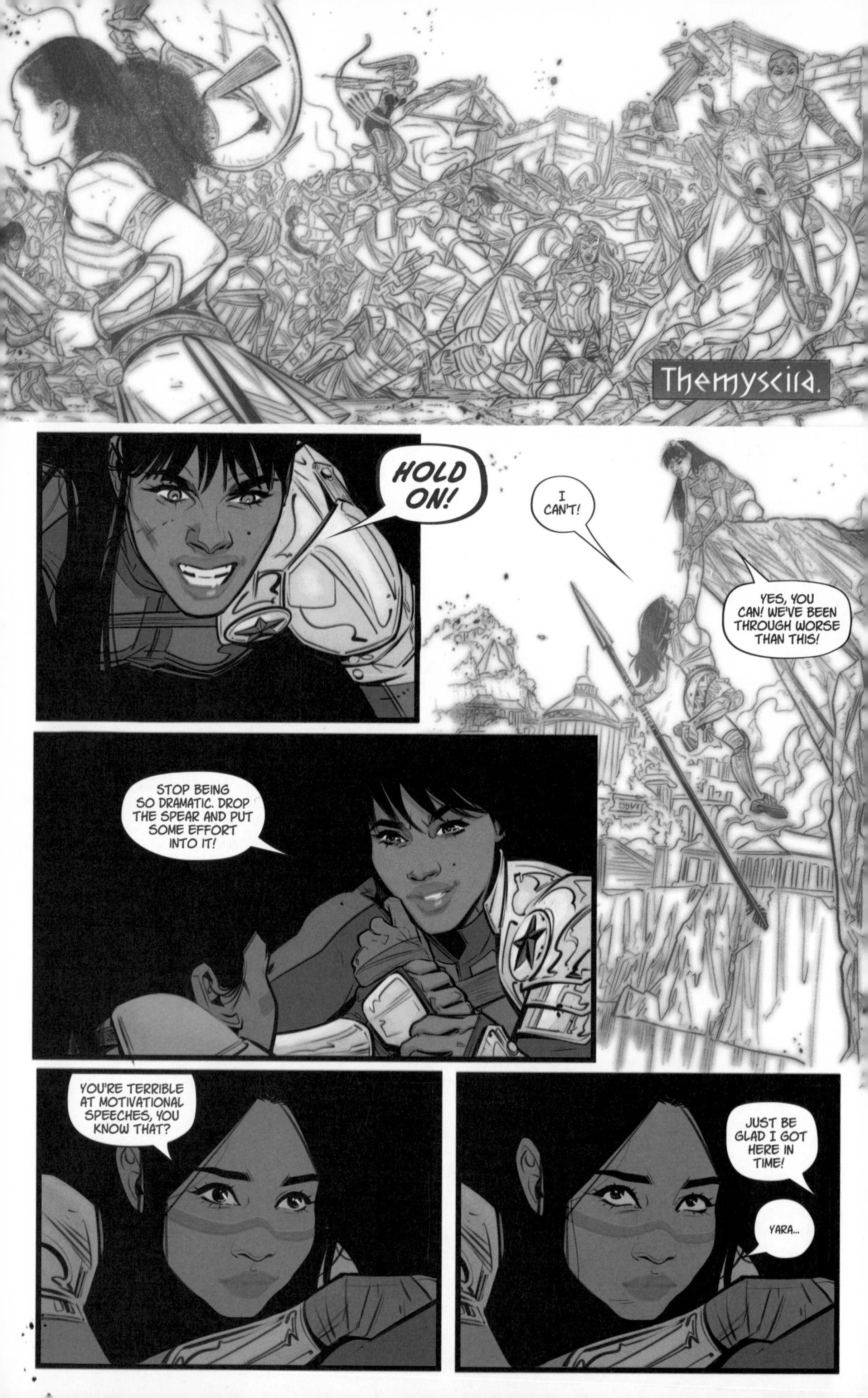
Themyscira.
HOLD ON!
I CAN'T!
YES, YOU CAN! WE'VE BEEN THROUGH WORSE THAN THIS!
STOP BEING SO DRAMATIC. DROP THE SPEAR AND PUT SOME EFFORT INTO IT!
YOU'RE TERRIBLE AT MOTIVATIONAL SPEECHES, YOU KNOW THAT?
JUST BE GLAD I GOT HERE IN TIME!
YARA...

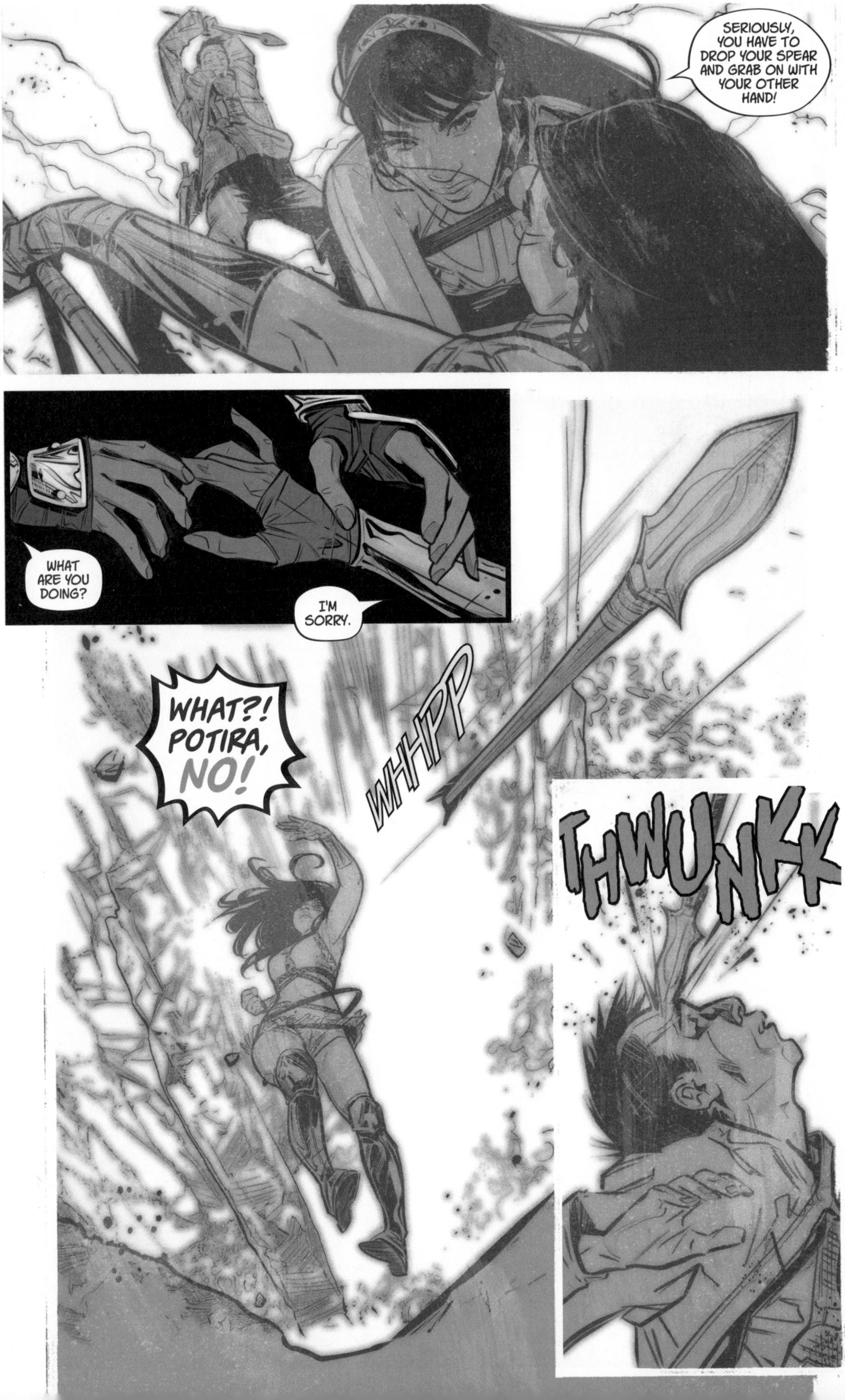
SERIOUSLY, YOU HAVE TO DROP YOUR SPEAR AND GRAB ON WITH YOUR OTHER HAND!
WHAT ARE YOU DOING?
I'M SORRY.
WHAT?! POTIRA, NO!
WHPP
THWUNKK

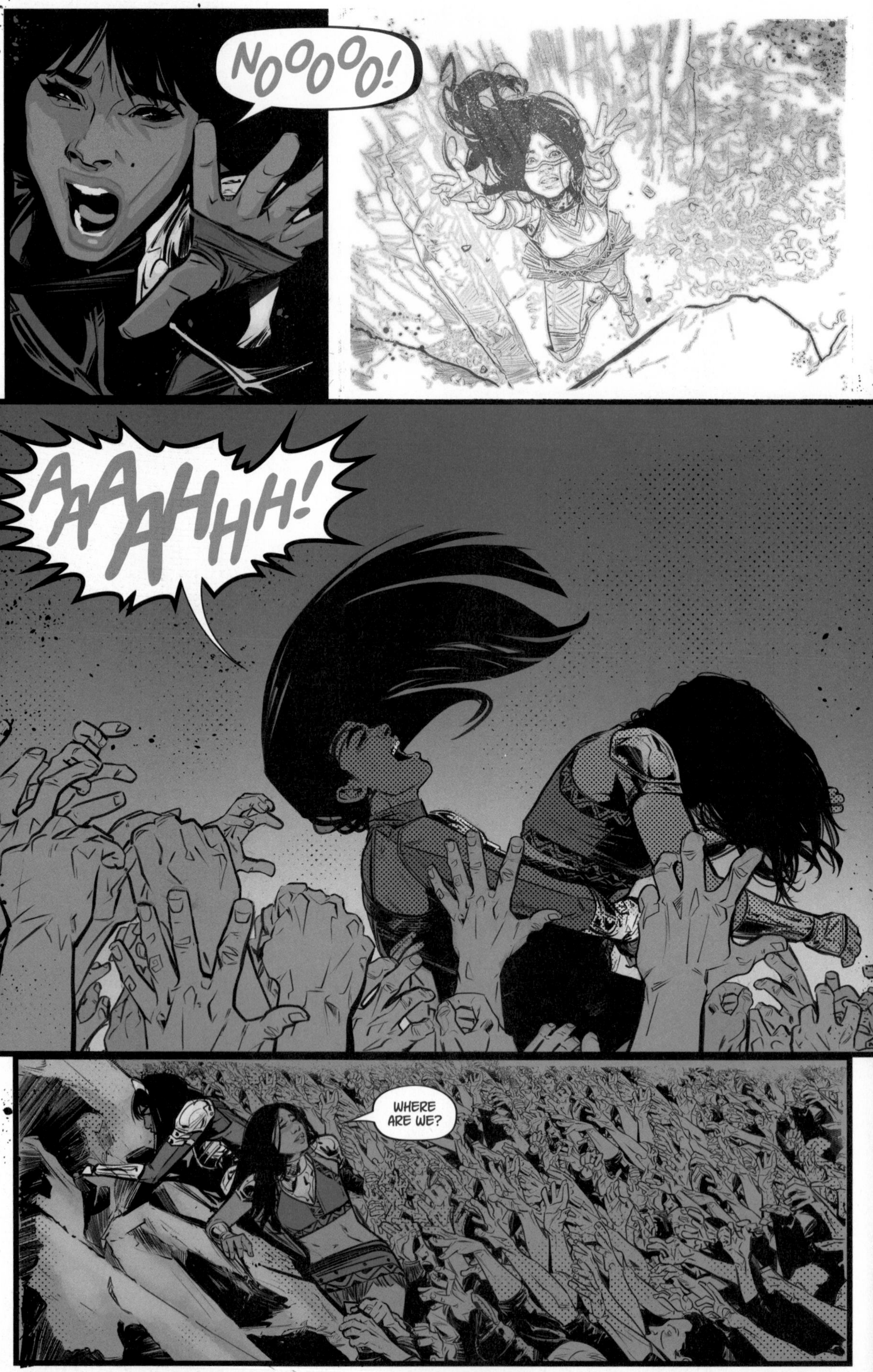
NOOOOO!
AAAAHHH!
WHERE ARE WE?

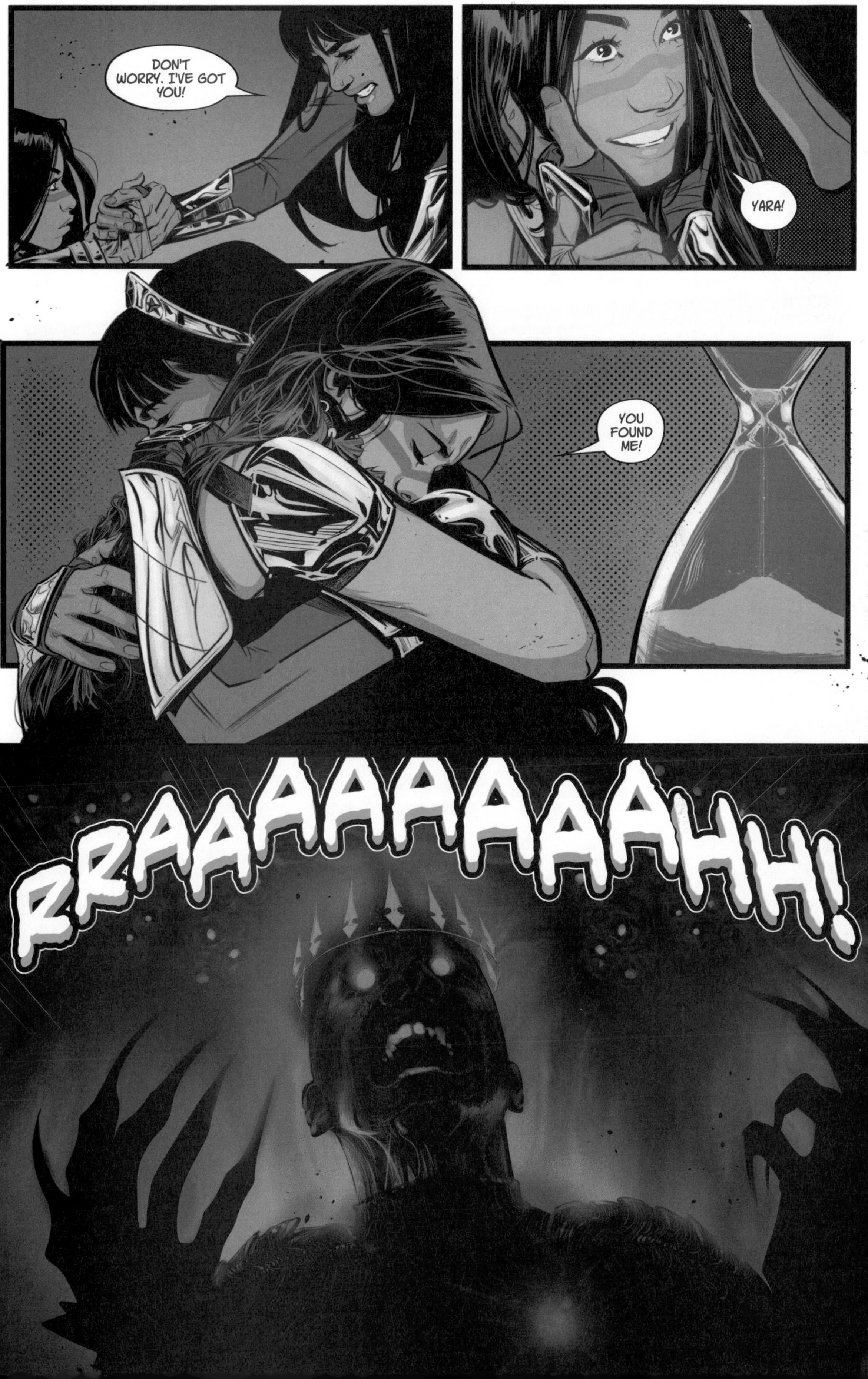
DON'T WORRY. I'VE GOT YOU!
YARA!
YOU FOUND ME!
RRAAAAAAAAAAHH!

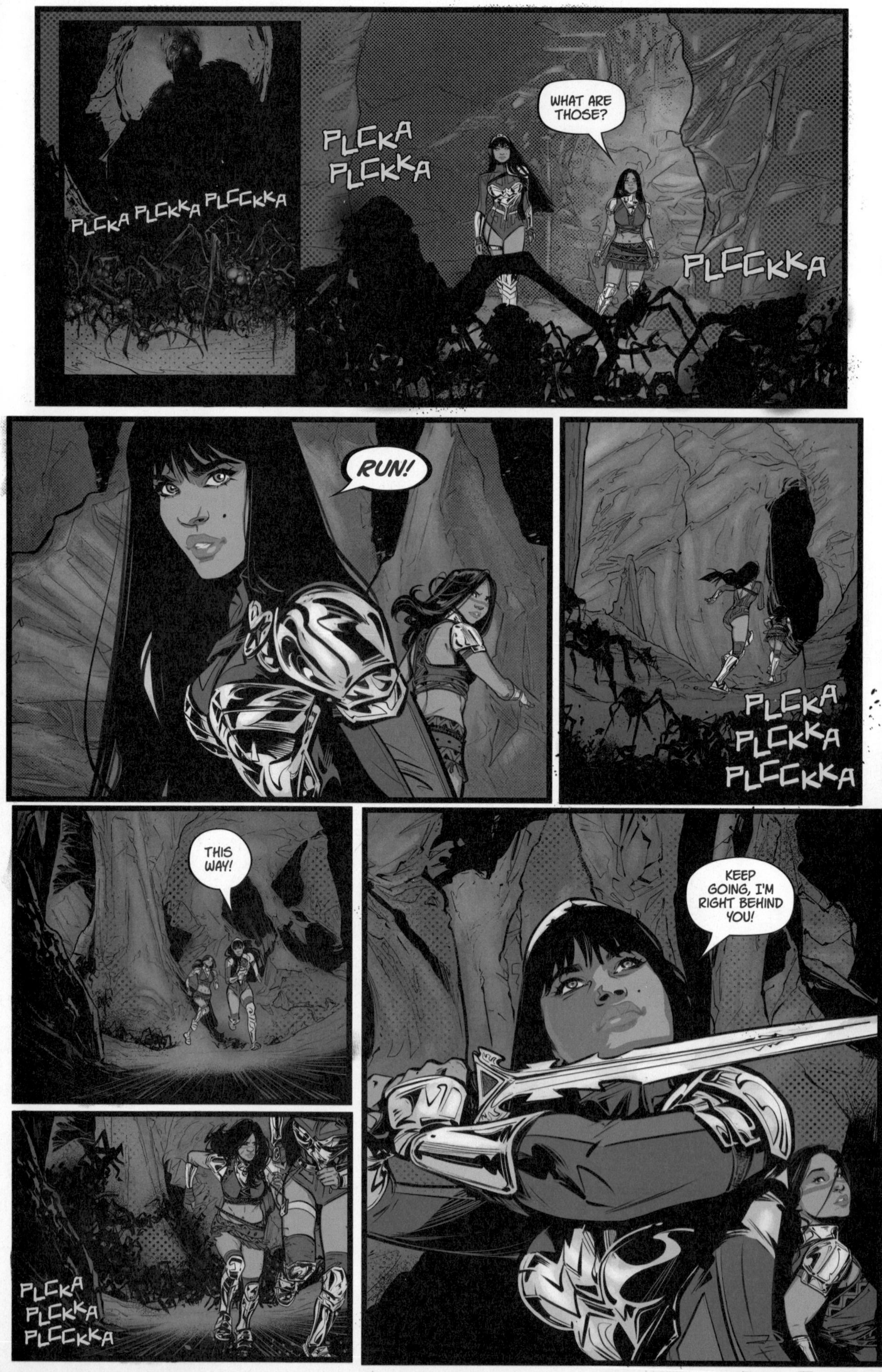
PLCKA PLCKKA PLCCKKA
PLCKA
PLCKKA
WHAT ARE THOSE?
PLCCKKA
RUN!
PLCKA
PLCKKA
PLCCKKA
THIS WAY!
PLCKA
PLCKKA
PLCCKKA
KEEP GOING, I'M RIGHT BEHIND YOU!

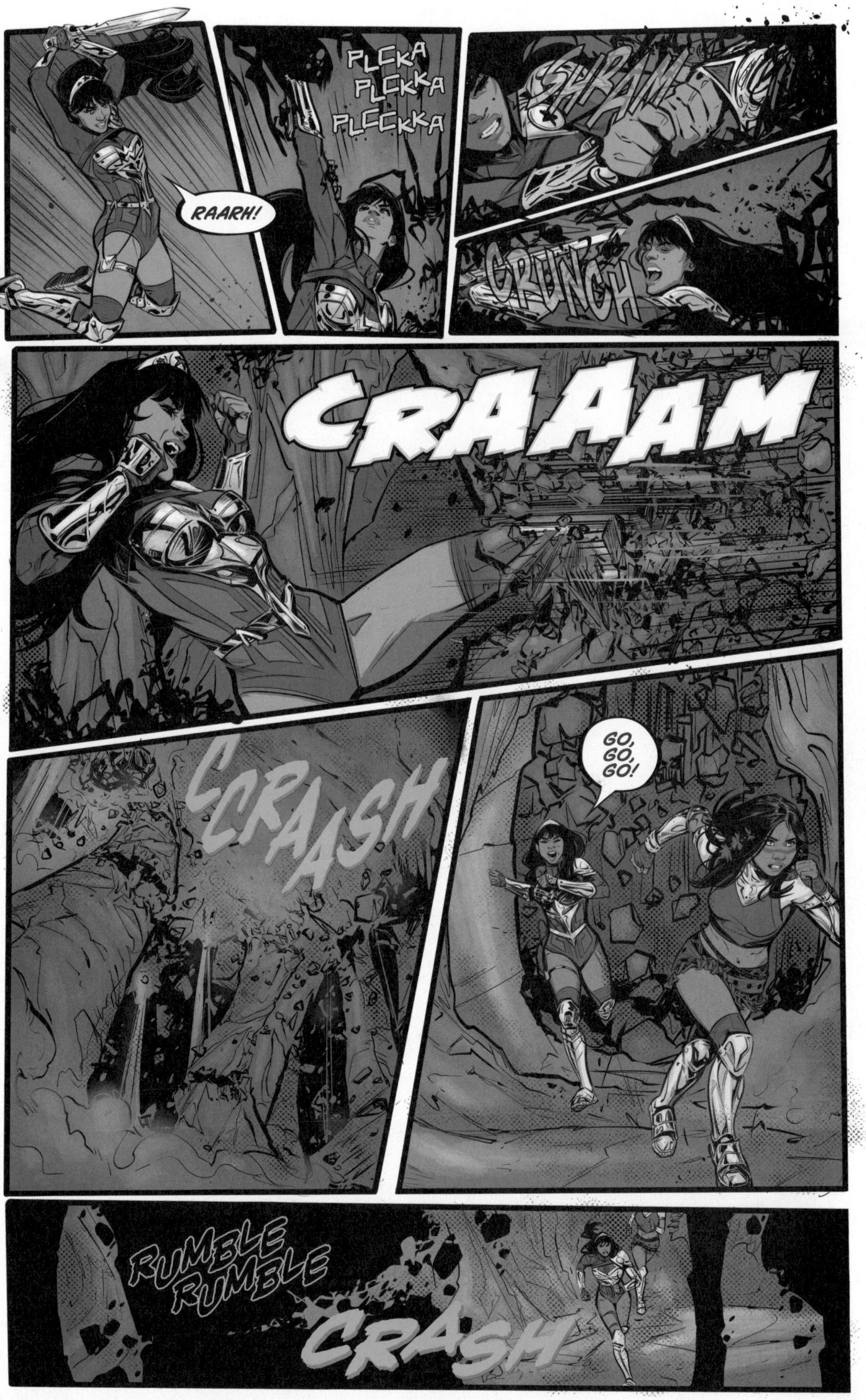
RAARH!
PLCKA
PLCKKA
PLCCKKA
SHRAM
CRUNCH
CRAAAM
CCRAASH
GO, GO, GO!
RUMBLE RUMBLE
CRASH

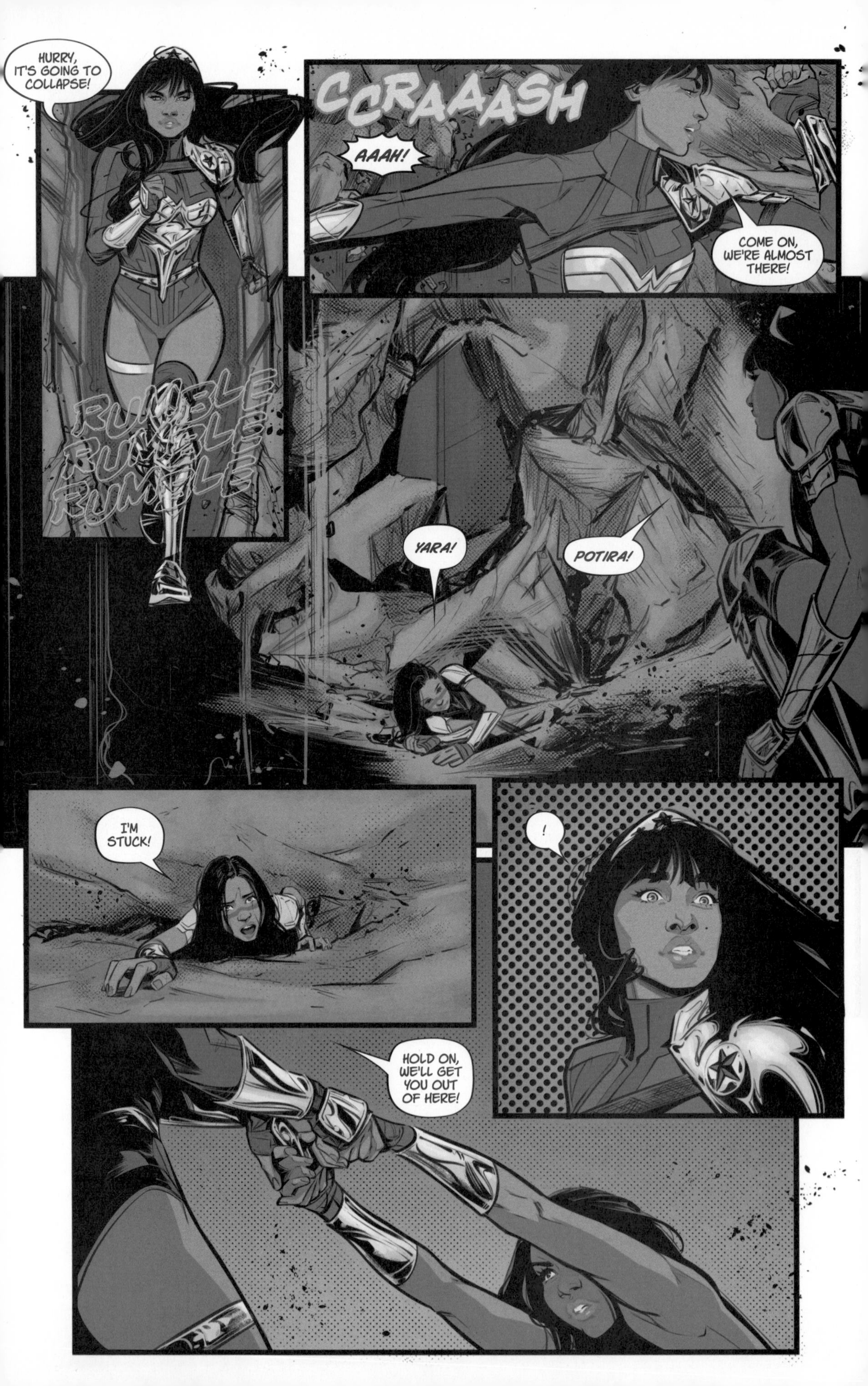
HURRY, IT'S GOING TO COLLAPSE!
RUMBLE RUMBLE RUMBLE
CCRAAASH
AAAH!
COME ON, WE'RE ALMOST THERE!
YARA!
POTIRA!
I'M STUCK!
!
HOLD ON, WE'LL GET YOU OUT OF HERE!

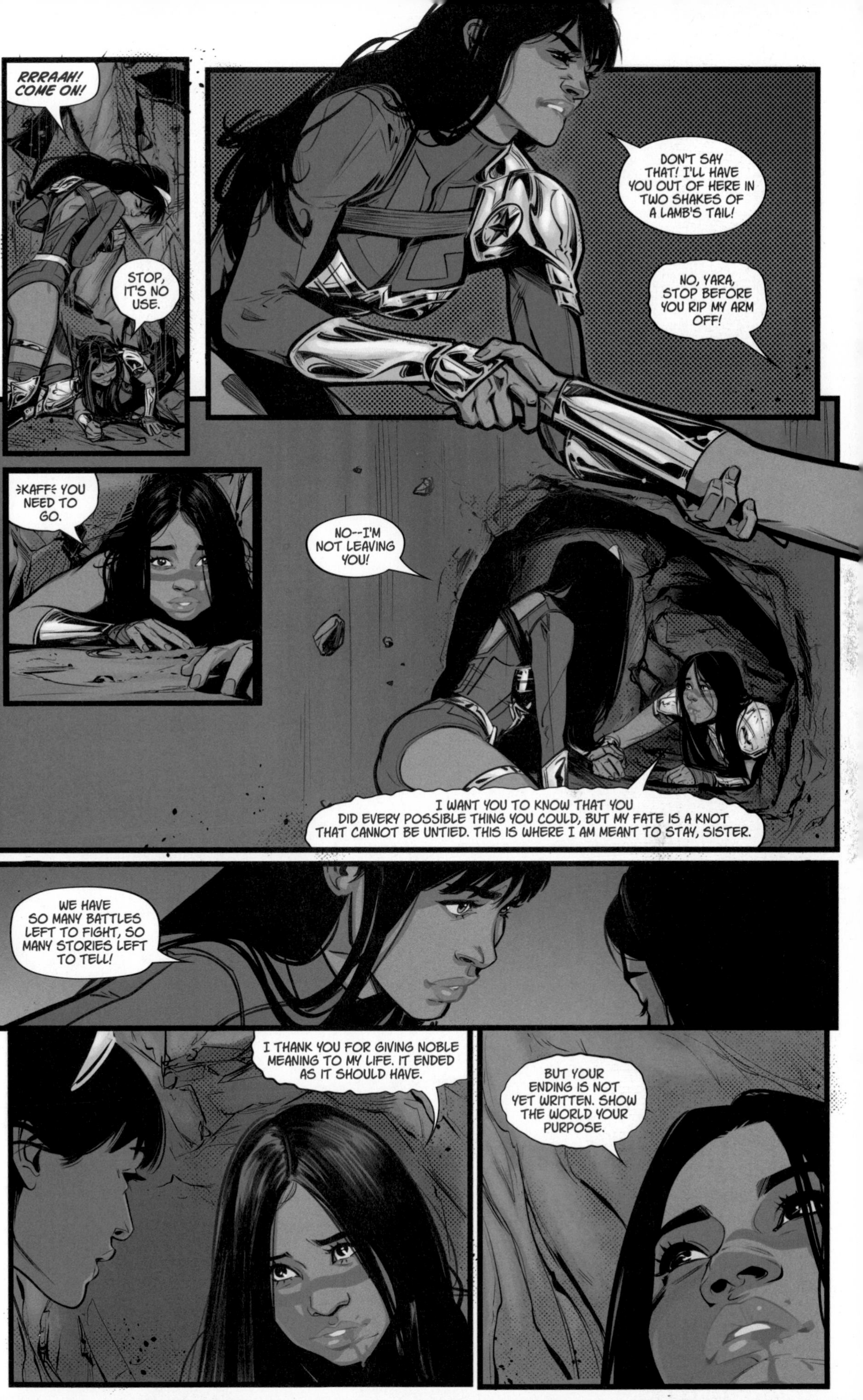

RRRAAH! COME ON!
STOP, IT'S NO USE.
DON'T SAY THAT! I'LL HAVE YOU OUT OF HERE IN TWO SHAKES OF A LAMB'S TAIL!
NO, YARA, STOP BEFORE YOU RIP MY ARM OFF!
≶KAFF≶ YOU NEED TO GO.
NO--I'M NOT LEAVING YOU!
I WANT YOU TO KNOW THAT YOU DID EVERY POSSIBLE THING YOU COULD, BUT MY FATE IS A KNOT THAT CANNOT BE UNTIED. THIS IS WHERE I AM MEANT TO STAY, SISTER.
WE HAVE SO MANY BATTLES LEFT TO FIGHT, SO MANY STORIES LEFT TO TELL!
I THANK YOU FOR GIVING NOBLE MEANING TO MY LIFE. IT ENDED AS IT SHOULD HAVE.
BUT YOUR ENDING IS NOT YET WRITTEN. SHOW THE WORLD YOUR PURPOSE.

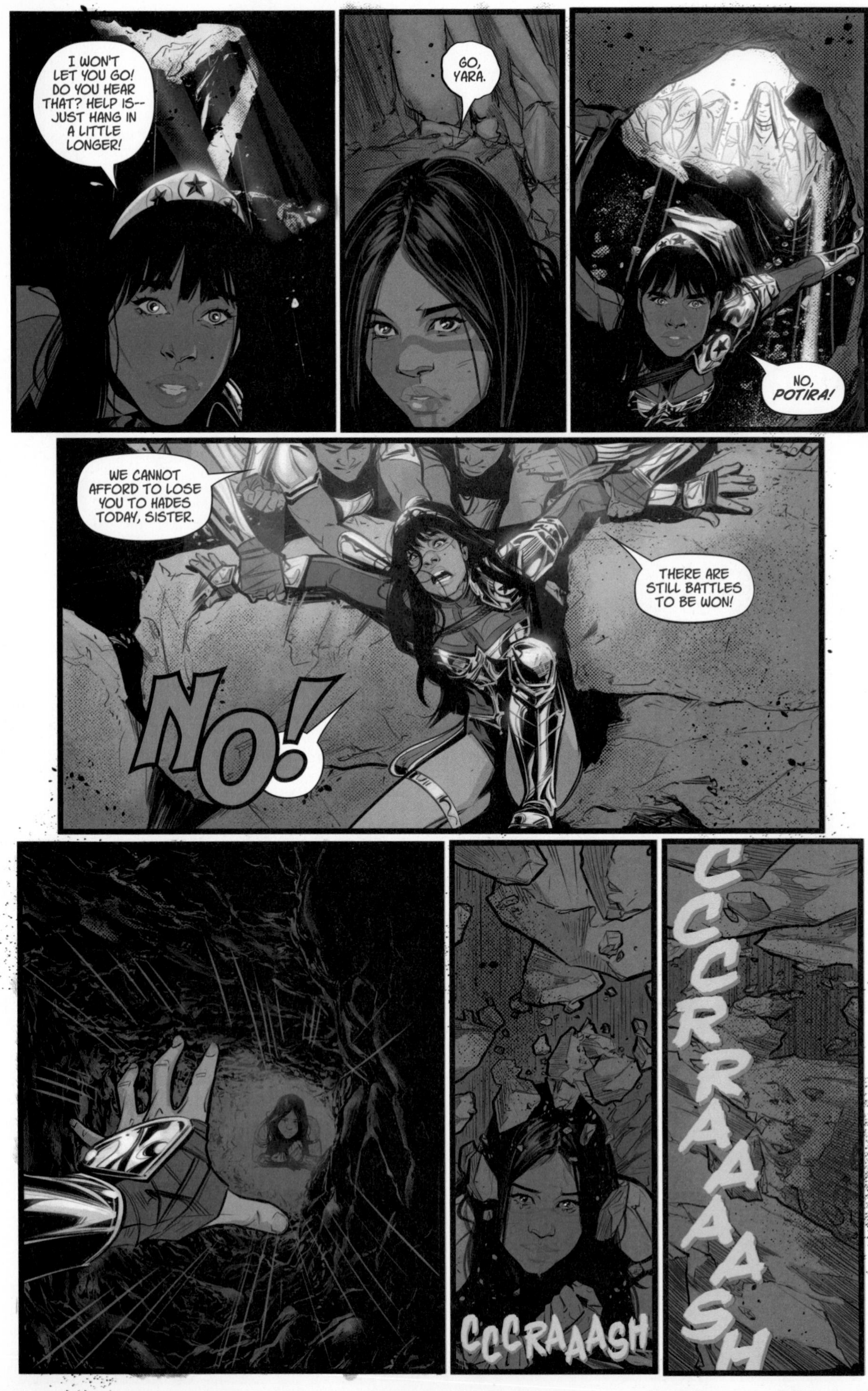
I WON'T LET YOU GO! DO YOU HEAR THAT? HELP IS-- JUST HANG IN A LITTLE LONGER!
GO, YARA.
NO, POTIRA!
WE CANNOT AFFORD TO LOSE YOU TO HADES TODAY, SISTER.
THERE ARE STILL BATTLES TO BE WON!
NO!
CCCRAAASH
CCCRRAAAASH

MUCH LIKE A PEARL FORMING IN AN OYSTER, ALL HERO LEGENDS GROW OUT OF A GRAIN OF TRUTH...

CCCRRASSHHHH

NOOOOO!

NO! STOP!

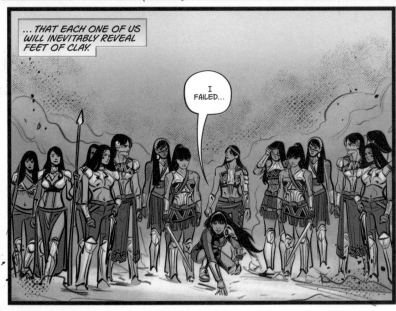

... THAT EACH ONE OF US WILL INEVITABLY REVEAL FEET OF CLAY.

I FAILED...

I FAILED YOU.

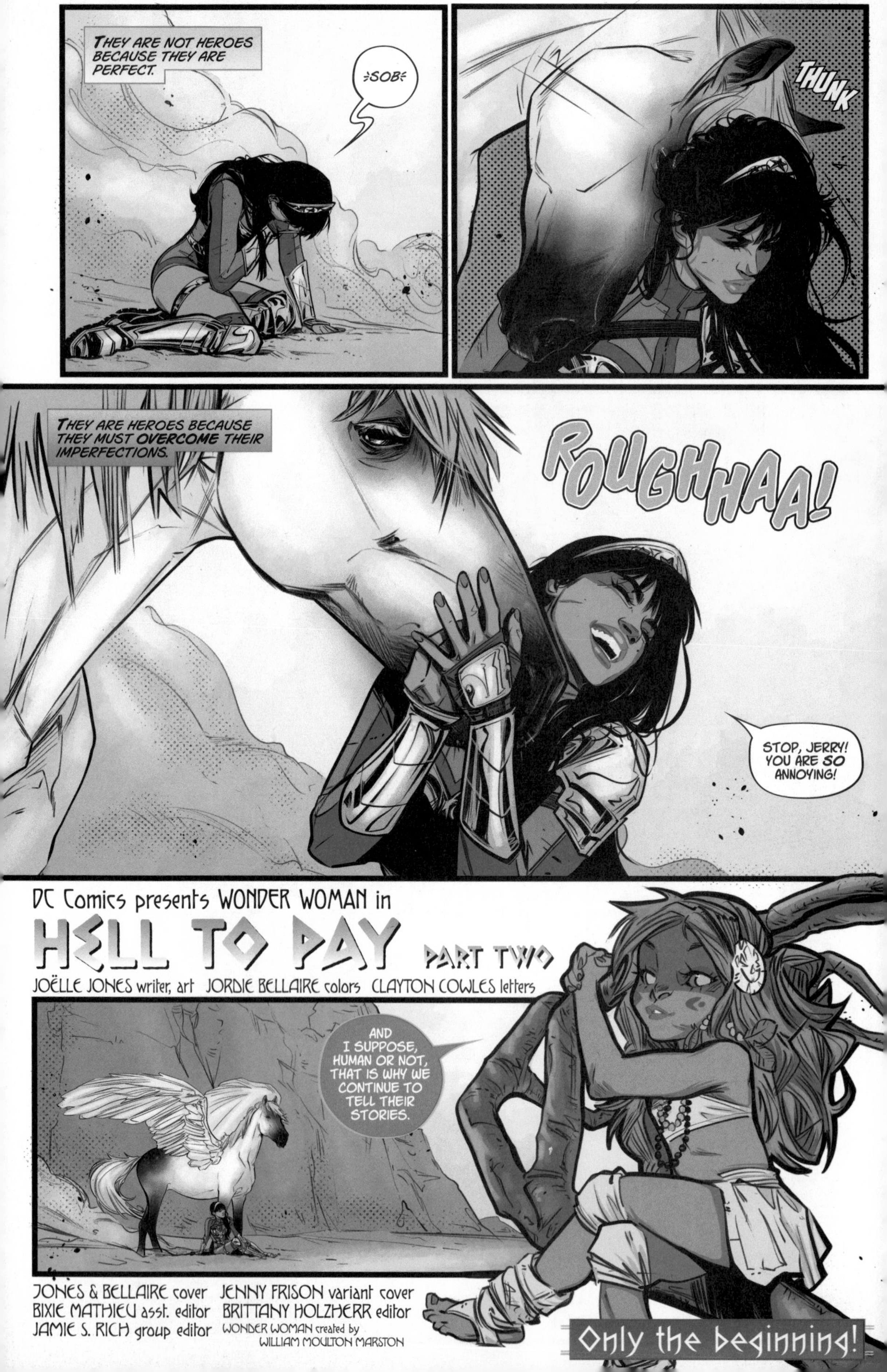
THEY ARE NOT HEROES BECAUSE THEY ARE PERFECT.
SOB
THUNK
THEY ARE HEROES BECAUSE THEY MUST OVERCOME THEIR IMPERFECTIONS.
ROUGHHAA!
STOP, JERRY! YOU ARE SO ANNOYING!
DC Comics presents WONDER WOMAN in
HELL TO PAY PART TWO
JOËLLE JONES writer, art JORDIE BELLAIRE colors CLAYTON COWLES letters
AND I SUPPOSE, HUMAN OR NOT, THAT IS WHY WE CONTINUE TO TELL THEIR STORIES.
JONES & BELLAIRE cover JENNY FRISON variant cover
BIXIE MATHIEU asst. editor BRITTANY HOLZHERR editor
JAMIE S. RICH group editor WONDER WOMAN created by WILLIAM MOULTON MARSTON
Only the beginning!

Future State: Superman/Wonder Woman #1
Cover Art by **LEE WEEKS** and **BRAD ANDERSON**

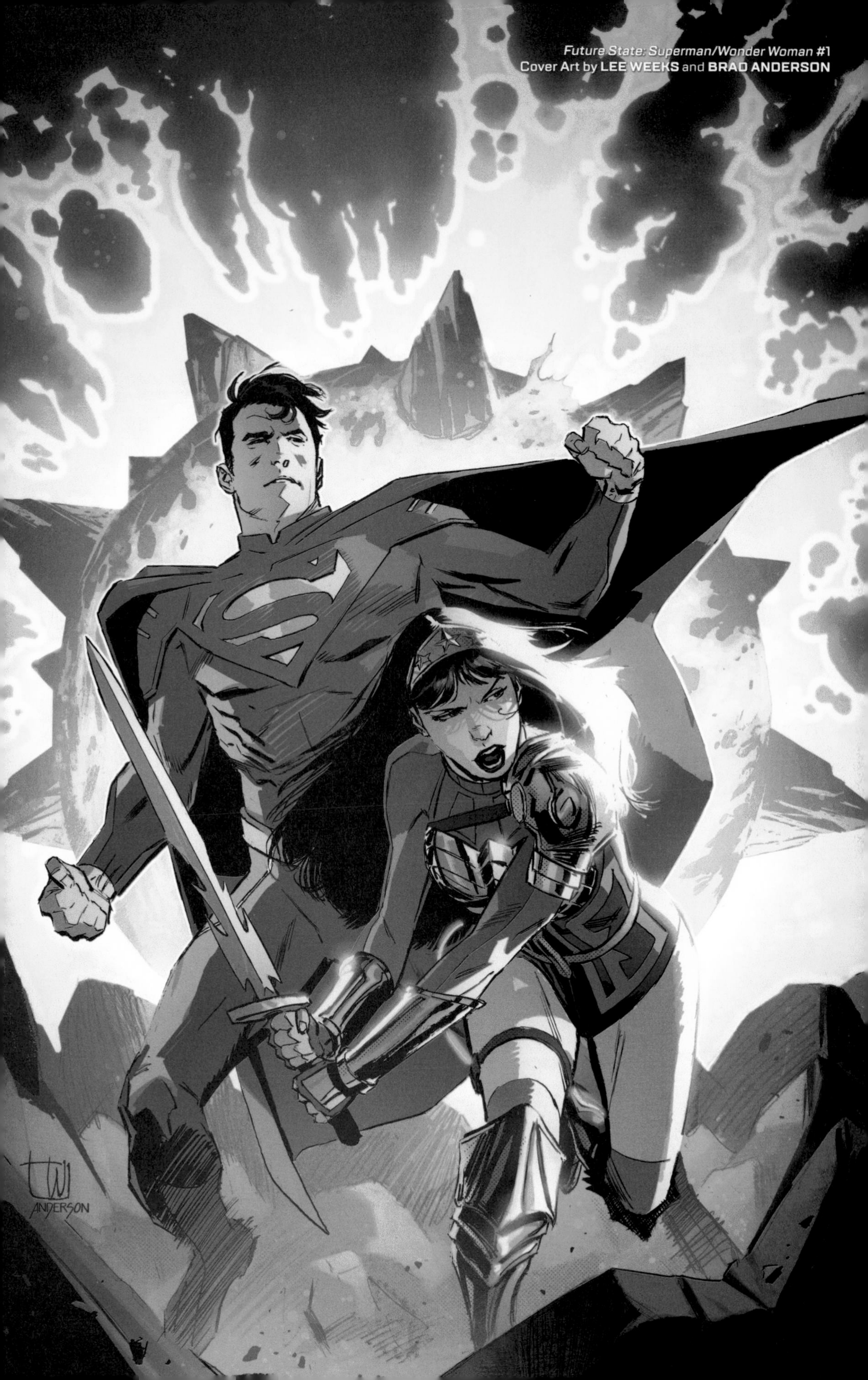
ANDERSON

FUTURE STATE

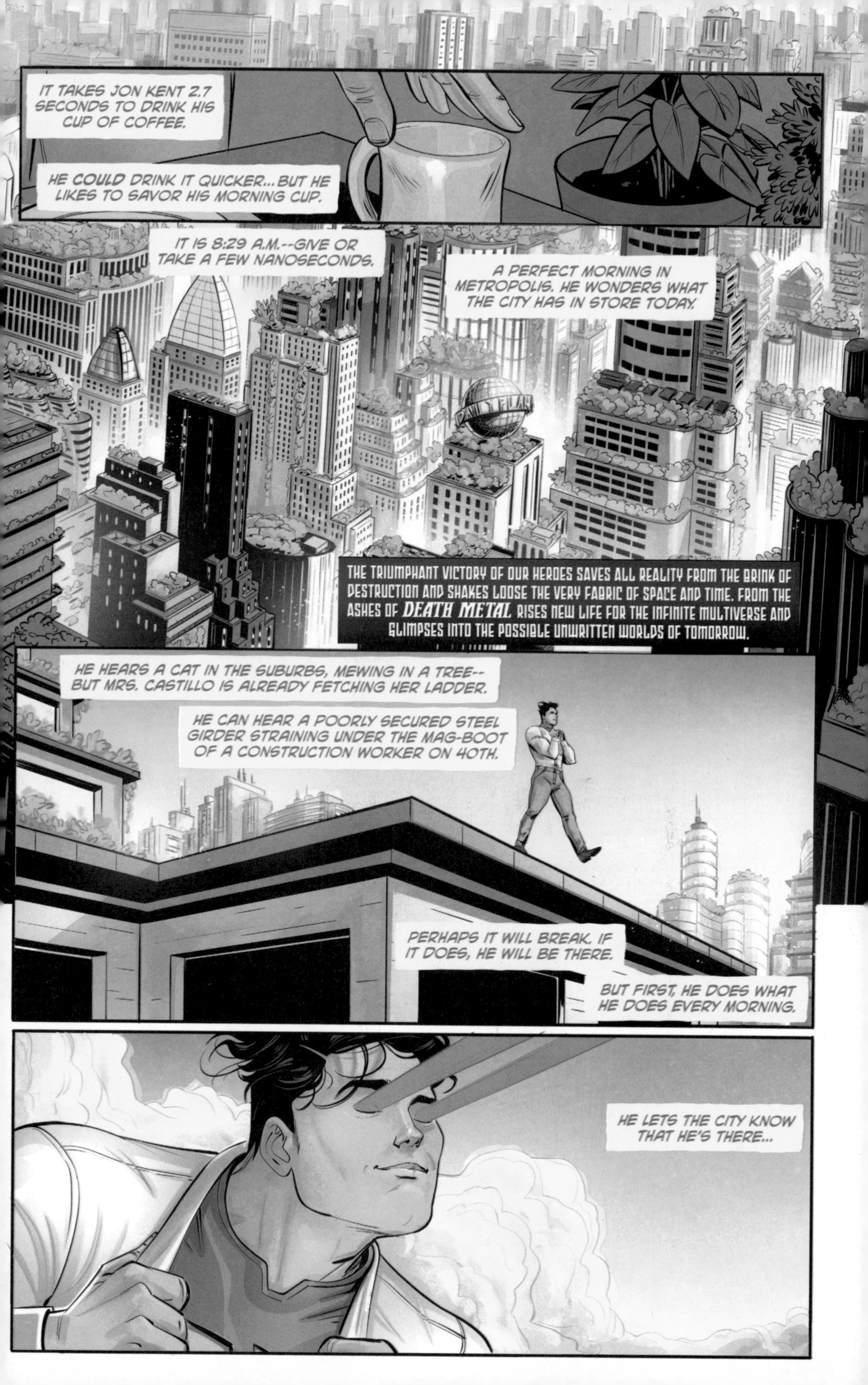
IT TAKES JON KENT 2.7 SECONDS TO DRINK HIS CUP OF COFFEE.
HE COULD DRINK IT QUICKER... BUT HE LIKES TO SAVOR HIS MORNING CUP.
IT IS 8:29 A.M.--GIVE OR TAKE A FEW NANOSECONDS.
A PERFECT MORNING IN METROPOLIS. HE WONDERS WHAT THE CITY HAS IN STORE TODAY.
THE TRIUMPHANT VICTORY OF OUR HEROES SAVES ALL REALITY FROM THE BRINK OF DESTRUCTION AND SHAKES LOOSE THE VERY FABRIC OF SPACE AND TIME. FROM THE ASHES OF DEATH METAL RISES NEW LIFE FOR THE INFINITE MULTIVERSE AND GLIMPSES INTO THE POSSIBLE UNWRITTEN WORLDS OF TOMORROW.
HE HEARS A CAT IN THE SUBURBS, MEWING IN A TREE--BUT MRS. CASTILLO IS ALREADY FETCHING HER LADDER.
HE CAN HEAR A POORLY SECURED STEEL GIRDER STRAINING UNDER THE MAG-BOOT OF A CONSTRUCTION WORKER ON 40TH.
PERHAPS IT WILL BREAK. IF IT DOES, HE WILL BE THERE.
BUT FIRST, HE DOES WHAT HE DOES EVERY MORNING.
HE LETS THE CITY KNOW THAT HE'S THERE...

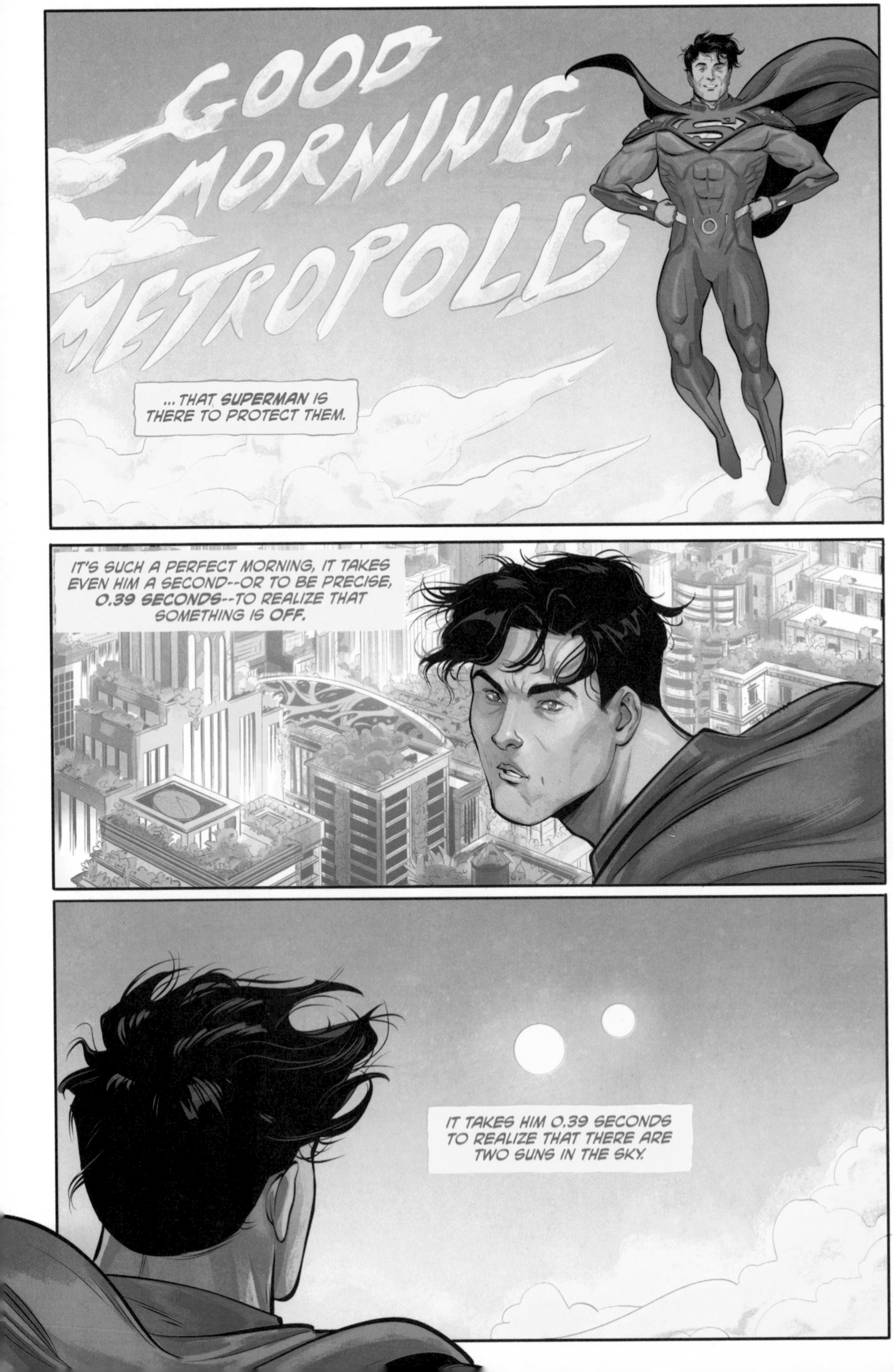
GOOD MORNING, METROPOLIS
...THAT SUPERMAN IS THERE TO PROTECT THEM.
IT'S SUCH A PERFECT MORNING, IT TAKES EVEN HIM A SECOND--OR TO BE PRECISE, 0.39 SECONDS--TO REALIZE THAT SOMETHING IS OFF.
IT TAKES HIM 0.39 SECONDS TO REALIZE THAT THERE ARE TWO SUNS IN THE SKY.

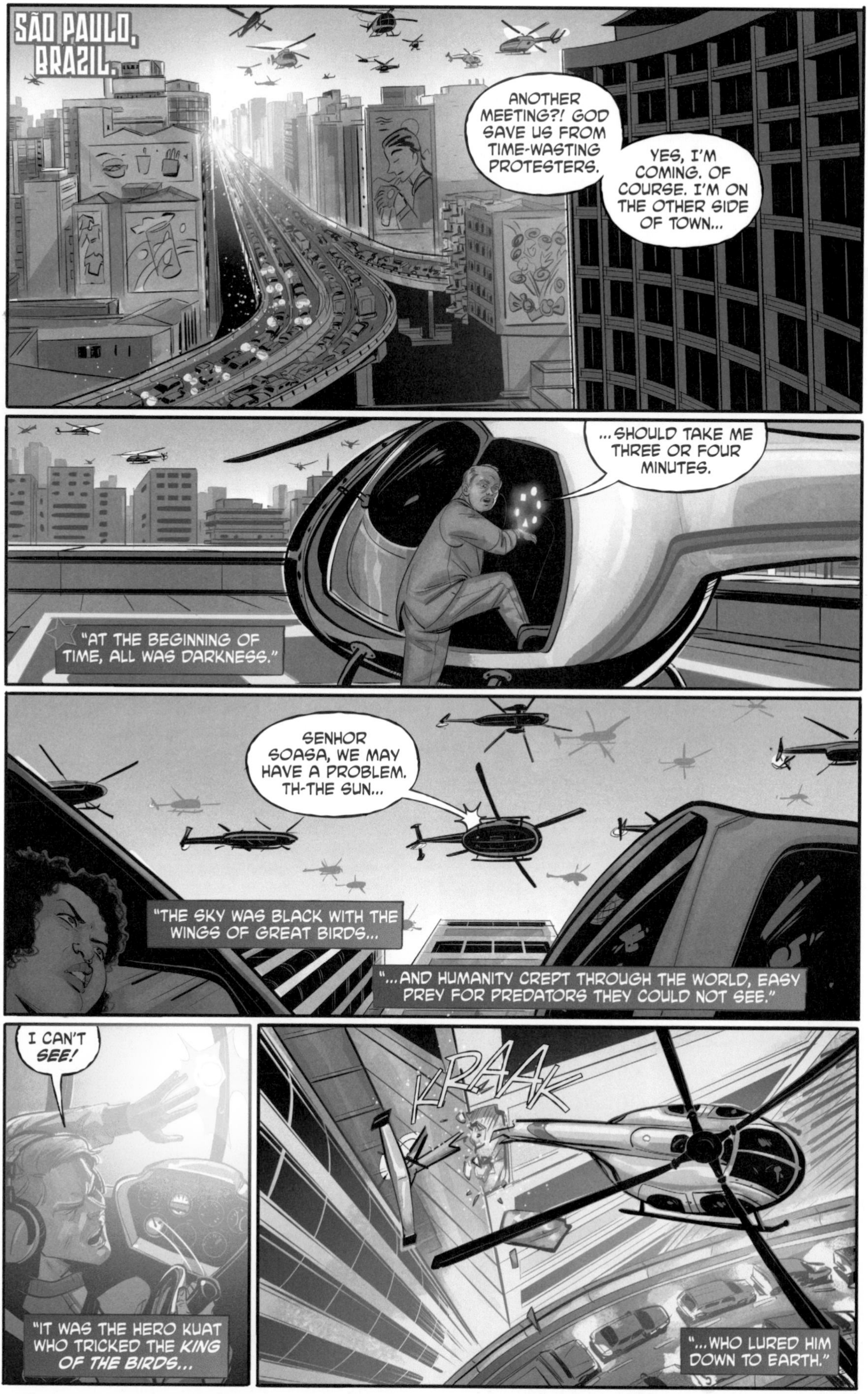
SÃO PAULO, BRAZIL.
ANOTHER MEETING?! GOD SAVE US FROM TIME-WASTING PROTESTERS.
YES, I'M COMING. OF COURSE. I'M ON THE OTHER SIDE OF TOWN...
...SHOULD TAKE ME THREE OR FOUR MINUTES.
"AT THE BEGINNING OF TIME, ALL WAS DARKNESS."
SENHOR SOASA, WE MAY HAVE A PROBLEM. TH-THE SUN...
"THE SKY WAS BLACK WITH THE WINGS OF GREAT BIRDS...
"...AND HUMANITY CREPT THROUGH THE WORLD, EASY PREY FOR PREDATORS THEY COULD NOT SEE."
I CAN'T *SEE!*
"IT WAS THE HERO KUAT WHO TRICKED THE *KING OF THE BIRDS...*
KRAAK
"...WHO LURED HIM DOWN TO EARTH."

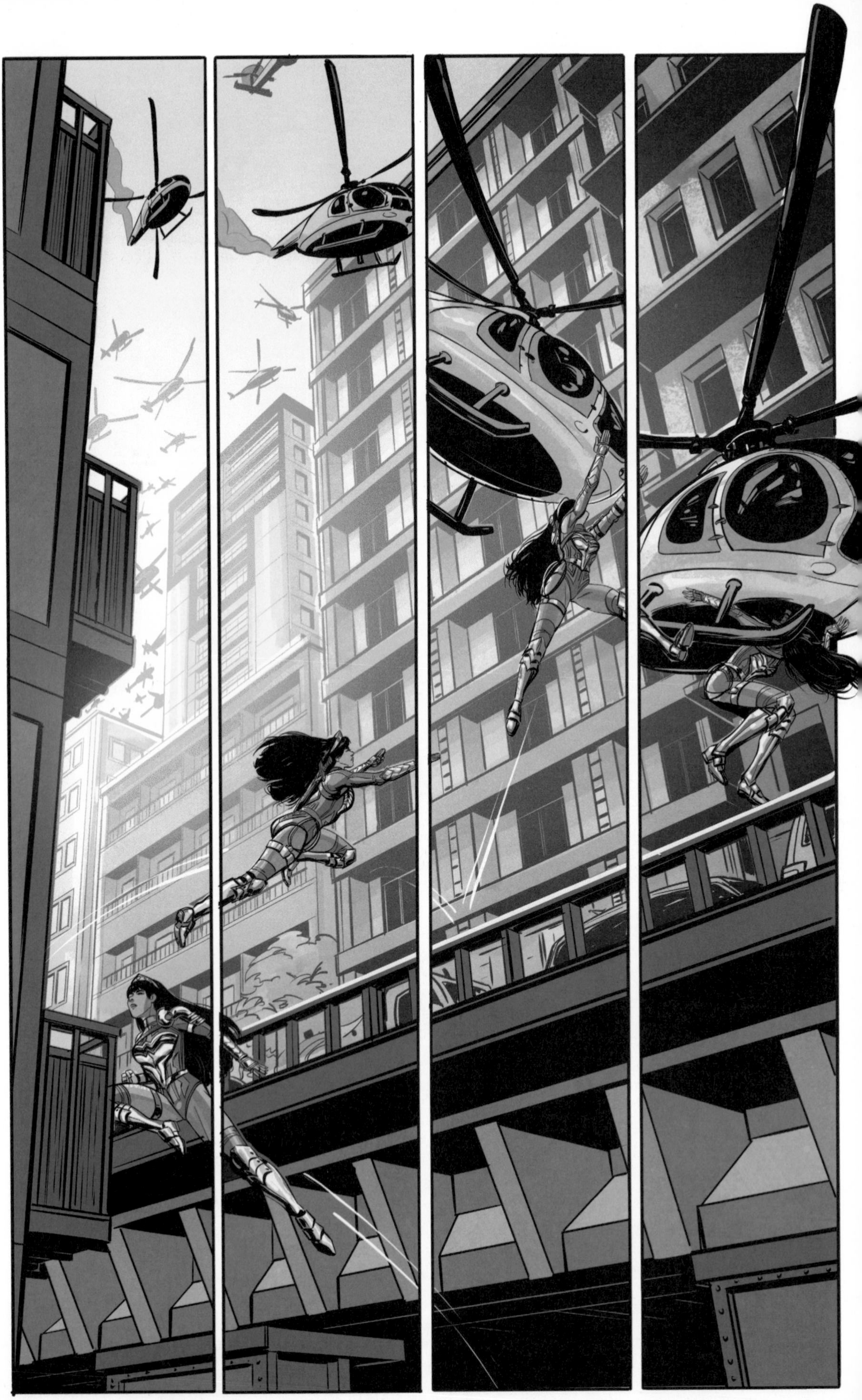

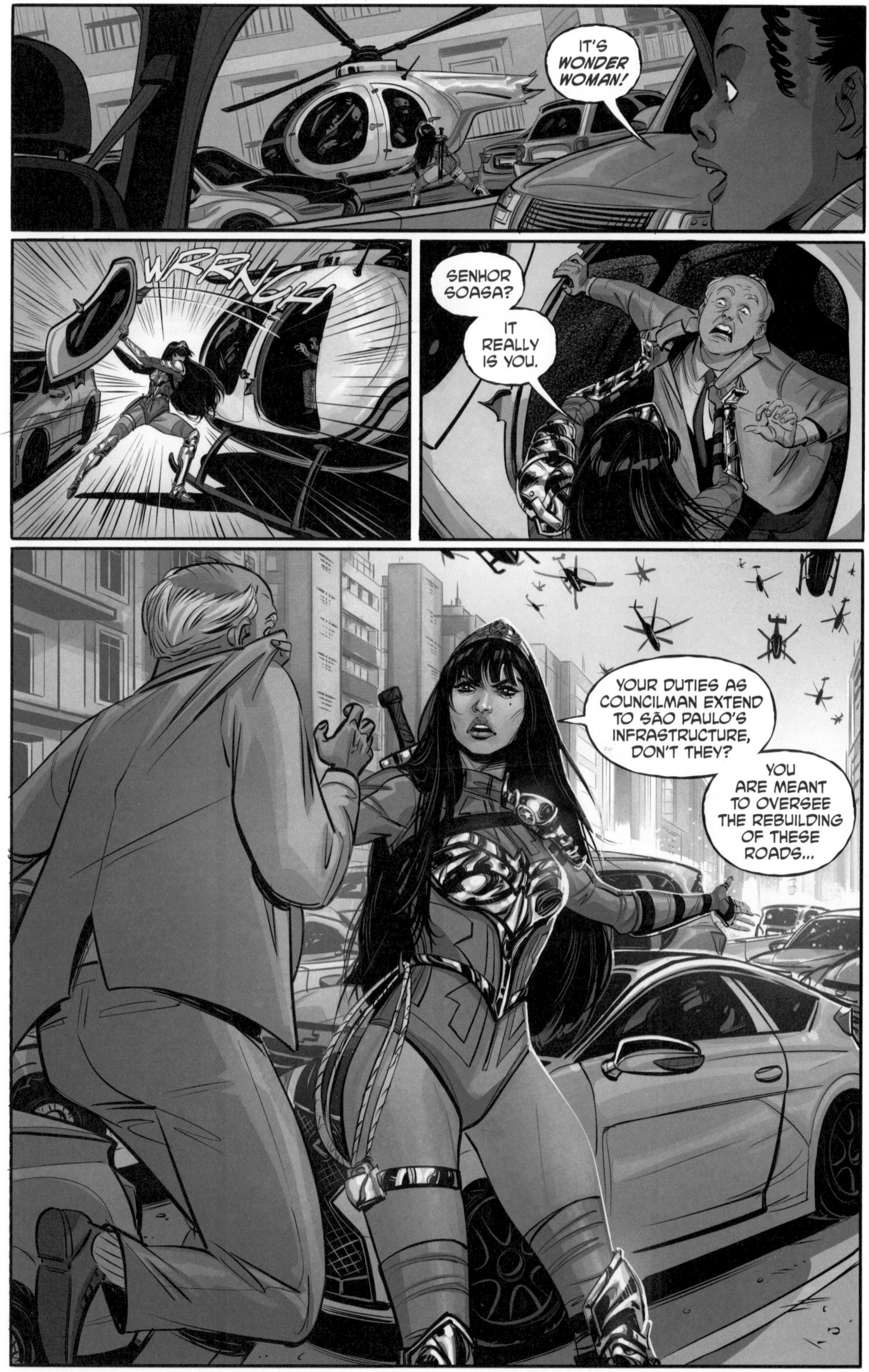
IT'S WONDER WOMAN!
WRRNGH
SENHOR SOASA?
IT REALLY IS YOU.
YOUR DUTIES AS COUNCILMAN EXTEND TO SÃO PAULO'S INFRASTRUCTURE, DON'T THEY?
YOU ARE MEANT TO OVERSEE THE REBUILDING OF THESE ROADS...

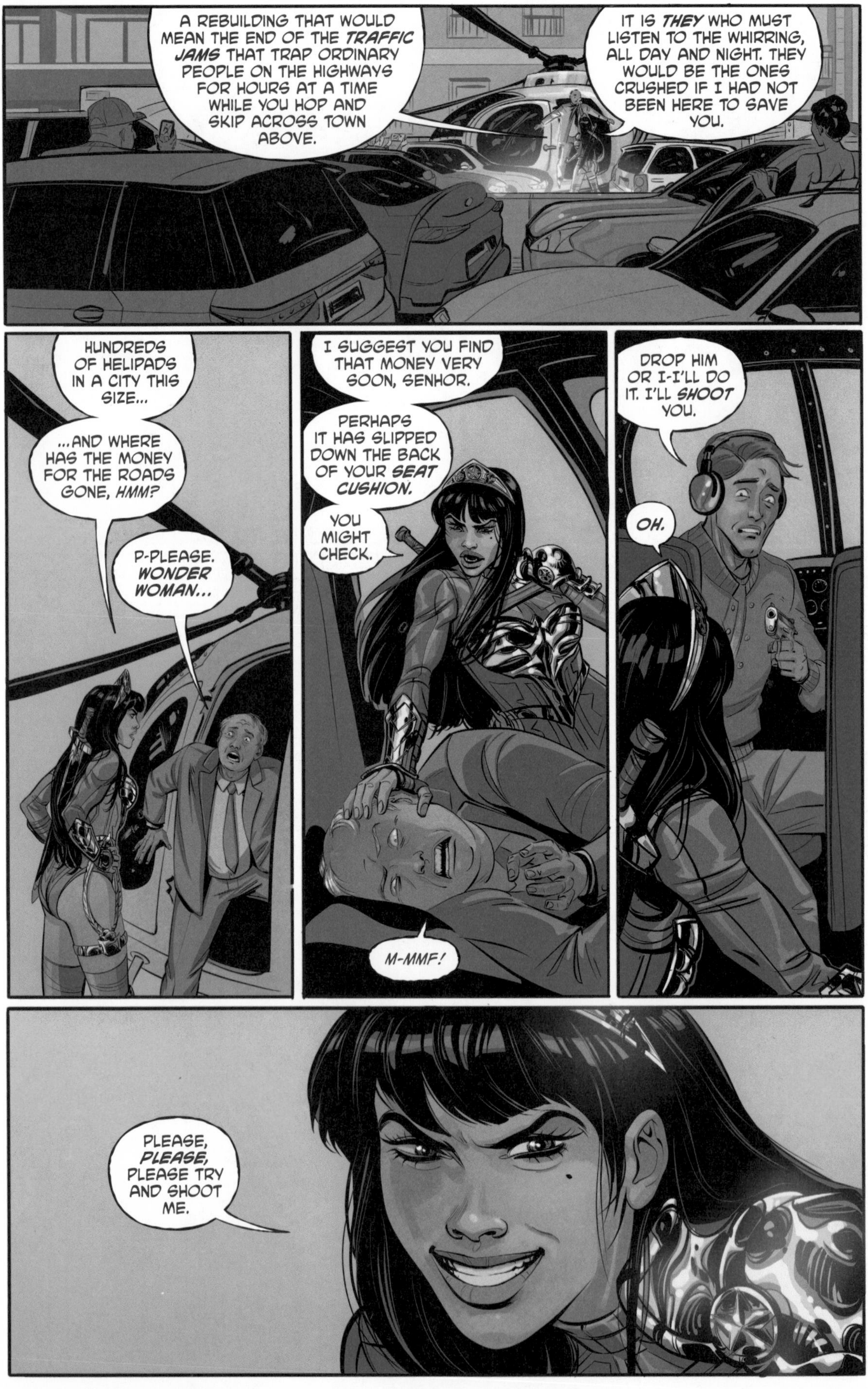
A REBUILDING THAT WOULD MEAN THE END OF THE TRAFFIC JAMS THAT TRAP ORDINARY PEOPLE ON THE HIGHWAYS FOR HOURS AT A TIME WHILE YOU HOP AND SKIP ACROSS TOWN ABOVE.
IT IS THEY WHO MUST LISTEN TO THE WHIRRING, ALL DAY AND NIGHT. THEY WOULD BE THE ONES CRUSHED IF I HAD NOT BEEN HERE TO SAVE YOU.
HUNDREDS OF HELIPADS IN A CITY THIS SIZE...
...AND WHERE HAS THE MONEY FOR THE ROADS GONE, HMM?
P-PLEASE. WONDER WOMAN...
I SUGGEST YOU FIND THAT MONEY VERY SOON, SENHOR.
PERHAPS IT HAS SLIPPED DOWN THE BACK OF YOUR SEAT CUSHION.
YOU MIGHT CHECK.
M-MMF!
DROP HIM OR I-I'LL DO IT. I'LL SHOOT YOU.
OH.
PLEASE, PLEASE, PLEASE TRY AND SHOOT ME.

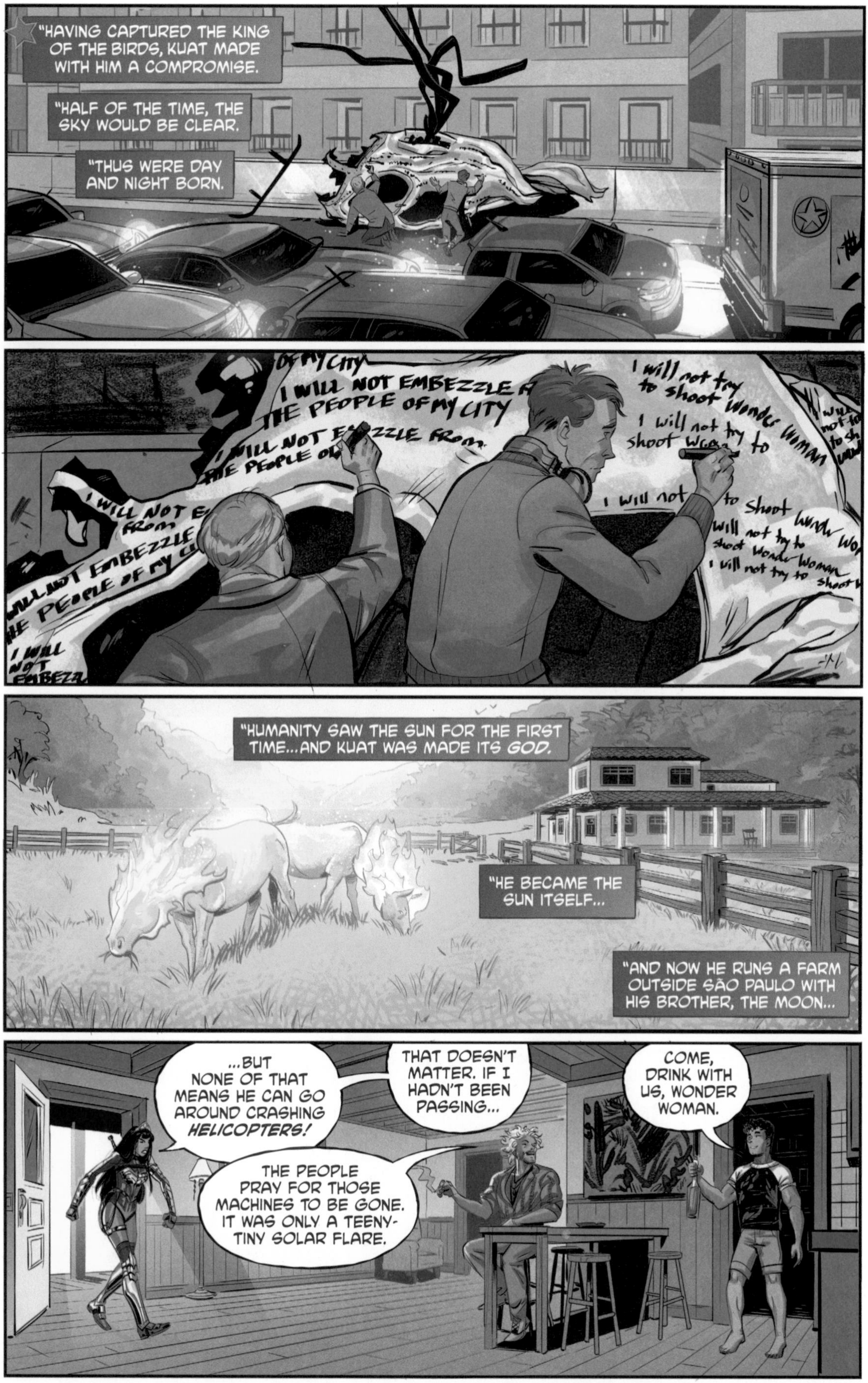
"HAVING CAPTURED THE KING OF THE BIRDS, KUAT MADE WITH HIM A COMPROMISE.
"HALF OF THE TIME, THE SKY WOULD BE CLEAR.
"THUS WERE DAY AND NIGHT BORN.
I WILL NOT EMBEZZLE FROM THE PEOPLE OF MY CITY
I will not try to shoot Wonder Woman
"HUMANITY SAW THE SUN FOR THE FIRST TIME...AND KUAT WAS MADE ITS *GOD*.
"HE BECAME THE SUN ITSELF...
"AND NOW HE RUNS A FARM OUTSIDE SÃO PAULO WITH HIS BROTHER, THE MOON...
...BUT NONE OF THAT MEANS HE CAN GO AROUND CRASHING ***HELICOPTERS!***
THAT DOESN'T MATTER. IF I HADN'T BEEN PASSING...
THE PEOPLE PRAY FOR THOSE MACHINES TO BE GONE. IT WAS ONLY A TEENY-TINY SOLAR FLARE.
COME, DRINK WITH US, WONDER WOMAN.

IT IS 9:30 A.M. I HAVE NOT COME HERE TO GET *DRUNK*, IAE. I HAVE COME HERE TO ADMONISH YOUR BROTHER.

...WE DISTILL OUR OWN CACHAÇA.

SEE, KUAT...WHY CAN'T THE SUN BE AS ACCOMMODATING AS THE MOON?

OH, GO WITH THE PIGS, THE BOTH OF YOU.

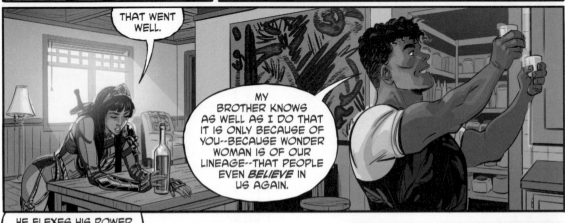

THAT WENT WELL.

MY BROTHER KNOWS AS WELL AS I DO THAT IT IS ONLY BECAUSE OF YOU--BECAUSE WONDER WOMAN IS OF OUR LINEAGE--THAT PEOPLE EVEN *BELIEVE* IN US AGAIN.

HE FLEXES HIS POWER FOR THEY *BELIEVE* THAT HE IS THE SUN AGAIN-- AND THEREFORE HE *IS* THE SUN AGAIN.

HE FEARS THEY WILL FORGET.

DRINK WITH HIM ON THE PORCH, UNDER HIS OWN RAYS. HE'LL SOON CHEER UP.

YOUR *OWN* CACHAÇA?

THE VERY BEST. AND VERY STRONG.

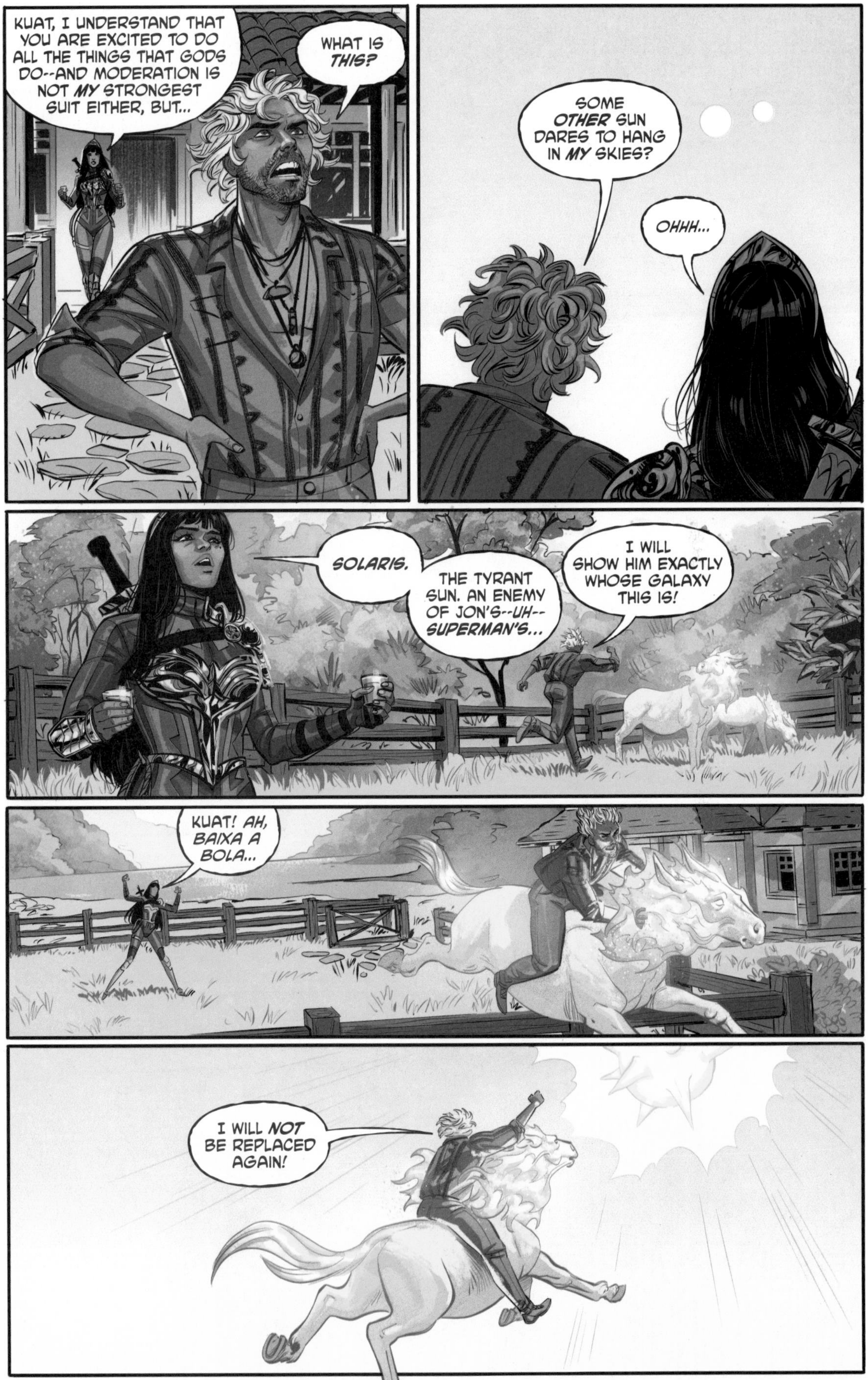
KUAT, I UNDERSTAND THAT YOU ARE EXCITED TO DO ALL THE THINGS THAT GODS DO--AND MODERATION IS NOT MY STRONGEST SUIT EITHER, BUT...
WHAT IS THIS?
SOME OTHER SUN DARES TO HANG IN MY SKIES?
OHHH...
SOLARIS.
THE TYRANT SUN. AN ENEMY OF JON'S--UH--SUPERMAN'S...
I WILL SHOW HIM EXACTLY WHOSE GALAXY THIS IS!
KUAT! AH, BAIXA A BOLA...
I WILL NOT BE REPLACED AGAIN!

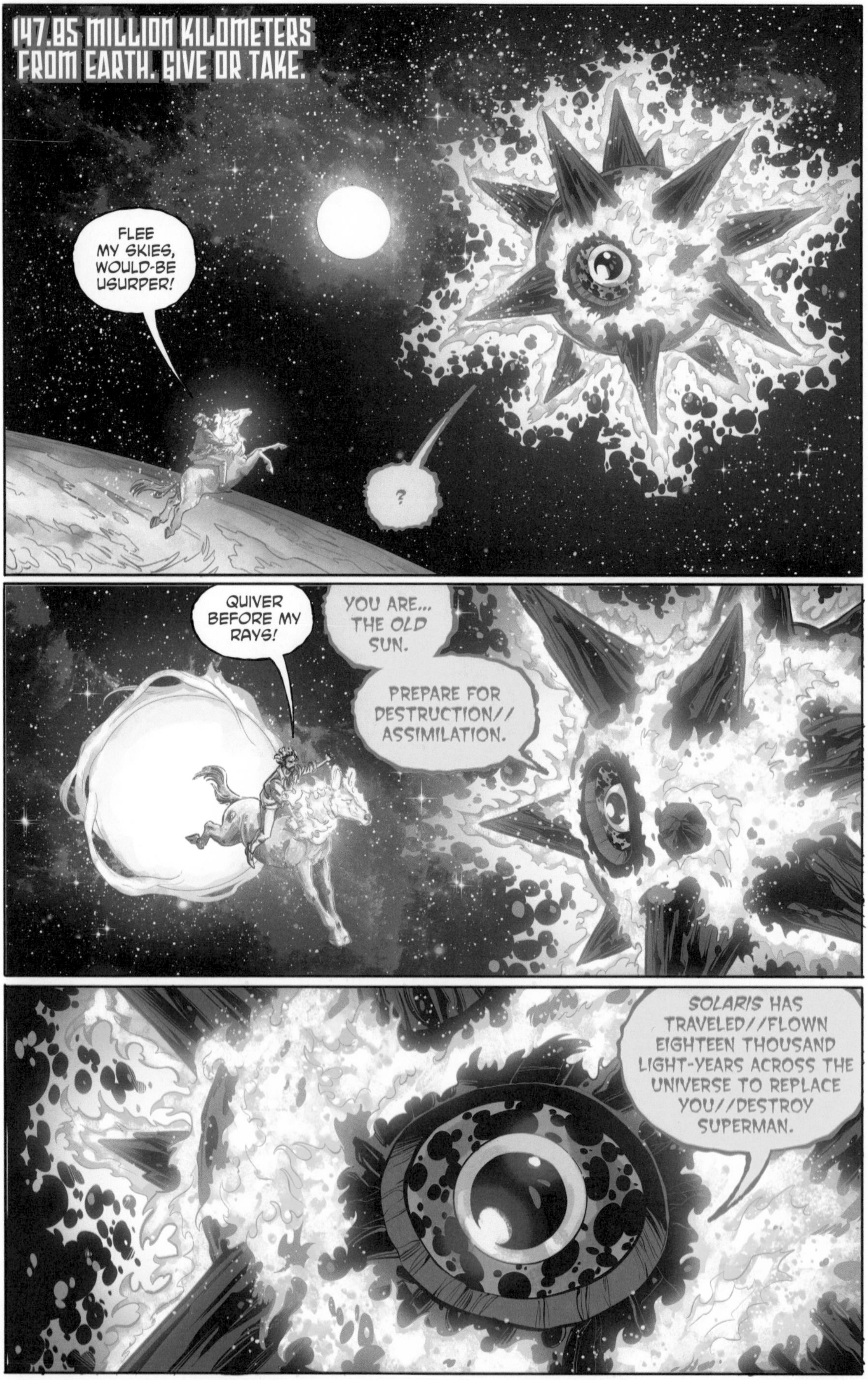
147.85 MILLION KILOMETERS FROM EARTH. GIVE OR TAKE.
FLEE MY SKIES, WOULD-BE USURPER!
?
QUIVER BEFORE MY RAYS!
YOU ARE... THE OLD SUN.
PREPARE FOR DESTRUCTION// ASSIMILATION.
SOLARIS HAS TRAVELED//FLOWN EIGHTEEN THOUSAND LIGHT-YEARS ACROSS THE UNIVERSE TO REPLACE YOU//DESTROY SUPERMAN.

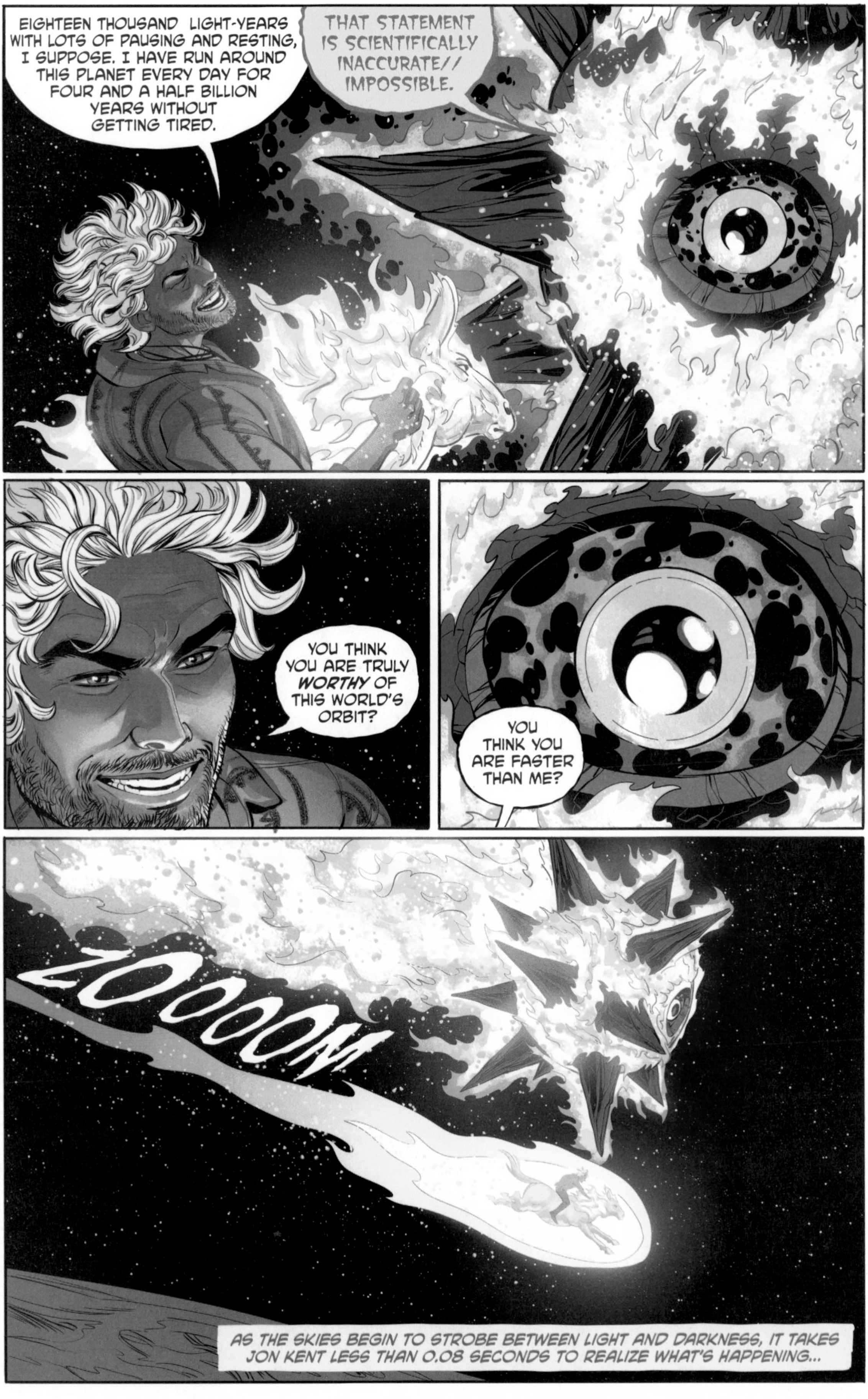
EIGHTEEN THOUSAND LIGHT-YEARS WITH LOTS OF PAUSING AND RESTING, I SUPPOSE. I HAVE RUN AROUND THIS PLANET EVERY DAY FOR FOUR AND A HALF BILLION YEARS WITHOUT GETTING TIRED.
THAT STATEMENT IS SCIENTIFICALLY INACCURATE// IMPOSSIBLE.
YOU THINK YOU ARE TRULY WORTHY OF THIS WORLD'S ORBIT?
YOU THINK YOU ARE FASTER THAN ME?
ZOOOOM
AS THE SKIES BEGIN TO STROBE BETWEEN LIGHT AND DARKNESS, IT TAKES JON KENT LESS THAN 0.08 SECONDS TO REALIZE WHAT'S HAPPENING...

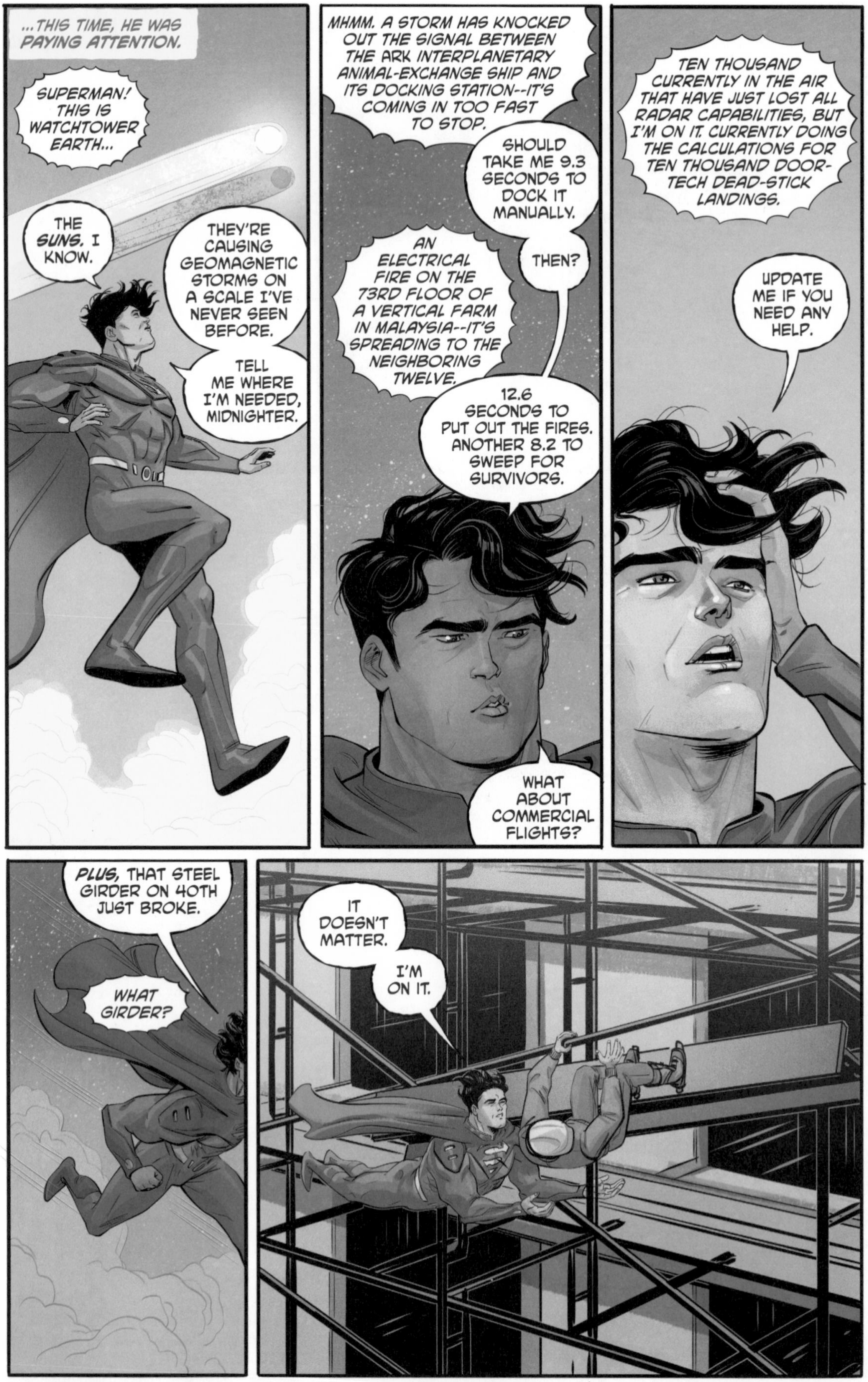
...THIS TIME, HE WAS PAYING ATTENTION.
SUPERMAN! THIS IS WATCHTOWER EARTH...
THE SUNS. I KNOW.
THEY'RE CAUSING GEOMAGNETIC STORMS ON A SCALE I'VE NEVER SEEN BEFORE.
TELL ME WHERE I'M NEEDED, MIDNIGHTER.
MHMM. A STORM HAS KNOCKED OUT THE SIGNAL BETWEEN THE ARK INTERPLANETARY ANIMAL-EXCHANGE SHIP AND ITS DOCKING STATION--IT'S COMING IN TOO FAST TO STOP.
SHOULD TAKE ME 9.3 SECONDS TO DOCK IT MANUALLY.
THEN?
AN ELECTRICAL FIRE ON THE 73RD FLOOR OF A VERTICAL FARM IN MALAYSIA--IT'S SPREADING TO THE NEIGHBORING TWELVE.
12.6 SECONDS TO PUT OUT THE FIRES. ANOTHER 8.2 TO SWEEP FOR SURVIVORS.
WHAT ABOUT COMMERCIAL FLIGHTS?
TEN THOUSAND CURRENTLY IN THE AIR THAT HAVE JUST LOST ALL RADAR CAPABILITIES, BUT I'M ON IT. CURRENTLY DOING THE CALCULATIONS FOR TEN THOUSAND DOOR-TECH DEAD-STICK LANDINGS.
UPDATE ME IF YOU NEED ANY HELP.
PLUS, THAT STEEL GIRDER ON 40TH JUST BROKE.
WHAT GIRDER?
IT DOESN'T MATTER.
I'M ON IT.

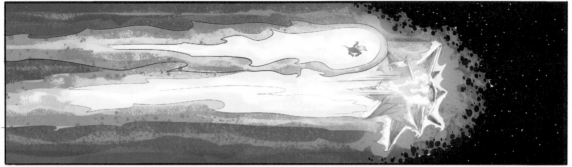

COME ON, COME ON, YOU IDIOT BEAST!

AHAH// HEHE.

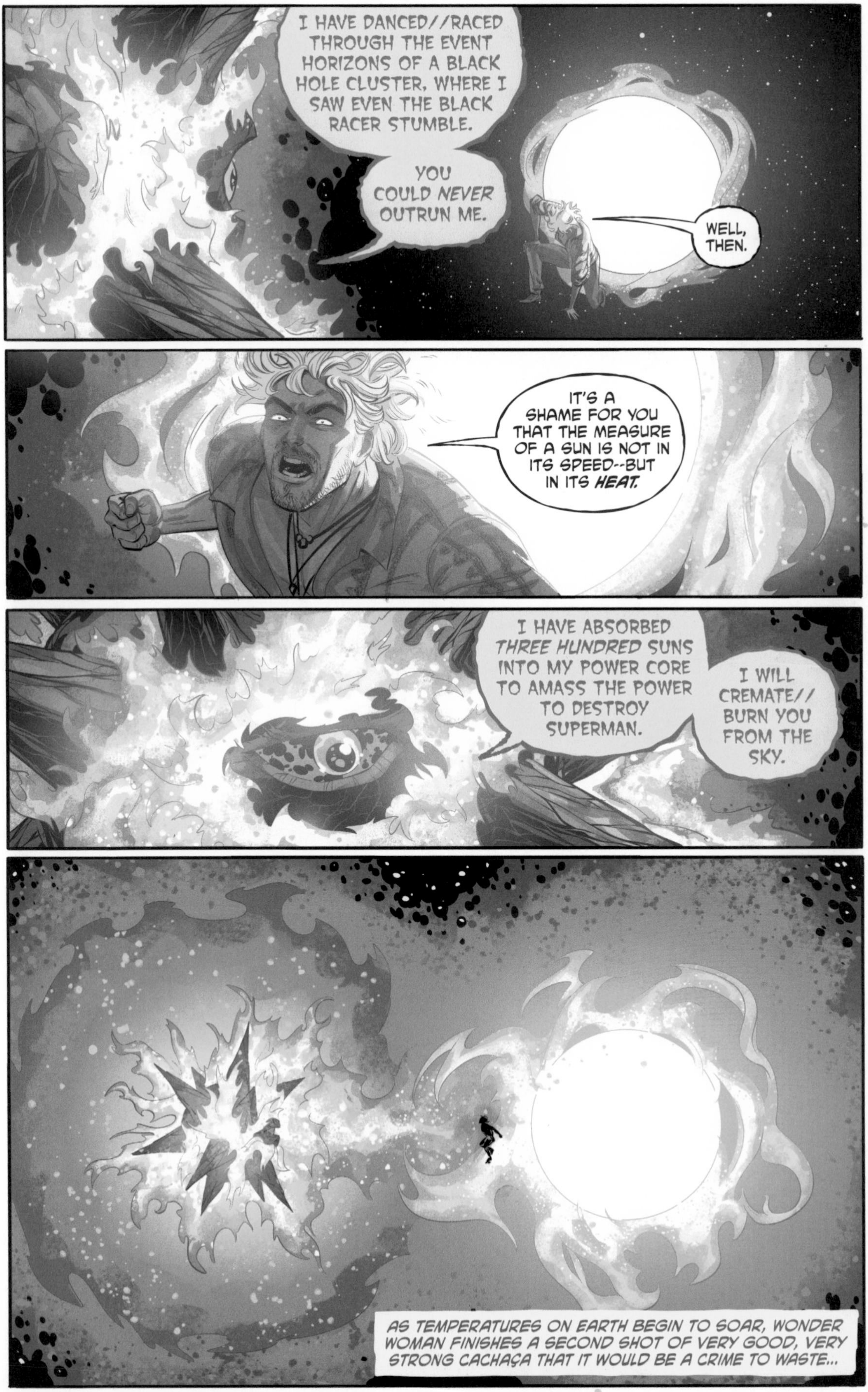

I HAVE DANCED//RACED THROUGH THE EVENT HORIZONS OF A BLACK HOLE CLUSTER, WHERE I SAW EVEN THE BLACK RACER STUMBLE.
YOU COULD *NEVER* OUTRUN ME.
WELL, THEN.
IT'S A SHAME FOR YOU THAT THE MEASURE OF A SUN IS NOT IN ITS SPEED--BUT IN ITS ***HEAT.***
I HAVE ABSORBED *THREE HUNDRED* SUNS INTO MY POWER CORE TO AMASS THE POWER TO DESTROY SUPERMAN.
I WILL CREMATE// BURN YOU FROM THE SKY.
AS TEMPERATURES ON EARTH BEGIN TO SOAR, WONDER WOMAN FINISHES A SECOND SHOT OF VERY GOOD, VERY STRONG CACHAÇA THAT IT WOULD BE A CRIME TO WASTE...

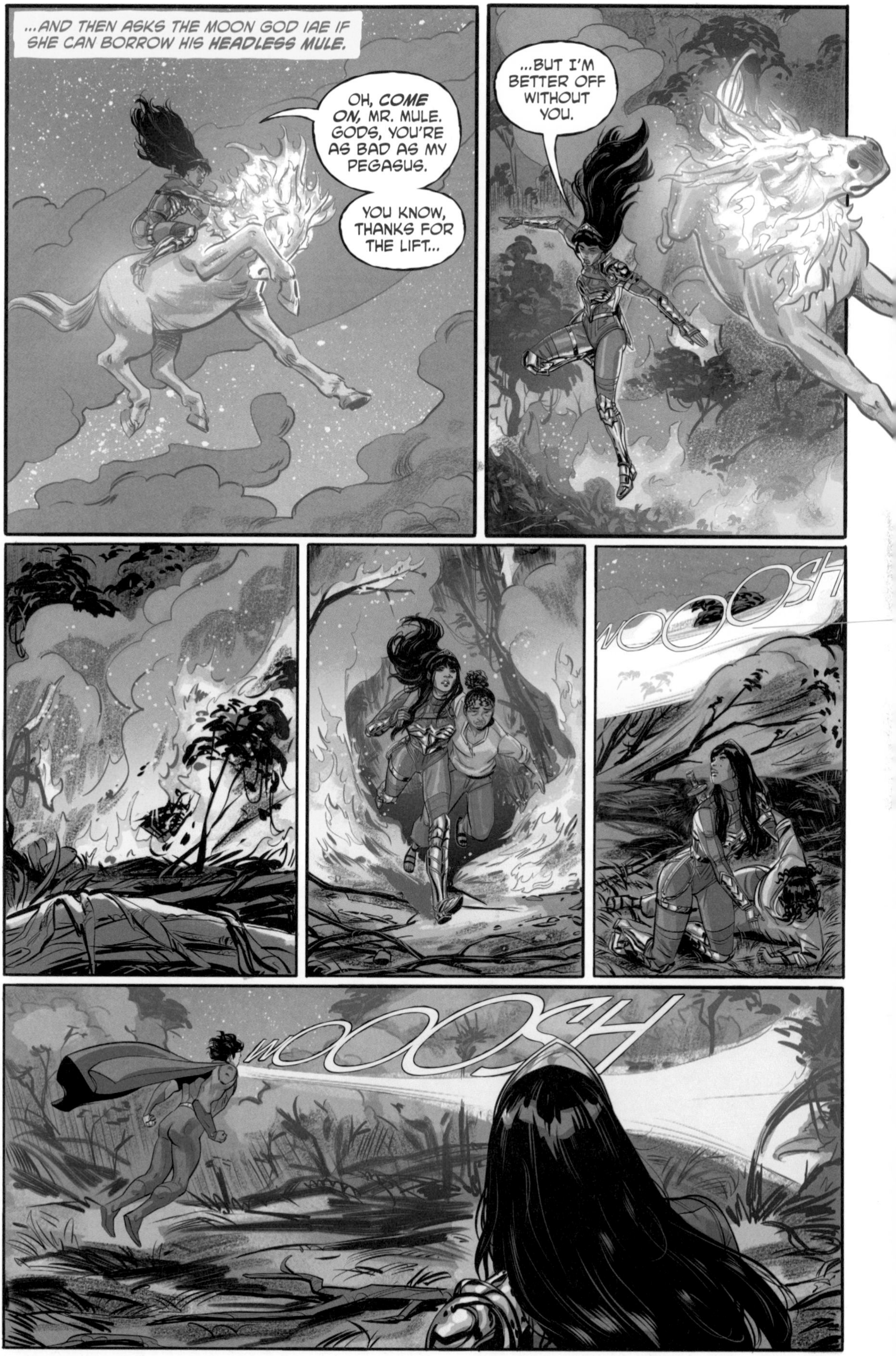
...AND THEN ASKS THE MOON GOD IAE IF SHE CAN BORROW HIS HEADLESS MULE.
OH, COME ON, MR. MULE. GODS, YOU'RE AS BAD AS MY PEGASUS.
YOU KNOW, THANKS FOR THE LIFT...
...BUT I'M BETTER OFF WITHOUT YOU.
WOOOOSH
WOOOOSH

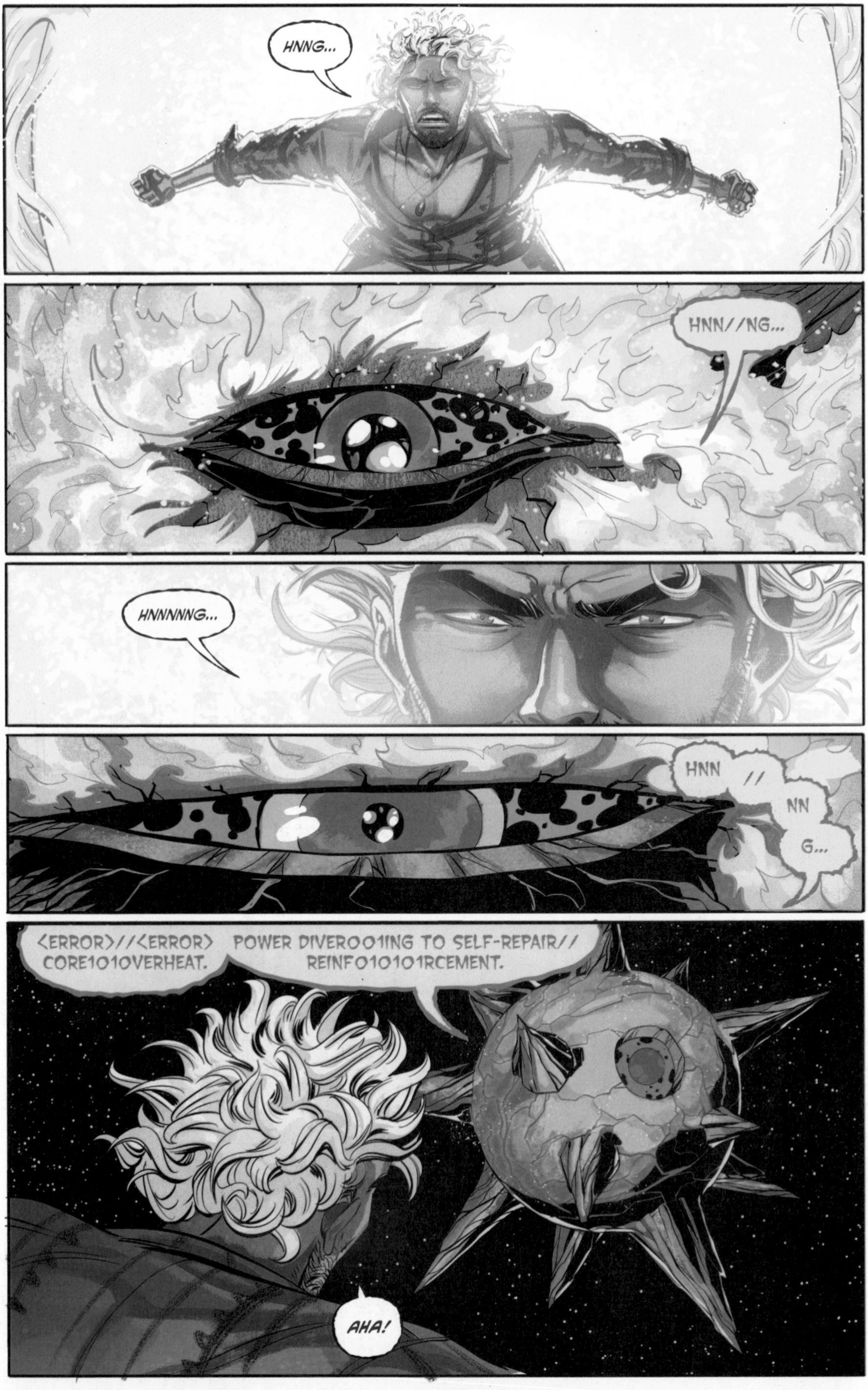
HNNG...
HNN//NG...
HNNNNNG...
HNN // NN G...
<ERROR>//<ERROR> CORE1010VERHEAT.
POWER DIVEROO11NG TO SELF-REPAIR// REINFO10101RCEMENT.
AHA!

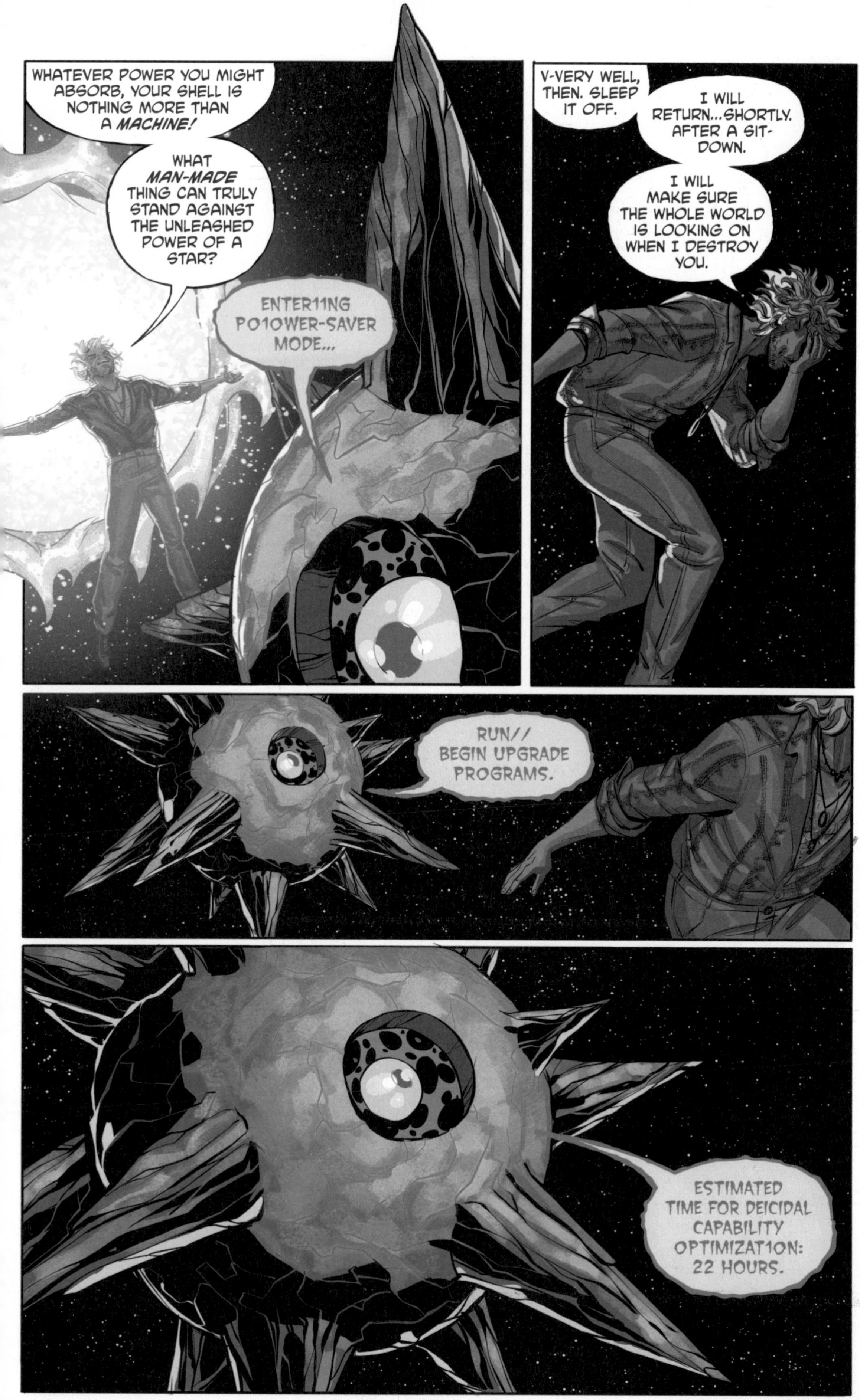
WHATEVER POWER YOU MIGHT ABSORB, YOUR SHELL IS NOTHING MORE THAN A *MACHINE!*
WHAT *MAN-MADE* THING CAN TRULY STAND AGAINST THE UNLEASHED POWER OF A STAR?
ENTER11NG PO1OWER-SAVER MODE...
V-VERY WELL, THEN. SLEEP IT OFF.
I WILL RETURN...SHORTLY. AFTER A SIT-DOWN.
I WILL MAKE SURE THE WHOLE WORLD IS LOOKING ON WHEN I DESTROY YOU.
RUN// BEGIN UPGRADE PROGRAMS.
ESTIMATED TIME FOR DEICIDAL CAPABILITY OPTIMIZAT1ON: 22 HOURS.

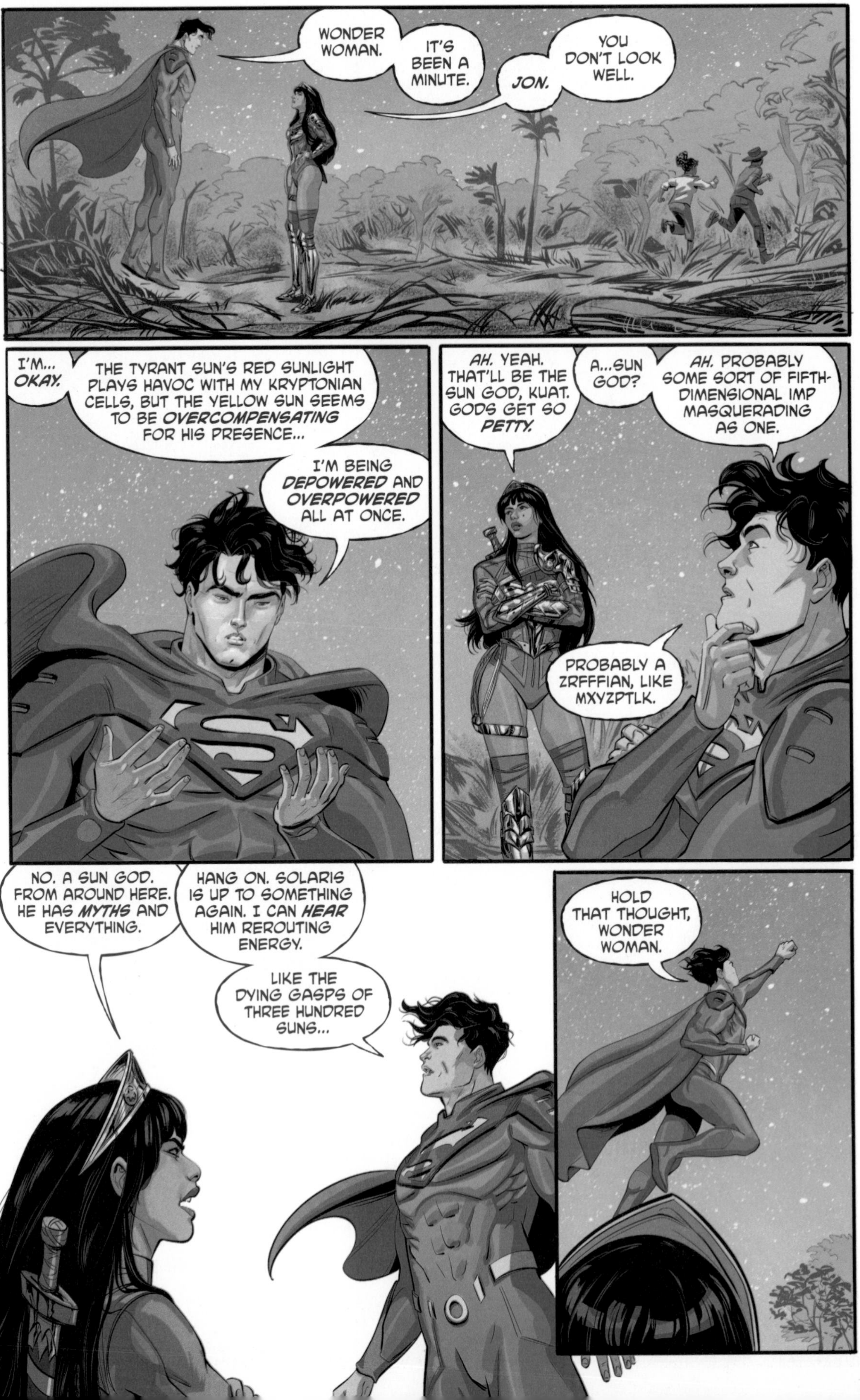
WONDER WOMAN.
IT'S BEEN A MINUTE.
JON.
YOU DON'T LOOK WELL.
I'M... OKAY.
THE TYRANT SUN'S RED SUNLIGHT PLAYS HAVOC WITH MY KRYPTONIAN CELLS, BUT THE YELLOW SUN SEEMS TO BE OVERCOMPENSATING FOR HIS PRESENCE...
I'M BEING DEPOWERED AND OVERPOWERED ALL AT ONCE.
AH. YEAH. THAT'LL BE THE SUN GOD, KUAT. GODS GET SO PETTY.
A...SUN GOD?
AH. PROBABLY SOME SORT OF FIFTH-DIMENSIONAL IMP MASQUERADING AS ONE.
PROBABLY A ZRFFFIAN, LIKE MXYZPTLK.
NO. A SUN GOD. FROM AROUND HERE. HE HAS MYTHS AND EVERYTHING.
HANG ON. SOLARIS IS UP TO SOMETHING AGAIN. I CAN HEAR HIM REROUTING ENERGY.
LIKE THE DYING GASPS OF THREE HUNDRED SUNS...
HOLD THAT THOUGHT, WONDER WOMAN.

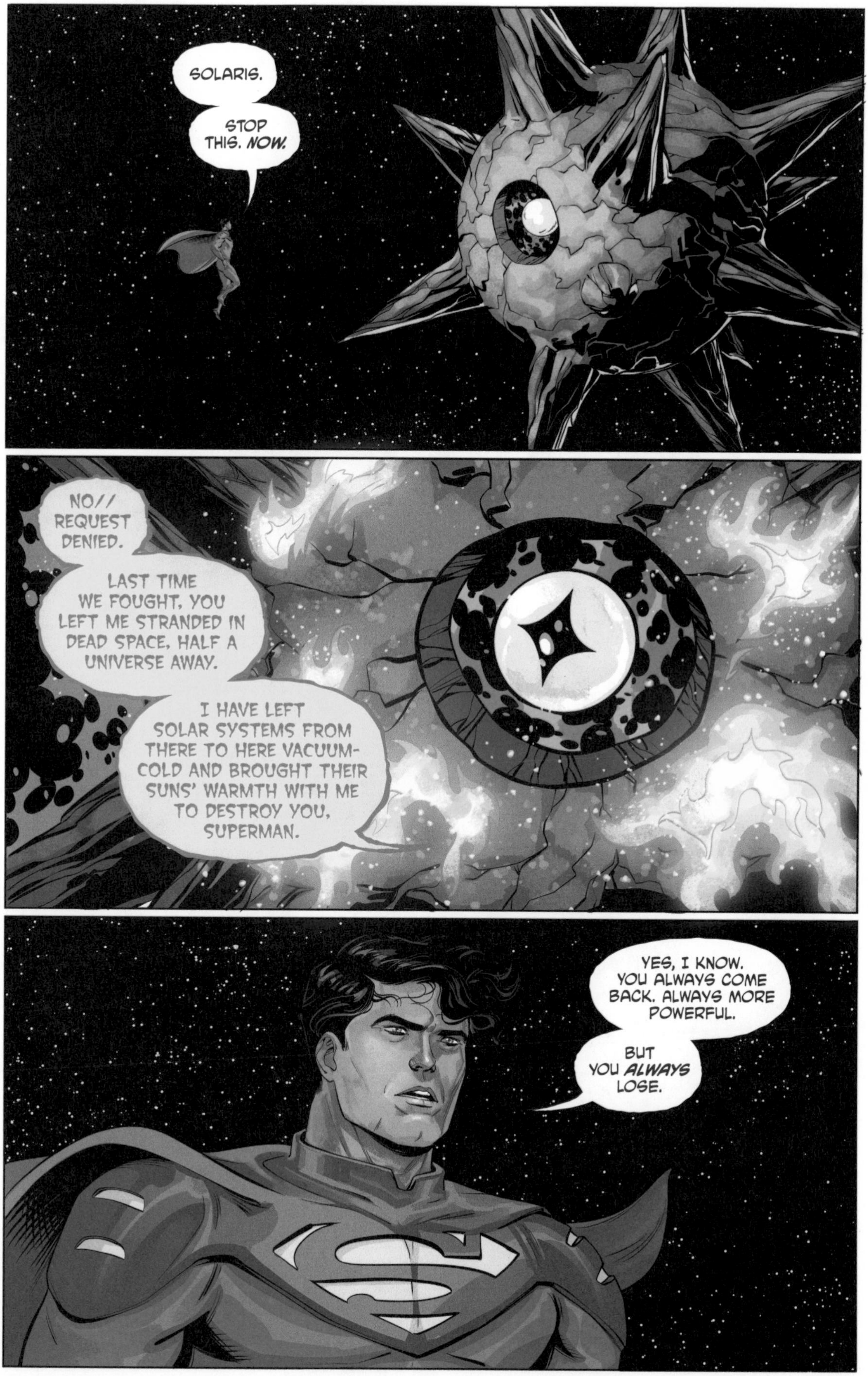
SOLARIS.
STOP THIS. *NOW.*
NO// REQUEST DENIED.
LAST TIME WE FOUGHT, YOU LEFT ME STRANDED IN DEAD SPACE, HALF A UNIVERSE AWAY.
I HAVE LEFT SOLAR SYSTEMS FROM THERE TO HERE VACUUM-COLD AND BROUGHT THEIR SUNS' WARMTH WITH ME TO DESTROY YOU, SUPERMAN.
YES, I KNOW. YOU ALWAYS COME BACK. ALWAYS MORE POWERFUL.
BUT YOU *ALWAYS* LOSE.

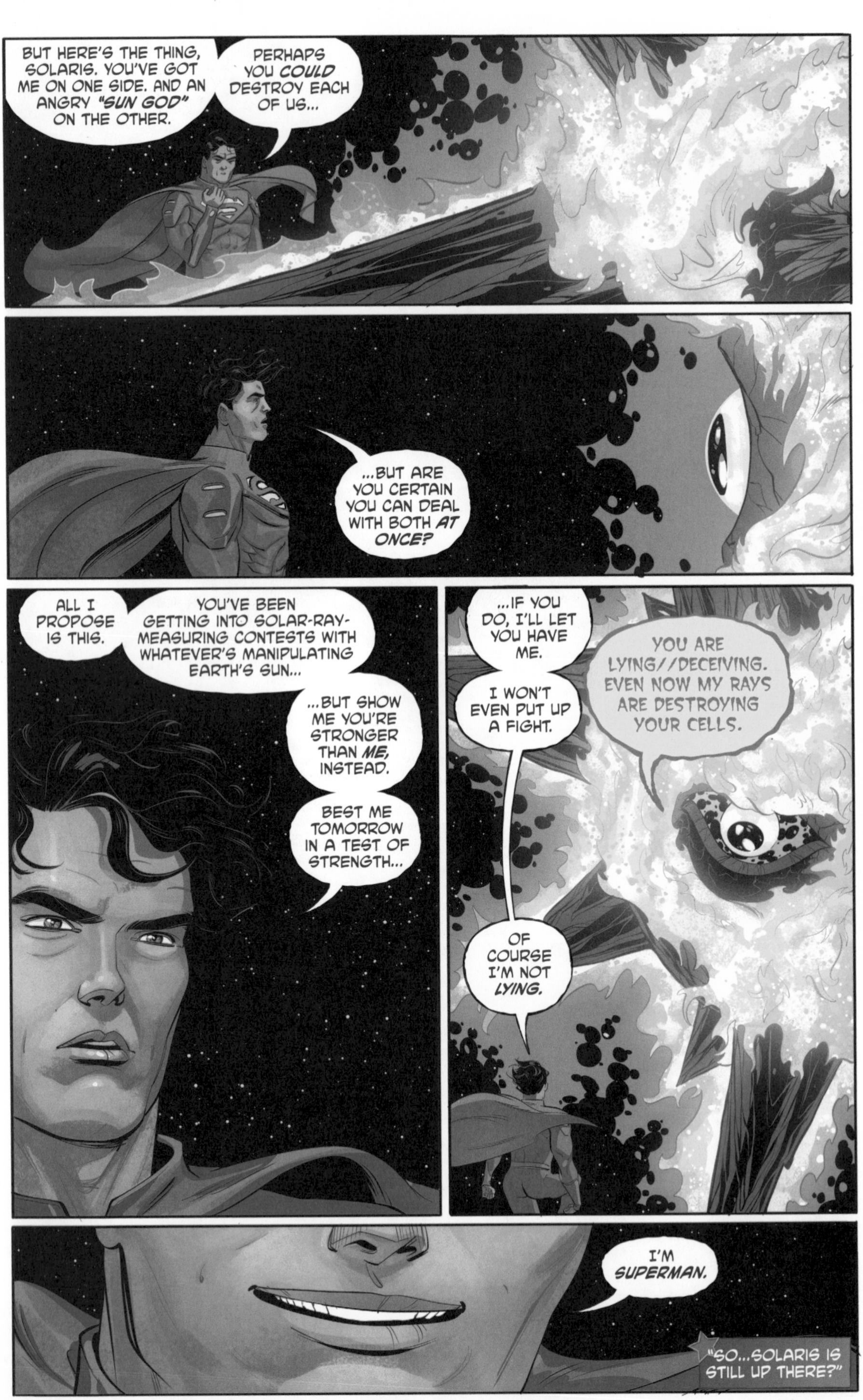
BUT HERE'S THE THING, SOLARIS. YOU'VE GOT ME ON ONE SIDE. AND AN ANGRY "SUN GOD" ON THE OTHER.
PERHAPS YOU COULD DESTROY EACH OF US...
...BUT ARE YOU CERTAIN YOU CAN DEAL WITH BOTH AT ONCE?
ALL I PROPOSE IS THIS.
YOU'VE BEEN GETTING INTO SOLAR-RAY-MEASURING CONTESTS WITH WHATEVER'S MANIPULATING EARTH'S SUN...
...BUT SHOW ME YOU'RE STRONGER THAN ME, INSTEAD.
BEST ME TOMORROW IN A TEST OF STRENGTH...
...IF YOU DO, I'LL LET YOU HAVE ME.
I WON'T EVEN PUT UP A FIGHT.
YOU ARE LYING//DECEIVING. EVEN NOW MY RAYS ARE DESTROYING YOUR CELLS.
OF COURSE I'M NOT LYING.
I'M SUPERMAN.
"SO...SOLARIS IS STILL UP THERE?"

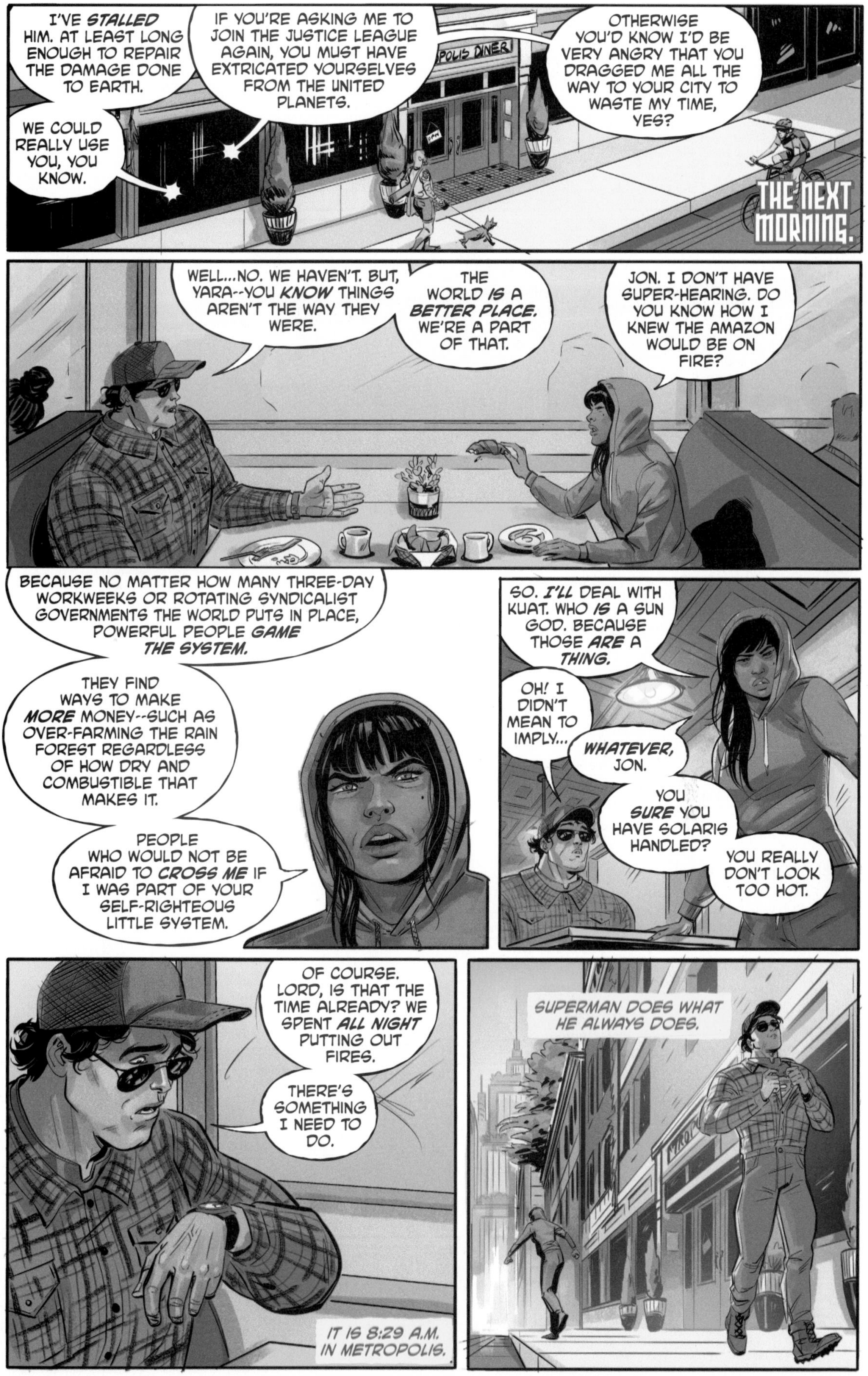
I'VE STALLED HIM. AT LEAST LONG ENOUGH TO REPAIR THE DAMAGE DONE TO EARTH.
WE COULD REALLY USE YOU, YOU KNOW.
IF YOU'RE ASKING ME TO JOIN THE JUSTICE LEAGUE AGAIN, YOU MUST HAVE EXTRICATED YOURSELVES FROM THE UNITED PLANETS.
OTHERWISE YOU'D KNOW I'D BE VERY ANGRY THAT YOU DRAGGED ME ALL THE WAY TO YOUR CITY TO WASTE MY TIME, YES?
POLIS DINER
THE NEXT MORNING.
WELL...NO. WE HAVEN'T. BUT, YARA--YOU KNOW THINGS AREN'T THE WAY THEY WERE.
THE WORLD IS A BETTER PLACE. WE'RE A PART OF THAT.
JON. I DON'T HAVE SUPER-HEARING. DO YOU KNOW HOW I KNEW THE AMAZON WOULD BE ON FIRE?
BECAUSE NO MATTER HOW MANY THREE-DAY WORKWEEKS OR ROTATING SYNDICALIST GOVERNMENTS THE WORLD PUTS IN PLACE, POWERFUL PEOPLE GAME THE SYSTEM.
THEY FIND WAYS TO MAKE MORE MONEY--SUCH AS OVER-FARMING THE RAIN FOREST REGARDLESS OF HOW DRY AND COMBUSTIBLE THAT MAKES IT.
PEOPLE WHO WOULD NOT BE AFRAID TO CROSS ME IF I WAS PART OF YOUR SELF-RIGHTEOUS LITTLE SYSTEM.
SO. I'LL DEAL WITH KUAT. WHO IS A SUN GOD. BECAUSE THOSE ARE A THING.
OH! I DIDN'T MEAN TO IMPLY...
WHATEVER, JON.
YOU SURE YOU HAVE SOLARIS HANDLED?
YOU REALLY DON'T LOOK TOO HOT.
OF COURSE. LORD, IS THAT THE TIME ALREADY? WE SPENT ALL NIGHT PUTTING OUT FIRES.
THERE'S SOMETHING I NEED TO DO.
IT IS 8:29 A.M. IN METROPOLIS.
SUPERMAN DOES WHAT HE ALWAYS DOES.

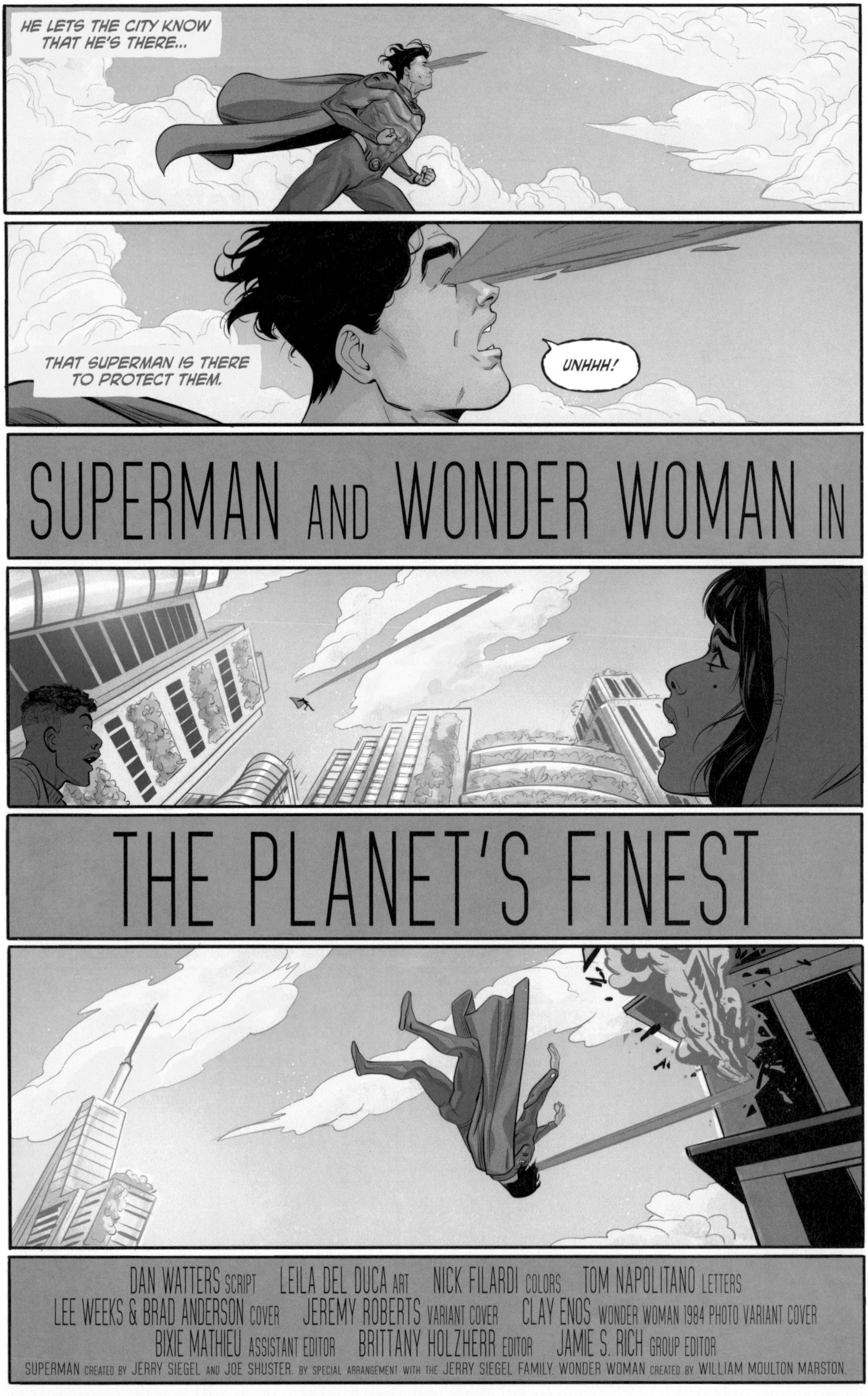
HE LETS THE CITY KNOW THAT HE'S THERE...
THAT SUPERMAN IS THERE TO PROTECT THEM.
UNHHH!
SUPERMAN AND WONDER WOMAN IN
THE PLANET'S FINEST
DAN WATTERS SCRIPT LEILA DEL DUCA ART NICK FILARDI COLORS TOM NAPOLITANO LETTERS
LEE WEEKS & BRAD ANDERSON COVER JEREMY ROBERTS VARIANT COVER CLAY ENOS WONDER WOMAN 1984 PHOTO VARIANT COVER
BIXIE MATHIEU ASSISTANT EDITOR BRITTANY HOLZHERR EDITOR JAMIE S. RICH GROUP EDITOR
SUPERMAN CREATED BY JERRY SIEGEL AND JOE SHUSTER. BY SPECIAL ARRANGEMENT WITH THE JERRY SIEGEL FAMILY. WONDER WOMAN CREATED BY WILLIAM MOULTON MARSTON.

Future State: Superman/Wonder Woman #2
Cover Art by **LEE WEEKS** and **BRAD ANDERSON**

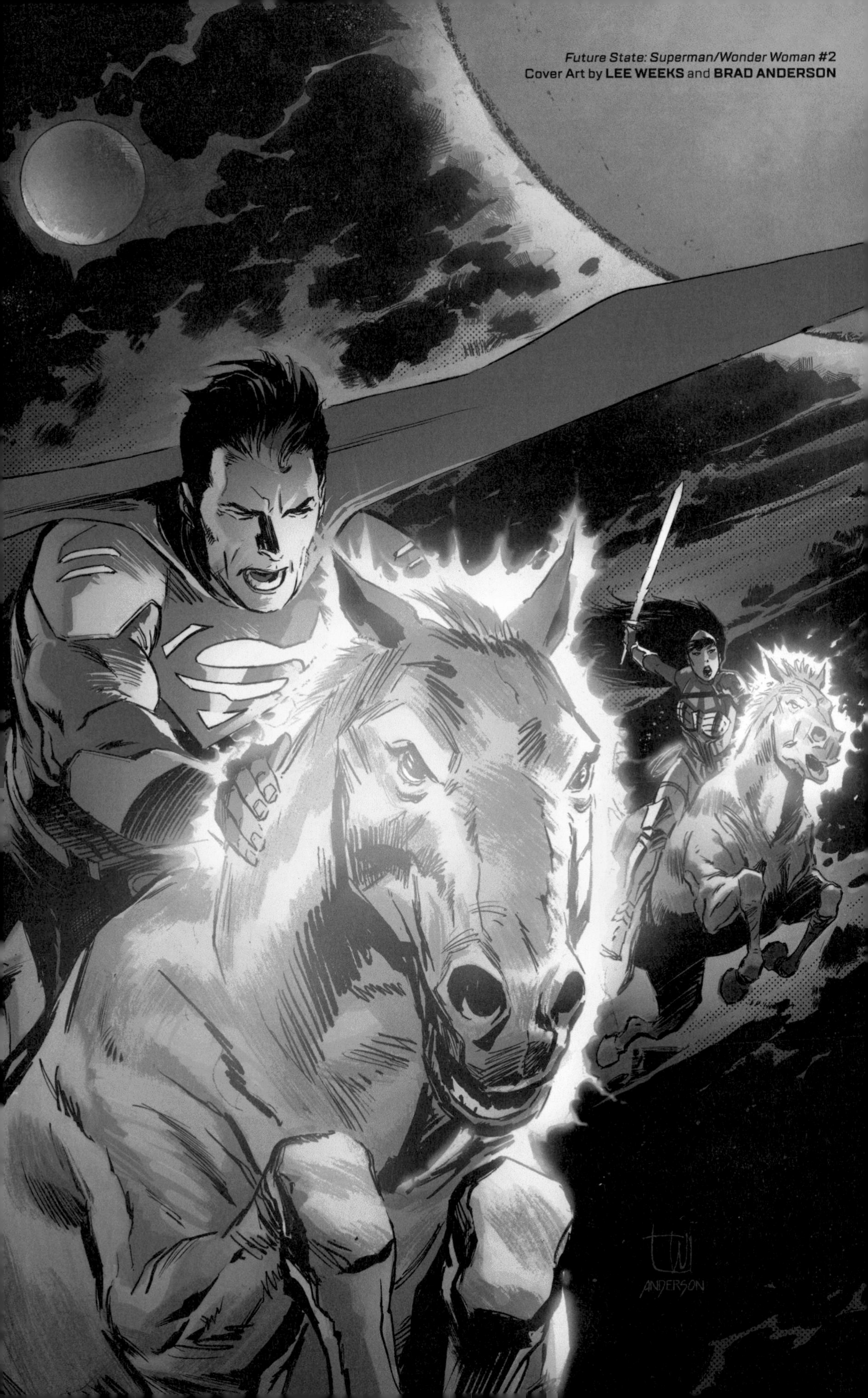
ANDERSON

FUTURE
STATE

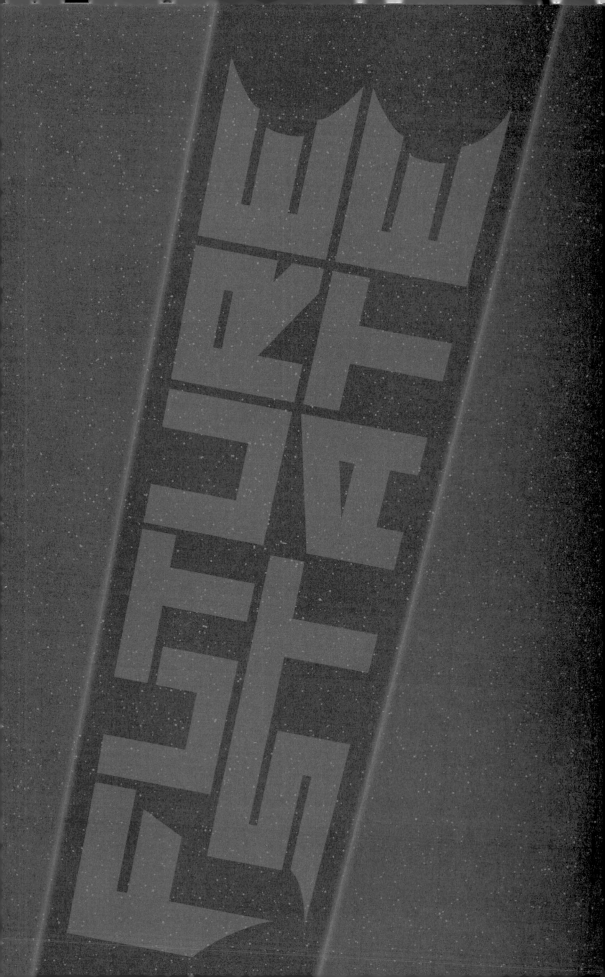

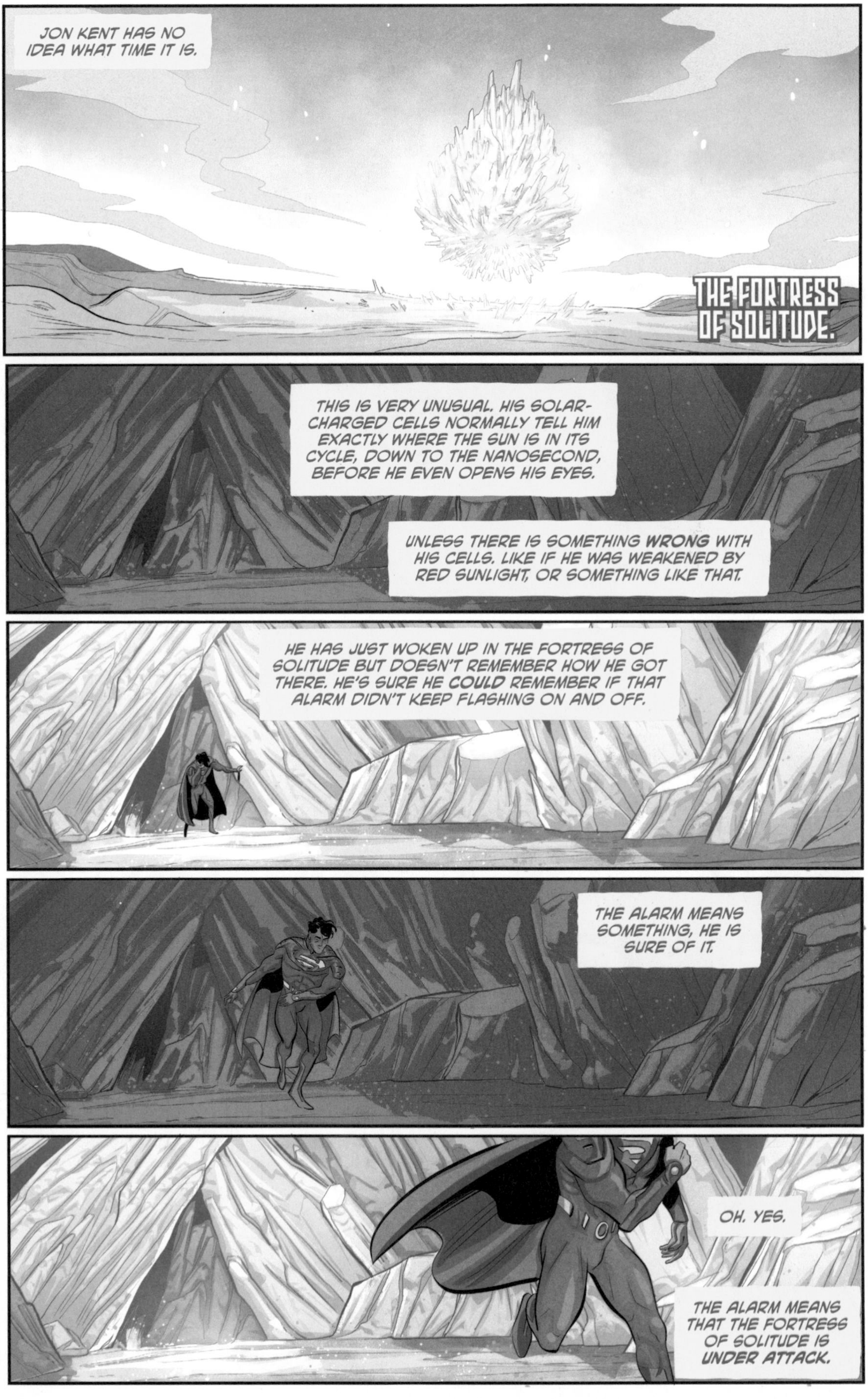
JON KENT HAS NO IDEA WHAT TIME IT IS.
THE FORTRESS OF SOLITUDE.
THIS IS VERY UNUSUAL. HIS SOLAR-CHARGED CELLS NORMALLY TELL HIM EXACTLY WHERE THE SUN IS IN ITS CYCLE, DOWN TO THE NANOSECOND, BEFORE HE EVEN OPENS HIS EYES.
UNLESS THERE IS SOMETHING WRONG WITH HIS CELLS. LIKE IF HE WAS WEAKENED BY RED SUNLIGHT, OR SOMETHING LIKE THAT.
HE HAS JUST WOKEN UP IN THE FORTRESS OF SOLITUDE BUT DOESN'T REMEMBER HOW HE GOT THERE. HE'S SURE HE COULD REMEMBER IF THAT ALARM DIDN'T KEEP FLASHING ON AND OFF.
THE ALARM MEANS SOMETHING, HE IS SURE OF IT.
OH. YES.
THE ALARM MEANS THAT THE FORTRESS OF SOLITUDE IS UNDER ATTACK.

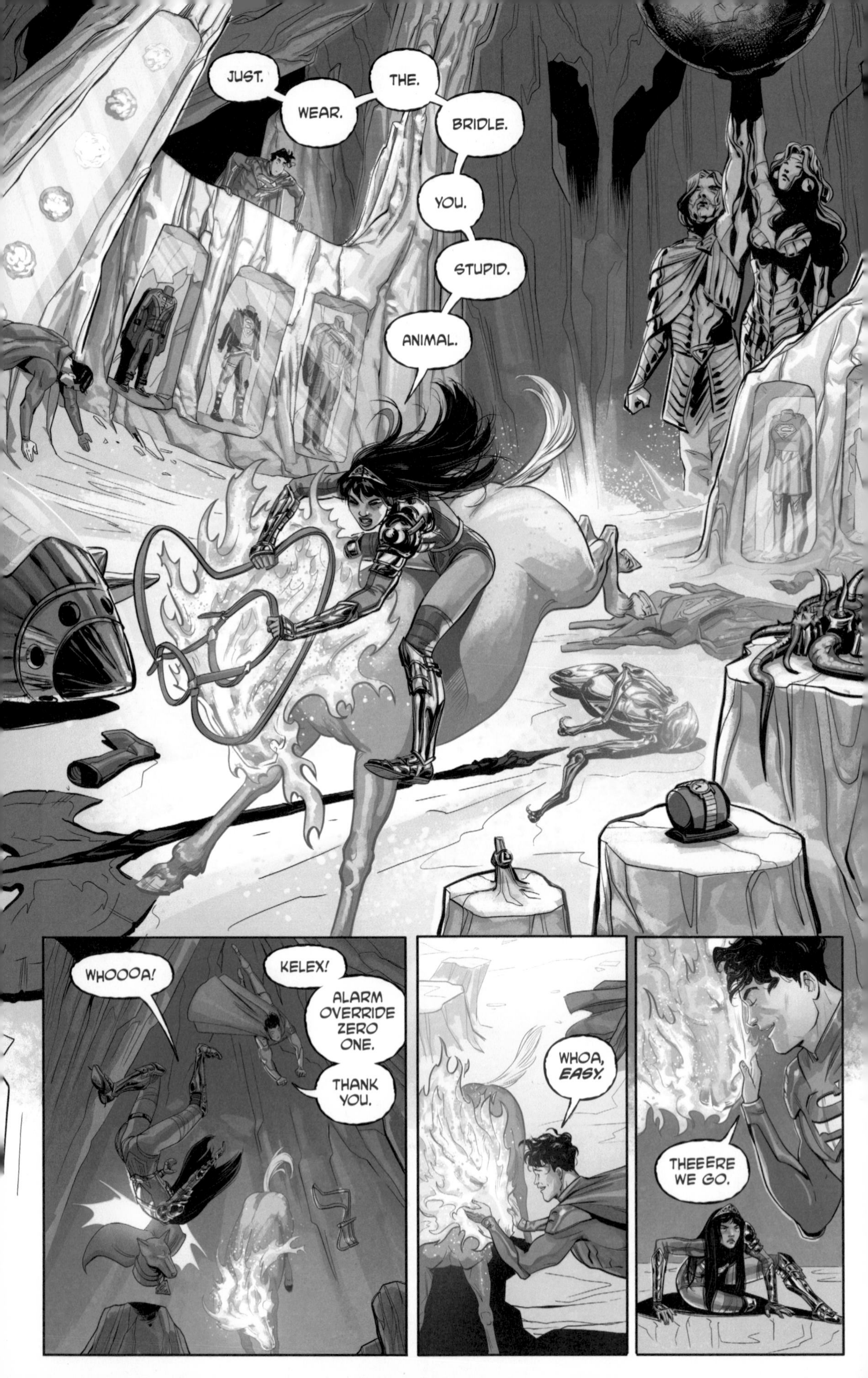
JUST.
WEAR.
THE.
BRIDLE.
YOU.
STUPID.
ANIMAL.
WHOOOA!
KELEX!
ALARM OVERRIDE ZERO ONE.
THANK YOU.
WHOA, *EASY.*
THEEERE WE GO.

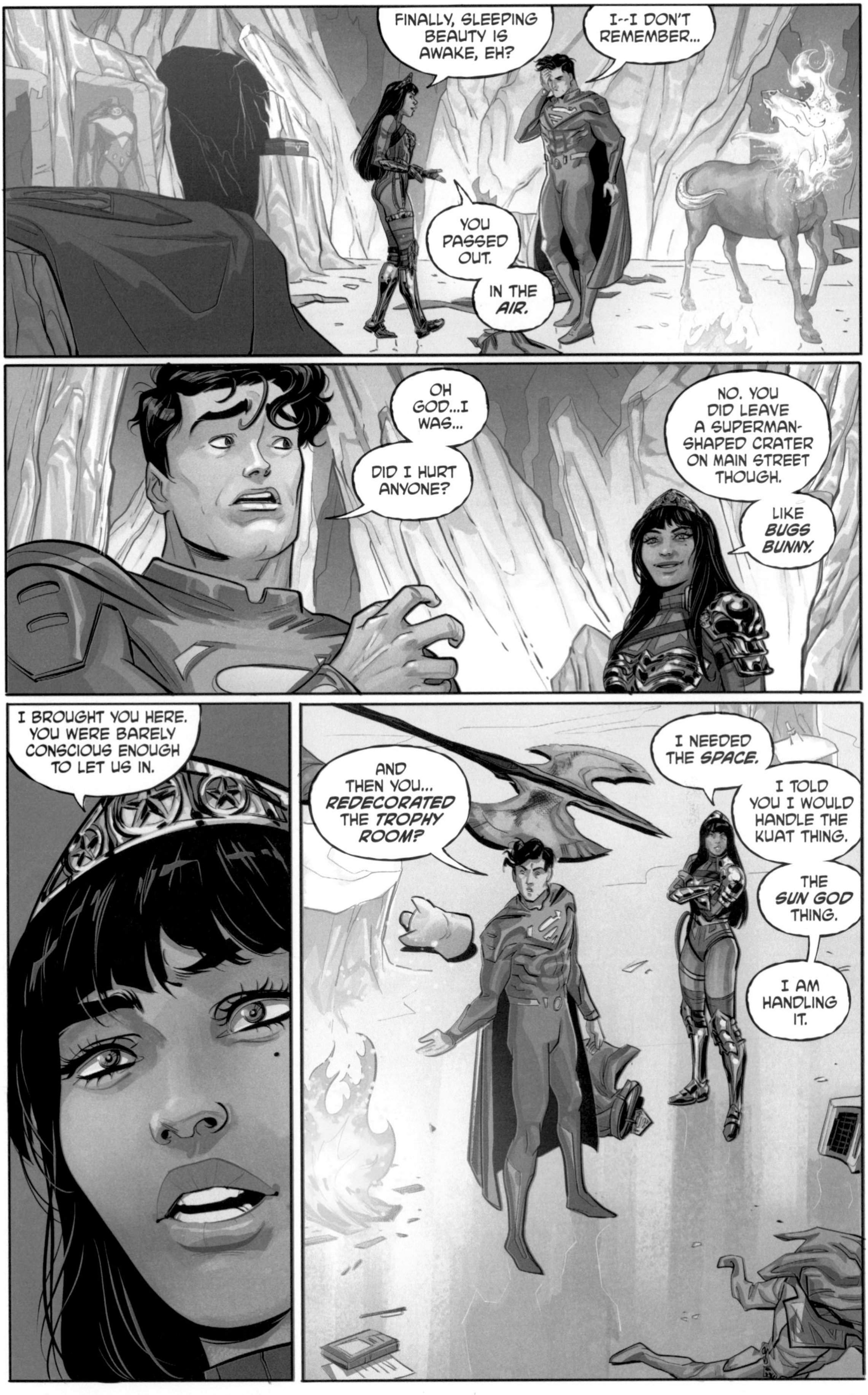
FINALLY, SLEEPING BEAUTY IS AWAKE, EH?
I--I DON'T REMEMBER...
YOU PASSED OUT.
IN THE *AIR.*
OH GOD...I WAS...
DID I HURT ANYONE?
NO. YOU DID LEAVE A SUPERMAN-SHAPED CRATER ON MAIN STREET THOUGH.
LIKE *BUGS BUNNY.*
I BROUGHT YOU HERE. YOU WERE BARELY CONSCIOUS ENOUGH TO LET US IN.
AND THEN YOU... *REDECORATED* THE *TROPHY ROOM?*
I NEEDED THE *SPACE.*
I TOLD YOU I WOULD HANDLE THE KUAT THING.
THE *SUN GOD* THING.
I AM HANDLING IT.

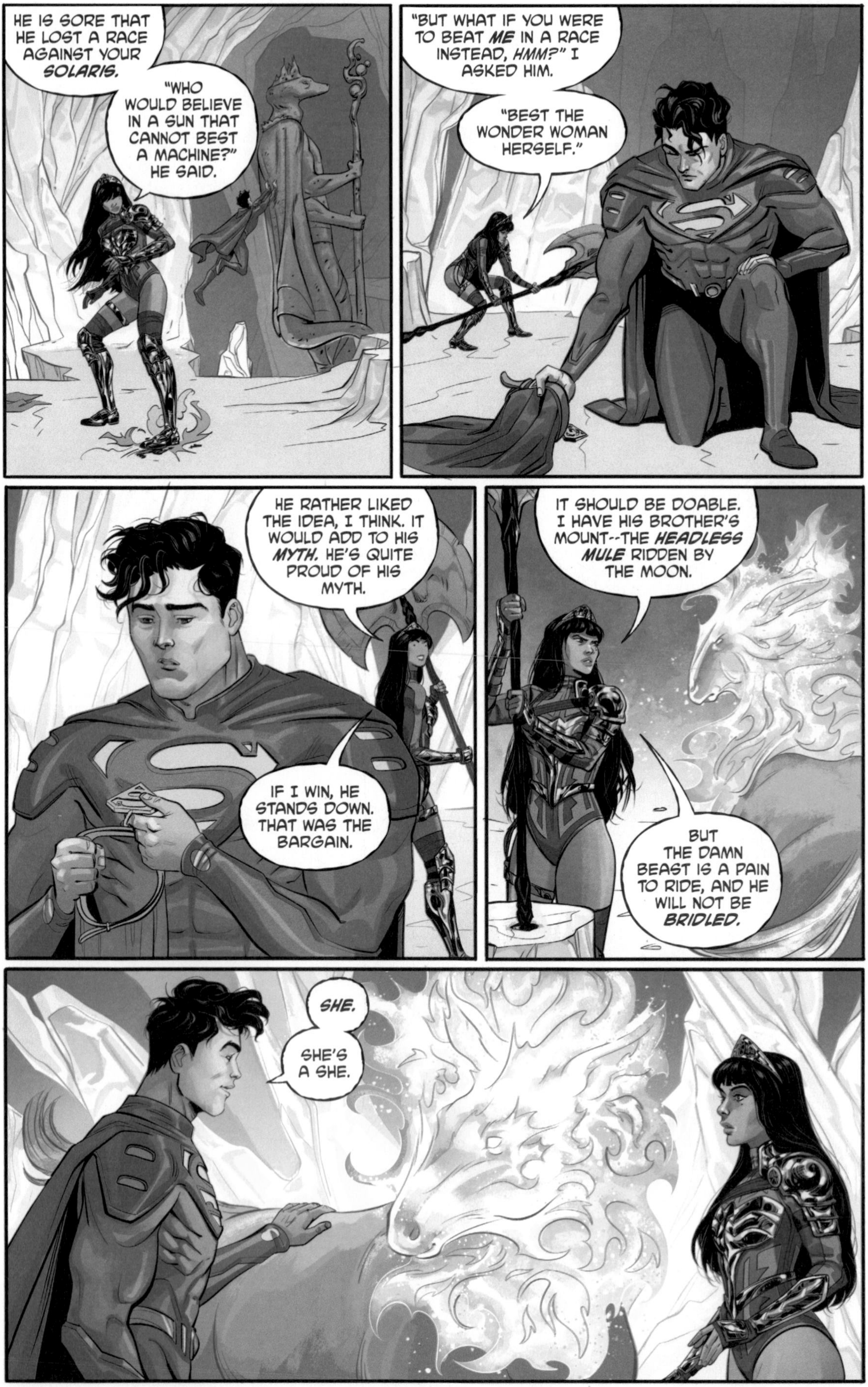
HE IS SORE THAT HE LOST A RACE AGAINST YOUR SOLARIS.
"WHO WOULD BELIEVE IN A SUN THAT CANNOT BEST A MACHINE?" HE SAID.
"BUT WHAT IF YOU WERE TO BEAT ME IN A RACE INSTEAD, HMM?" I ASKED HIM.
"BEST THE WONDER WOMAN HERSELF."
HE RATHER LIKED THE IDEA, I THINK. IT WOULD ADD TO HIS MYTH. HE'S QUITE PROUD OF HIS MYTH.
IF I WIN, HE STANDS DOWN. THAT WAS THE BARGAIN.
IT SHOULD BE DOABLE. I HAVE HIS BROTHER'S MOUNT--THE HEADLESS MULE RIDDEN BY THE MOON.
BUT THE DAMN BEAST IS A PAIN TO RIDE, AND HE WILL NOT BE BRIDLED.
SHE.
SHE'S A SHE.

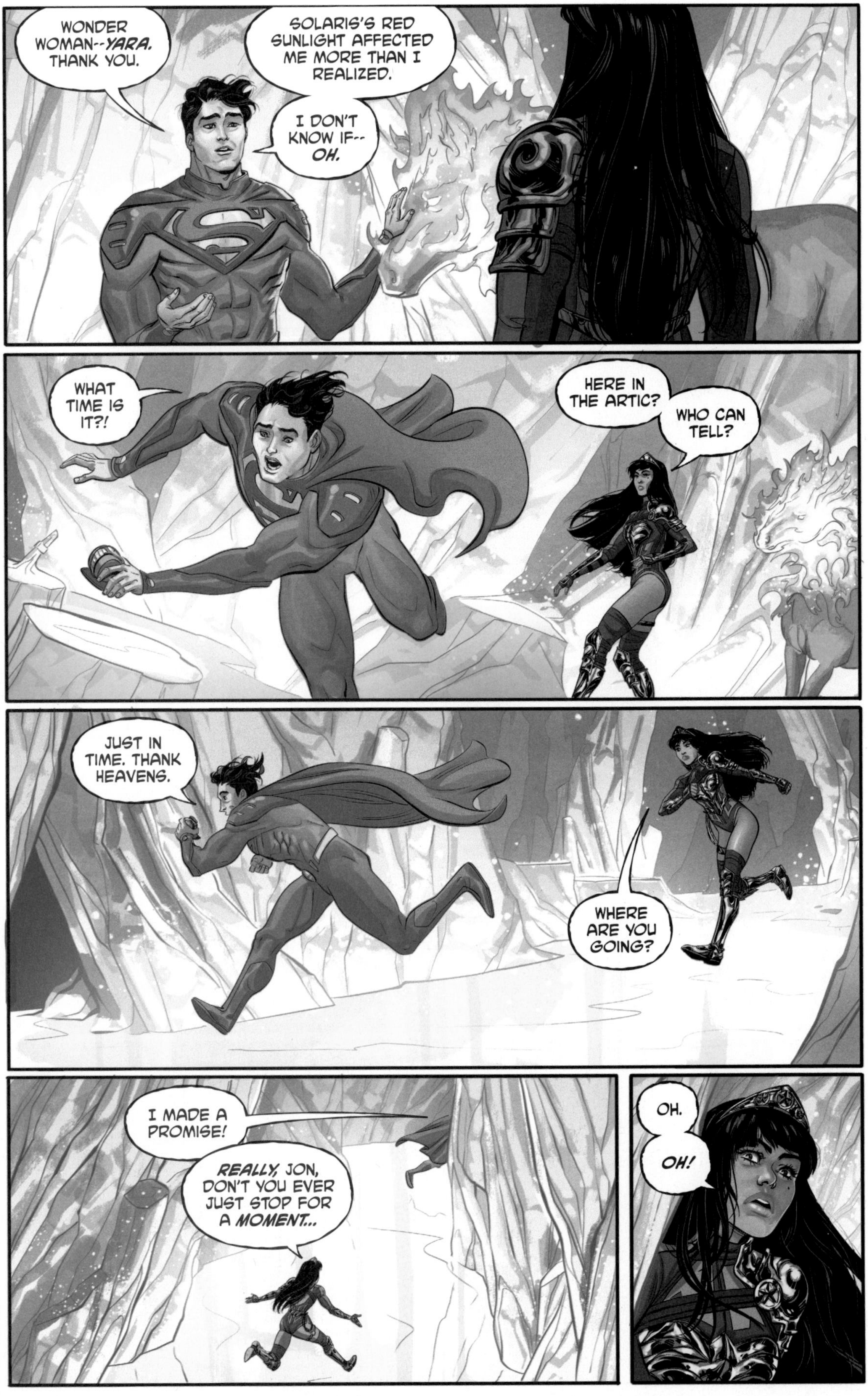
WONDER WOMAN--YARA. THANK YOU.
SOLARIS'S RED SUNLIGHT AFFECTED ME MORE THAN I REALIZED.
I DON'T KNOW IF-- OH.
WHAT TIME IS IT?!
HERE IN THE ARTIC?
WHO CAN TELL?
JUST IN TIME. THANK HEAVENS.
WHERE ARE YOU GOING?
I MADE A PROMISE!
REALLY, JON, DON'T YOU EVER JUST STOP FOR A MOMENT...
OH.
OH!

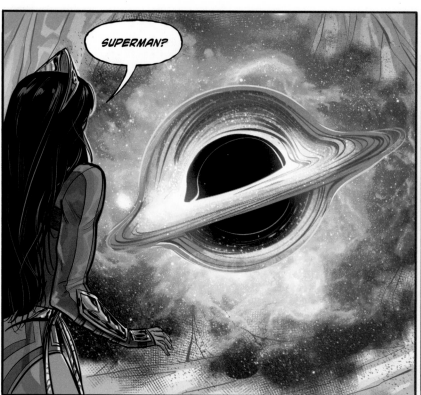

SUPERMAN?

BOOOM

AAAND *THERE.* IT'S DONE.

UH... *WHAT* IS DONE? WHAT IS *THAT?*

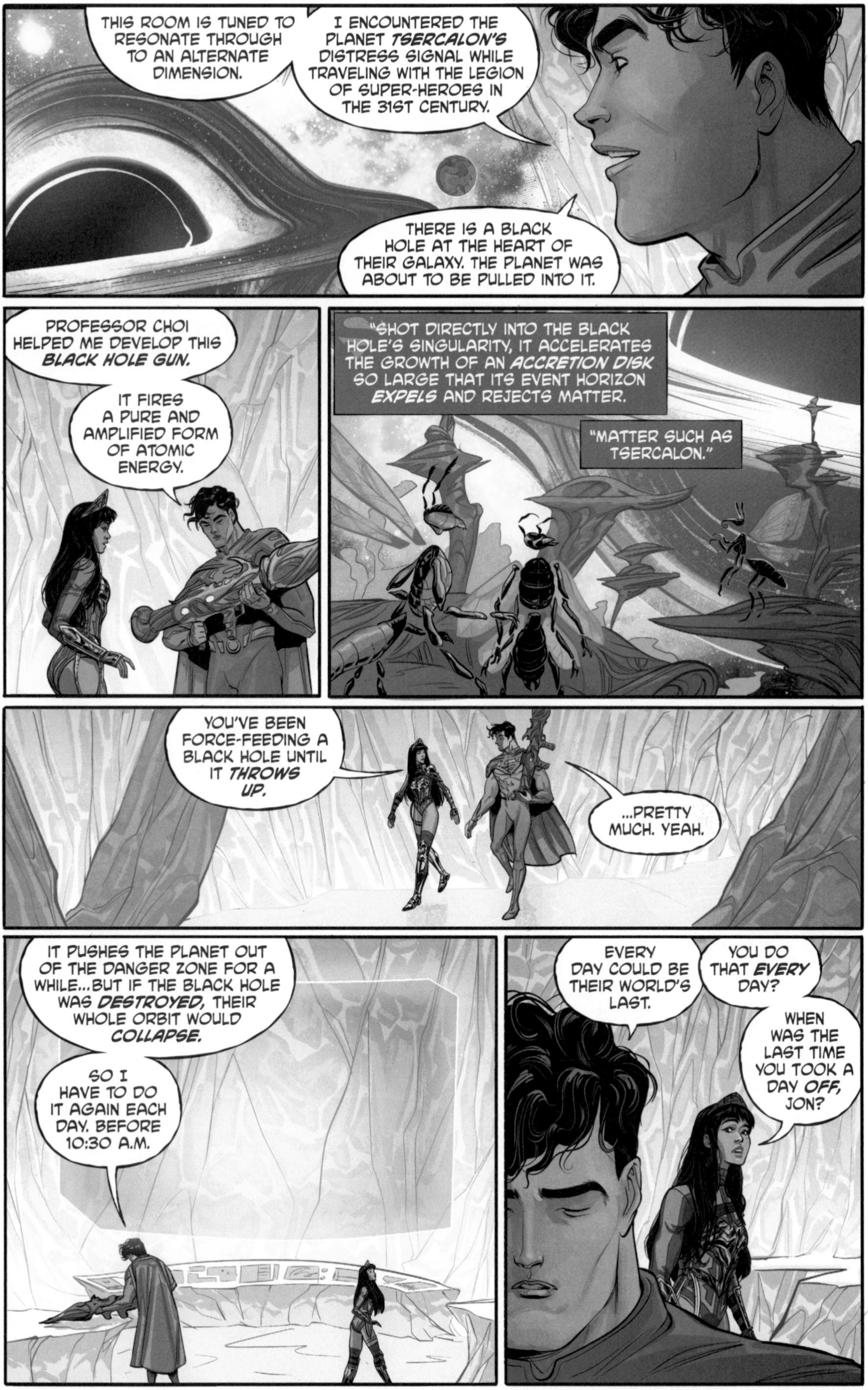
THIS ROOM IS TUNED TO RESONATE THROUGH TO AN ALTERNATE DIMENSION.
I ENCOUNTERED THE PLANET *TSERCALON'S* DISTRESS SIGNAL WHILE TRAVELING WITH THE LEGION OF SUPER-HEROES IN THE 31ST CENTURY.
THERE IS A BLACK HOLE AT THE HEART OF THEIR GALAXY. THE PLANET WAS ABOUT TO BE PULLED INTO IT.
PROFESSOR CHOI HELPED ME DEVELOP THIS *BLACK HOLE GUN.*
IT FIRES A PURE AND AMPLIFIED FORM OF ATOMIC ENERGY.
"SHOT DIRECTLY INTO THE BLACK HOLE'S SINGULARITY, IT ACCELERATES THE GROWTH OF AN *ACCRETION DISK* SO LARGE THAT ITS EVENT HORIZON *EXPELS* AND REJECTS MATTER.
"MATTER SUCH AS TSERCALON."
YOU'VE BEEN FORCE-FEEDING A BLACK HOLE UNTIL IT *THROWS UP.*
...PRETTY MUCH. YEAH.
IT PUSHES THE PLANET OUT OF THE DANGER ZONE FOR A WHILE...BUT IF THE BLACK HOLE WAS *DESTROYED,* THEIR WHOLE ORBIT WOULD *COLLAPSE.*
SO I HAVE TO DO IT AGAIN EACH DAY. BEFORE 10:30 A.M.
EVERY DAY COULD BE THEIR WORLD'S LAST.
YOU DO THAT *EVERY* DAY?
WHEN WAS THE LAST TIME YOU TOOK A DAY *OFF,* JON?

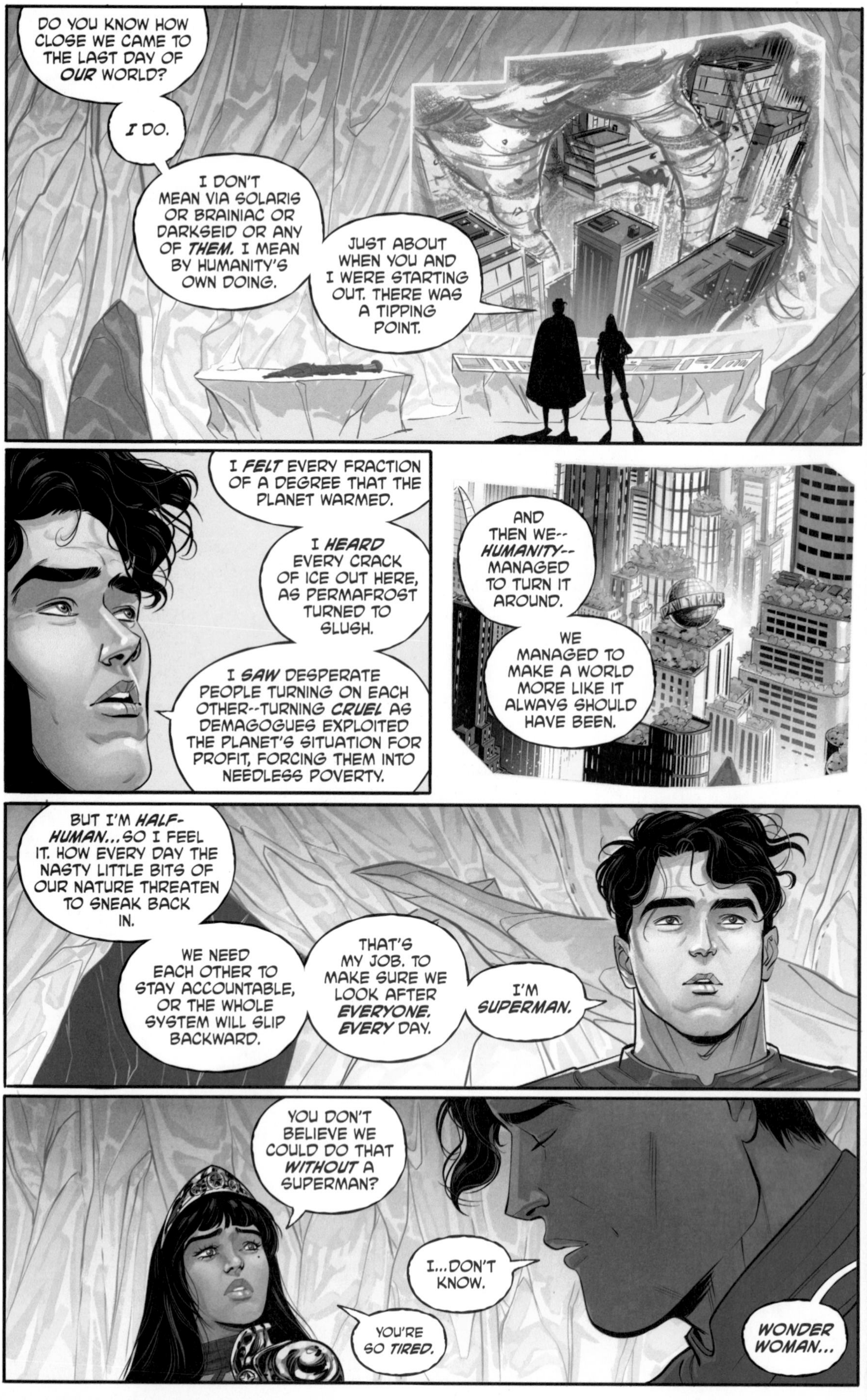
DO YOU KNOW HOW CLOSE WE CAME TO THE LAST DAY OF *OUR* WORLD?
I DO.
I DON'T MEAN VIA SOLARIS OR BRAINIAC OR DARKSEID OR ANY OF *THEM.* I MEAN BY HUMANITY'S OWN DOING.
JUST ABOUT WHEN YOU AND I WERE STARTING OUT. THERE WAS A TIPPING POINT.
I *FELT* EVERY FRACTION OF A DEGREE THAT THE PLANET WARMED.
I *HEARD* EVERY CRACK OF ICE OUT HERE, AS PERMAFROST TURNED TO SLUSH.
I *SAW* DESPERATE PEOPLE TURNING ON EACH OTHER--TURNING *CRUEL* AS DEMAGOGUES EXPLOITED THE PLANET'S SITUATION FOR PROFIT, FORCING THEM INTO NEEDLESS POVERTY.
AND THEN WE-- *HUMANITY*-- MANAGED TO TURN IT AROUND.
WE MANAGED TO MAKE A WORLD MORE LIKE IT ALWAYS SHOULD HAVE BEEN.
BUT I'M *HALF-HUMAN...* SO I FEEL IT. HOW EVERY DAY THE NASTY LITTLE BITS OF OUR NATURE THREATEN TO SNEAK BACK IN.
WE NEED EACH OTHER TO STAY ACCOUNTABLE, OR THE WHOLE SYSTEM WILL SLIP BACKWARD.
THAT'S MY JOB. TO MAKE SURE WE LOOK AFTER *EVERYONE. EVERY* DAY.
I'M *SUPERMAN.*
YOU DON'T BELIEVE WE COULD DO THAT *WITHOUT* A SUPERMAN?
I...DON'T KNOW.
YOU'RE SO *TIRED.*
WONDER WOMAN...

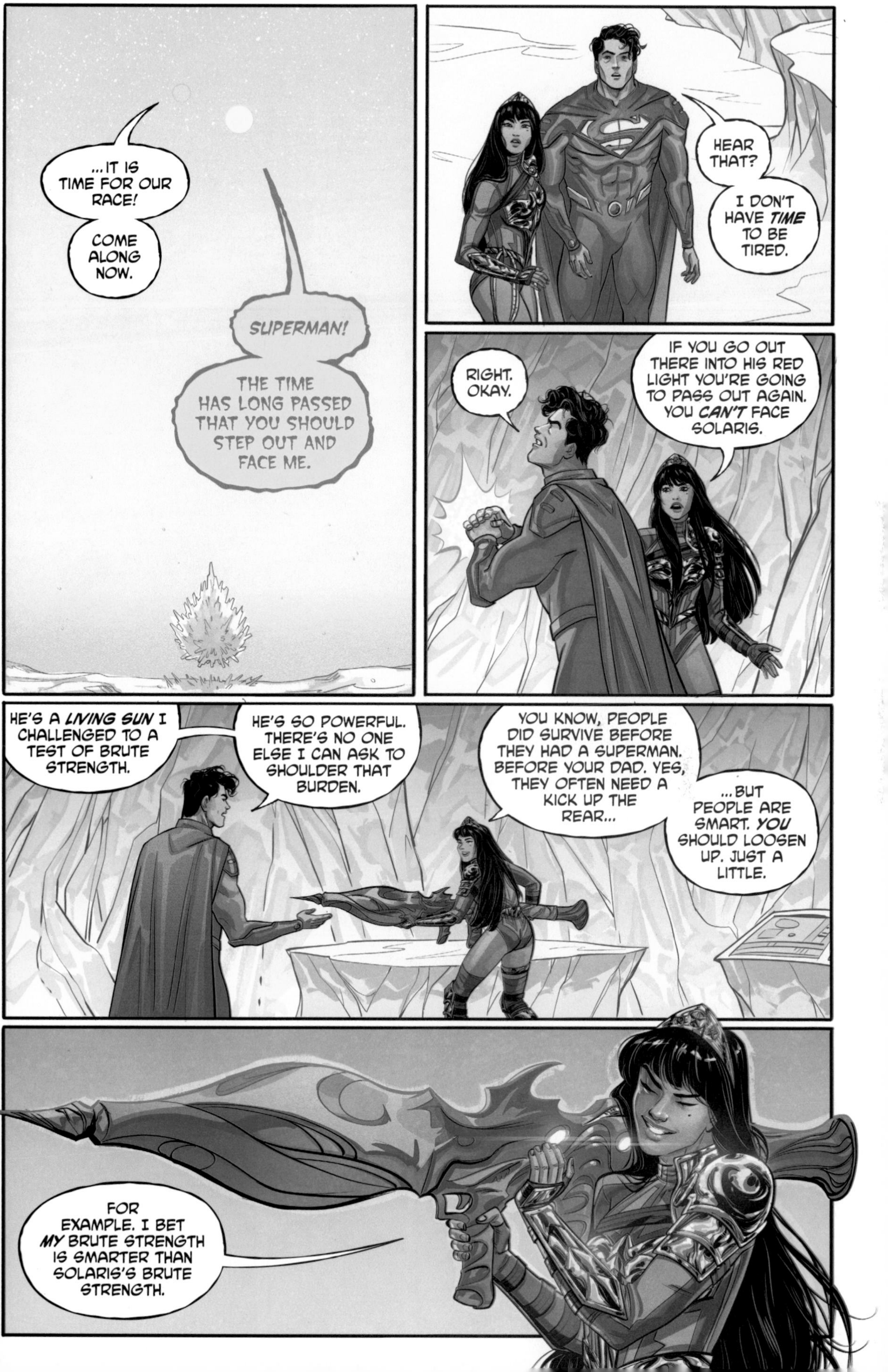
...IT IS TIME FOR OUR RACE!
COME ALONG NOW.
SUPERMAN!
THE TIME HAS LONG PASSED THAT YOU SHOULD STEP OUT AND FACE ME.
HEAR THAT?
I DON'T HAVE TIME TO BE TIRED.
RIGHT. OKAY.
IF YOU GO OUT THERE INTO HIS RED LIGHT YOU'RE GOING TO PASS OUT AGAIN. YOU CAN'T FACE SOLARIS.
HE'S A LIVING SUN I CHALLENGED TO A TEST OF BRUTE STRENGTH.
HE'S SO POWERFUL. THERE'S NO ONE ELSE I CAN ASK TO SHOULDER THAT BURDEN.
YOU KNOW, PEOPLE DID SURVIVE BEFORE THEY HAD A SUPERMAN. BEFORE YOUR DAD. YES, THEY OFTEN NEED A KICK UP THE REAR...
...BUT PEOPLE ARE SMART. YOU SHOULD LOOSEN UP. JUST A LITTLE.
FOR EXAMPLE. I BET MY BRUTE STRENGTH IS SMARTER THAN SOLARIS'S BRUTE STRENGTH.

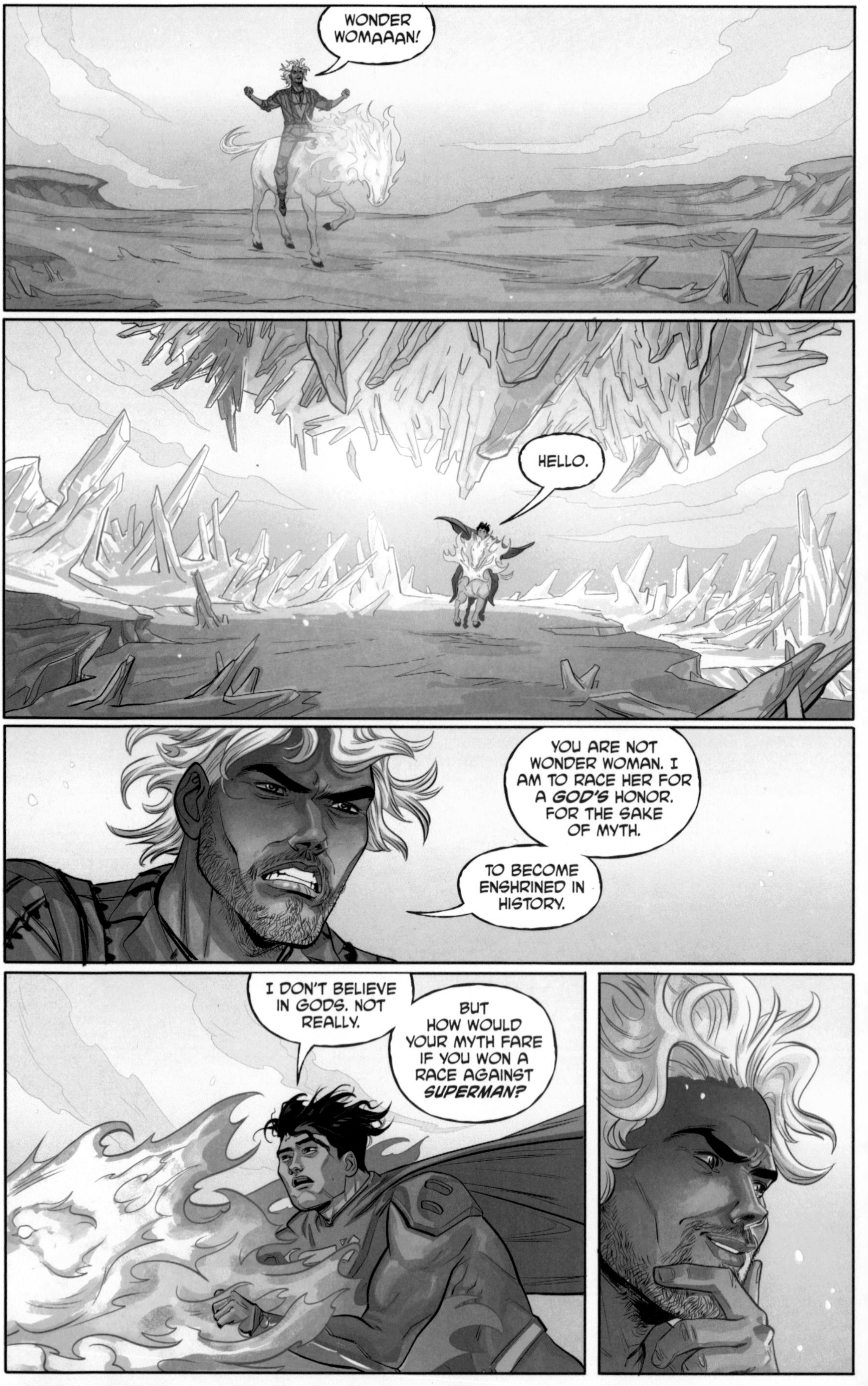
WONDER WOMAAAN!
HELLO.
YOU ARE NOT WONDER WOMAN. I AM TO RACE HER FOR A *GOD'S* HONOR. FOR THE SAKE OF MYTH.
TO BECOME ENSHRINED IN HISTORY.
I DON'T BELIEVE IN GODS. NOT REALLY.
BUT HOW WOULD YOUR MYTH FARE IF YOU WON A RACE AGAINST *SUPERMAN?*

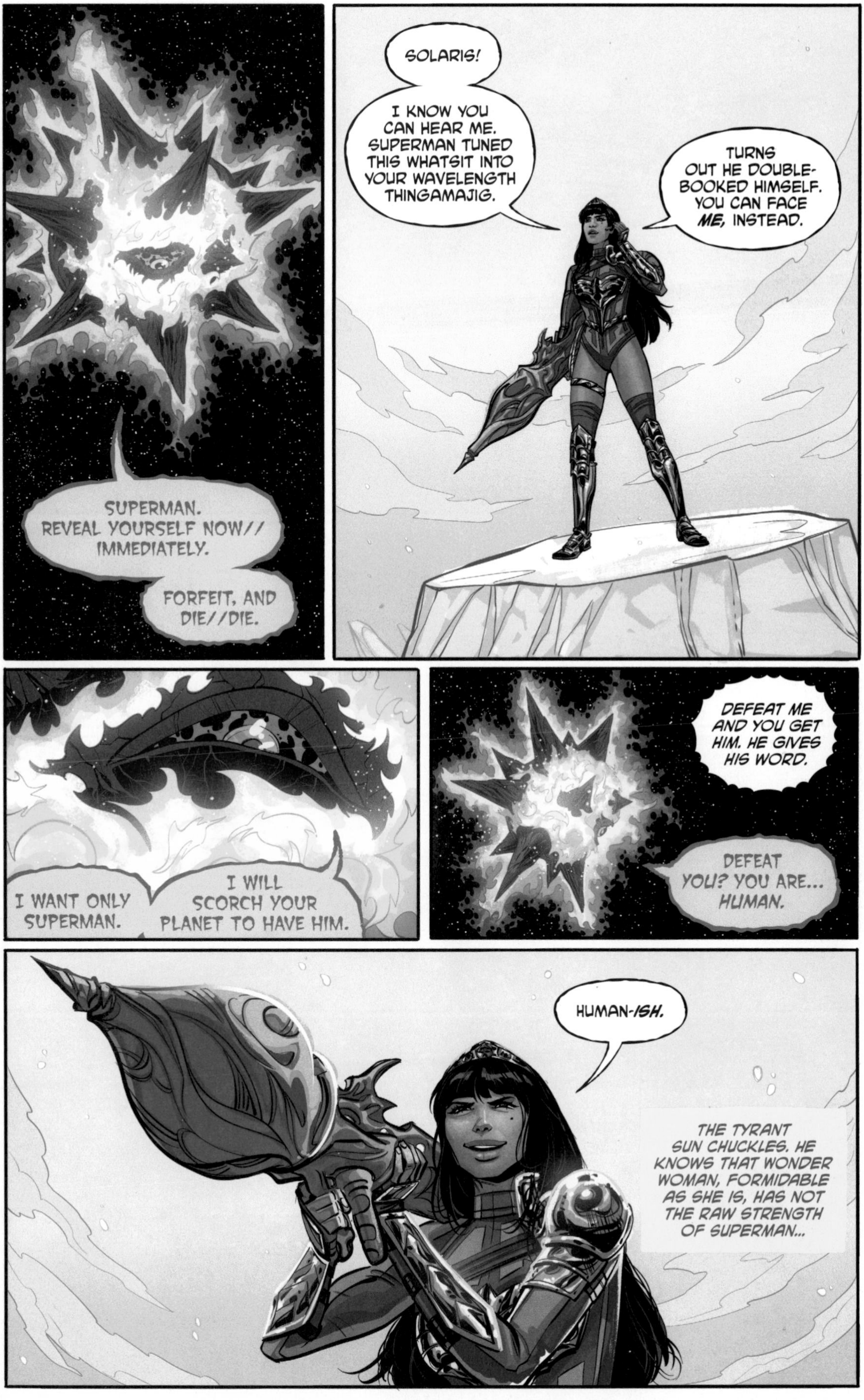
SUPERMAN. REVEAL YOURSELF NOW// IMMEDIATELY.
FORFEIT, AND DIE//DIE.
SOLARIS!
I KNOW YOU CAN HEAR ME. SUPERMAN TUNED THIS WHATSIT INTO YOUR WAVELENGTH THINGAMAJIG.
TURNS OUT HE DOUBLE-BOOKED HIMSELF. YOU CAN FACE *ME,* INSTEAD.
I WANT ONLY SUPERMAN.
I WILL SCORCH YOUR PLANET TO HAVE HIM.
DEFEAT ME AND YOU GET HIM. HE GIVES HIS WORD.
DEFEAT YOU? YOU ARE... HUMAN.
HUMAN-*ISH.*
THE TYRANT SUN CHUCKLES. HE KNOWS THAT WONDER WOMAN, FORMIDABLE AS SHE IS, HAS NOT THE RAW STRENGTH OF SUPERMAN...

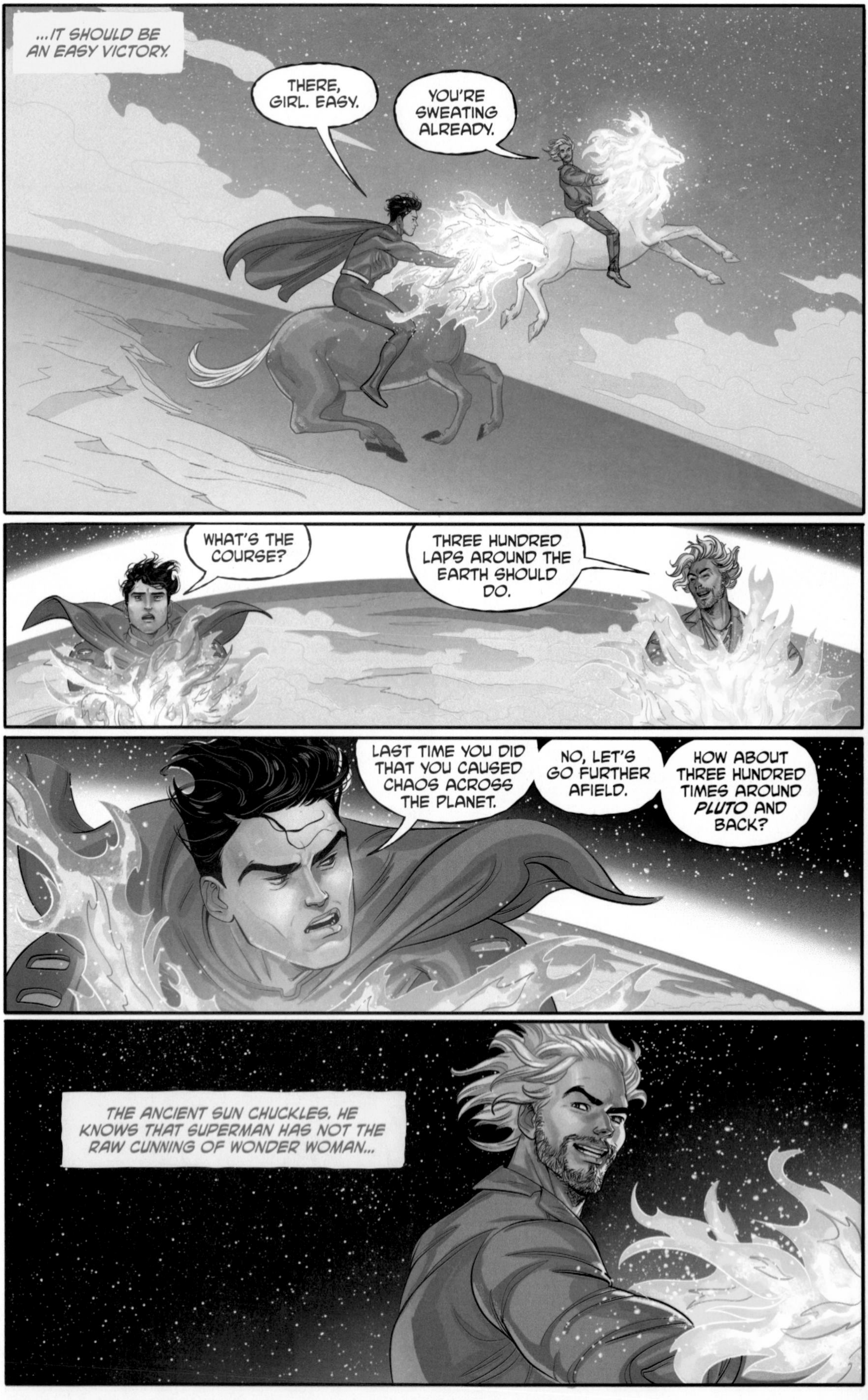
...IT SHOULD BE AN EASY VICTORY.
THERE, GIRL. EASY.
YOU'RE SWEATING ALREADY.
WHAT'S THE COURSE?
THREE HUNDRED LAPS AROUND THE EARTH SHOULD DO.
LAST TIME YOU DID THAT YOU CAUSED CHAOS ACROSS THE PLANET.
NO, LET'S GO FURTHER AFIELD.
HOW ABOUT THREE HUNDRED TIMES AROUND *PLUTO* AND BACK?
THE ANCIENT SUN CHUCKLES. HE KNOWS THAT SUPERMAN HAS NOT THE RAW CUNNING OF WONDER WOMAN...

...ANOTHER EASY VICTORY TO BE HAD.

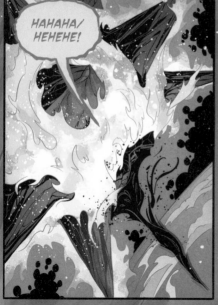

HAHAHA! HEHEHE!

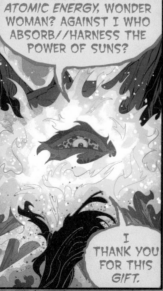

IS THIS...*PURE ATOMIC ENERGY*, WONDER WOMAN? AGAINST I WHO ABSORB//HARNESS THE POWER OF SUNS?

I THANK YOU FOR THIS *GIFT.*

I SHALL RETURN IT TENFOLD UPON YOUR LITTLE EARTH.

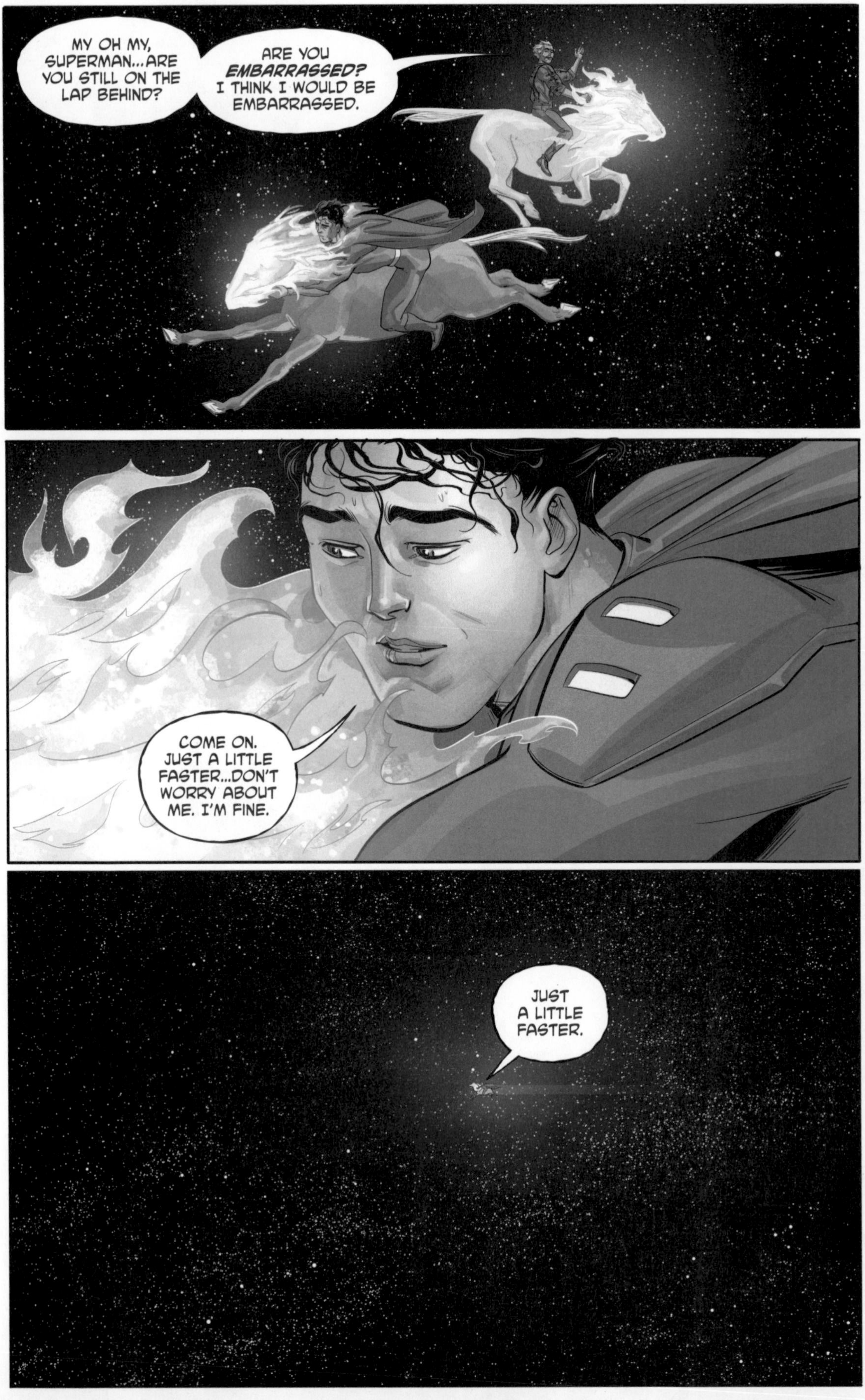
MY OH MY, SUPERMAN...ARE YOU STILL ON THE LAP BEHIND?
ARE YOU *EMBARRASSED?* I THINK I WOULD BE EMBARRASSED.
COME ON. JUST A LITTLE FASTER...DON'T WORRY ABOUT ME. I'M FINE.
JUST A LITTLE FASTER.

HEY, SOLARIS. SO SCIENCE ISN'T SO MUCH MY THING. BUT I GET AROUND. YOU KNOW HOW IT IS.

ONE TIME THE GREEK FATES PULLED ME THROUGH TIME TO THE END OF THE UNIVERSE. IT WAS A WHOLE "GHOST OF CHRISTMAS FUTURE" THING.

IT ENDED IN MORE *PUNCHING* THAN I REMEMBER FROM THAT BOOK, BUT STILL.

ANYWAY. THE ONE THING I REMEMBER ABOUT THE END OF THE UNIVERSE IS THE *STARS...*

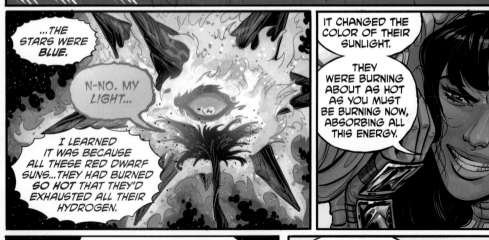

...THE STARS WERE *BLUE.*

N-NO. MY LIGHT...

I LEARNED IT WAS BECAUSE ALL THESE RED DWARF SUNS...THEY HAD BURNED SO HOT THAT THEY'D EXHAUSTED ALL THEIR HYDROGEN.

IT CHANGED THE COLOR OF THEIR SUNLIGHT.

THEY WERE BURNING ABOUT AS HOT AS YOU MUST BE BURNING NOW, ABSORBING ALL THIS ENERGY.

AND THE COLOR OF YOUR SUNLIGHT IS THE ONLY THING STOPPING SUPERMAN FROM PUNCHING YOU INTO LITTLE ROBOT BITS, RIGHT?

NOO-OOO-OOO!

SOLARIS RAN AWAY. I THINK THAT CONSTITUTES *OUT OF ORBIT,* SUPERMAN.

THE RED SUN'S GONE.

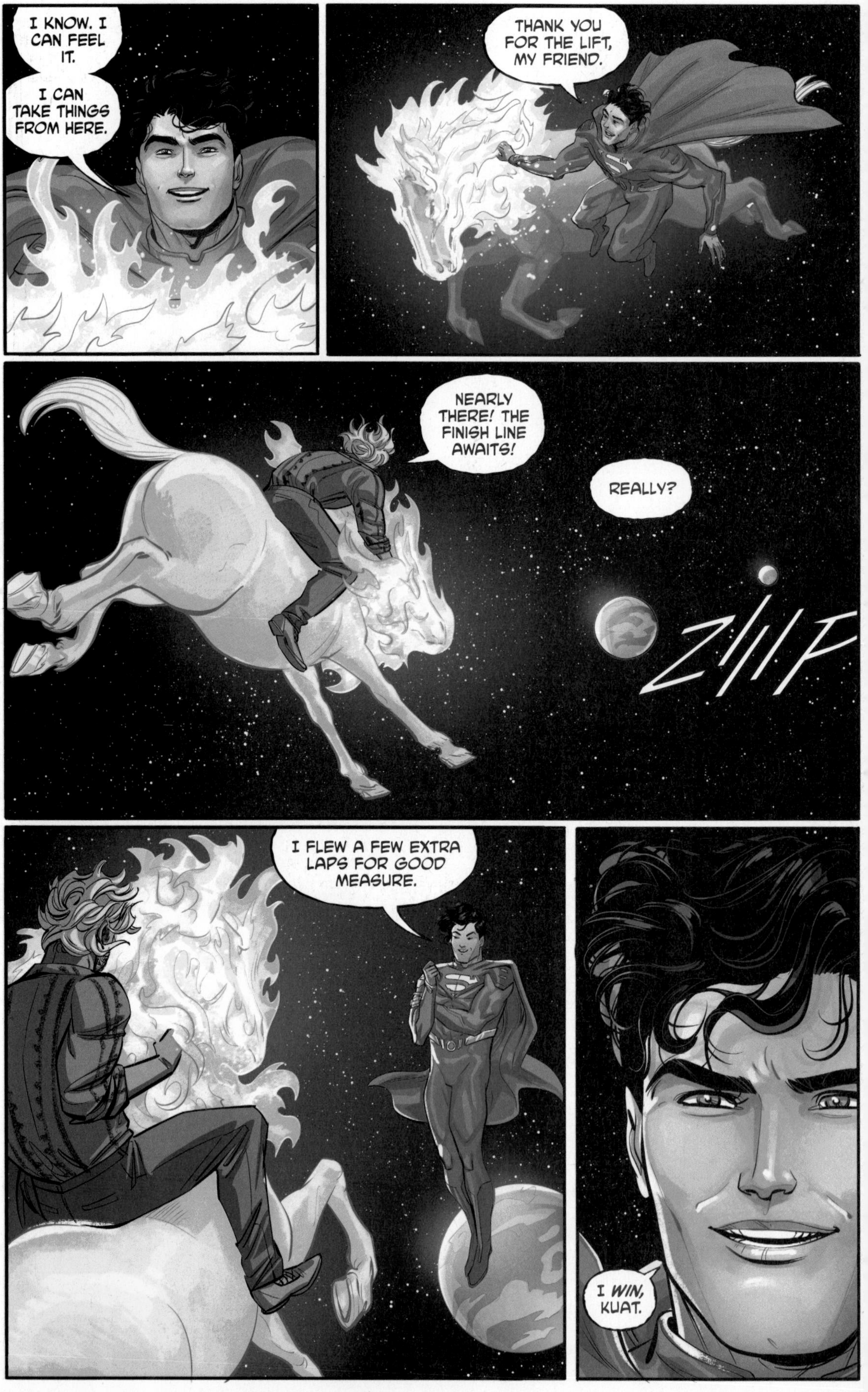
I KNOW. I CAN FEEL IT.
I CAN TAKE THINGS FROM HERE.
THANK YOU FOR THE LIFT, MY FRIEND.
NEARLY THERE! THE FINISH LINE AWAITS!
REALLY?
ZIIIF
I FLEW A FEW EXTRA LAPS FOR GOOD MEASURE.
I *WIN*, KUAT.

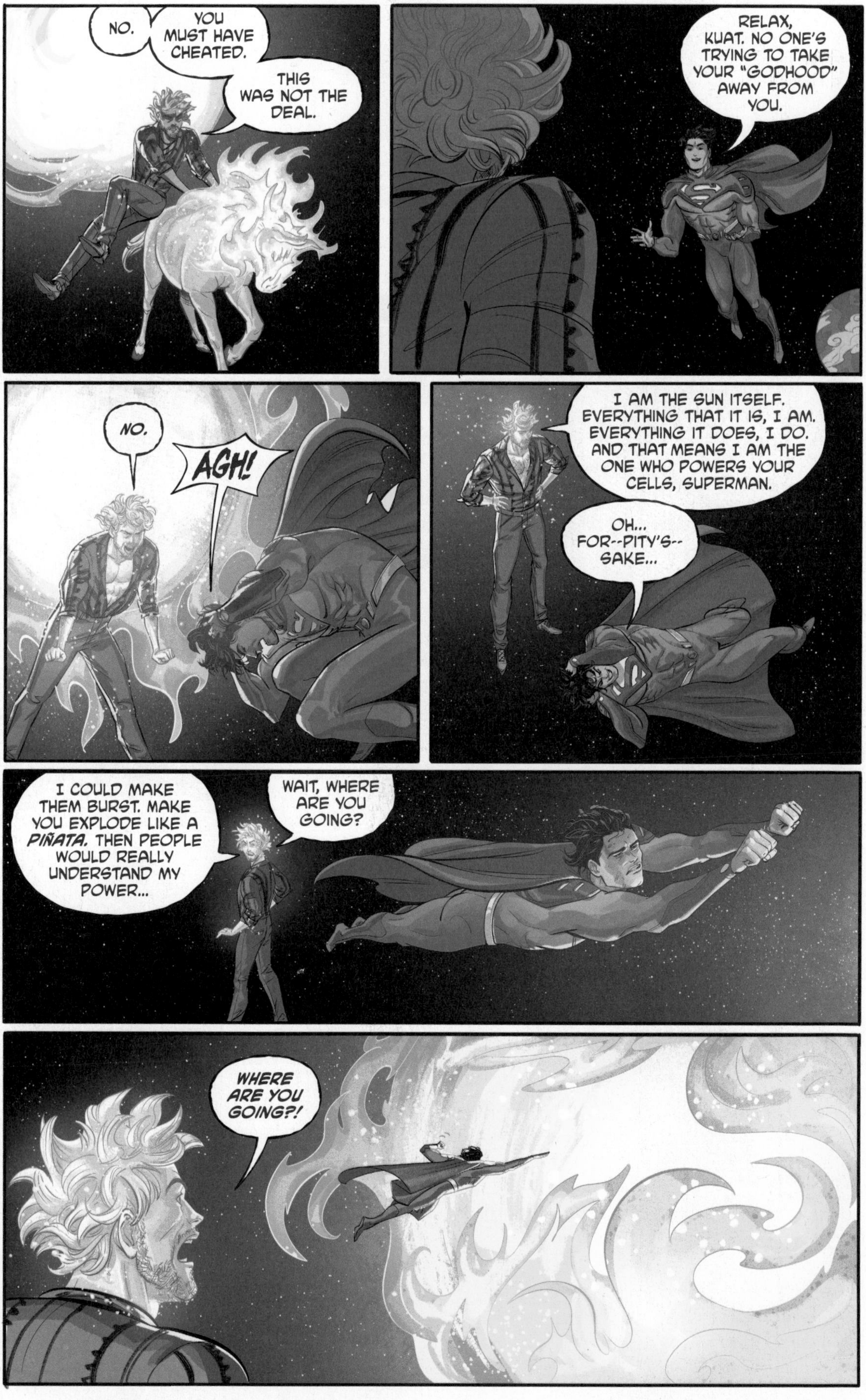
NO.
YOU MUST HAVE CHEATED.
THIS WAS NOT THE DEAL.
RELAX, KUAT. NO ONE'S TRYING TO TAKE YOUR "GODHOOD" AWAY FROM YOU.
NO.
AGH!
I AM THE SUN ITSELF. EVERYTHING THAT IT IS, I AM. EVERYTHING IT DOES, I DO. AND THAT MEANS I AM THE ONE WHO POWERS YOUR CELLS, SUPERMAN.
OH... FOR--PITY'S--SAKE...
I COULD MAKE THEM BURST. MAKE YOU EXPLODE LIKE A *PIÑATA.* THEN PEOPLE WOULD REALLY UNDERSTAND MY POWER...
WAIT, WHERE ARE YOU GOING?
WHERE ARE YOU GOING?!

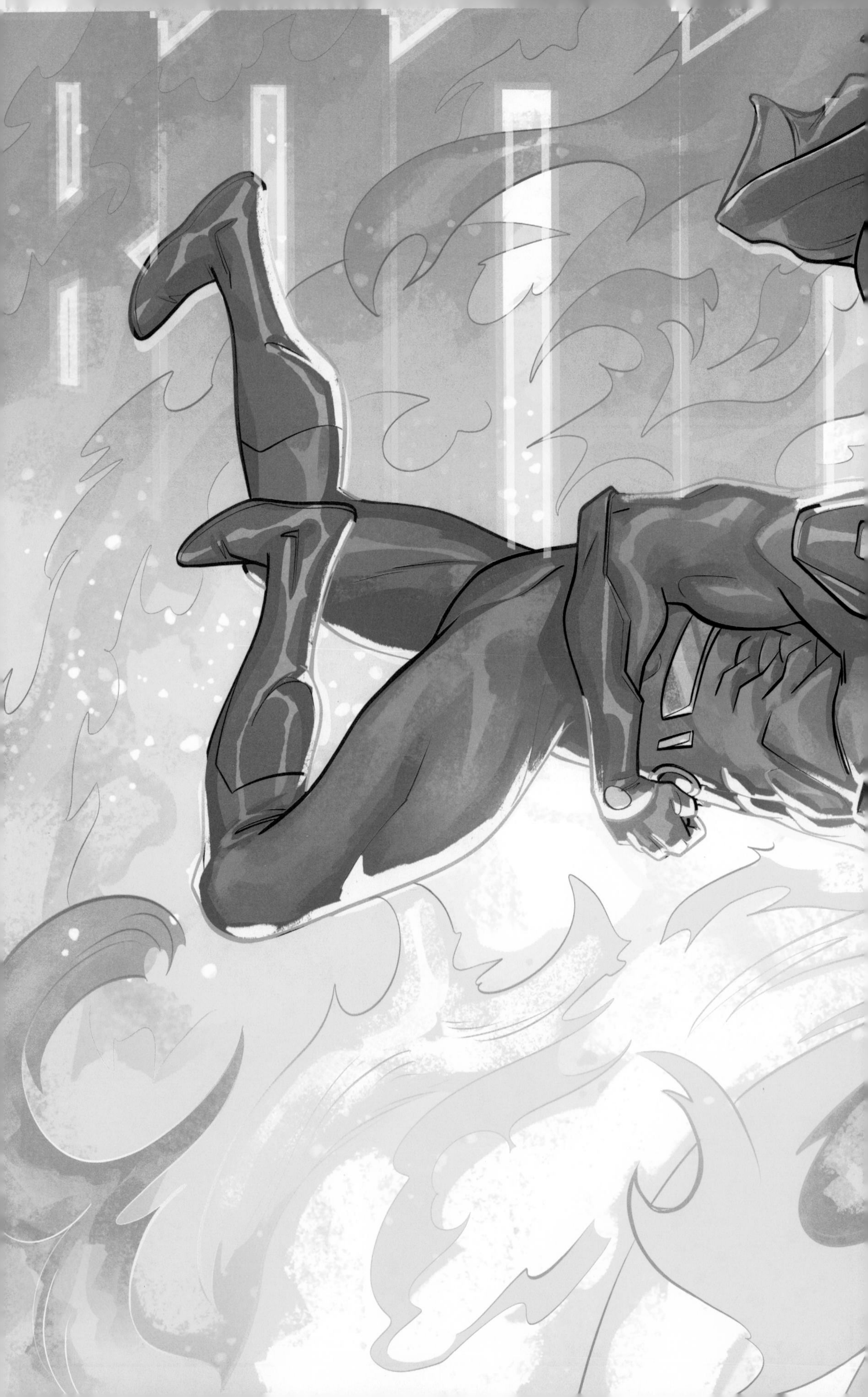

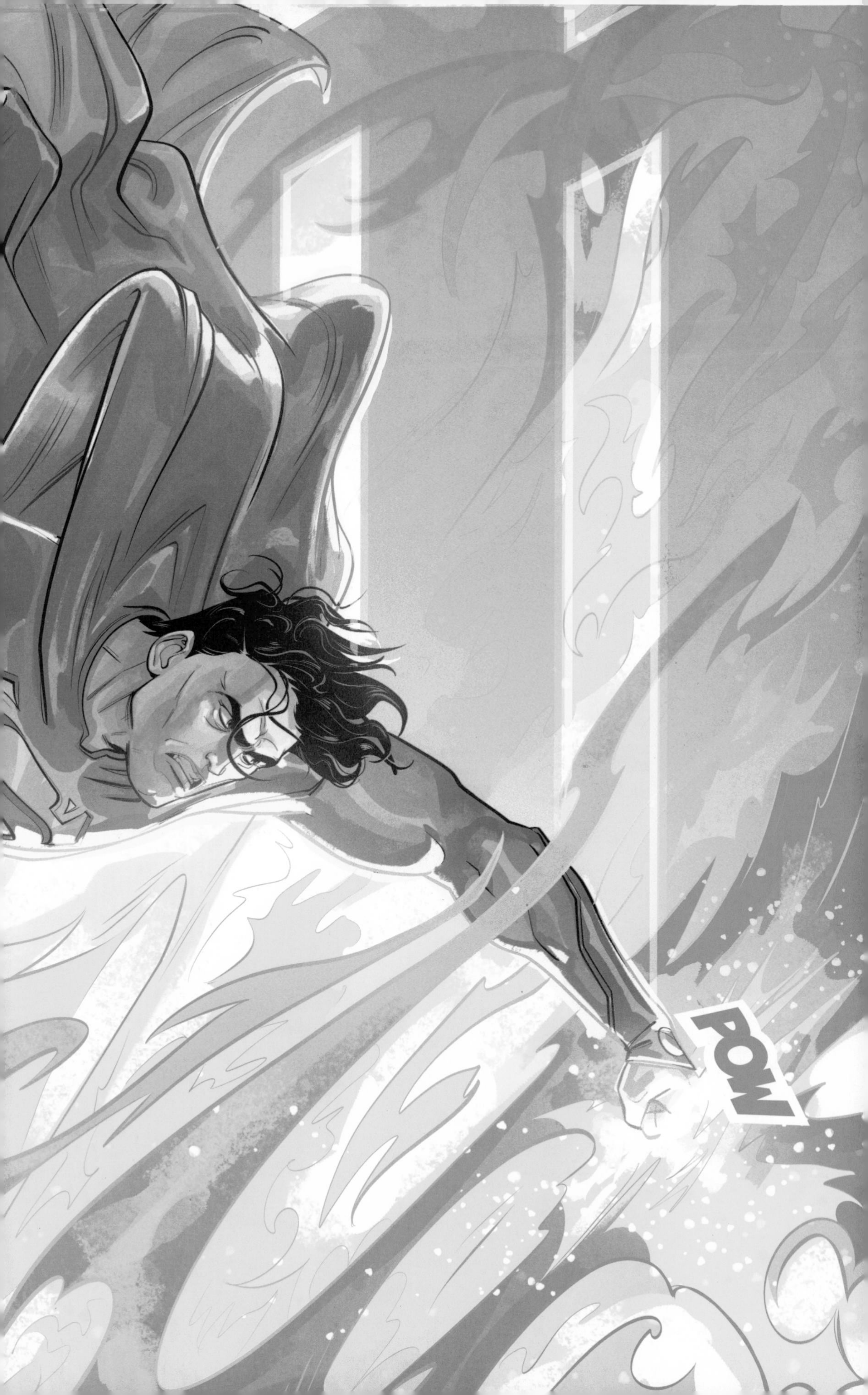
POW

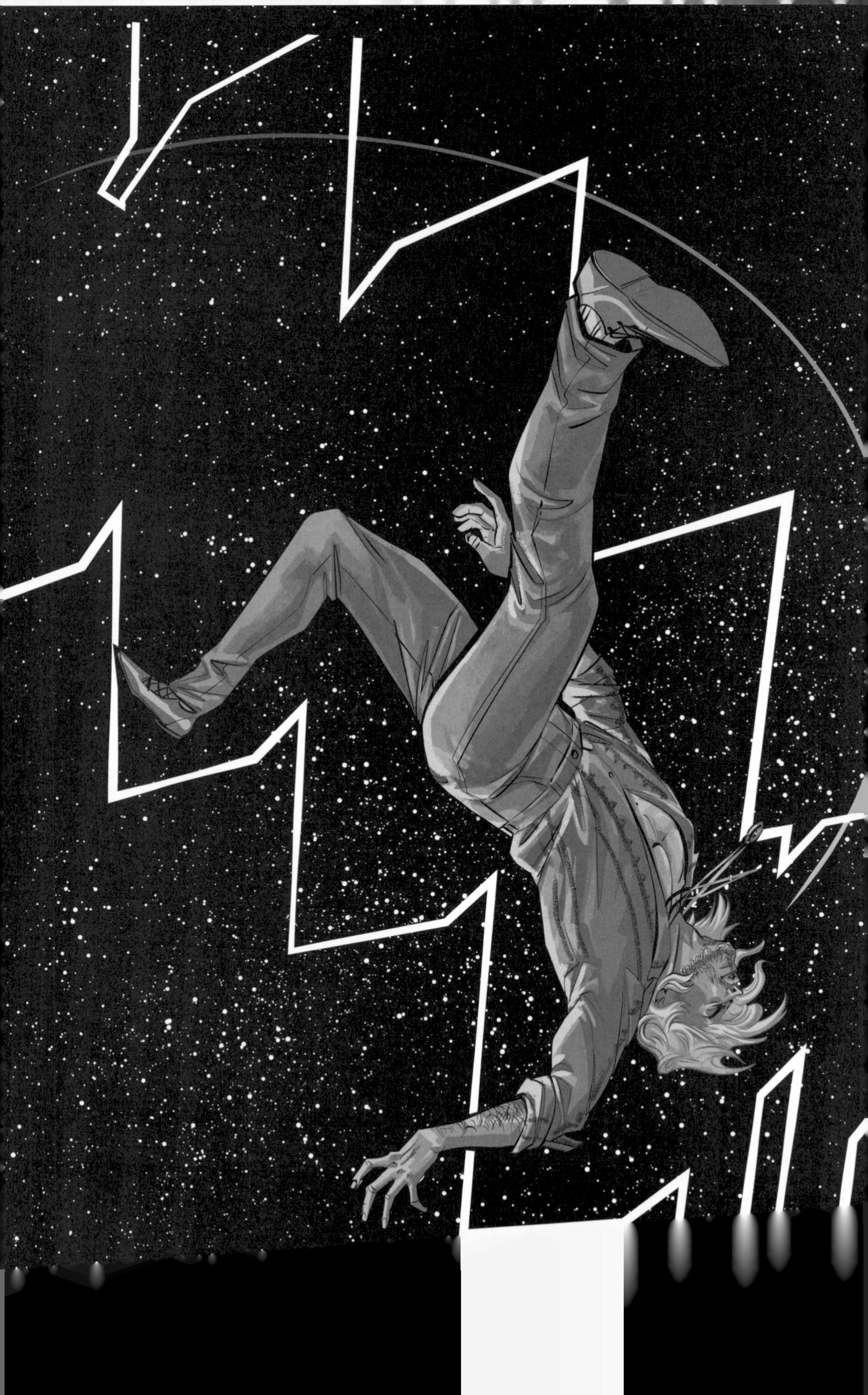

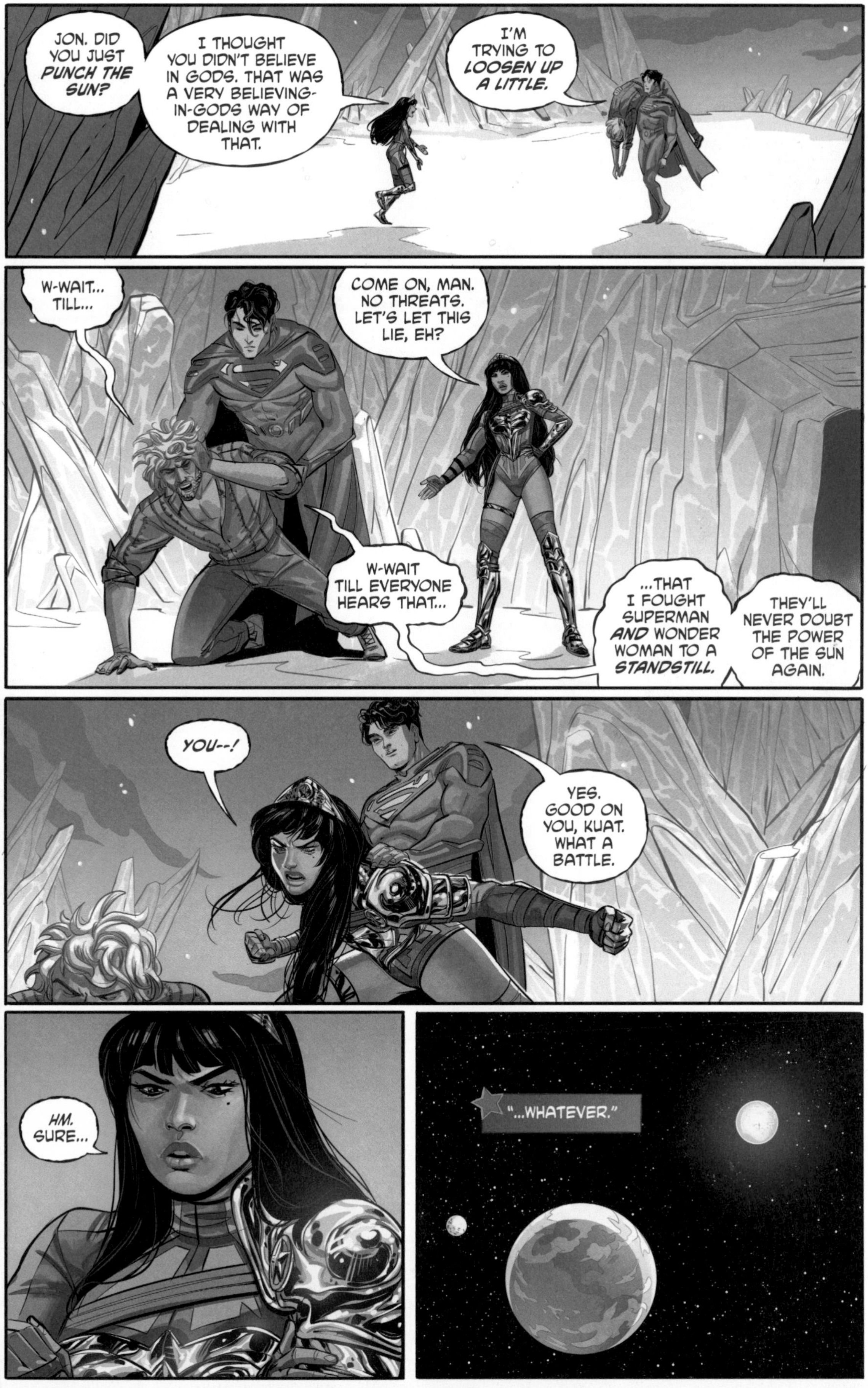
JON. DID YOU JUST PUNCH THE SUN?
I THOUGHT YOU DIDN'T BELIEVE IN GODS. THAT WAS A VERY BELIEVING-IN-GODS WAY OF DEALING WITH THAT.
I'M TRYING TO LOOSEN UP A LITTLE.
W-WAIT... TILL...
COME ON, MAN. NO THREATS. LET'S LET THIS LIE, EH?
W-WAIT TILL EVERYONE HEARS THAT...
...THAT I FOUGHT SUPERMAN AND WONDER WOMAN TO A STANDSTILL.
THEY'LL NEVER DOUBT THE POWER OF THE SUN AGAIN.
YOU--!
YES. GOOD ON YOU, KUAT. WHAT A BATTLE.
HM. SURE...
"...WHATEVER."

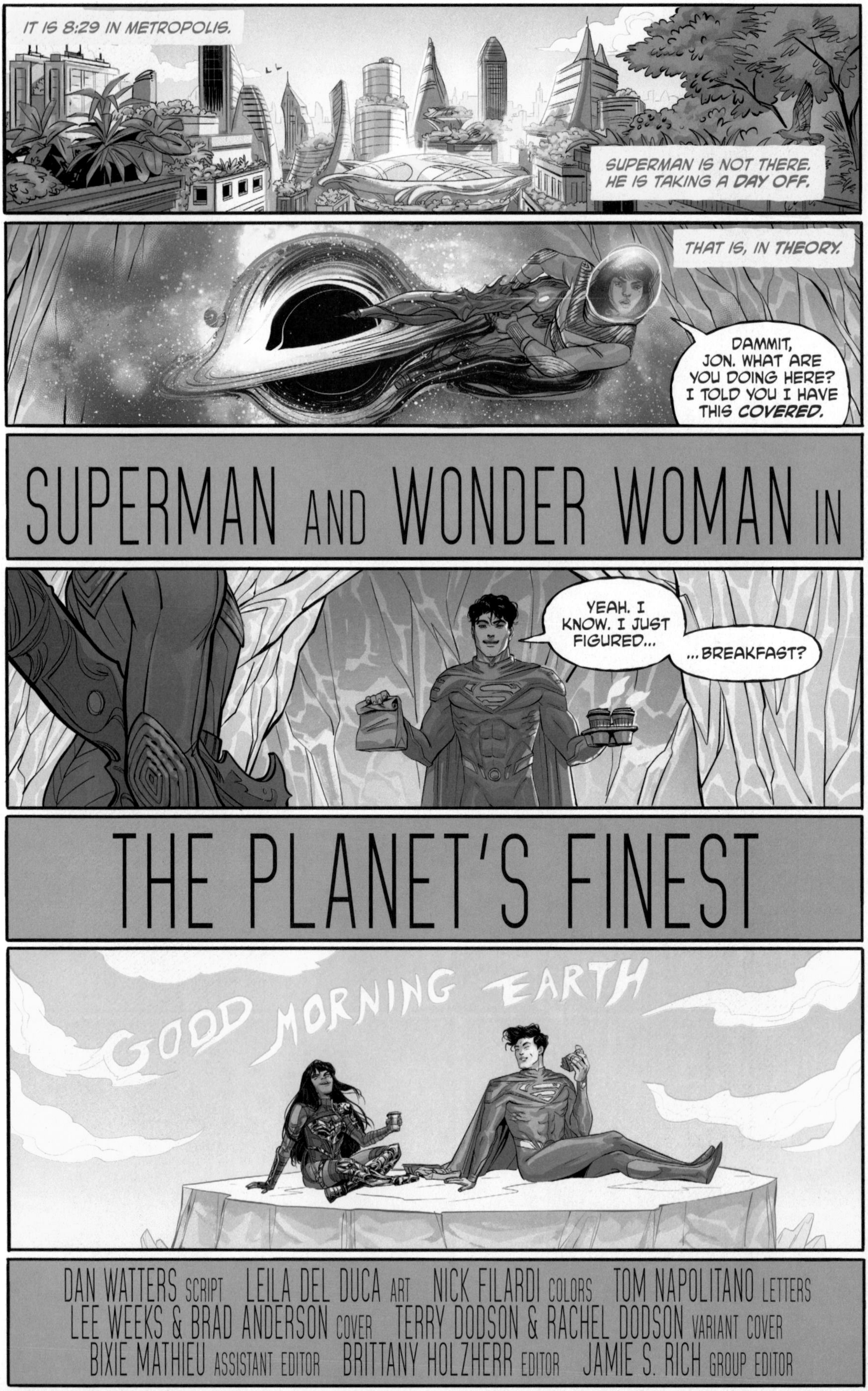
IT IS 8:29 IN METROPOLIS.
SUPERMAN IS NOT THERE. HE IS TAKING A DAY OFF.
THAT IS, IN THEORY.
DAMMIT, JON. WHAT ARE YOU DOING HERE? I TOLD YOU I HAVE THIS COVERED.
SUPERMAN AND WONDER WOMAN IN
YEAH. I KNOW. I JUST FIGURED...
...BREAKFAST?
THE PLANET'S FINEST
GOOD MORNING EARTH
DAN WATTERS SCRIPT LEILA DEL DUCA ART NICK FILARDI COLORS TOM NAPOLITANO LETTERS
LEE WEEKS & BRAD ANDERSON COVER TERRY DODSON & RACHEL DODSON VARIANT COVER
BIXIE MATHIEU ASSISTANT EDITOR BRITTANY HOLZHERR EDITOR JAMIE S. RICH GROUP EDITOR

SUPERMAN CREATED BY JERRY SIEGEL AND JOE SHUSTER. BY SPECIAL ARRANGEMENT WITH THE JERRY SIEGEL FAMILY. WONDER WOMAN CREATED BY WILLIAM MOULTON MARST

Future State: Immortal Wonder Woman #1
Cover Art by **JEN BARTEL**

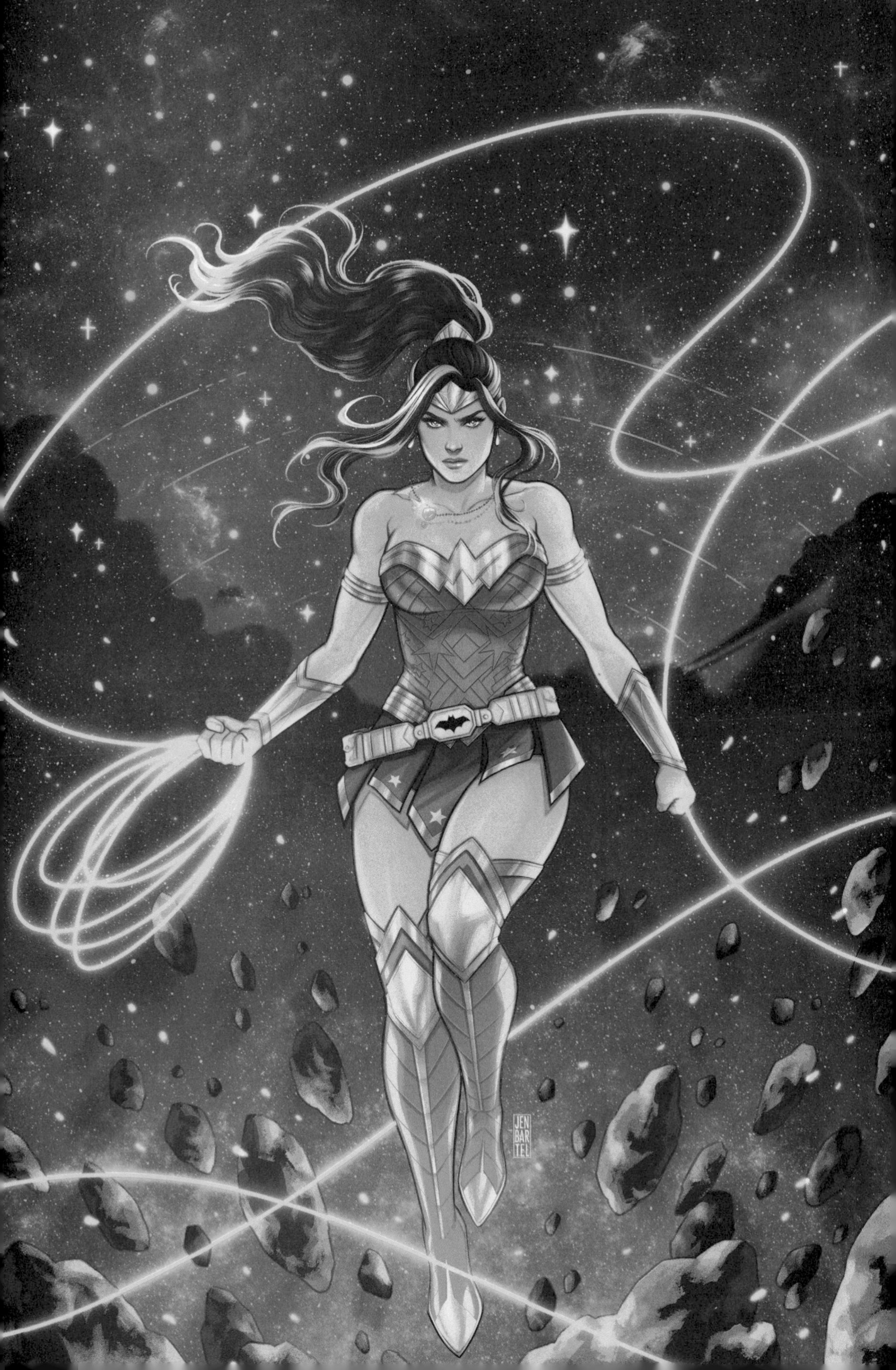
JEN
BAR
TEL

FUTURE STATE

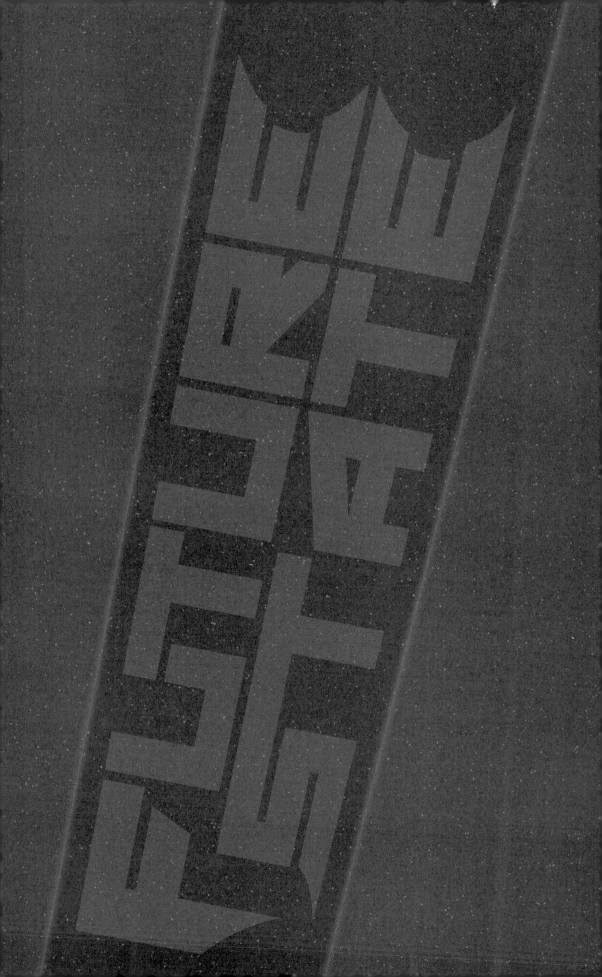

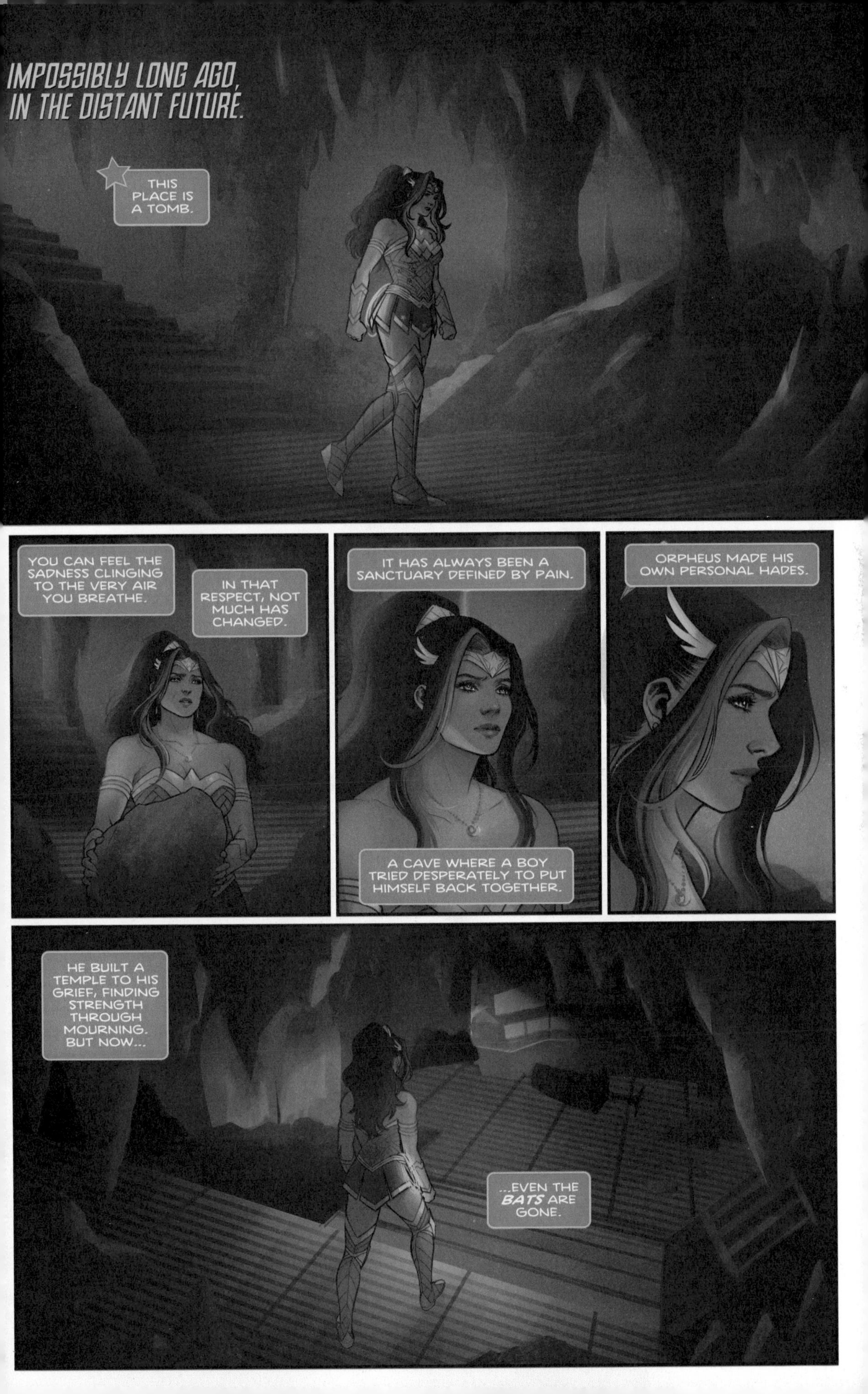
IMPOSSIBLY LONG AGO, IN THE DISTANT FUTURE.
THIS PLACE IS A TOMB.
YOU CAN FEEL THE SADNESS CLINGING TO THE VERY AIR YOU BREATHE.
IN THAT RESPECT, NOT MUCH HAS CHANGED.
IT HAS ALWAYS BEEN A SANCTUARY DEFINED BY PAIN.
A CAVE WHERE A BOY TRIED DESPERATELY TO PUT HIMSELF BACK TOGETHER.
ORPHEUS MADE HIS OWN PERSONAL HADES.
HE BUILT A TEMPLE TO HIS GRIEF, FINDING STRENGTH THROUGH MOURNING. BUT NOW...
...EVEN THE *BATS* ARE GONE.

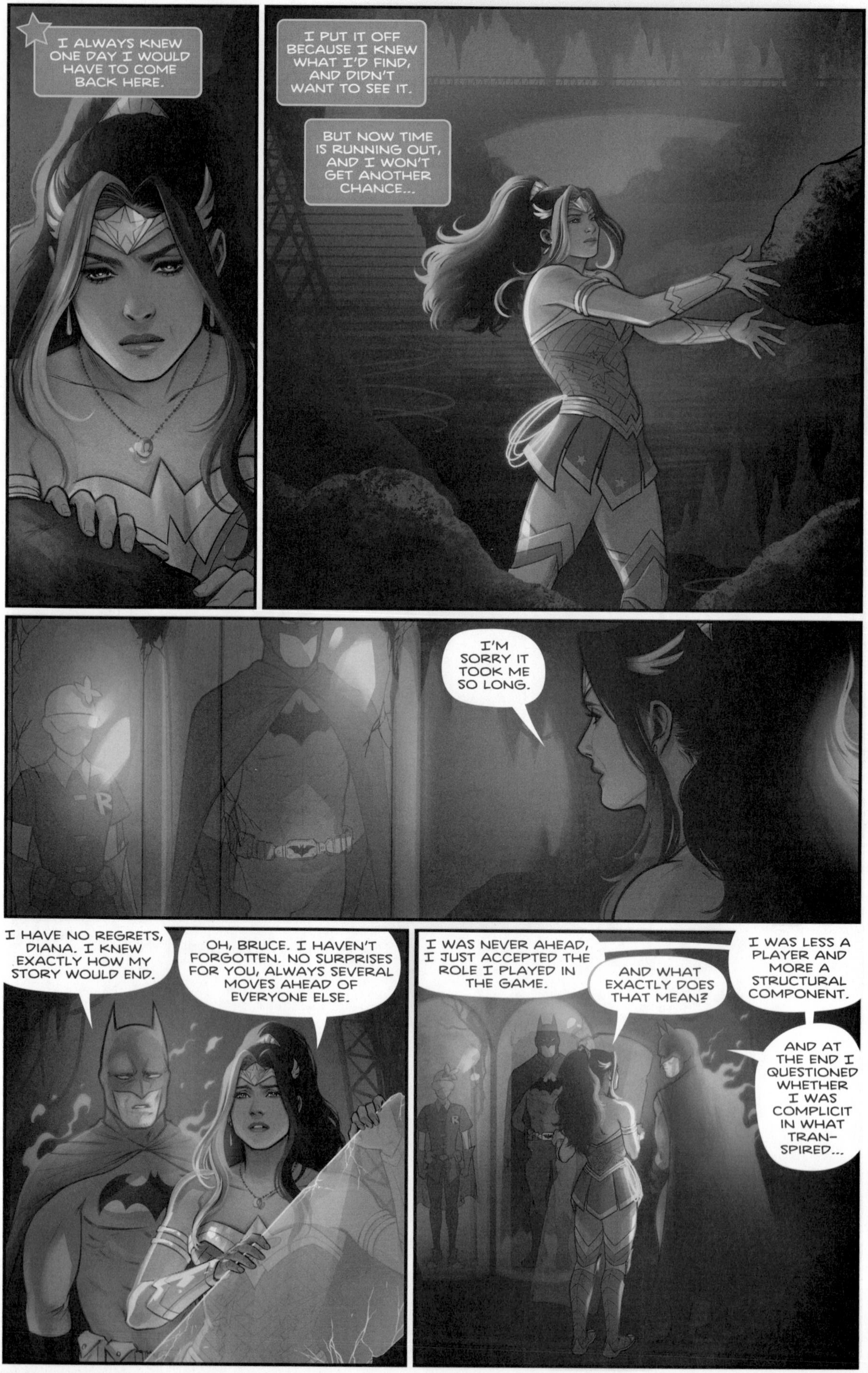

I ALWAYS KNEW ONE DAY I WOULD HAVE TO COME BACK HERE.
I PUT IT OFF BECAUSE I KNEW WHAT I'D FIND, AND DIDN'T WANT TO SEE IT.
BUT NOW TIME IS RUNNING OUT, AND I WON'T GET ANOTHER CHANCE...
I'M SORRY IT TOOK ME SO LONG.
I HAVE NO REGRETS, DIANA. I KNEW EXACTLY HOW MY STORY WOULD END.
OH, BRUCE. I HAVEN'T FORGOTTEN. NO SURPRISES FOR YOU, ALWAYS SEVERAL MOVES AHEAD OF EVERYONE ELSE.
I WAS NEVER AHEAD, I JUST ACCEPTED THE ROLE I PLAYED IN THE GAME.
AND WHAT EXACTLY DOES THAT MEAN?
I WAS LESS A PLAYER AND MORE A STRUCTURAL COMPONENT.
AND AT THE END I QUESTIONED WHETHER I WAS COMPLICIT IN WHAT TRAN-SPIRED...

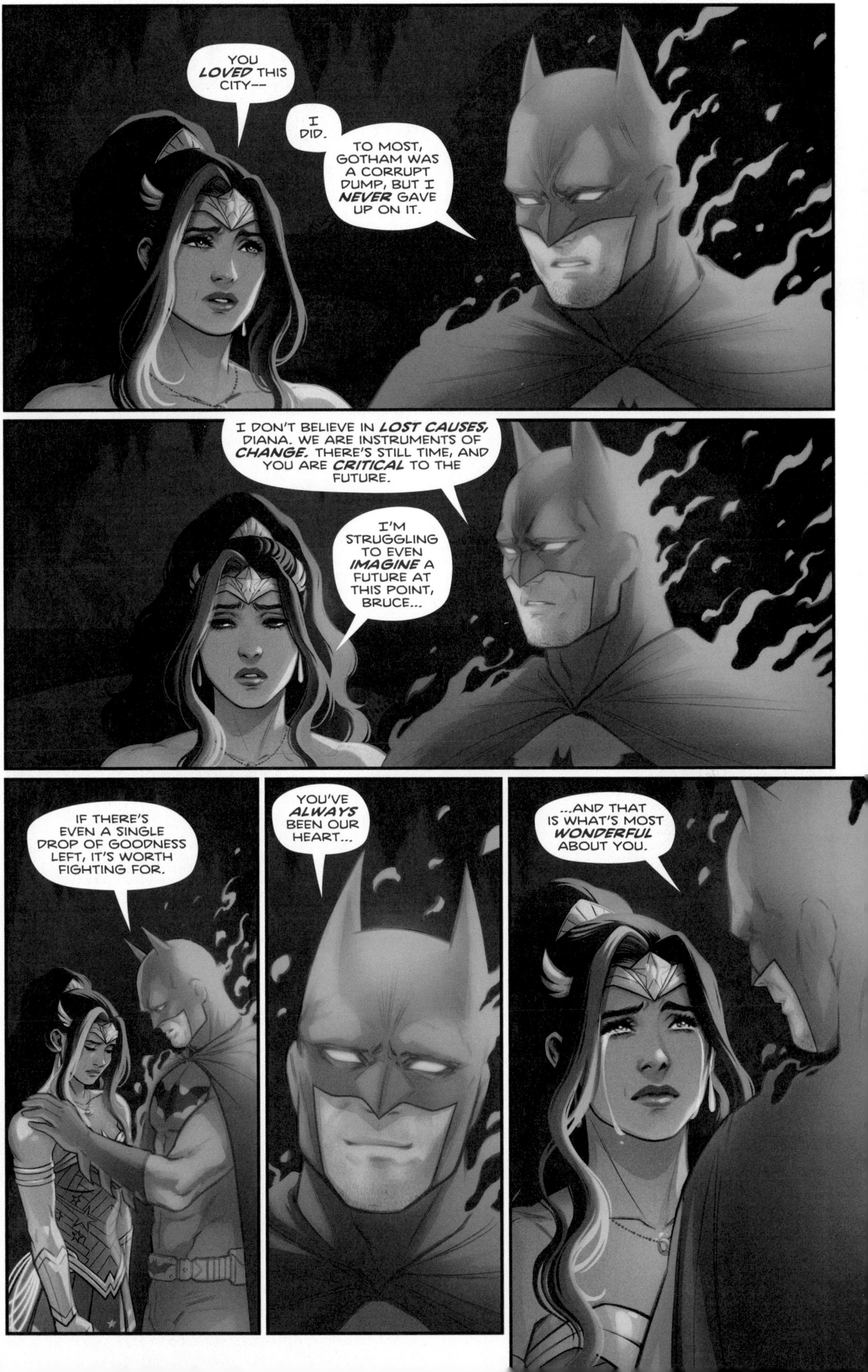
YOU LOVED THIS CITY--
I DID.
TO MOST, GOTHAM WAS A CORRUPT DUMP, BUT I NEVER GAVE UP ON IT.
I DON'T BELIEVE IN LOST CAUSES, DIANA. WE ARE INSTRUMENTS OF CHANGE. THERE'S STILL TIME, AND YOU ARE CRITICAL TO THE FUTURE.
I'M STRUGGLING TO EVEN IMAGINE A FUTURE AT THIS POINT, BRUCE...
IF THERE'S EVEN A SINGLE DROP OF GOODNESS LEFT, IT'S WORTH FIGHTING FOR.
YOU'VE ALWAYS BEEN OUR HEART...
...AND THAT IS WHAT'S MOST WONDERFUL ABOUT YOU.

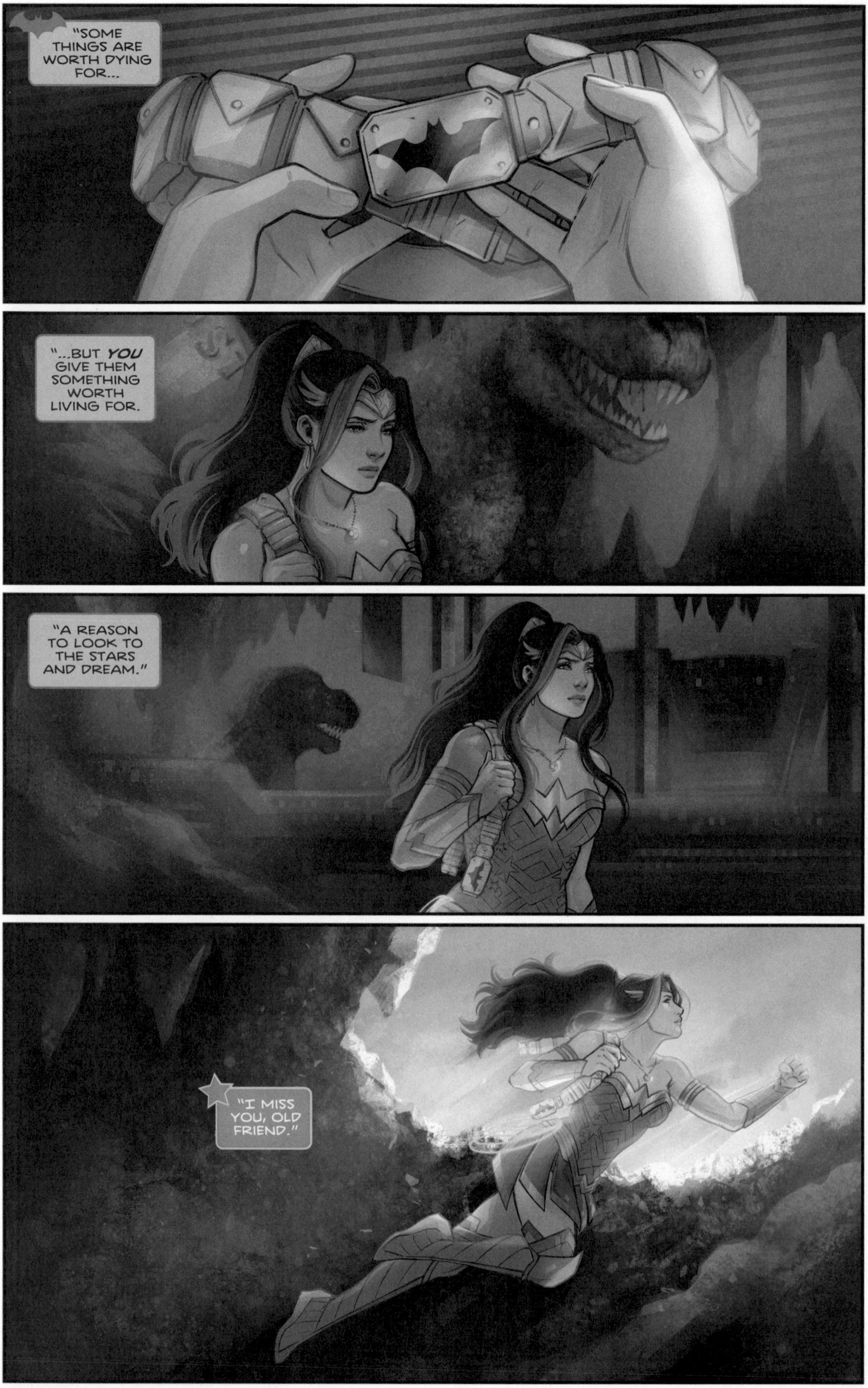
"SOME THINGS ARE WORTH DYING FOR...
"...BUT *YOU* GIVE THEM SOMETHING WORTH LIVING FOR.
"A REASON TO LOOK TO THE STARS AND DREAM."
"I MISS YOU, OLD FRIEND."

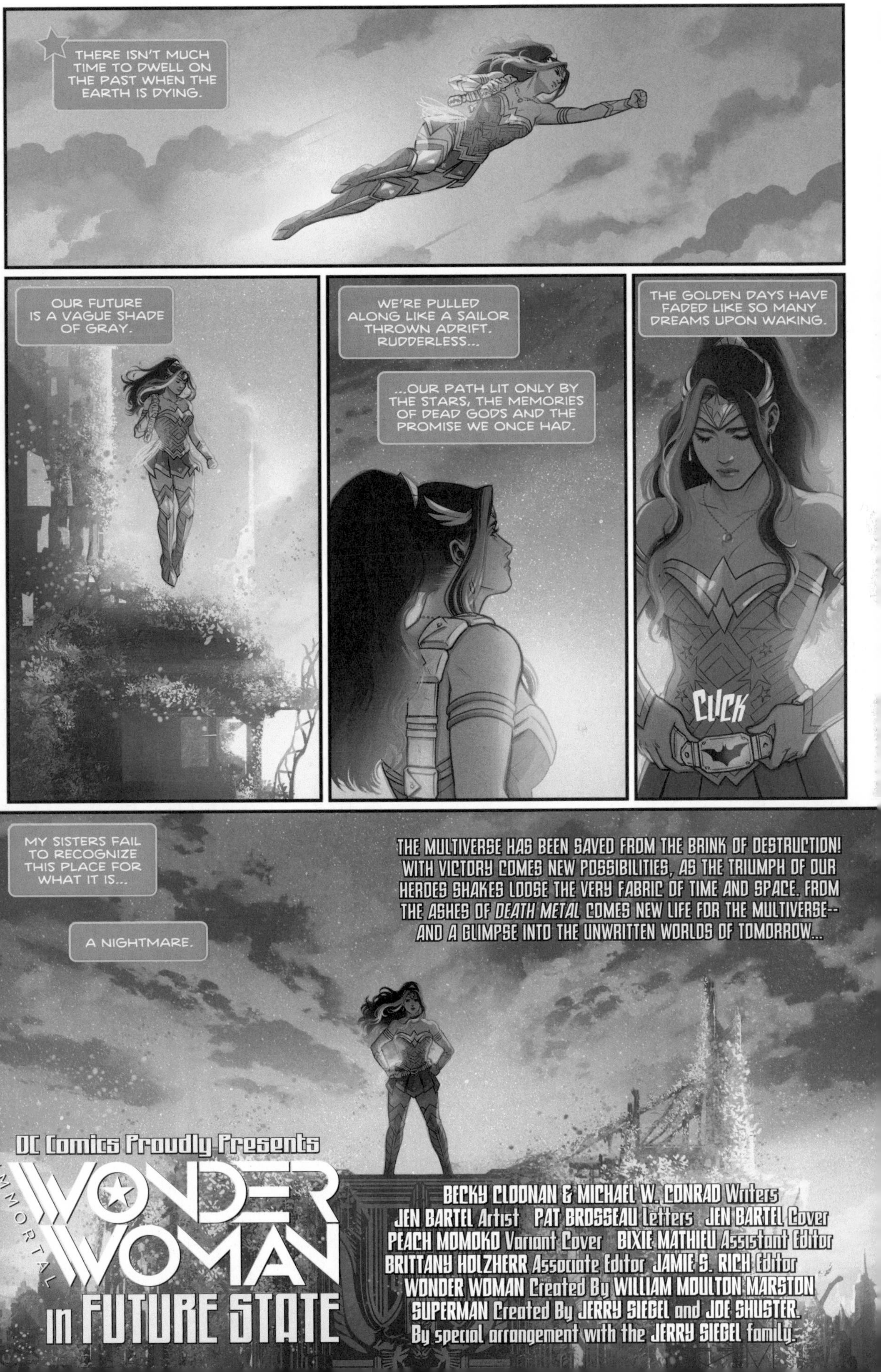
THERE ISN'T MUCH TIME TO DWELL ON THE PAST WHEN THE EARTH IS DYING.
OUR FUTURE IS A VAGUE SHADE OF GRAY.
WE'RE PULLED ALONG LIKE A SAILOR THROWN ADRIFT. RUDDERLESS...
...OUR PATH LIT ONLY BY THE STARS, THE MEMORIES OF DEAD GODS AND THE PROMISE WE ONCE HAD.
THE GOLDEN DAYS HAVE FADED LIKE SO MANY DREAMS UPON WAKING.
CLICK
MY SISTERS FAIL TO RECOGNIZE THIS PLACE FOR WHAT IT IS...
A NIGHTMARE.
THE MULTIVERSE HAS BEEN SAVED FROM THE BRINK OF DESTRUCTION! WITH VICTORY COMES NEW POSSIBILITIES, AS THE TRIUMPH OF OUR HEROES SHAKES LOOSE THE VERY FABRIC OF TIME AND SPACE. FROM THE ASHES OF *DEATH METAL* COMES NEW LIFE FOR THE MULTIVERSE--AND A GLIMPSE INTO THE UNWRITTEN WORLDS OF TOMORROW...
DC Comics Proudly Presents
IMMORTAL WONDER WOMAN in FUTURE STATE
BECKY CLOONAN & MICHAEL W. CONRAD Writers
JEN BARTEL Artist PAT BROSSEAU Letters JEN BARTEL Cover
PEACH MOMOKO Variant Cover BIXIE MATHIEU Assistant Editor
BRITTANY HOLZHERR Associate Editor JAMIE S. RICH Editor
WONDER WOMAN Created By WILLIAM MOULTON MARSTON
SUPERMAN Created By JERRY SIEGEL and JOE SHUSTER.
By special arrangement with the JERRY SIEGEL family.

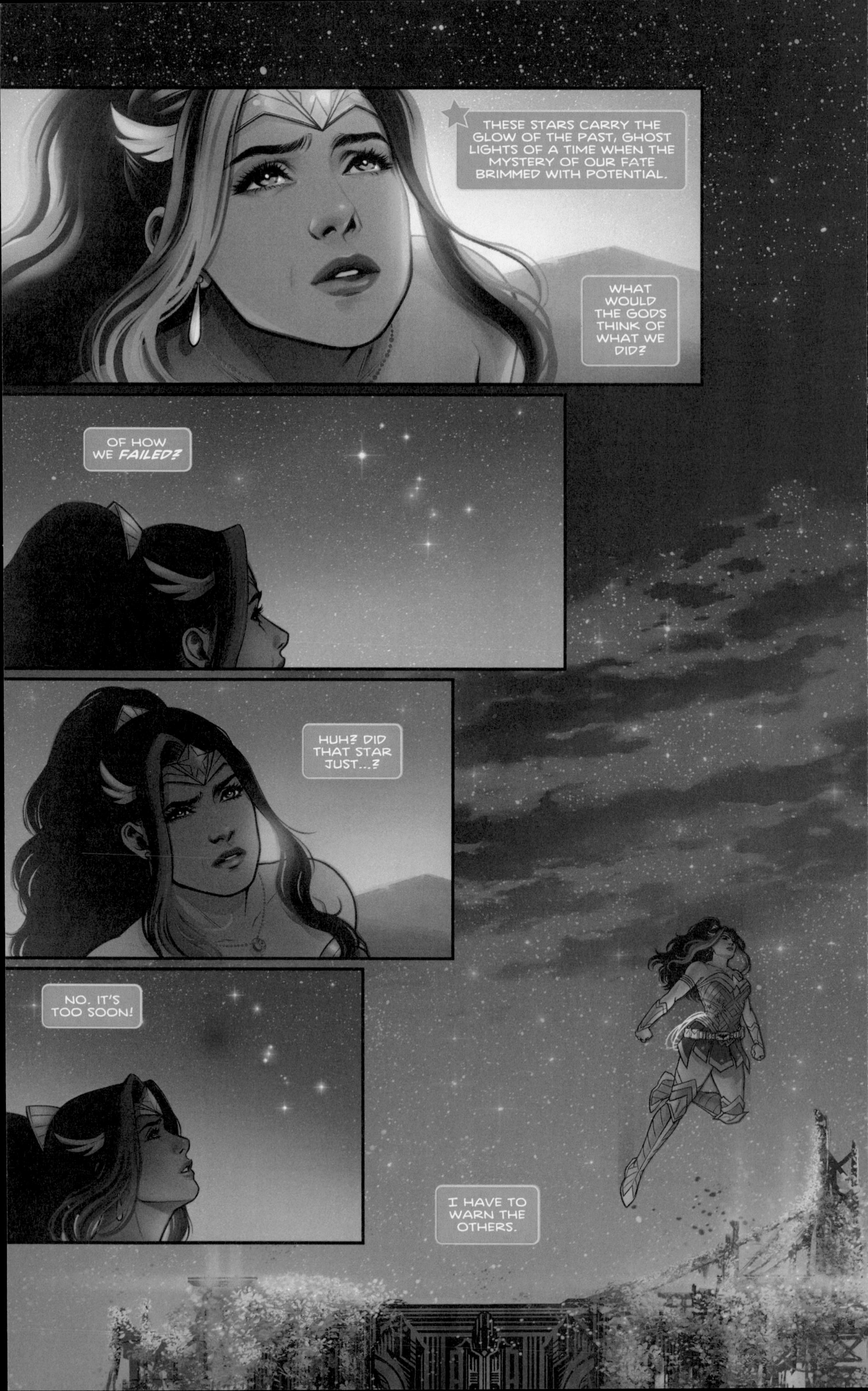
THESE STARS CARRY THE GLOW OF THE PAST, GHOST LIGHTS OF A TIME WHEN THE MYSTERY OF OUR FATE BRIMMED WITH POTENTIAL.
WHAT WOULD THE GODS THINK OF WHAT WE DID?
OF HOW WE *FAILED*?
HUH? DID THAT STAR JUST...?
NO. IT'S TOO SOON!
I HAVE TO WARN THE OTHERS.

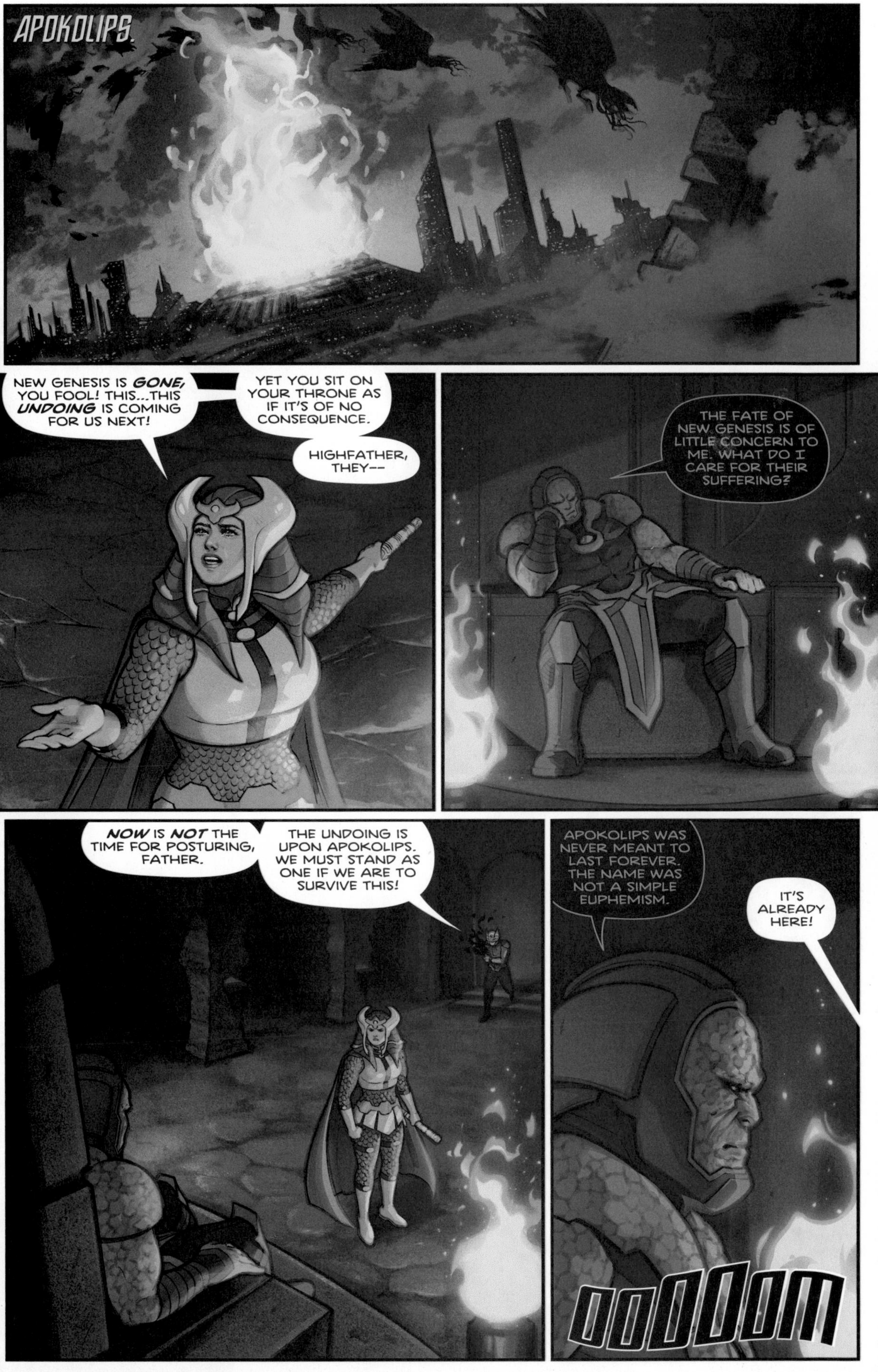
APOKOLIPS.
NEW GENESIS IS GONE, YOU FOOL! THIS...THIS UNDOING IS COMING FOR US NEXT!
YET YOU SIT ON YOUR THRONE AS IF IT'S OF NO CONSEQUENCE.
HIGHFATHER, THEY--
THE FATE OF NEW GENESIS IS OF LITTLE CONCERN TO ME. WHAT DO I CARE FOR THEIR SUFFERING?
NOW IS NOT THE TIME FOR POSTURING, FATHER.
THE UNDOING IS UPON APOKOLIPS. WE MUST STAND AS ONE IF WE ARE TO SURVIVE THIS!
APOKOLIPS WAS NEVER MEANT TO LAST FOREVER. THE NAME WAS NOT A SIMPLE EUPHEMISM.
IT'S ALREADY HERE!
OOOOOM

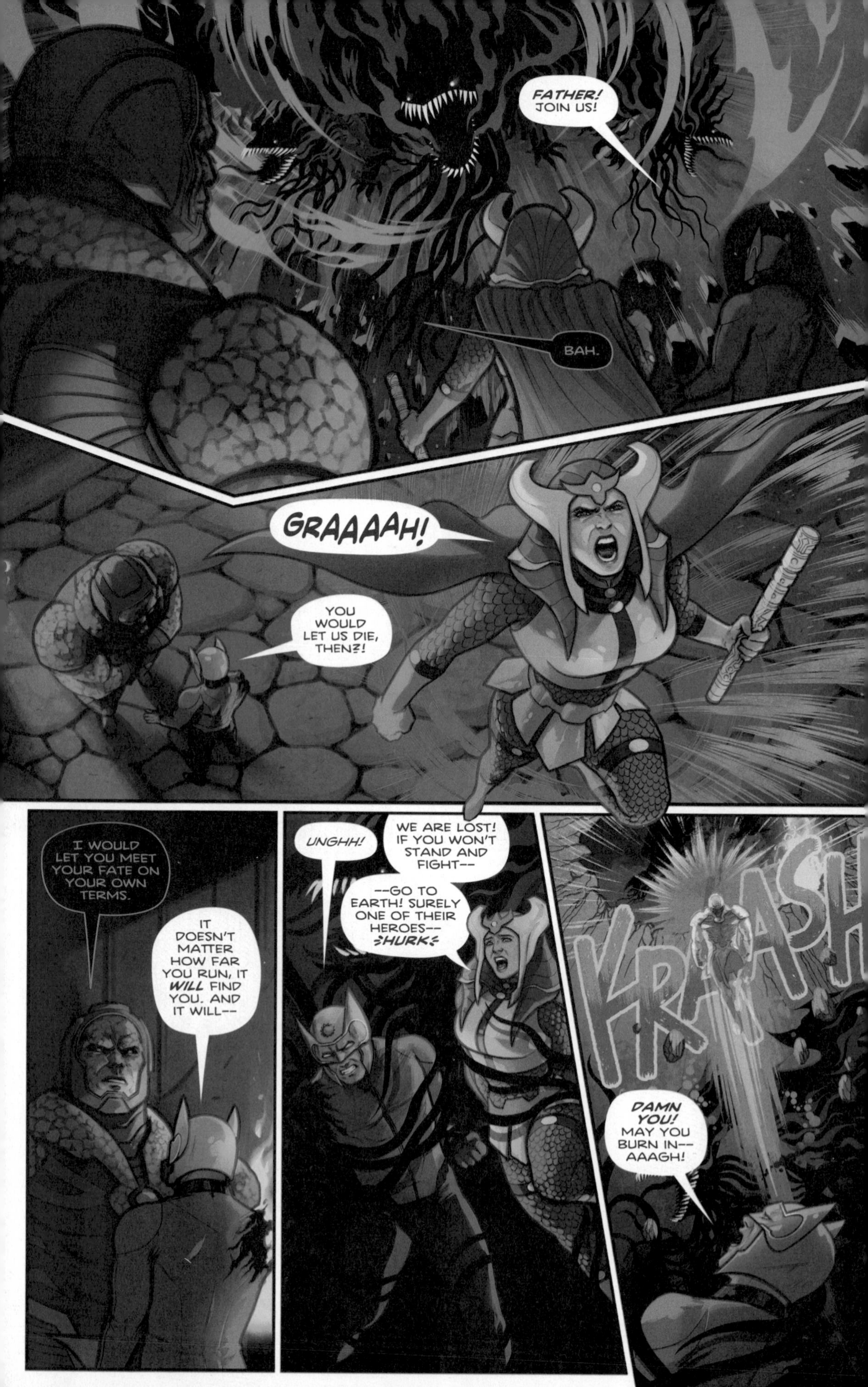
FATHER! JOIN US!
BAH.
GRAAAAH!
YOU WOULD LET US DIE, THEN?!
I WOULD LET YOU MEET YOUR FATE ON YOUR OWN TERMS.
IT DOESN'T MATTER HOW FAR YOU RUN, IT WILL FIND YOU. AND IT WILL--
UNGHH!
WE ARE LOST! IF YOU WON'T STAND AND FIGHT--
--GO TO EARTH! SURELY ONE OF THEIR HEROES-- HURK
KRAASH
DAMN YOU! MAY YOU BURN IN-- AAAGH!

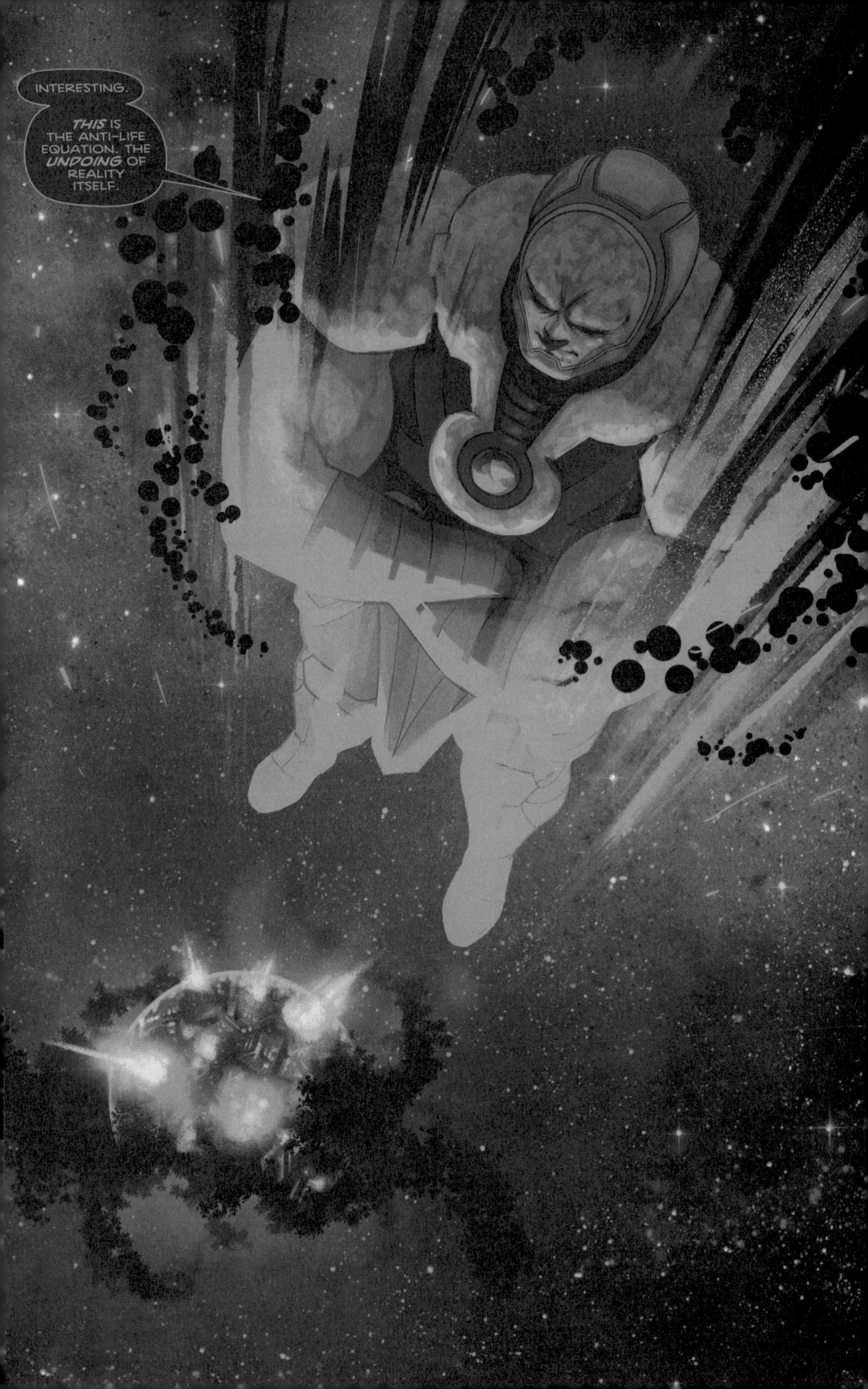
INTERESTING.
THIS IS THE ANTI-LIFE EQUATION. THE UNDOING OF REALITY ITSELF.

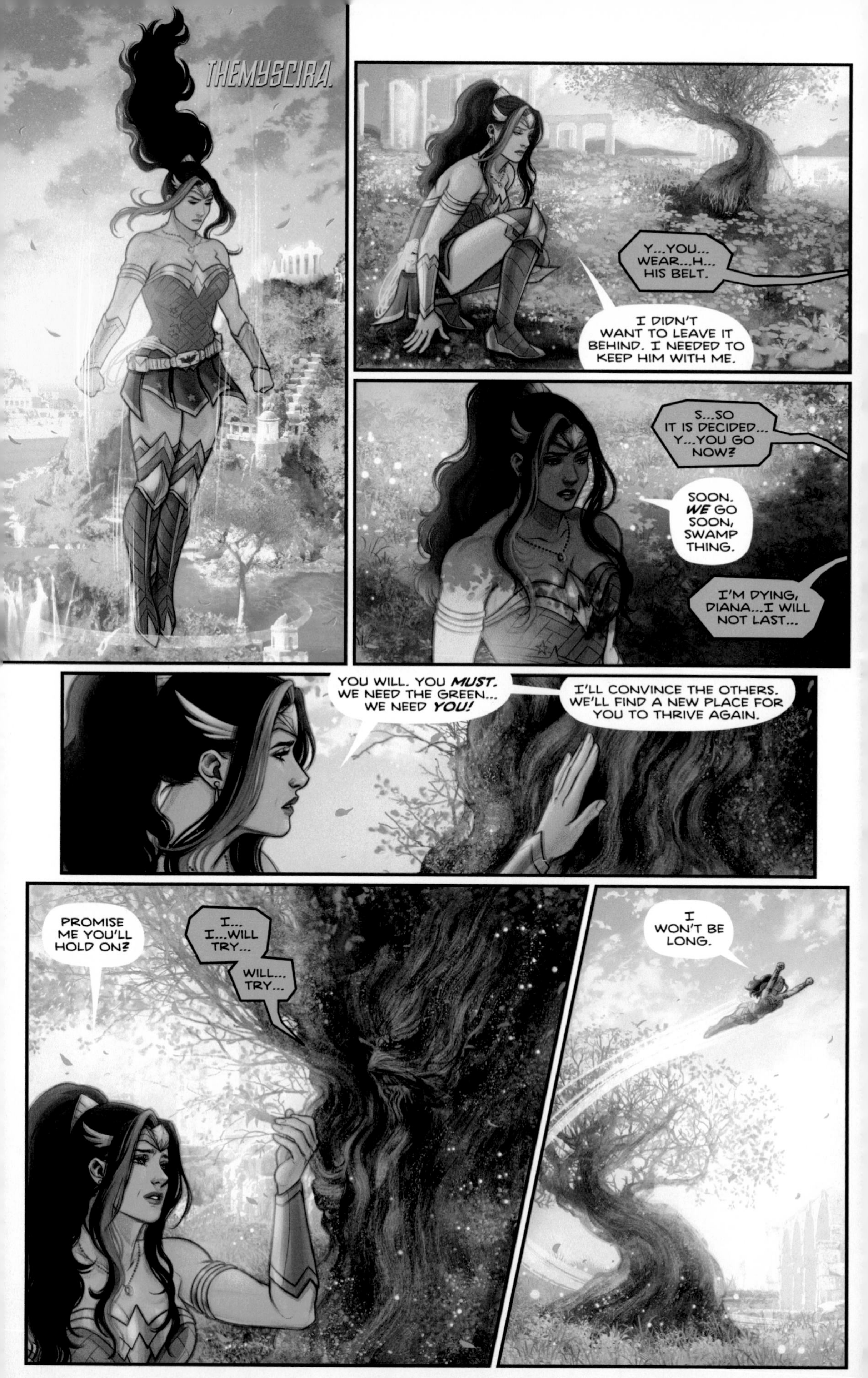
THEMYSCIRA.
Y...YOU... WEAR...H... HIS BELT.
I DIDN'T WANT TO LEAVE IT BEHIND. I NEEDED TO KEEP HIM WITH ME.
S...SO IT IS DECIDED... Y...YOU GO NOW?
SOON. **WE** GO SOON, SWAMP THING.
I'M DYING, DIANA...I WILL NOT LAST...
YOU WILL. YOU **MUST.** WE NEED THE GREEN... WE NEED **YOU!**
I'LL CONVINCE THE OTHERS. WE'LL FIND A NEW PLACE FOR YOU TO THRIVE AGAIN.
PROMISE ME YOU'LL HOLD ON?
I... I...WILL TRY...
WILL... TRY...
I WON'T BE LONG.

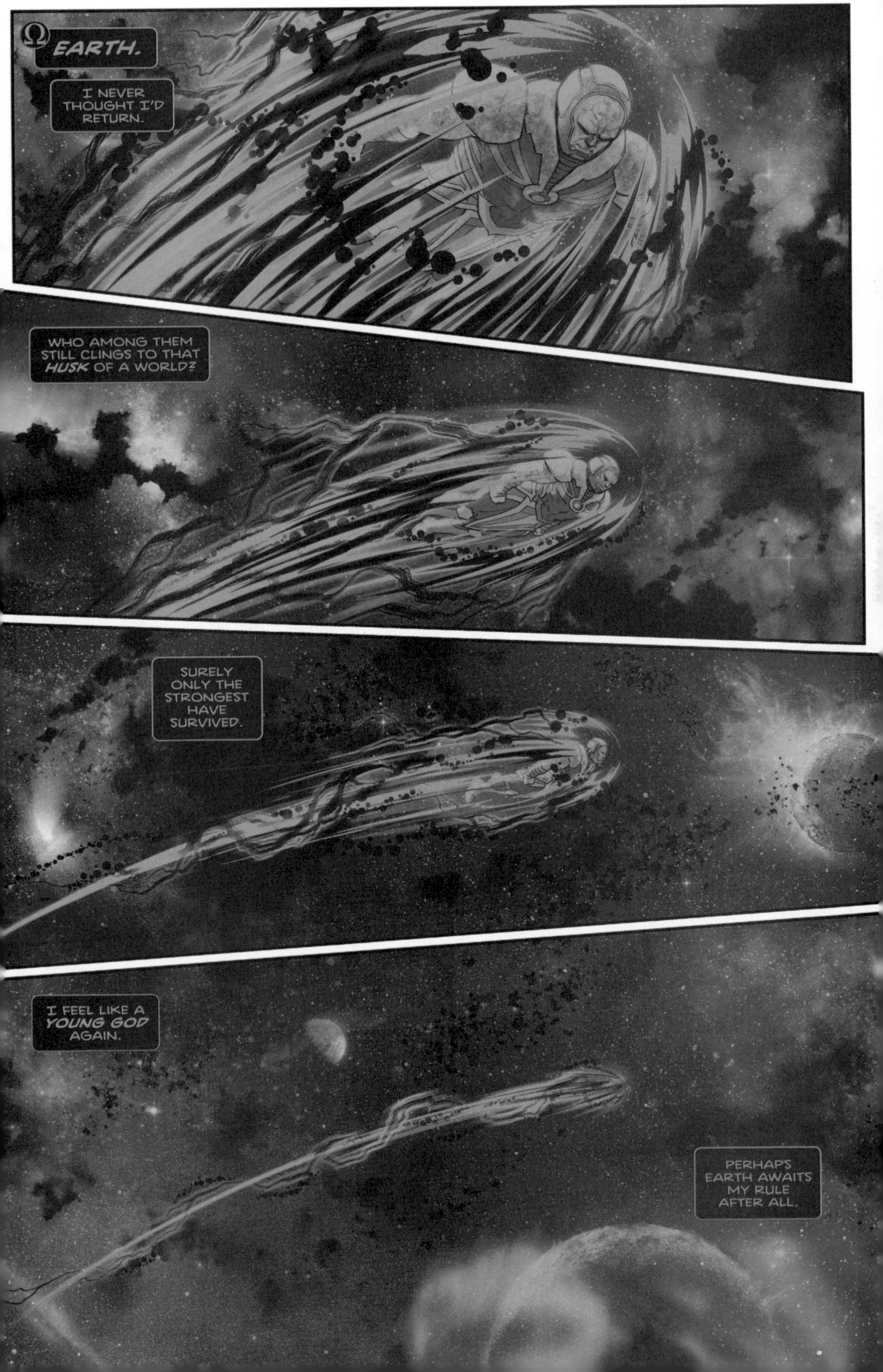
EARTH.
I NEVER THOUGHT I'D RETURN.
WHO AMONG THEM STILL CLINGS TO THAT HUSK OF A WORLD?
SURELY ONLY THE STRONGEST HAVE SURVIVED.
I FEEL LIKE A YOUNG GOD AGAIN.
PERHAPS EARTH AWAITS MY RULE AFTER ALL.

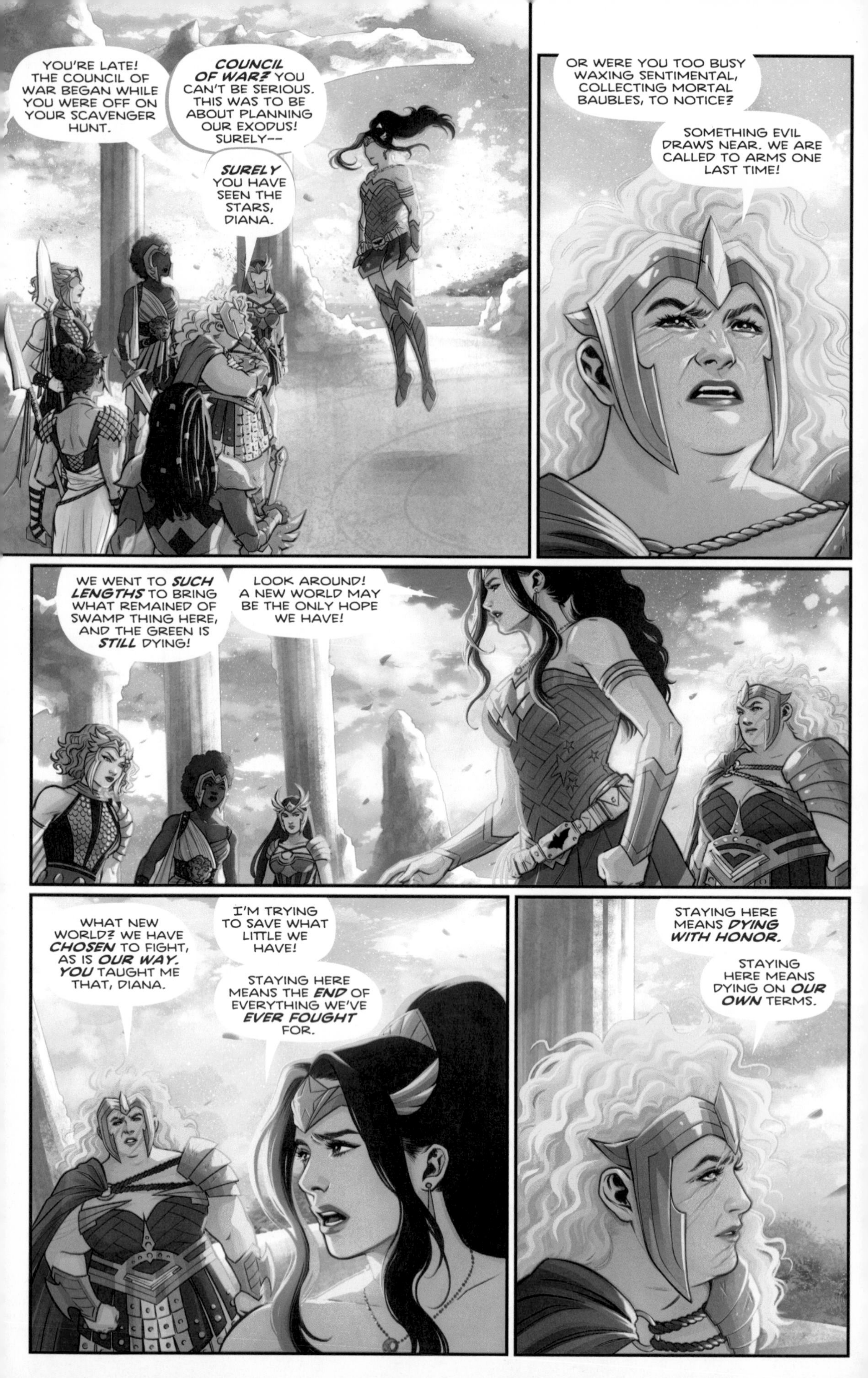

YOU'RE LATE! THE COUNCIL OF WAR BEGAN WHILE YOU WERE OFF ON YOUR SCAVENGER HUNT.
COUNCIL OF WAR? YOU CAN'T BE SERIOUS. THIS WAS TO BE ABOUT PLANNING OUR EXODUS! SURELY--
SURELY YOU HAVE SEEN THE STARS, DIANA.
OR WERE YOU TOO BUSY WAXING SENTIMENTAL, COLLECTING MORTAL BAUBLES, TO NOTICE?
SOMETHING EVIL DRAWS NEAR. WE ARE CALLED TO ARMS ONE LAST TIME!
WE WENT TO SUCH LENGTHS TO BRING WHAT REMAINED OF SWAMP THING HERE, AND THE GREEN IS STILL DYING!
LOOK AROUND! A NEW WORLD MAY BE THE ONLY HOPE WE HAVE!
WHAT NEW WORLD? WE HAVE CHOSEN TO FIGHT, AS IS OUR WAY. YOU TAUGHT ME THAT, DIANA.
I'M TRYING TO SAVE WHAT LITTLE WE HAVE!
STAYING HERE MEANS THE END OF EVERYTHING WE'VE EVER FOUGHT FOR.
STAYING HERE MEANS DYING WITH HONOR.
STAYING HERE MEANS DYING ON OUR OWN TERMS.

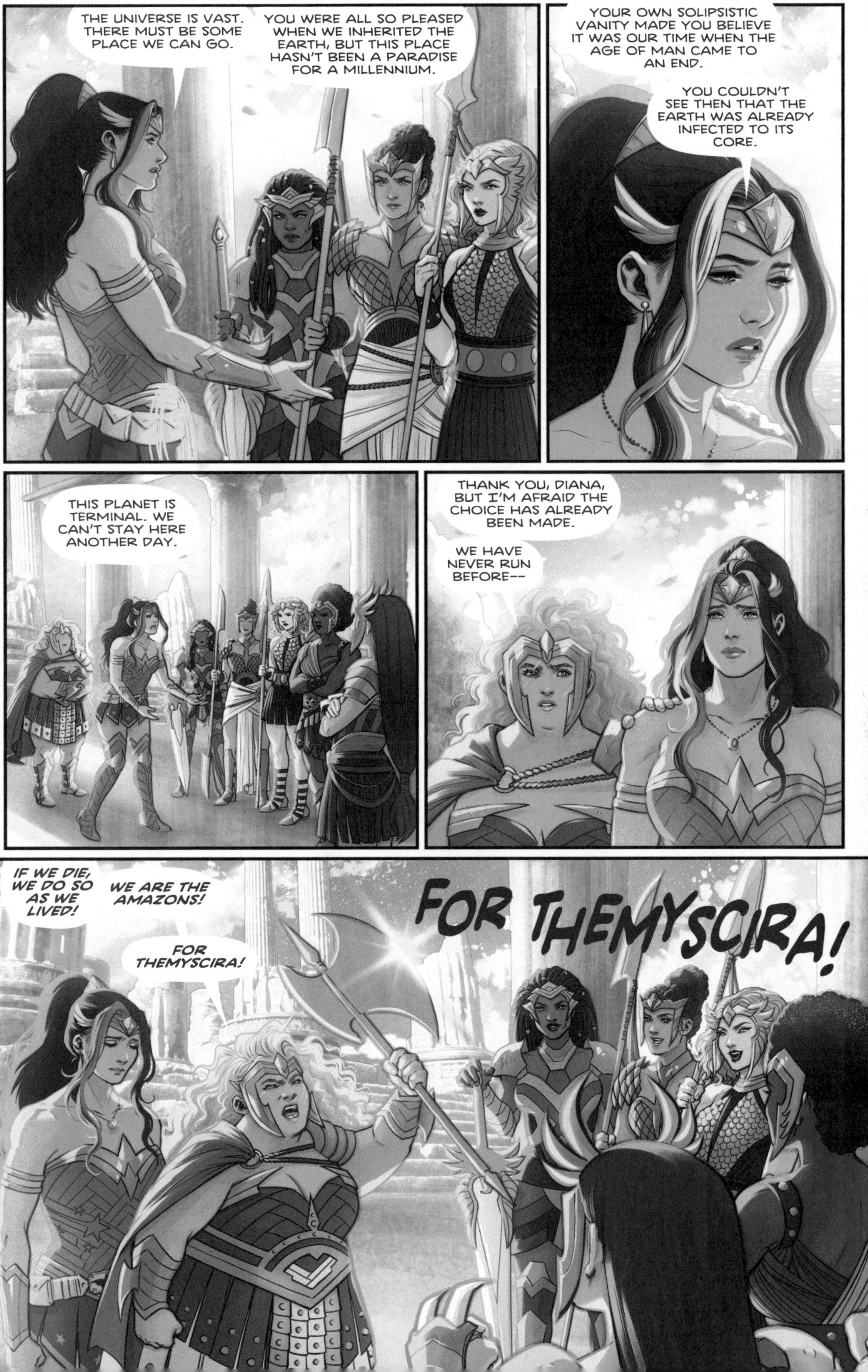
THE UNIVERSE IS VAST. THERE MUST BE SOME PLACE WE CAN GO.
YOU WERE ALL SO PLEASED WHEN WE INHERITED THE EARTH, BUT THIS PLACE HASN'T BEEN A PARADISE FOR A MILLENNIUM.
YOUR OWN SOLIPSISTIC VANITY MADE YOU BELIEVE IT WAS OUR TIME WHEN THE AGE OF MAN CAME TO AN END.
YOU COULDN'T SEE THEN THAT THE EARTH WAS ALREADY INFECTED TO ITS CORE.
THIS PLANET IS TERMINAL. WE CAN'T STAY HERE ANOTHER DAY.
THANK YOU, DIANA, BUT I'M AFRAID THE CHOICE HAS ALREADY BEEN MADE.
WE HAVE NEVER RUN BEFORE--
IF WE DIE, WE DO SO AS WE LIVED!
WE ARE THE AMAZONS!
FOR THEMYSCIRA!
FOR THEMYSCIRA!

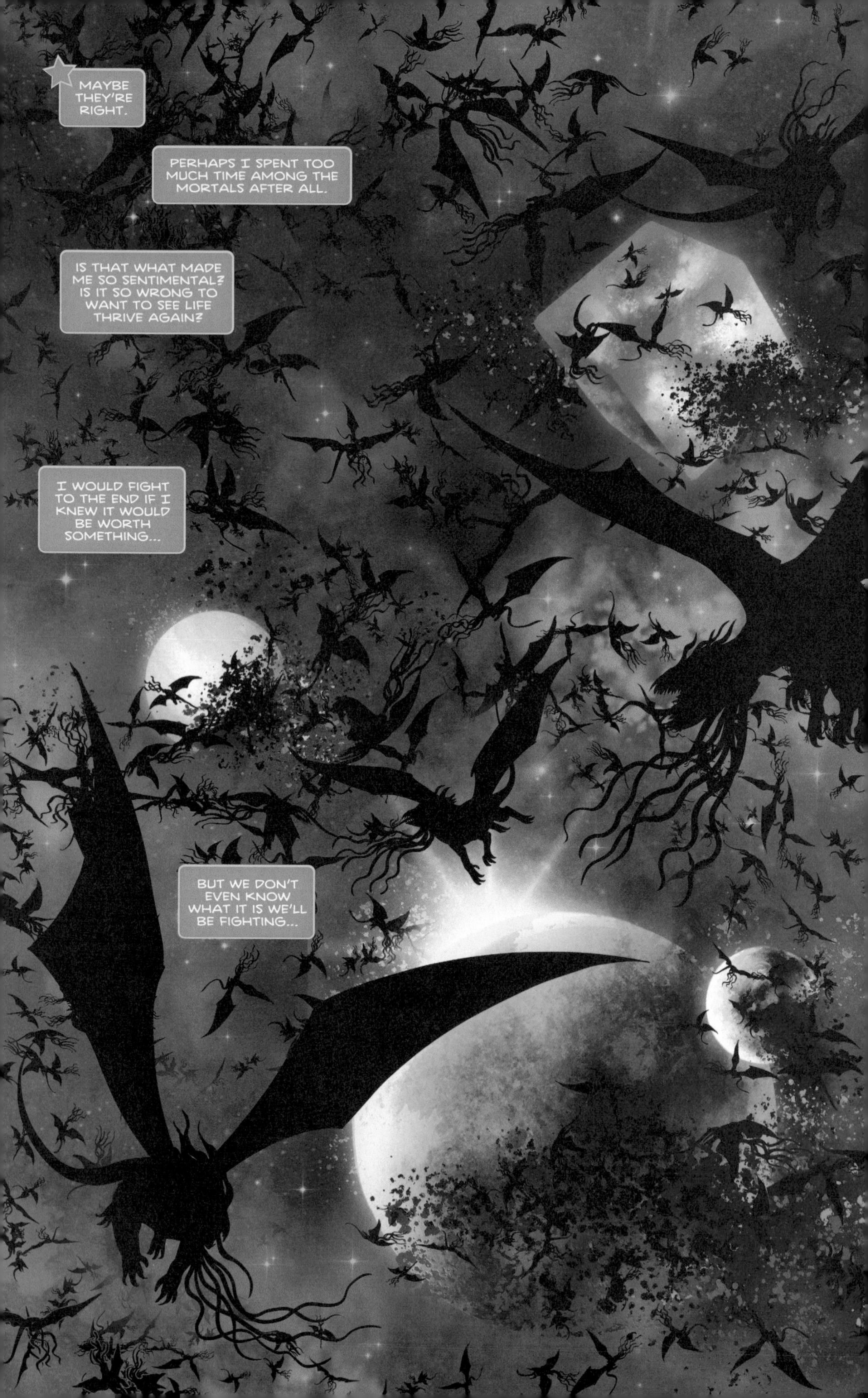
MAYBE THEY'RE RIGHT.
PERHAPS I SPENT TOO MUCH TIME AMONG THE MORTALS AFTER ALL.
IS THAT WHAT MADE ME SO SENTIMENTAL? IS IT SO WRONG TO WANT TO SEE LIFE THRIVE AGAIN?
I WOULD FIGHT TO THE END IF I KNEW IT WOULD BE WORTH SOMETHING...
BUT WE DON'T EVEN KNOW WHAT IT IS WE'LL BE FIGHTING...

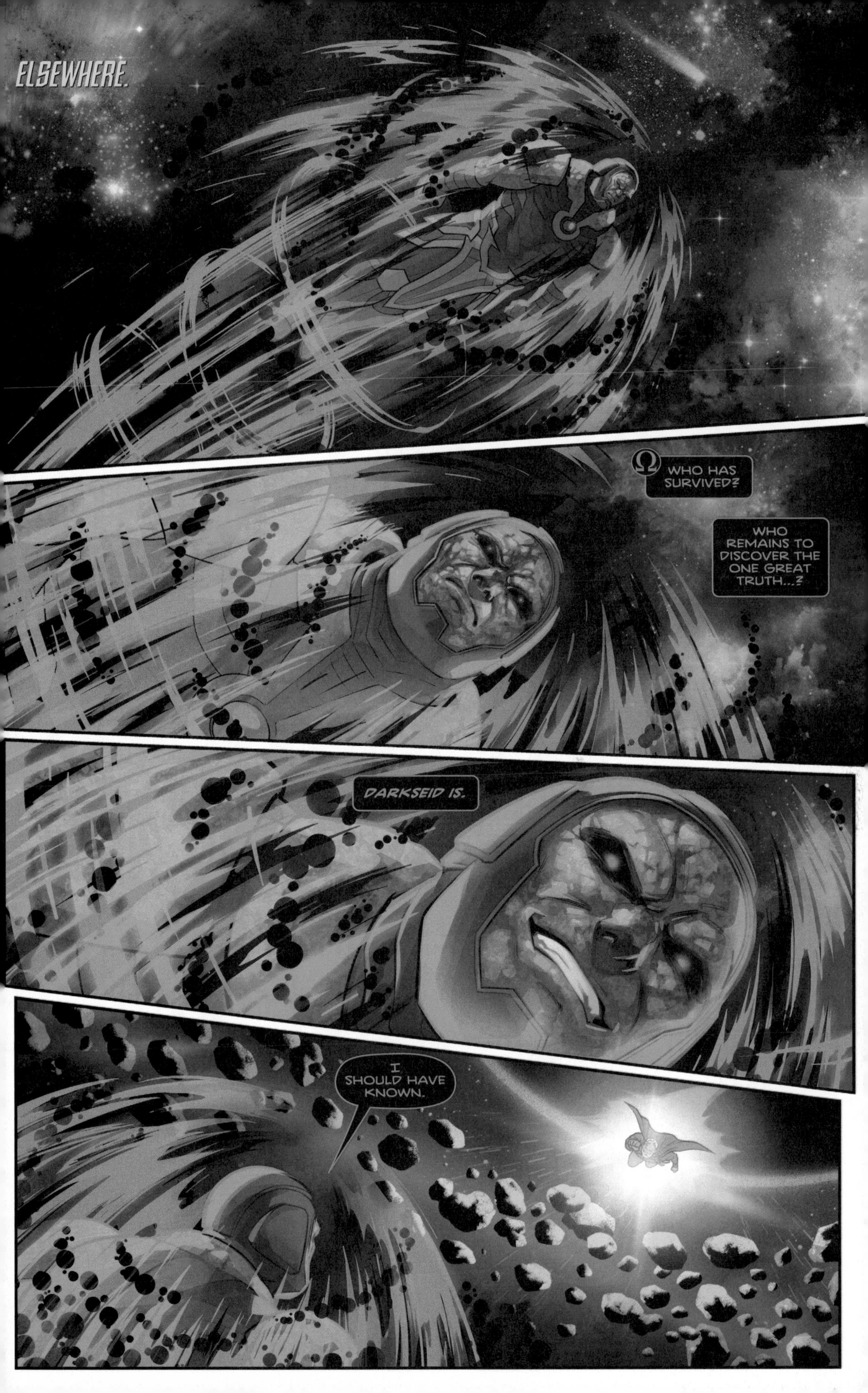
ELSEWHERE.
WHO HAS SURVIVED?
WHO REMAINS TO DISCOVER THE ONE GREAT TRUTH...?
DARKSEID IS.
I SHOULD HAVE KNOWN.

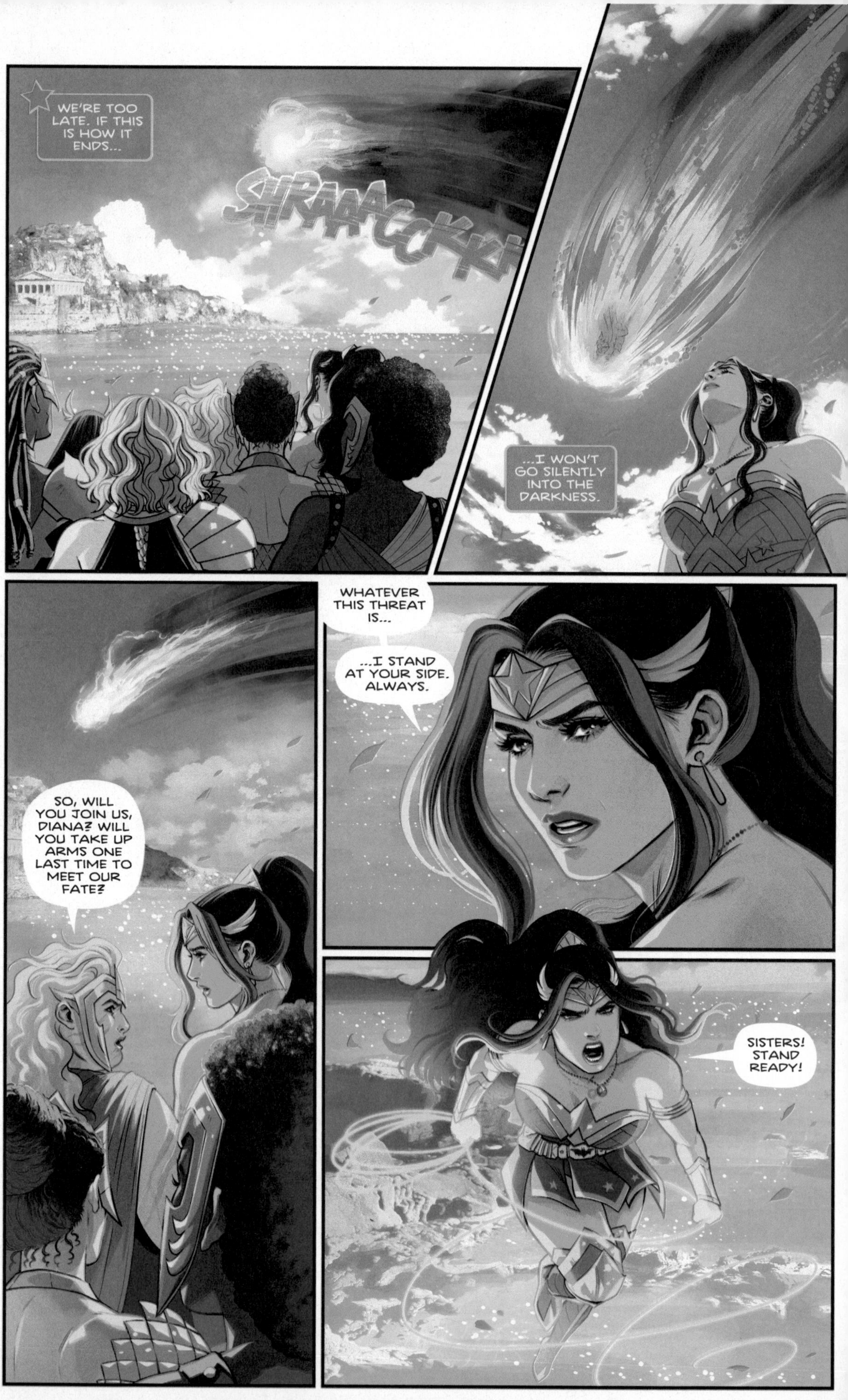
WE'RE TOO LATE. IF THIS IS HOW IT ENDS...
SHRAAACKKK!
...I WON'T GO SILENTLY INTO THE DARKNESS.
SO, WILL YOU JOIN US, DIANA? WILL YOU TAKE UP ARMS ONE LAST TIME TO MEET OUR FATE?
WHATEVER THIS THREAT IS...
...I STAND AT YOUR SIDE. ALWAYS.
SISTERS! STAND READY!

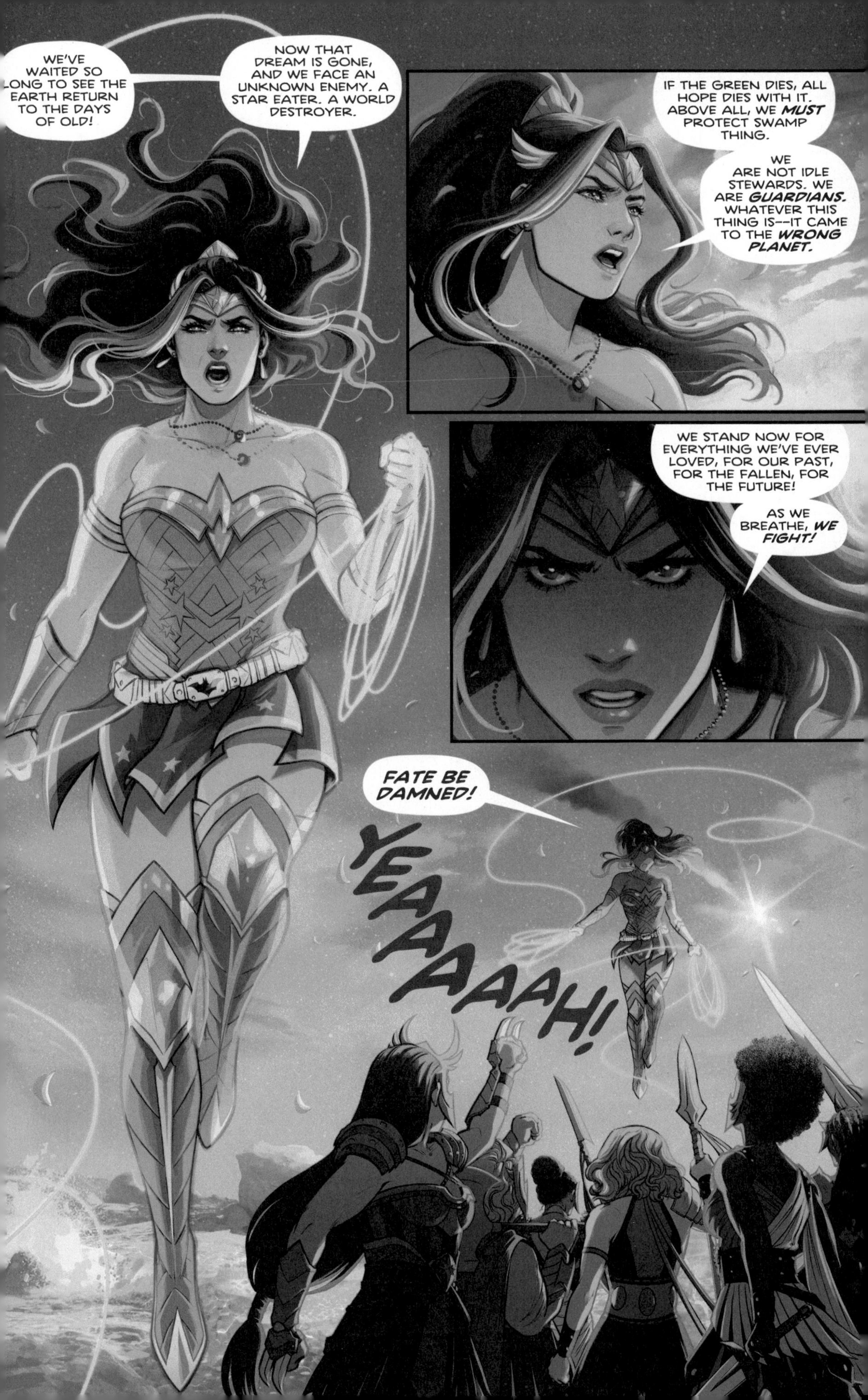
WE'VE WAITED SO LONG TO SEE THE EARTH RETURN TO THE DAYS OF OLD!
NOW THAT DREAM IS GONE, AND WE FACE AN UNKNOWN ENEMY. A STAR EATER. A WORLD DESTROYER.
IF THE GREEN DIES, ALL HOPE DIES WITH IT. ABOVE ALL, WE MUST PROTECT SWAMP THING.
WE ARE NOT IDLE STEWARDS. WE ARE GUARDIANS. WHATEVER THIS THING IS--IT CAME TO THE WRONG PLANET.
WE STAND NOW FOR EVERYTHING WE'VE EVER LOVED, FOR OUR PAST, FOR THE FALLEN, FOR THE FUTURE!
AS WE BREATHE, WE FIGHT!
FATE BE DAMNED!
YEAAAAAH!

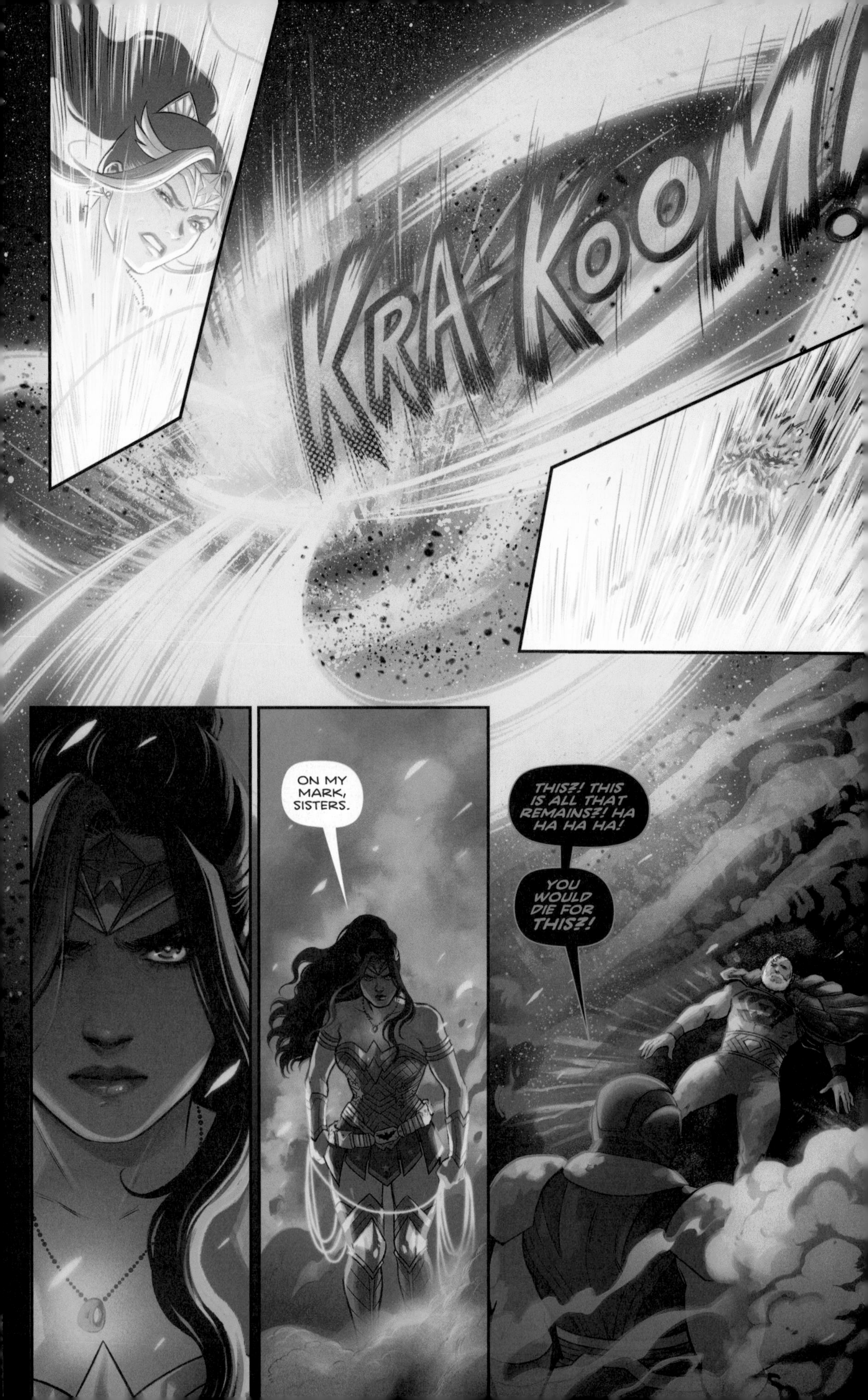
KRA-KOOM!
ON MY MARK, SISTERS.
THIS?! THIS IS ALL THAT REMAINS?! HA HA HA HA!
YOU WOULD DIE FOR THIS?!

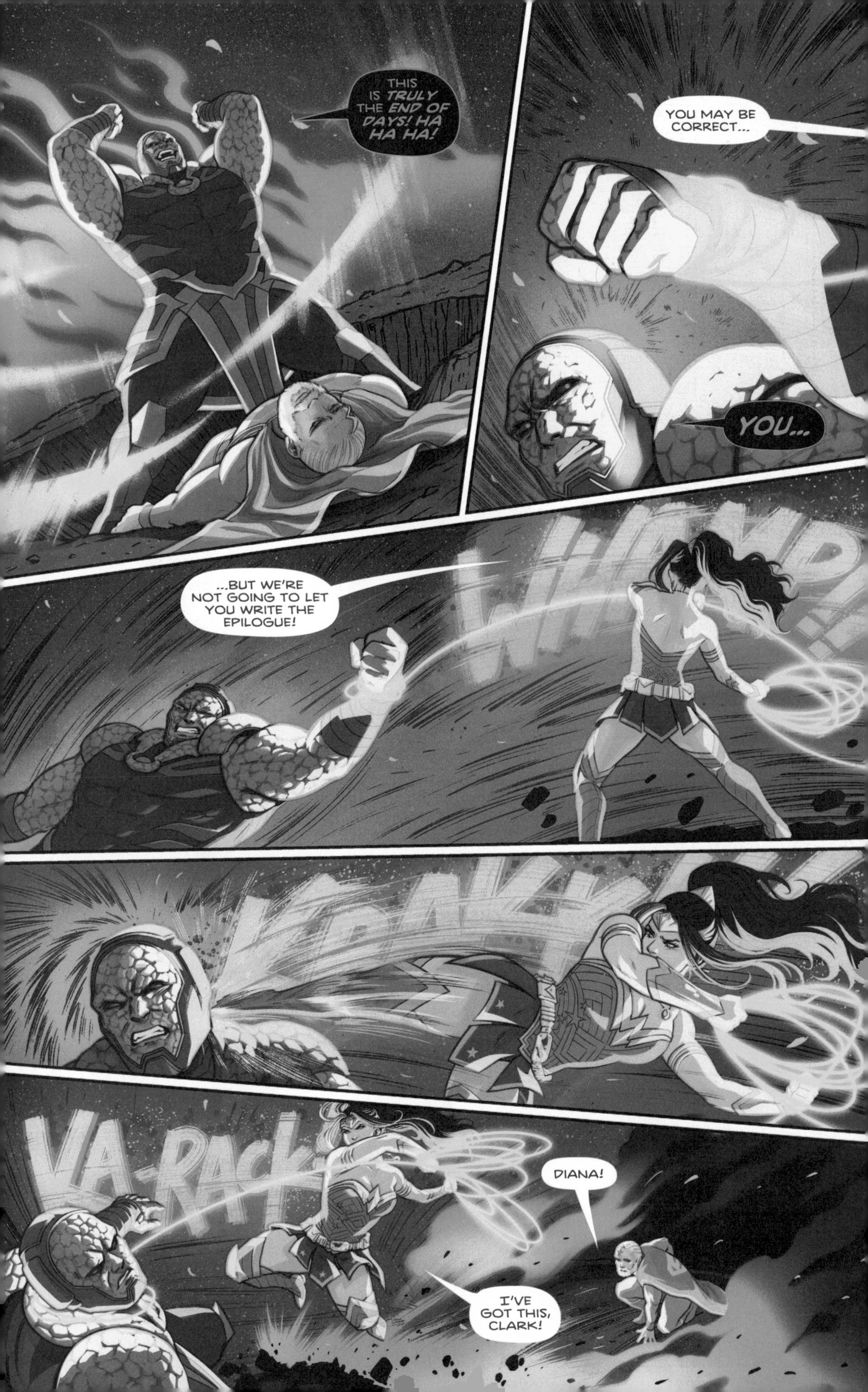

THIS IS *TRULY* THE *END OF DAYS!* HA HA HA!
YOU MAY BE CORRECT...
YOU...
...BUT WE'RE NOT GOING TO LET YOU WRITE THE EPILOGUE!
VA-RACK
DIANA!
I'VE GOT THIS, CLARK!

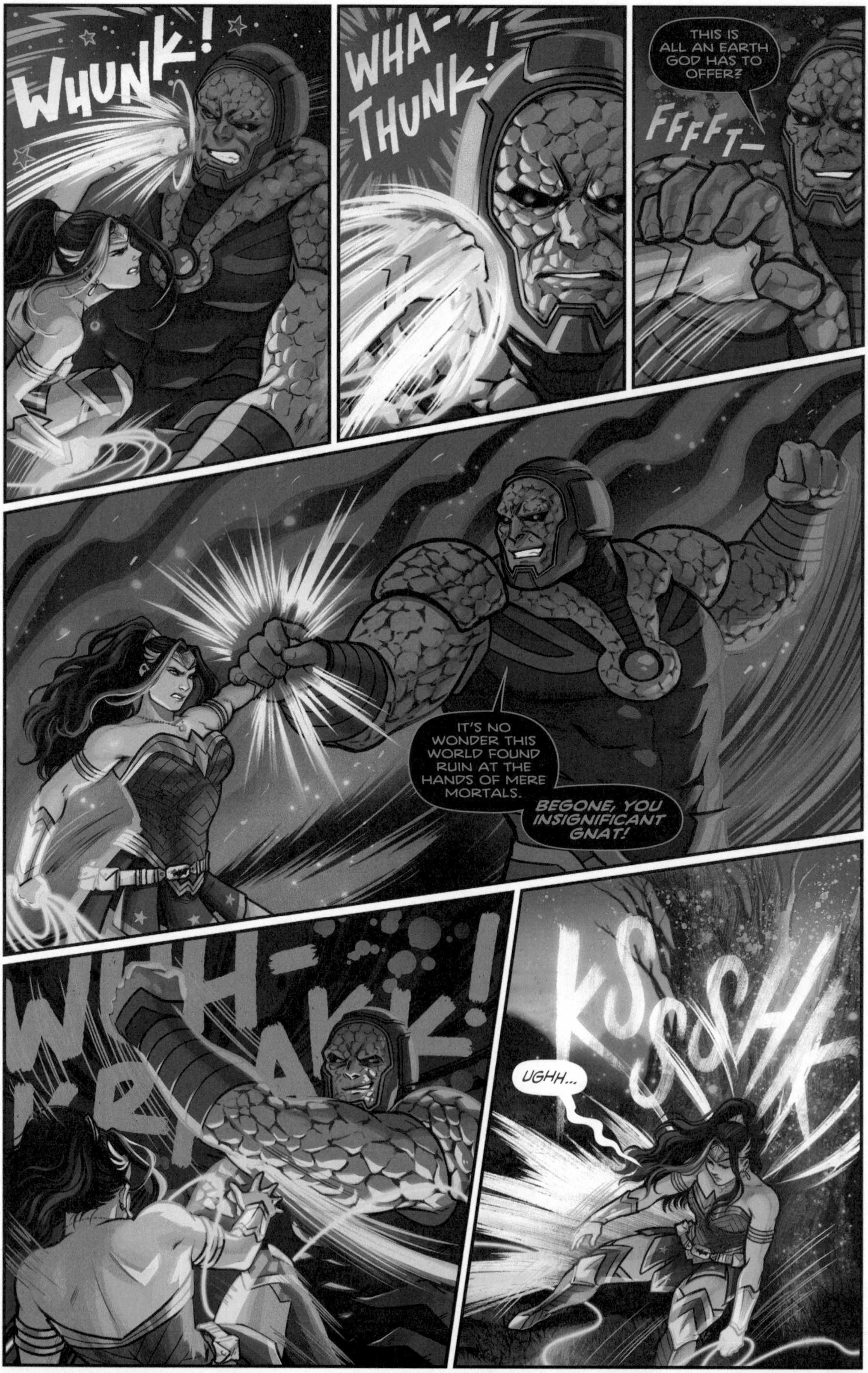
WHUNK!
WHA-THUNK!
THIS IS ALL AN EARTH GOD HAS TO OFFER?
FFFFT-
IT'S NO WONDER THIS WORLD FOUND RUIN AT THE HANDS OF MERE MORTALS.
BEGONE, YOU INSIGNIFICANT GNAT!
KSSSH
UGHH...

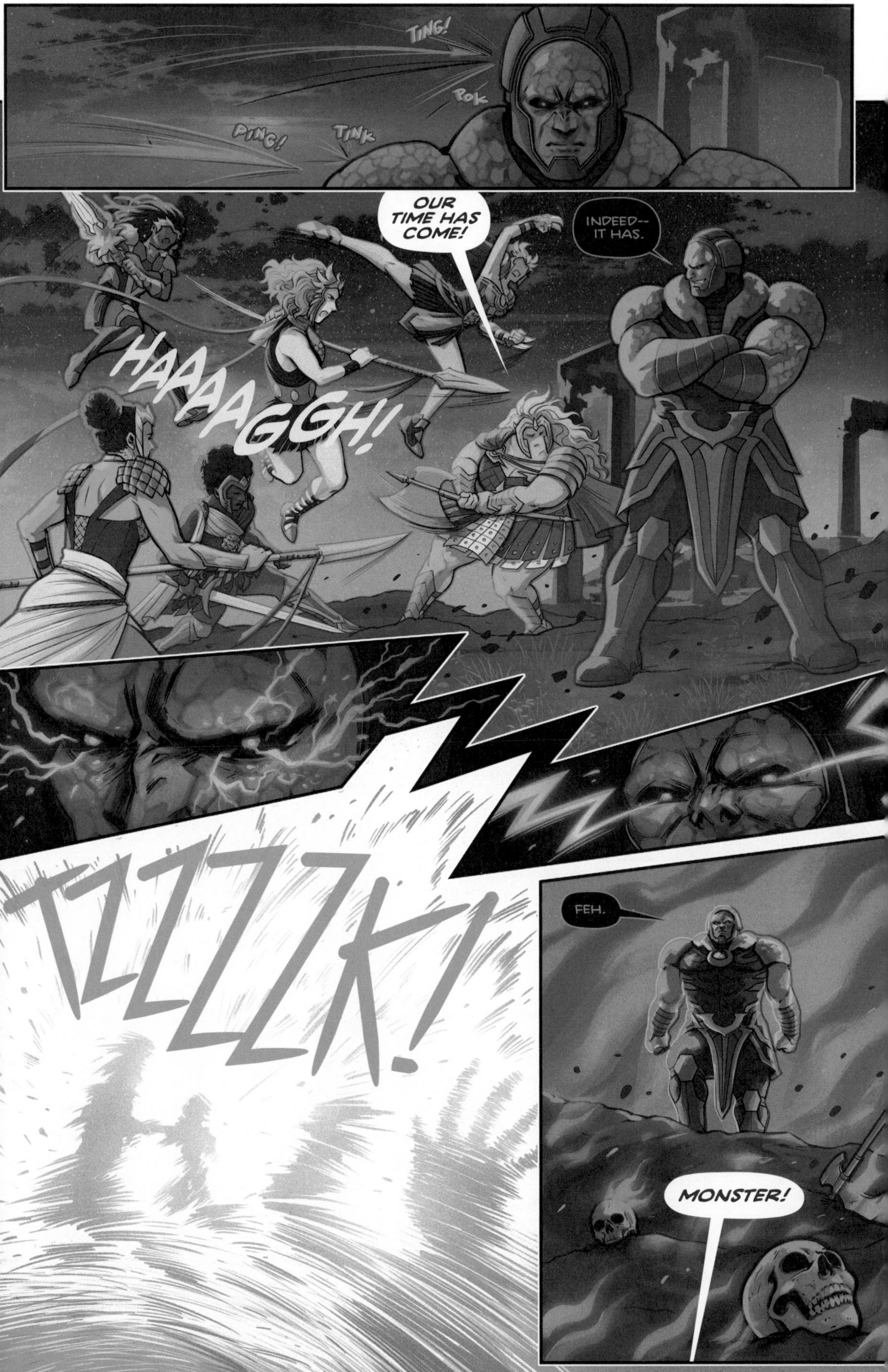
TING!
POK
PING!
TINK
OUR TIME HAS COME!
INDEED-- IT HAS.
HAAAAGGH!
TZZZZK!
FEH.
MONSTER!

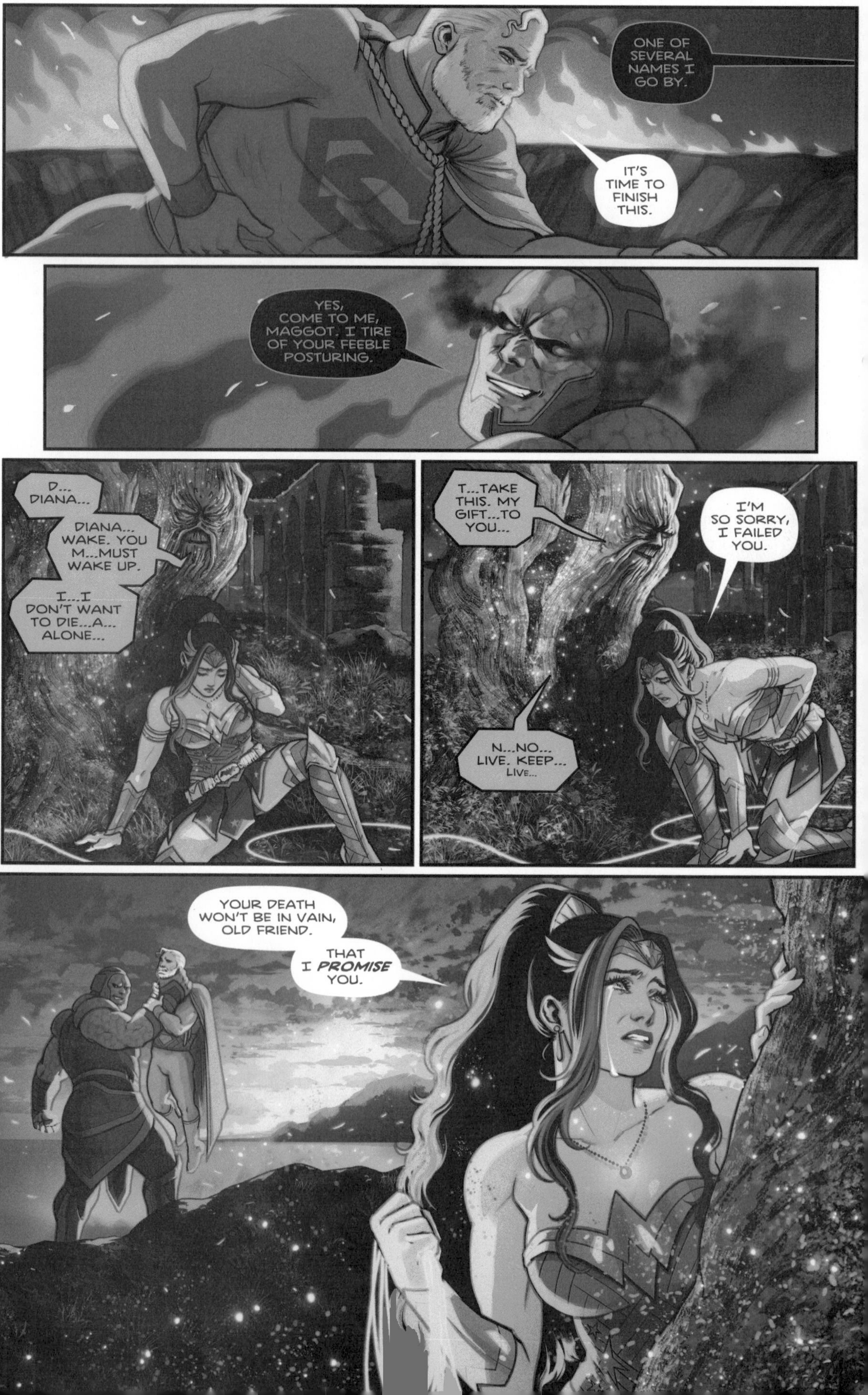

ONE OF SEVERAL NAMES I GO BY.
IT'S TIME TO FINISH THIS.
YES, COME TO ME, MAGGOT. I TIRE OF YOUR FEEBLE POSTURING.
D... DIANA...
DIANA... WAKE. YOU M...MUST WAKE UP.
I...I DON'T WANT TO DIE...A... ALONE...
T...TAKE THIS. MY GIFT...TO YOU...
I'M SO SORRY, I FAILED YOU.
N...NO... LIVE. KEEP... LIVE...
YOUR DEATH WON'T BE IN VAIN, OLD FRIEND.
THAT I *PROMISE* YOU.

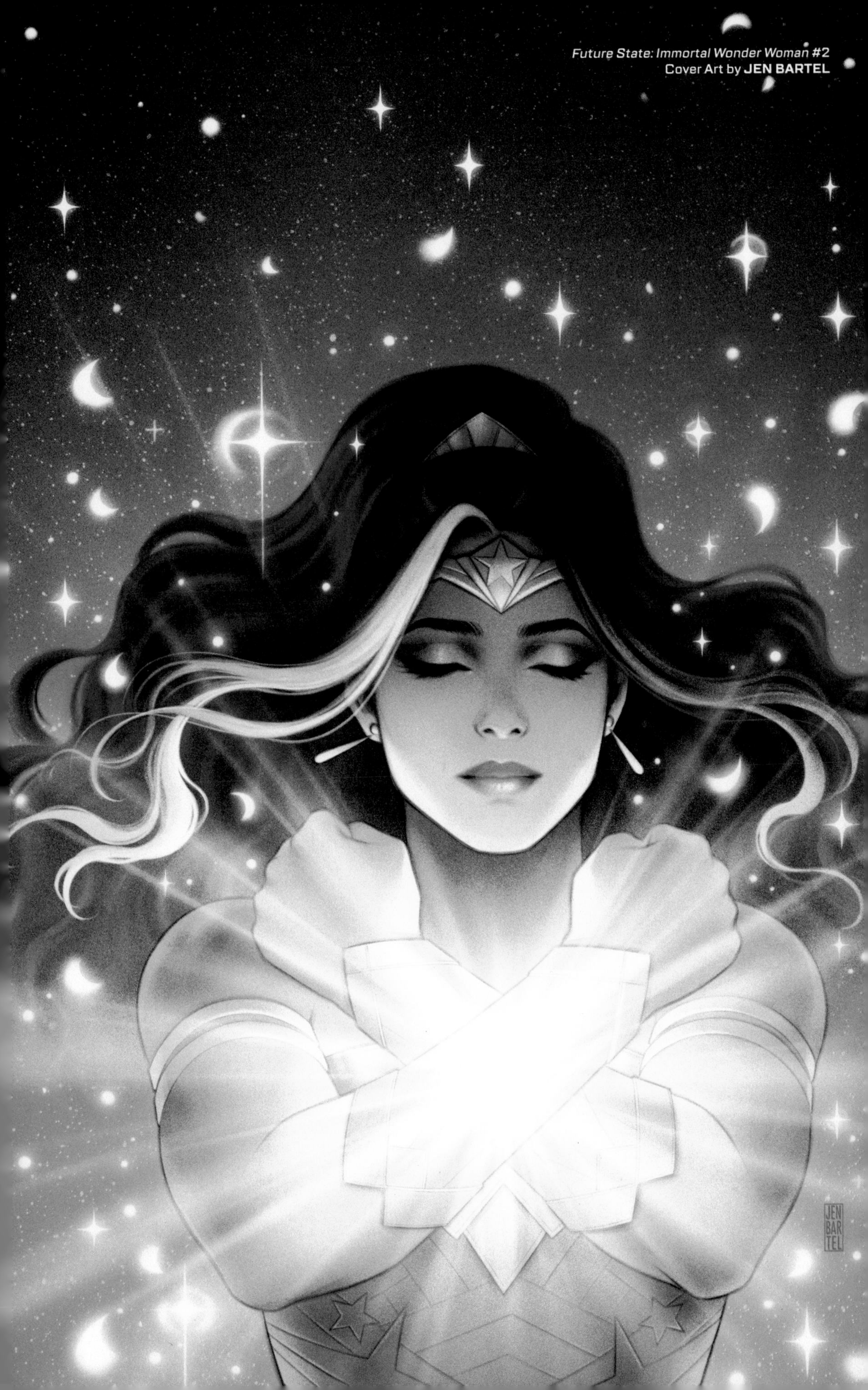
JEN BARTEL

Future State: Immortal Wonder Woman #2
Cover Art by **JEN BARTEL**

FUTURE STATE

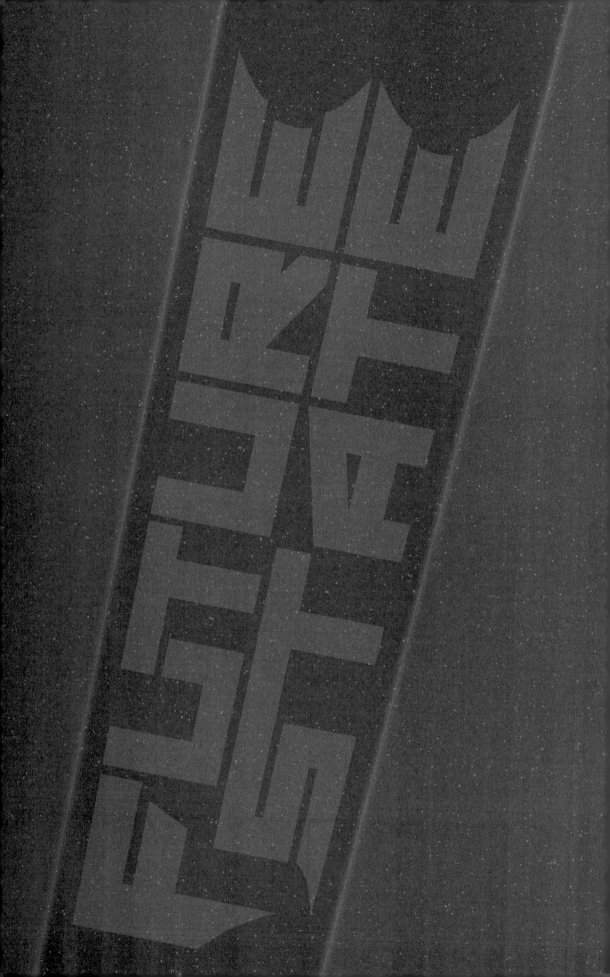

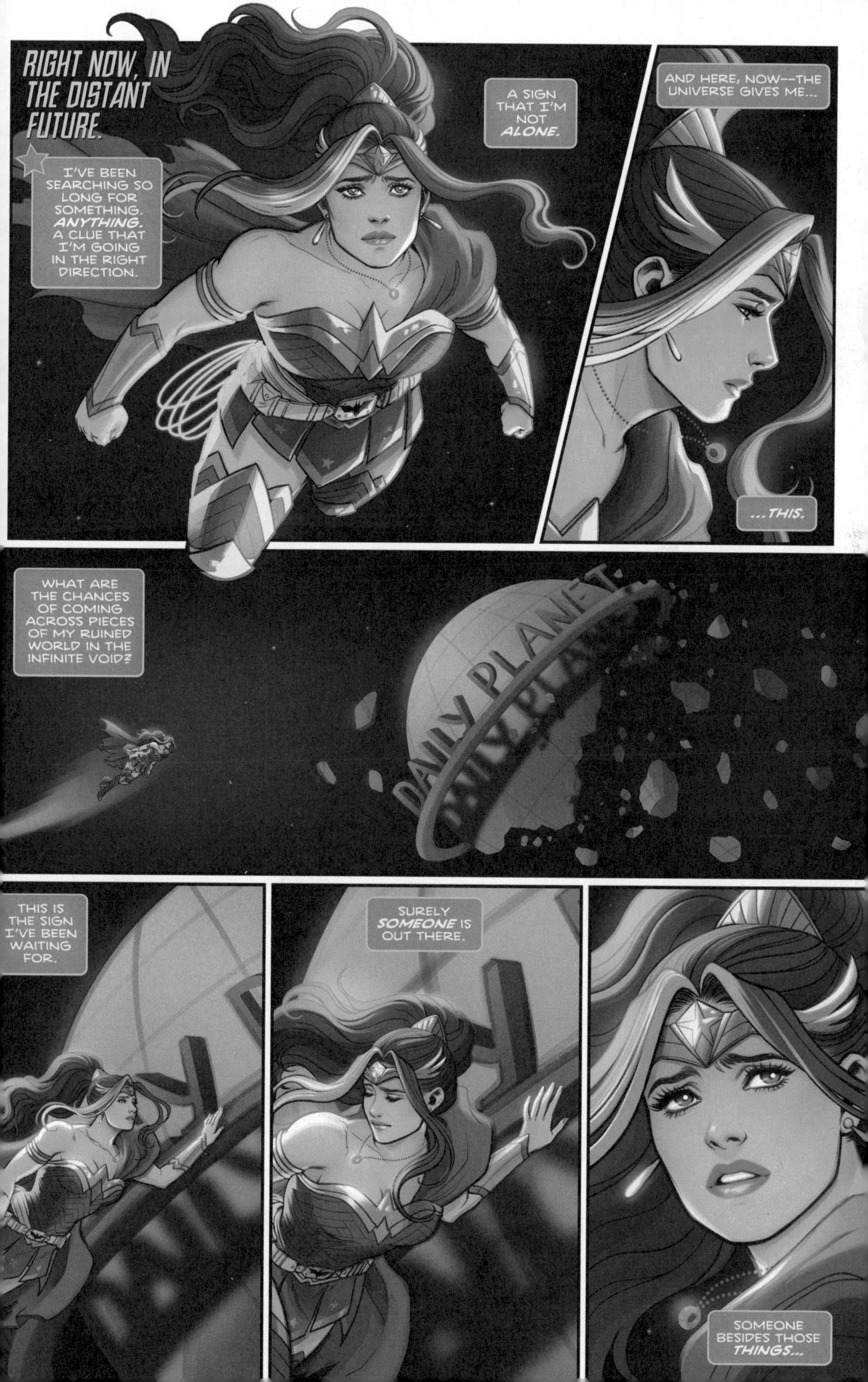
RIGHT NOW, IN THE DISTANT FUTURE.
I'VE BEEN SEARCHING SO LONG FOR SOMETHING. ANYTHING. A CLUE THAT I'M GOING IN THE RIGHT DIRECTION.
A SIGN THAT I'M NOT ALONE.
AND HERE, NOW--THE UNIVERSE GIVES ME...
...THIS.
WHAT ARE THE CHANCES OF COMING ACROSS PIECES OF MY RUINED WORLD IN THE INFINITE VOID?
DAILY PLANET
THIS IS THE SIGN I'VE BEEN WAITING FOR.
SURELY SOMEONE IS OUT THERE.
SOMEONE BESIDES THOSE THINGS...

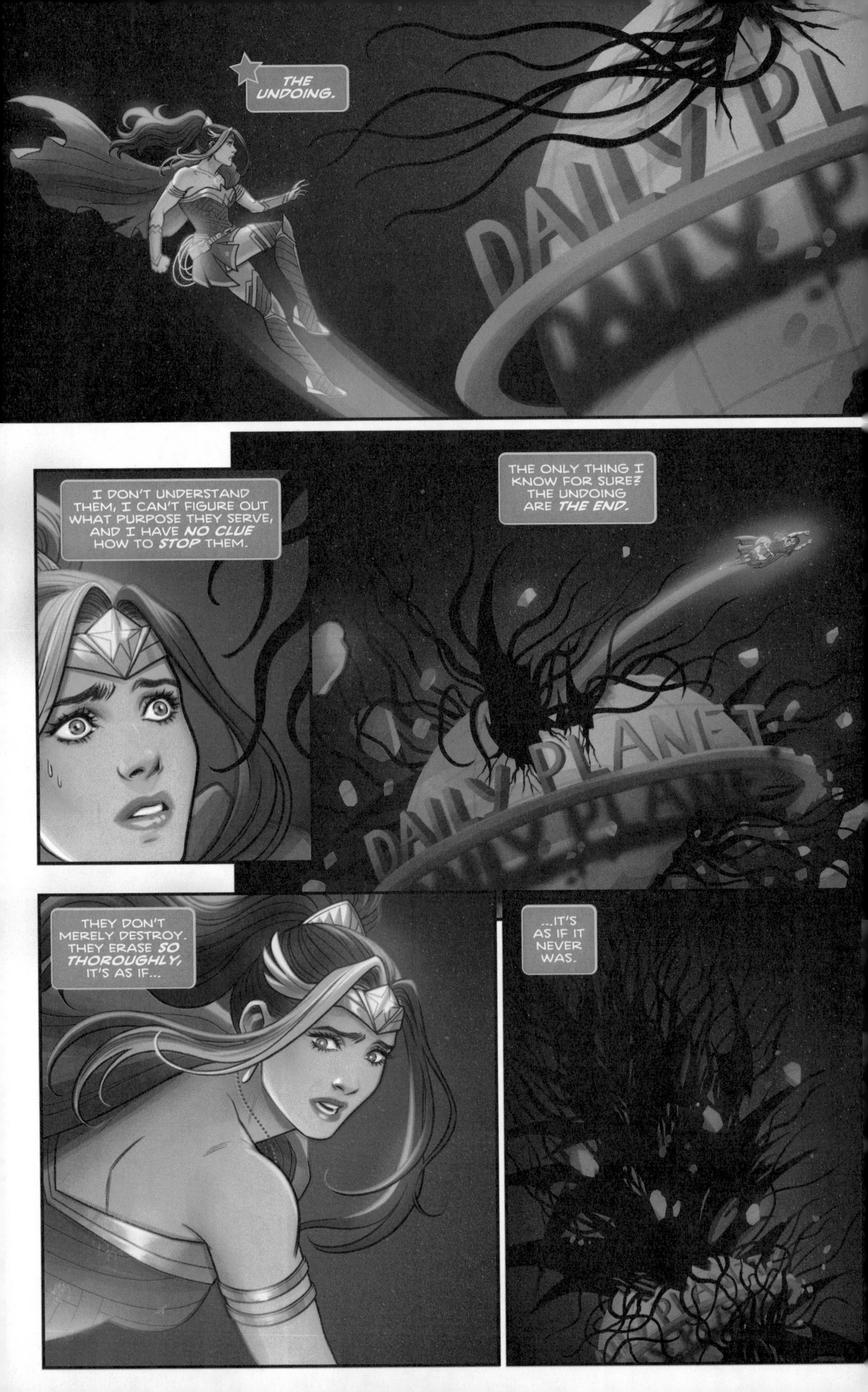
THE UNDOING.
DAILY PL
I DON'T UNDERSTAND THEM, I CAN'T FIGURE OUT WHAT PURPOSE THEY SERVE, AND I HAVE NO CLUE HOW TO STOP THEM.
THE ONLY THING I KNOW FOR SURE? THE UNDOING ARE THE END.
DAILY PLANET
THEY DON'T MERELY DESTROY. THEY ERASE SO THOROUGHLY, IT'S AS IF...
...IT'S AS IF IT NEVER WAS.

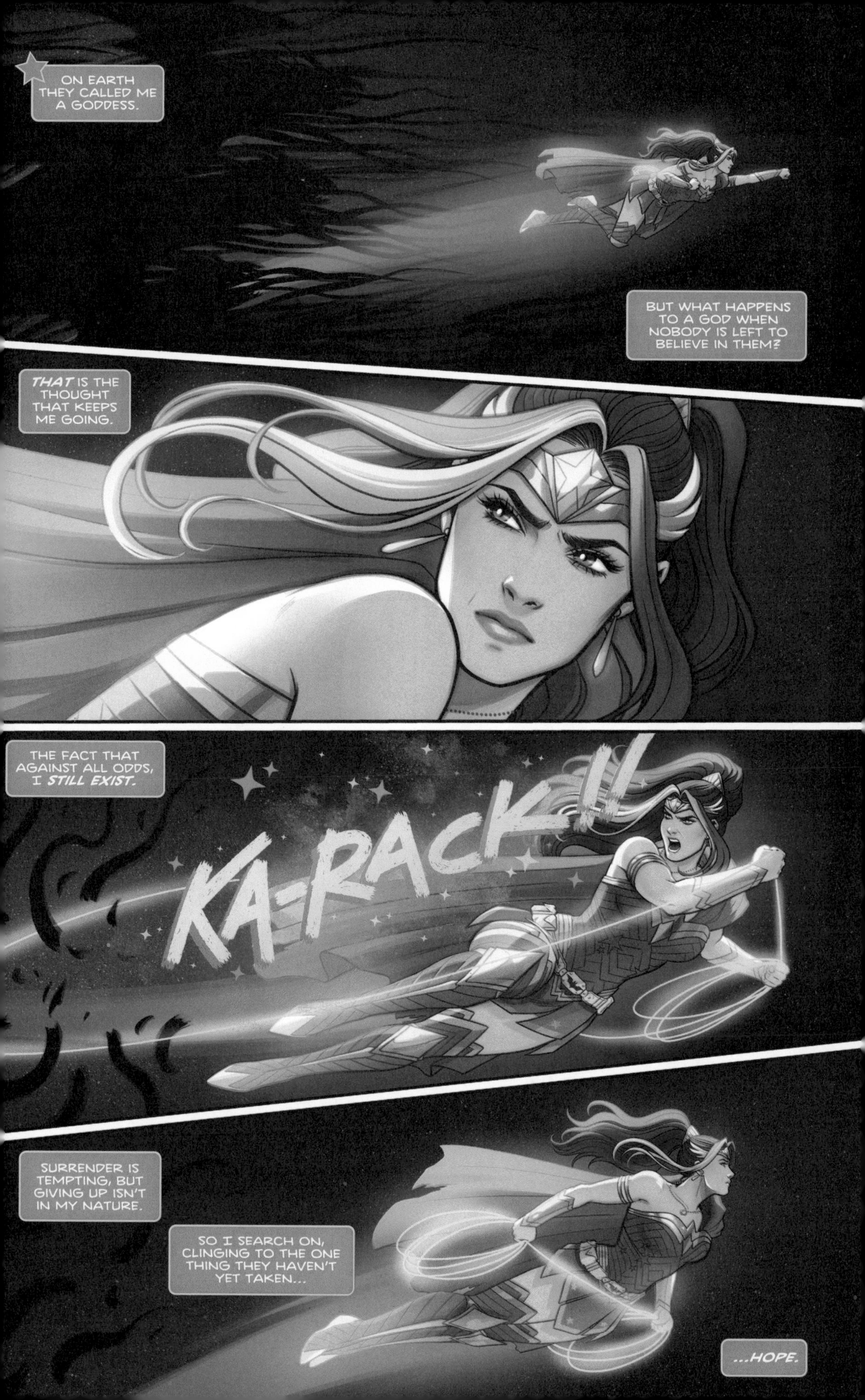
ON EARTH THEY CALLED ME A GODDESS.
BUT WHAT HAPPENS TO A GOD WHEN NOBODY IS LEFT TO BELIEVE IN THEM?
THAT IS THE THOUGHT THAT KEEPS ME GOING.
THE FACT THAT AGAINST ALL ODDS, I STILL EXIST.
KA-RACK!!
SURRENDER IS TEMPTING, BUT GIVING UP ISN'T IN MY NATURE.
SO I SEARCH ON, CLINGING TO THE ONE THING THEY HAVEN'T YET TAKEN...
...HOPE.

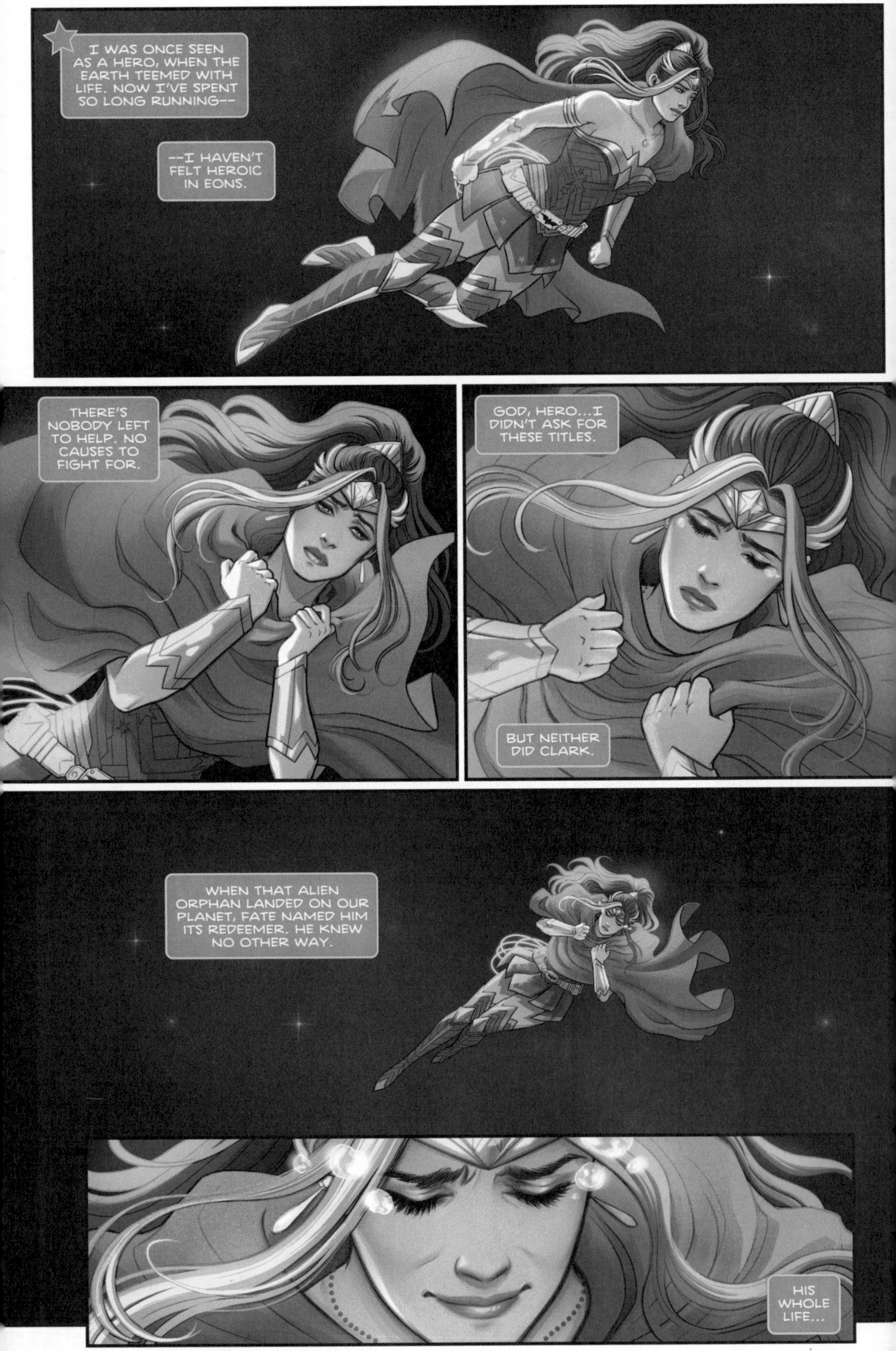
I WAS ONCE SEEN AS A HERO, WHEN THE EARTH TEEMED WITH LIFE. NOW I'VE SPENT SO LONG RUNNING--
--I HAVEN'T FELT HEROIC IN EONS.
THERE'S NOBODY LEFT TO HELP. NO CAUSES TO FIGHT FOR.
GOD, HERO...I DIDN'T ASK FOR THESE TITLES.
BUT NEITHER DID CLARK.
WHEN THAT ALIEN ORPHAN LANDED ON OUR PLANET, FATE NAMED HIM ITS REDEEMER. HE KNEW NO OTHER WAY.
HIS WHOLE LIFE...

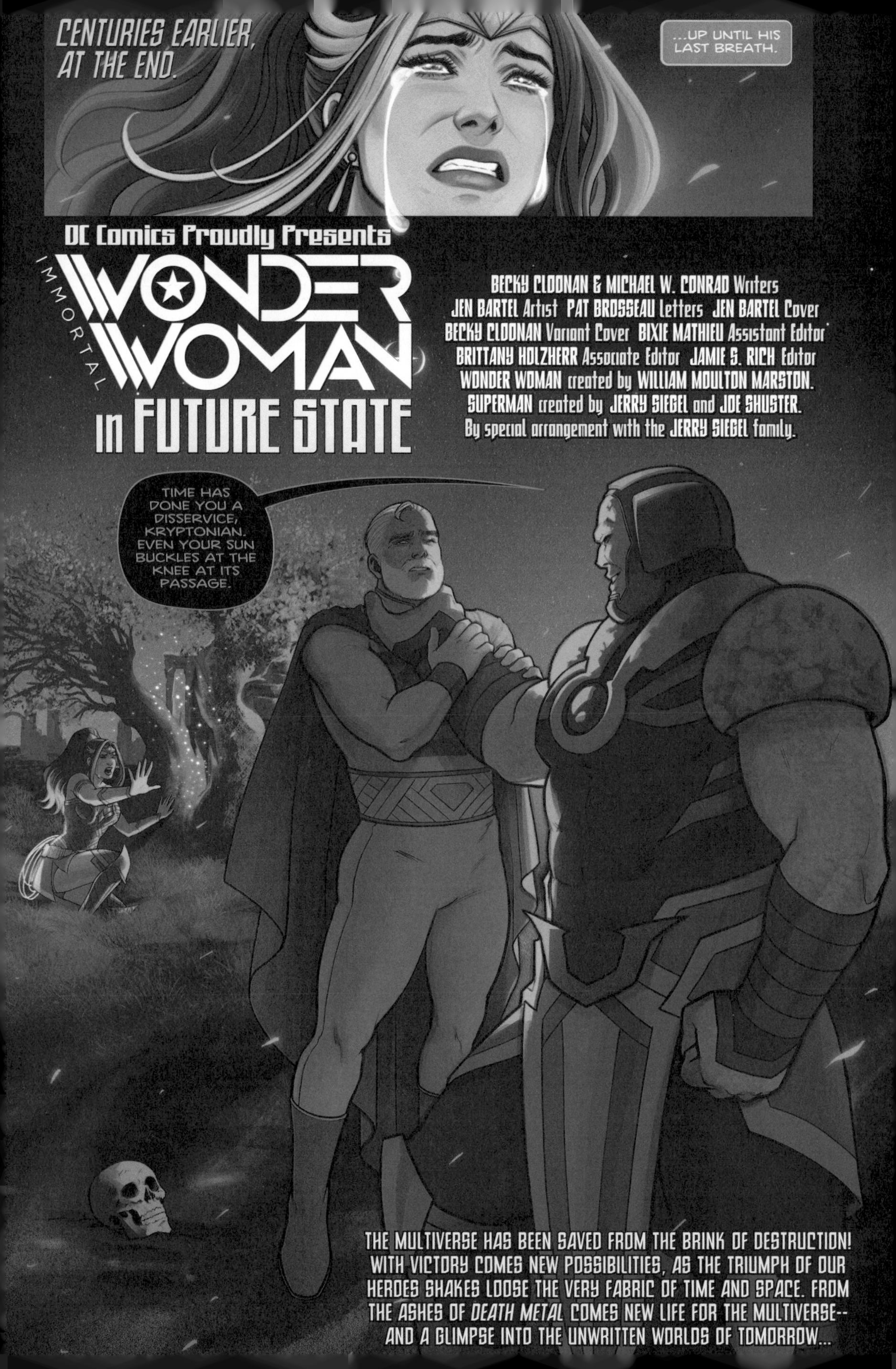
CENTURIES EARLIER, AT THE END.
...UP UNTIL HIS LAST BREATH.
DC Comics Proudly Presents
IMMORTAL WONDER WOMAN in FUTURE STATE
BECKY CLOONAN & MICHAEL W. CONRAD Writers
JEN BARTEL Artist PAT BROSSEAU Letters JEN BARTEL Cover
BECKY CLOONAN Variant Cover BIXIE MATHIEU Assistant Editor
BRITTANY HOLZHERR Associate Editor JAMIE S. RICH Editor
WONDER WOMAN created by WILLIAM MOULTON MARSTON.
SUPERMAN created by JERRY SIEGEL and JOE SHUSTER.
By special arrangement with the JERRY SIEGEL family.
TIME HAS DONE YOU A DISSERVICE, KRYPTONIAN. EVEN YOUR SUN BUCKLES AT THE KNEE AT ITS PASSAGE.
THE MULTIVERSE HAS BEEN SAVED FROM THE BRINK OF DESTRUCTION! WITH VICTORY COMES NEW POSSIBILITIES, AS THE TRIUMPH OF OUR HEROES SHAKES LOOSE THE VERY FABRIC OF TIME AND SPACE. FROM THE ASHES OF *DEATH METAL* COMES NEW LIFE FOR THE MULTIVERSE--AND A GLIMPSE INTO THE UNWRITTEN WORLDS OF TOMORROW...

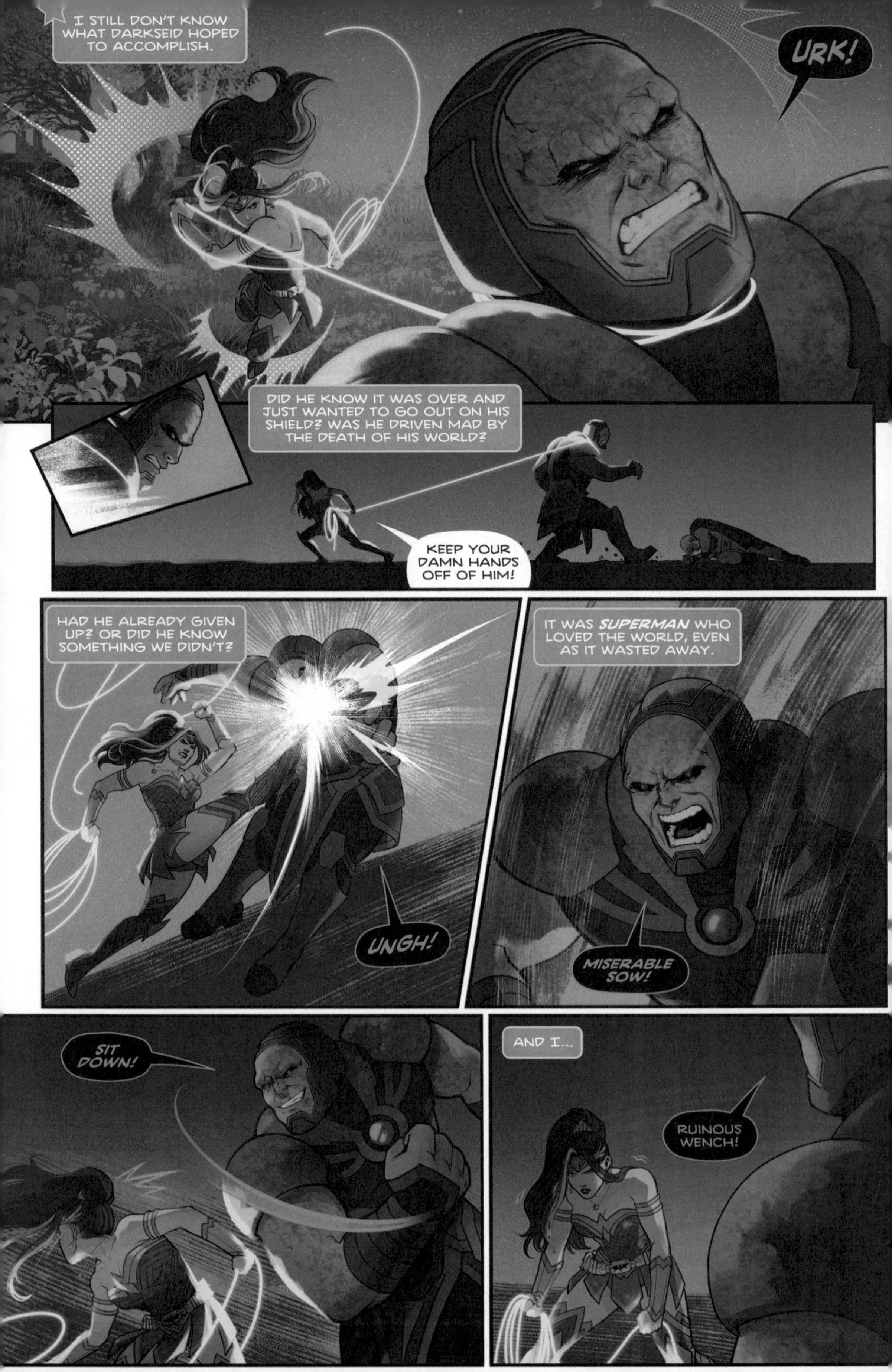
I STILL DON'T KNOW WHAT DARKSEID HOPED TO ACCOMPLISH.
URK!
DID HE KNOW IT WAS OVER AND JUST WANTED TO GO OUT ON HIS SHIELD? WAS HE DRIVEN MAD BY THE DEATH OF HIS WORLD?
KEEP YOUR DAMN HANDS OFF OF HIM!
HAD HE ALREADY GIVEN UP? OR DID HE KNOW SOMETHING WE DIDN'T?
UNGH!
IT WAS SUPERMAN WHO LOVED THE WORLD, EVEN AS IT WASTED AWAY.
MISERABLE SOW!
SIT DOWN!
AND I...
RUINOUS WENCH!

...I LOVED HIM ALL THE MORE FOR IT.

NO!

WHOOSH

NOW DARKSEID IS NOTHING.

BARELY A MEMORY, AND EVEN THAT IS FADING.

BUT WHEN I THINK OF CLARK...

I'M SORRY.

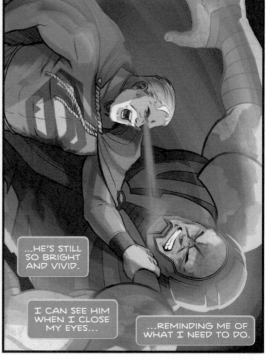

...HE'S STILL SO BRIGHT AND VIVID.

I CAN SEE HIM WHEN I CLOSE MY EYES...

...REMINDING ME OF WHAT I NEED TO DO.

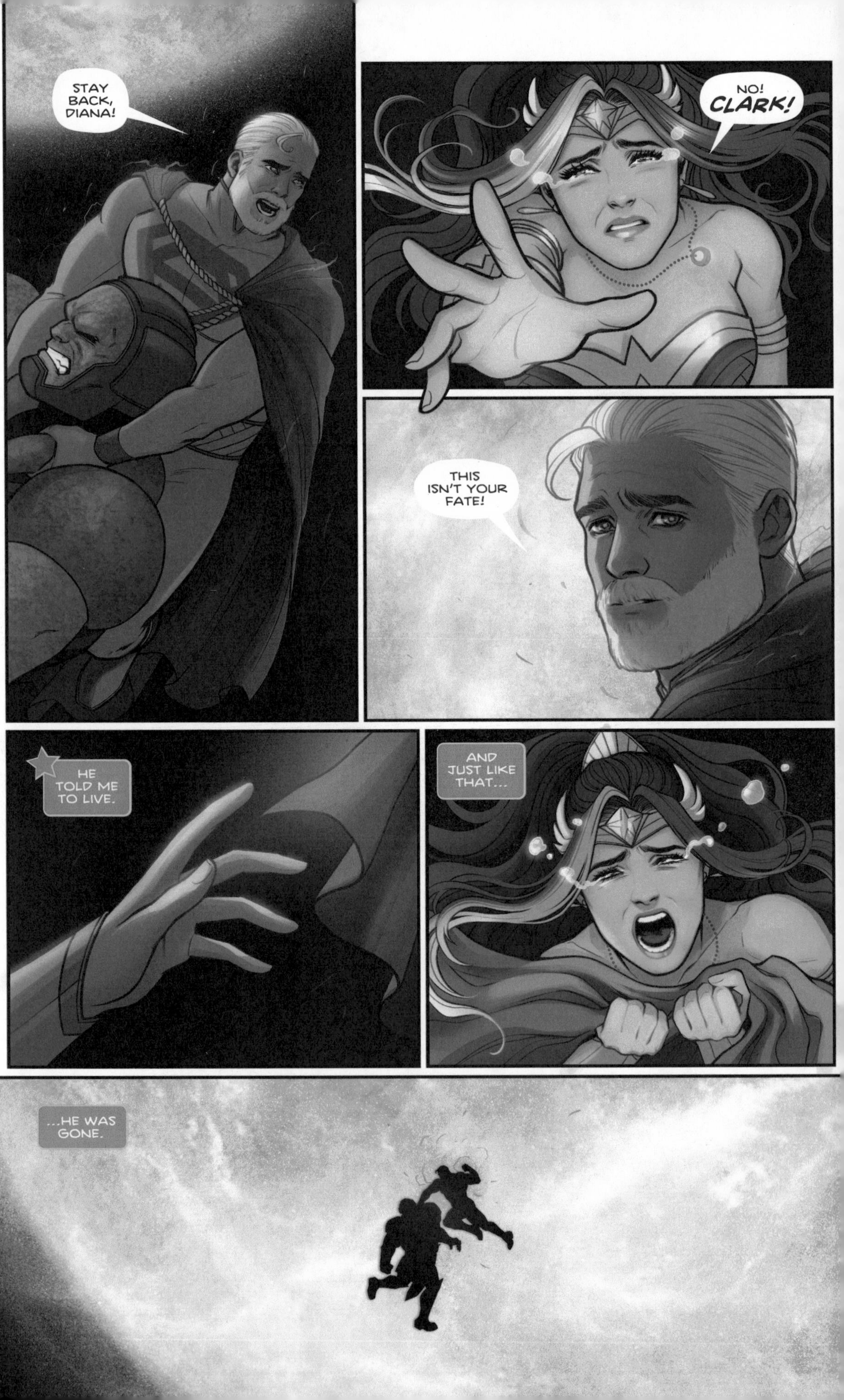
STAY BACK, DIANA!
NO! CLARK!
THIS ISN'T YOUR FATE!
HE TOLD ME TO LIVE.
AND JUST LIKE THAT...
...HE WAS GONE.

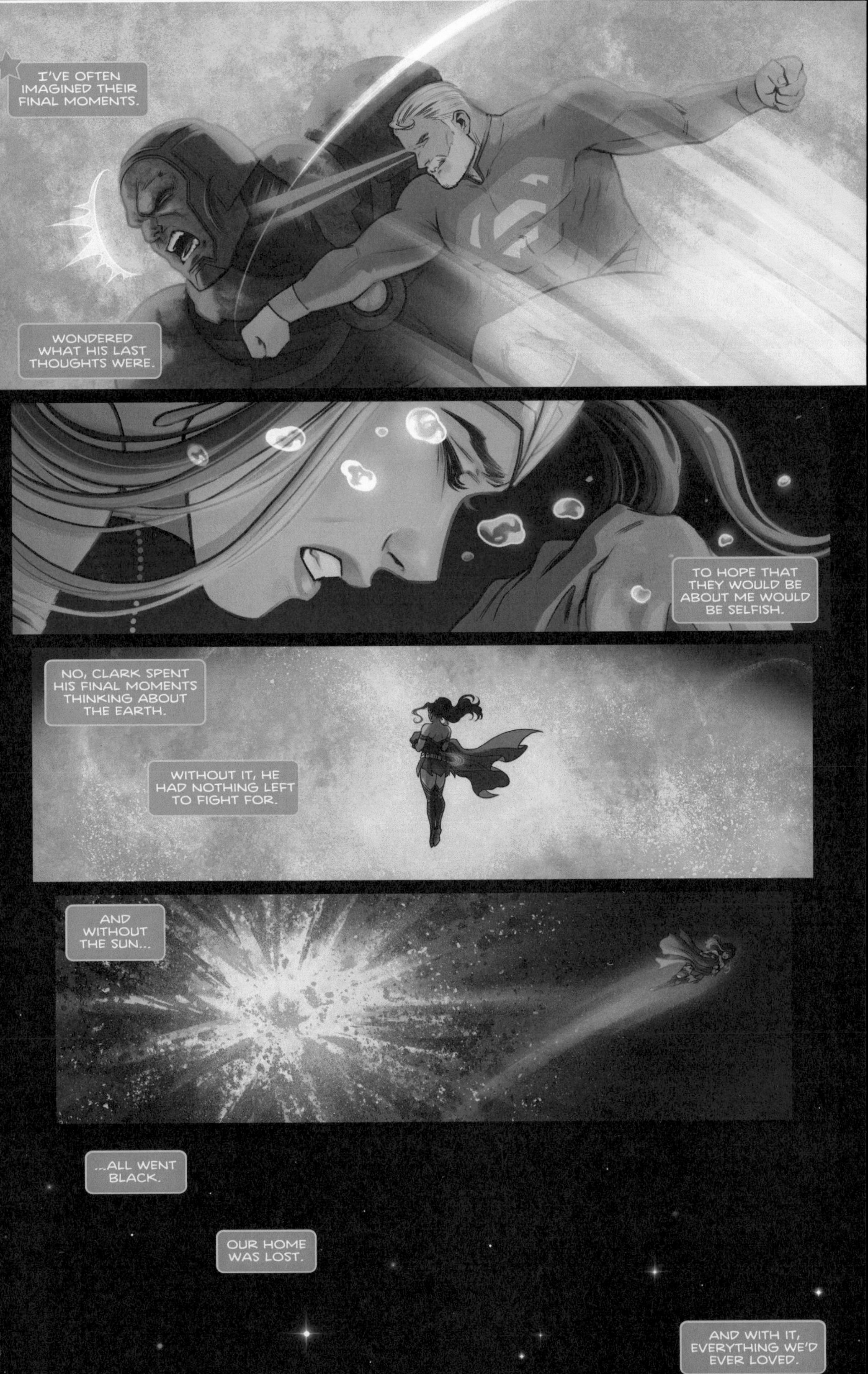
I'VE OFTEN IMAGINED THEIR FINAL MOMENTS.
WONDERED WHAT HIS LAST THOUGHTS WERE.
TO HOPE THAT THEY WOULD BE ABOUT ME WOULD BE SELFISH.
NO, CLARK SPENT HIS FINAL MOMENTS THINKING ABOUT THE EARTH.
WITHOUT IT, HE HAD NOTHING LEFT TO FIGHT FOR.
AND WITHOUT THE SUN...
...ALL WENT BLACK.
OUR HOME WAS LOST.
AND WITH IT, EVERYTHING WE'D EVER LOVED.

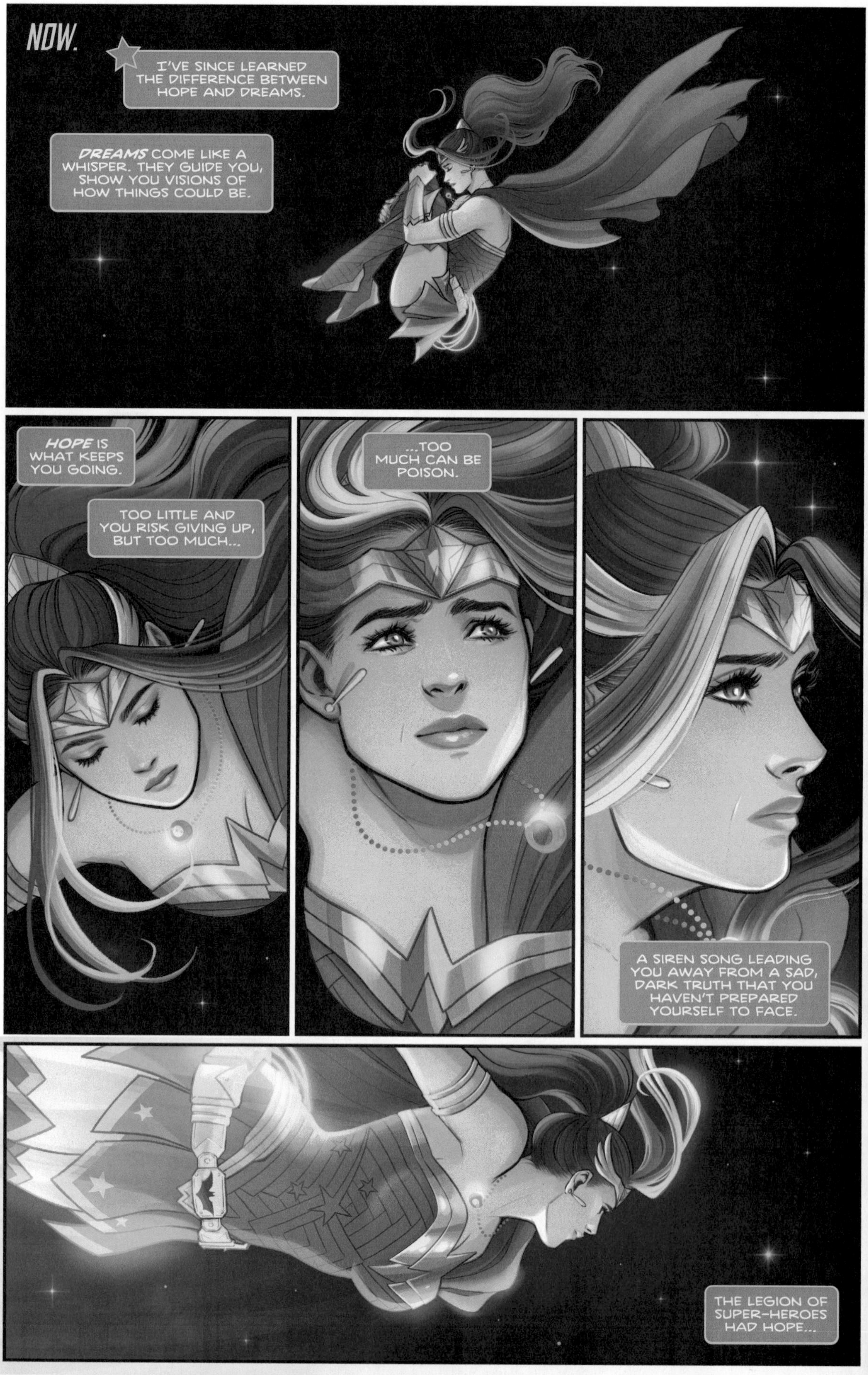
NOW.
I'VE SINCE LEARNED THE DIFFERENCE BETWEEN HOPE AND DREAMS.
DREAMS COME LIKE A WHISPER. THEY GUIDE YOU, SHOW YOU VISIONS OF HOW THINGS COULD BE.
HOPE IS WHAT KEEPS YOU GOING.
TOO LITTLE AND YOU RISK GIVING UP, BUT TOO MUCH...
...TOO MUCH CAN BE POISON.
A SIREN SONG LEADING YOU AWAY FROM A SAD, DARK TRUTH THAT YOU HAVEN'T PREPARED YOURSELF TO FACE.
THE LEGION OF SUPER-HEROES HAD HOPE...

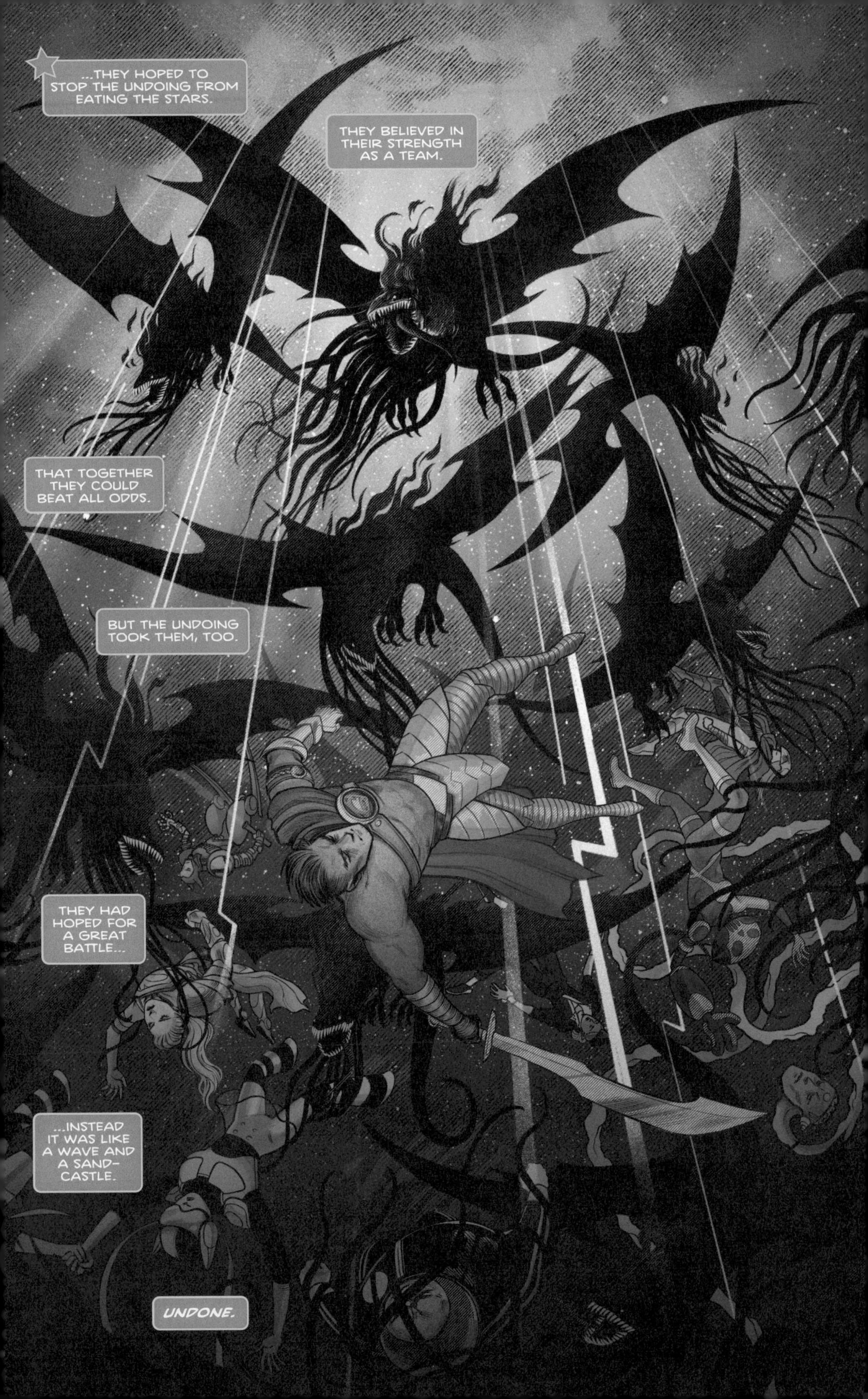
...THEY HOPED TO STOP THE UNDOING FROM EATING THE STARS.
THEY BELIEVED IN THEIR STRENGTH AS A TEAM.
THAT TOGETHER THEY COULD BEAT ALL ODDS.
BUT THE UNDOING TOOK THEM, TOO.
THEY HAD HOPED FOR A GREAT BATTLE...
...INSTEAD IT WAS LIKE A WAVE AND A SAND-CASTLE.
UNDONE.

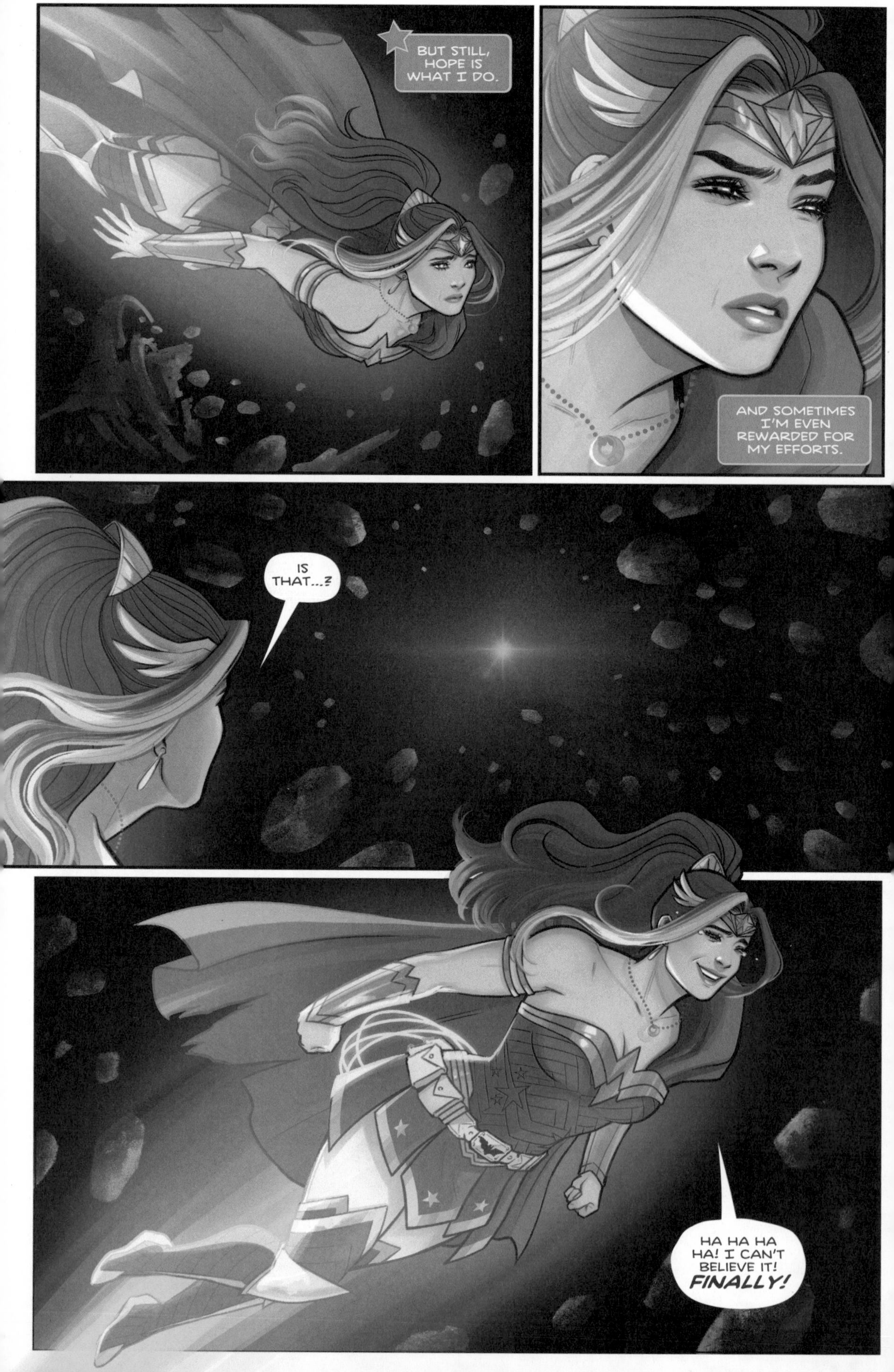
BUT STILL, HOPE IS WHAT I DO.
AND SOMETIMES I'M EVEN REWARDED FOR MY EFFORTS.
IS THAT...?
HA HA HA HA! I CAN'T BELIEVE IT! FINALLY!

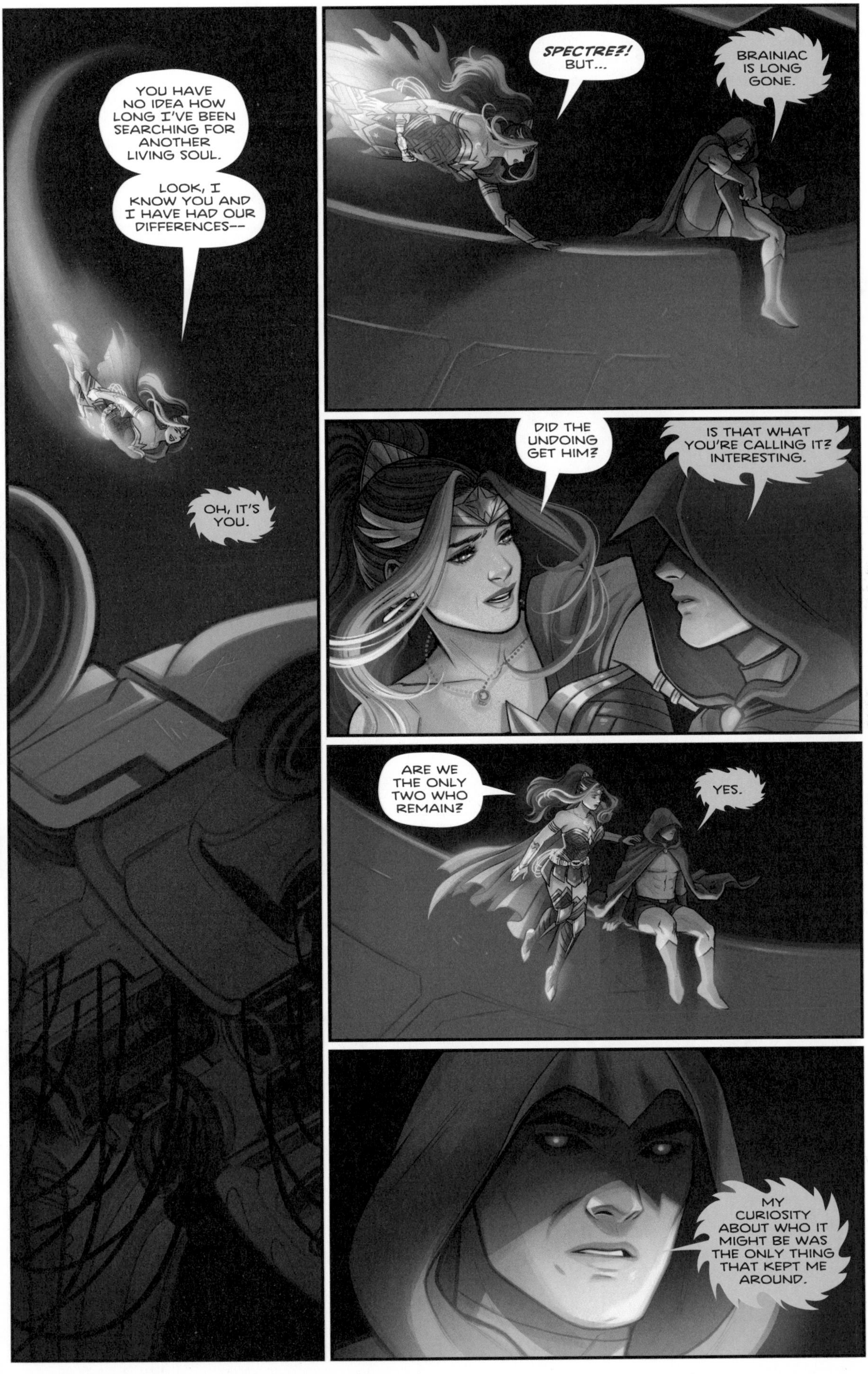
YOU HAVE NO IDEA HOW LONG I'VE BEEN SEARCHING FOR ANOTHER LIVING SOUL.
LOOK, I KNOW YOU AND I HAVE HAD OUR DIFFERENCES--
OH, IT'S YOU.
SPECTRE?! BUT...
BRAINIAC IS LONG GONE.
DID THE UNDOING GET HIM?
IS THAT WHAT YOU'RE CALLING IT? INTERESTING.
ARE WE THE ONLY TWO WHO REMAIN?
YES.
MY CURIOSITY ABOUT WHO IT MIGHT BE WAS THE ONLY THING THAT KEPT ME AROUND.

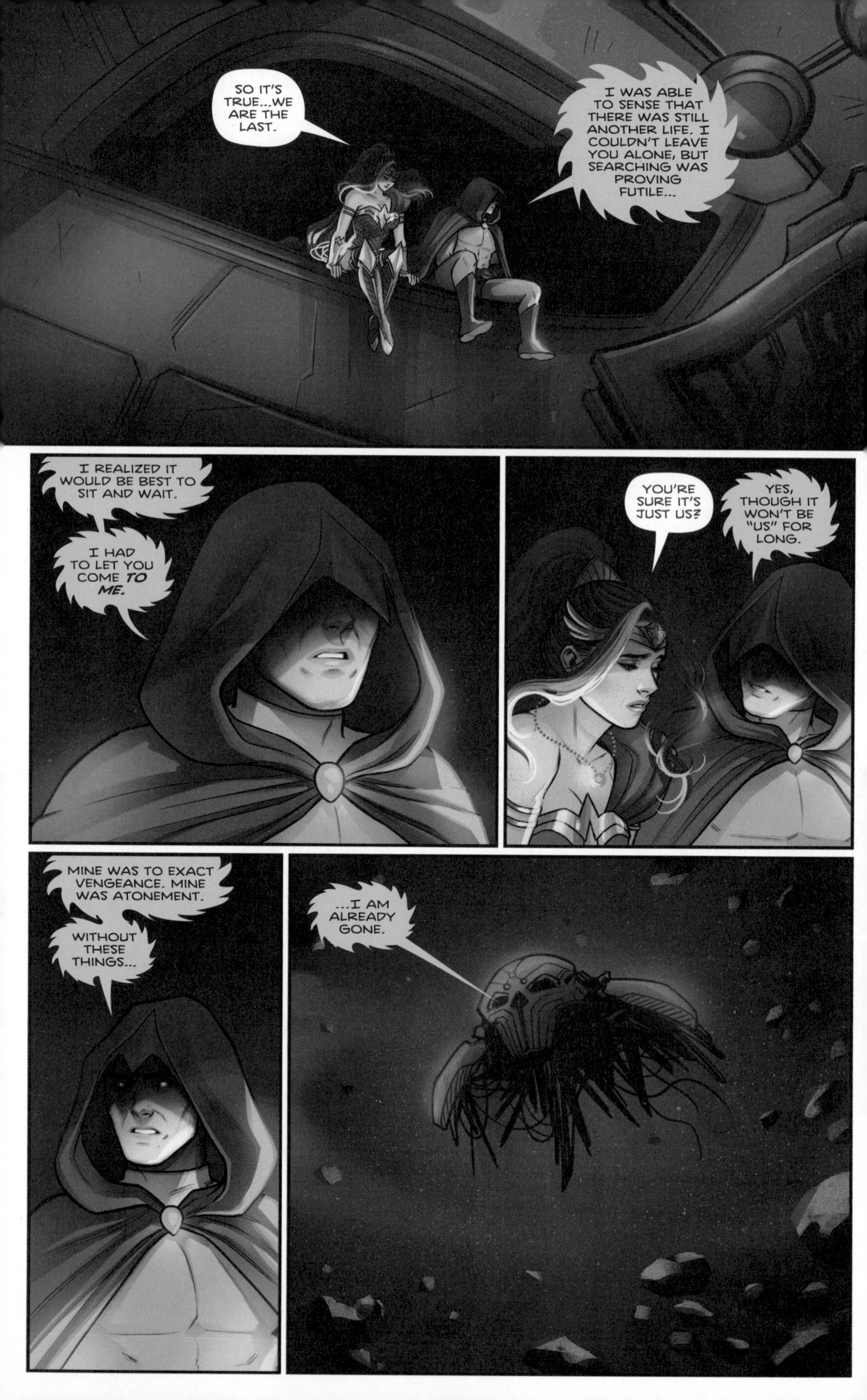
SO IT'S TRUE...WE ARE THE LAST.
I WAS ABLE TO SENSE THAT THERE WAS STILL ANOTHER LIFE. I COULDN'T LEAVE YOU ALONE, BUT SEARCHING WAS PROVING FUTILE...
I REALIZED IT WOULD BE BEST TO SIT AND WAIT.
I HAD TO LET YOU COME *TO ME.*
YOU'RE SURE IT'S JUST US?
YES, THOUGH IT WON'T BE "US" FOR LONG.
MINE WAS TO EXACT VENGEANCE. MINE WAS ATONEMENT.
WITHOUT THESE THINGS...
...I AM ALREADY GONE.

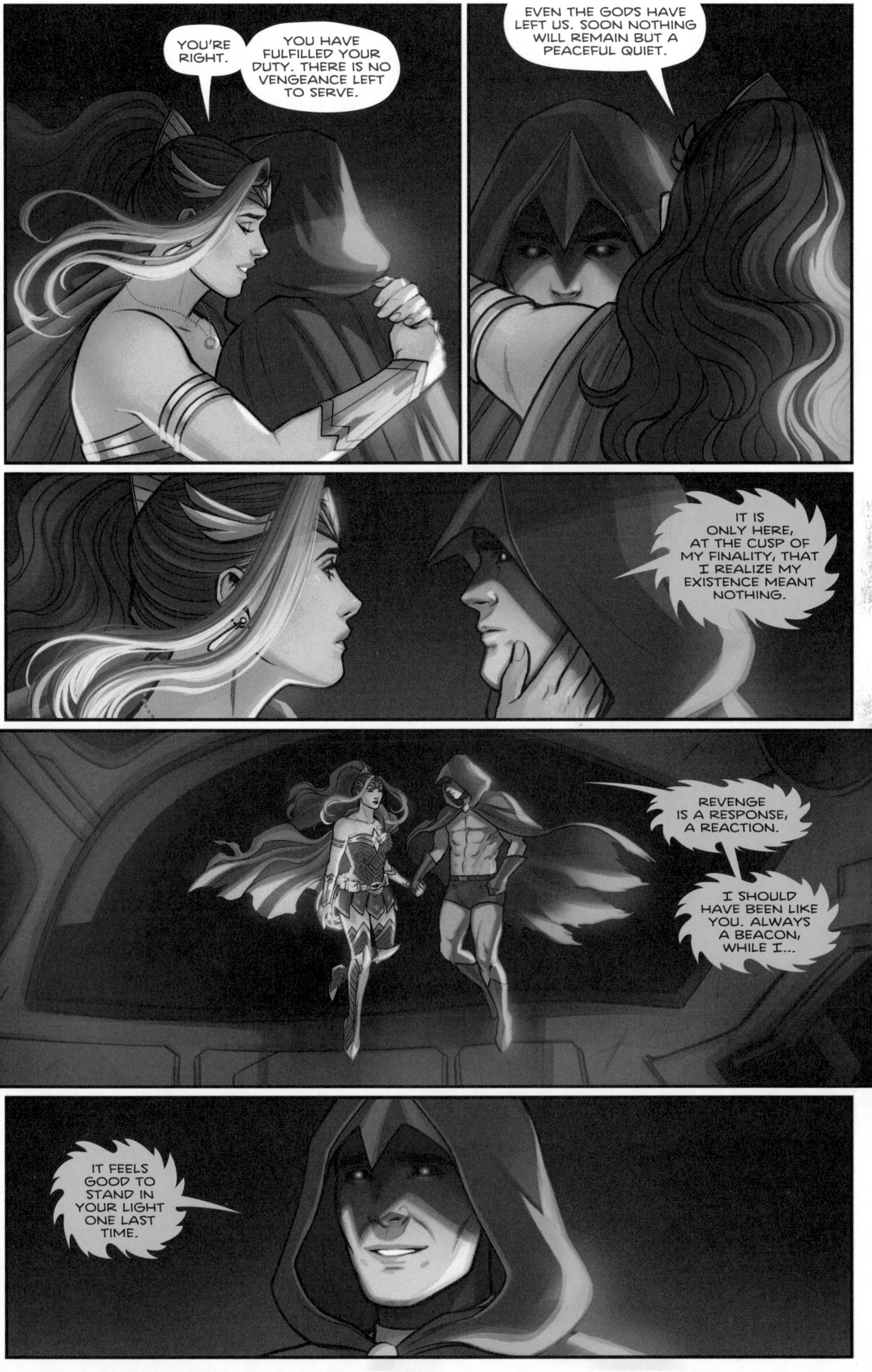
YOU'RE RIGHT.
YOU HAVE FULFILLED YOUR DUTY. THERE IS NO VENGEANCE LEFT TO SERVE.
EVEN THE GODS HAVE LEFT US. SOON NOTHING WILL REMAIN BUT A PEACEFUL QUIET.
IT IS ONLY HERE, AT THE CUSP OF MY FINALITY, THAT I REALIZE MY EXISTENCE MEANT NOTHING.
REVENGE IS A RESPONSE, A REACTION.
I SHOULD HAVE BEEN LIKE YOU. ALWAYS A BEACON, WHILE I...
IT FEELS GOOD TO STAND IN YOUR LIGHT ONE LAST TIME.

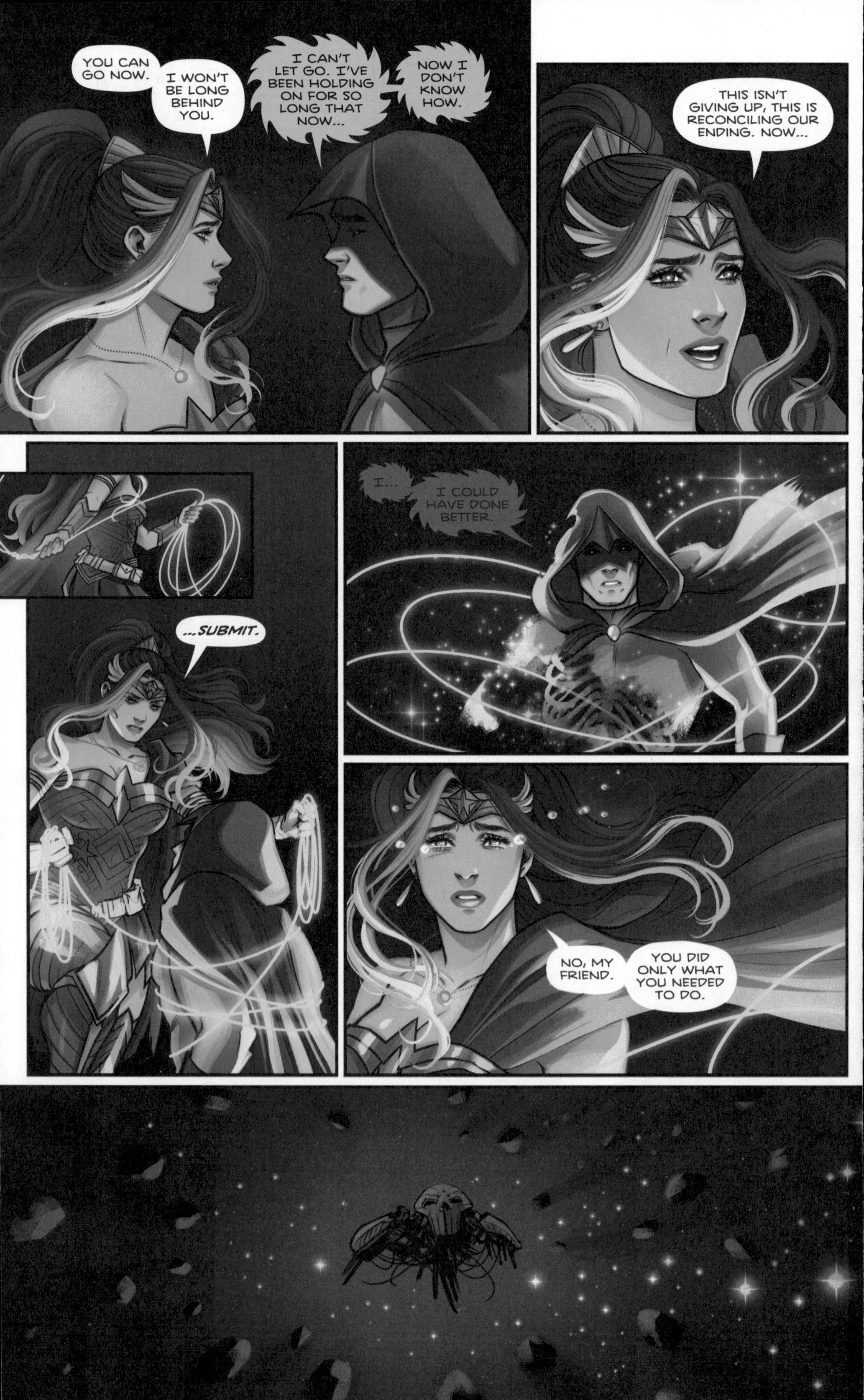
YOU CAN GO NOW.
I WON'T BE LONG BEHIND YOU.
I CAN'T LET GO. I'VE BEEN HOLDING ON FOR SO LONG THAT NOW...
NOW I DON'T KNOW HOW.
THIS ISN'T GIVING UP, THIS IS RECONCILING OUR ENDING. NOW...
...SUBMIT.
I...
I COULD HAVE DONE BETTER.
NO, MY FRIEND.
YOU DID ONLY WHAT YOU NEEDED TO DO.

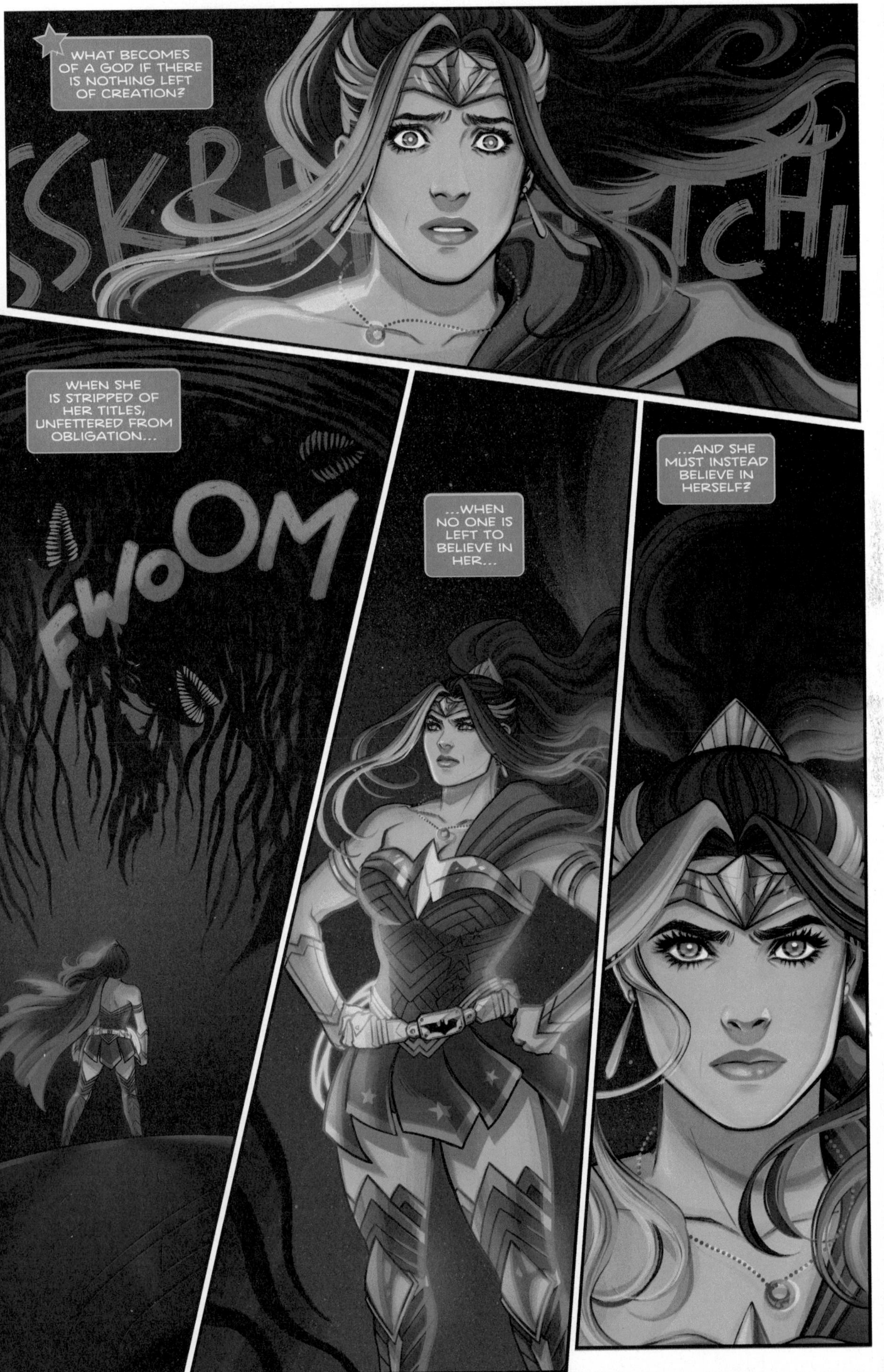

WHAT BECOMES OF A GOD IF THERE IS NOTHING LEFT OF CREATION?
WHEN SHE IS STRIPPED OF HER TITLES, UNFETTERED FROM OBLIGATION...
FWOOM
...WHEN NO ONE IS LEFT TO BELIEVE IN HER...
...AND SHE MUST INSTEAD BELIEVE IN HERSELF?

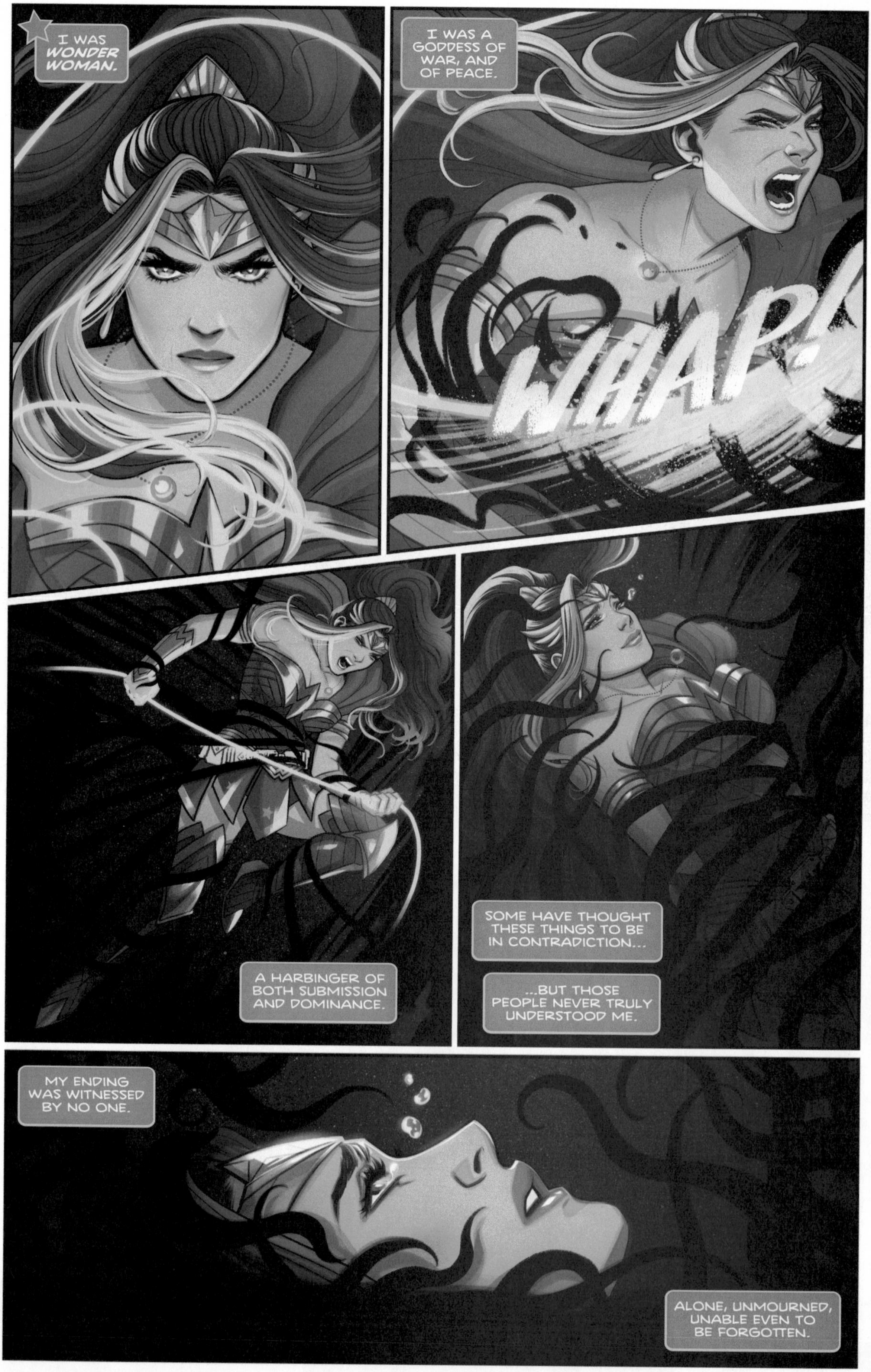
I WAS WONDER WOMAN.
I WAS A GODDESS OF WAR, AND OF PEACE.
WHAP!
A HARBINGER OF BOTH SUBMISSION AND DOMINANCE.
SOME HAVE THOUGHT THESE THINGS TO BE IN CONTRADICTION...
...BUT THOSE PEOPLE NEVER TRULY UNDERSTOOD ME.
MY ENDING WAS WITNESSED BY NO ONE.
ALONE, UNMOURNED, UNABLE EVEN TO BE FORGOTTEN.

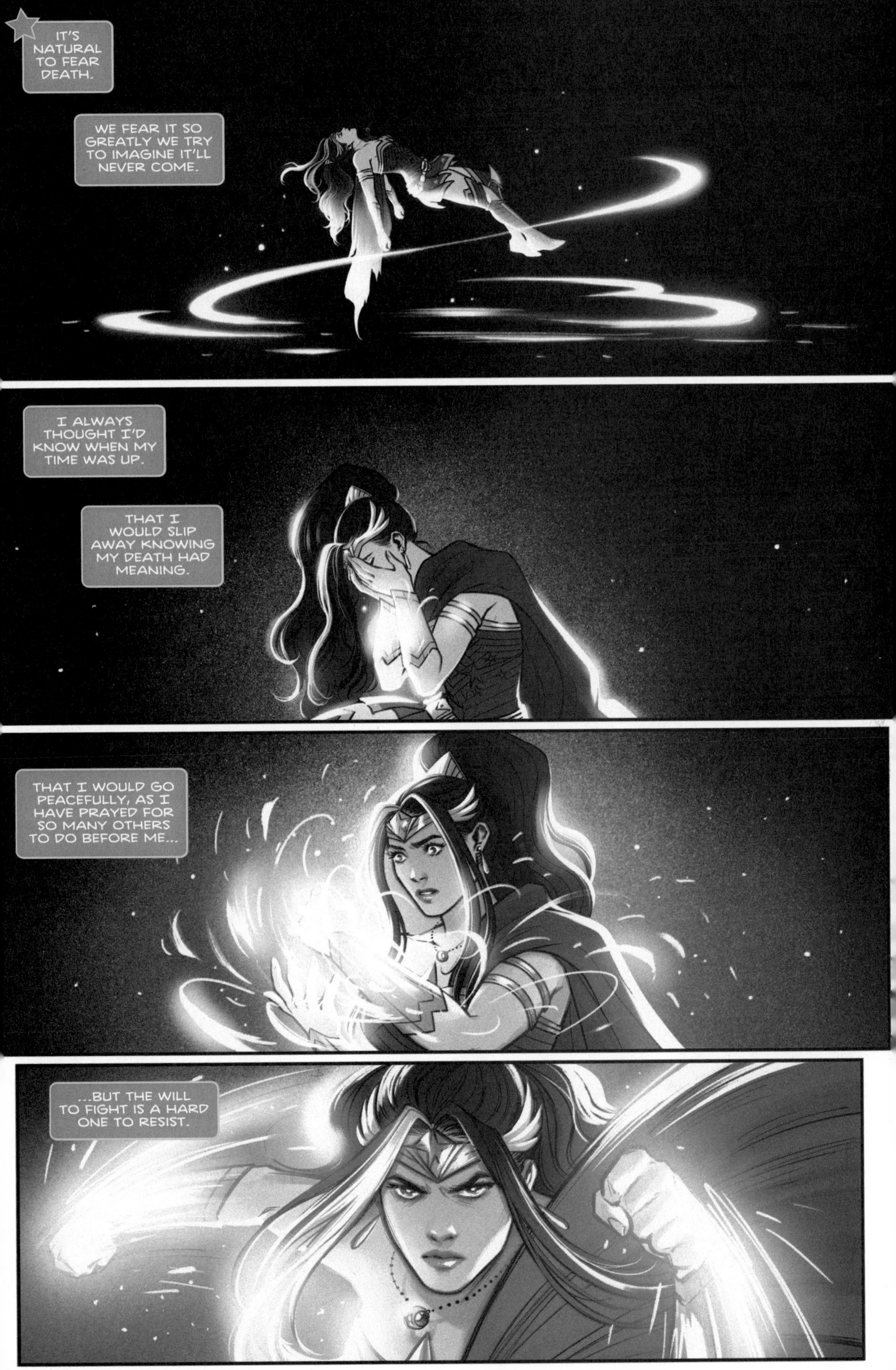
IT'S NATURAL TO FEAR DEATH.
WE FEAR IT SO GREATLY WE TRY TO IMAGINE IT'LL NEVER COME.
I ALWAYS THOUGHT I'D KNOW WHEN MY TIME WAS UP.
THAT I WOULD SLIP AWAY KNOWING MY DEATH HAD MEANING.
THAT I WOULD GO PEACEFULLY, AS I HAVE PRAYED FOR SO MANY OTHERS TO DO BEFORE ME...
...BUT THE WILL TO FIGHT IS A HARD ONE TO RESIST.

AN ENDING IS JUST ANOTHER WORD FOR CHANGE.

AND THIS IS NOT THE END OF MY STORY...

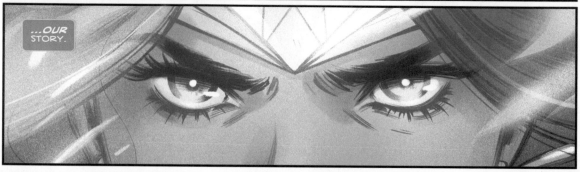

...*OUR* STORY.

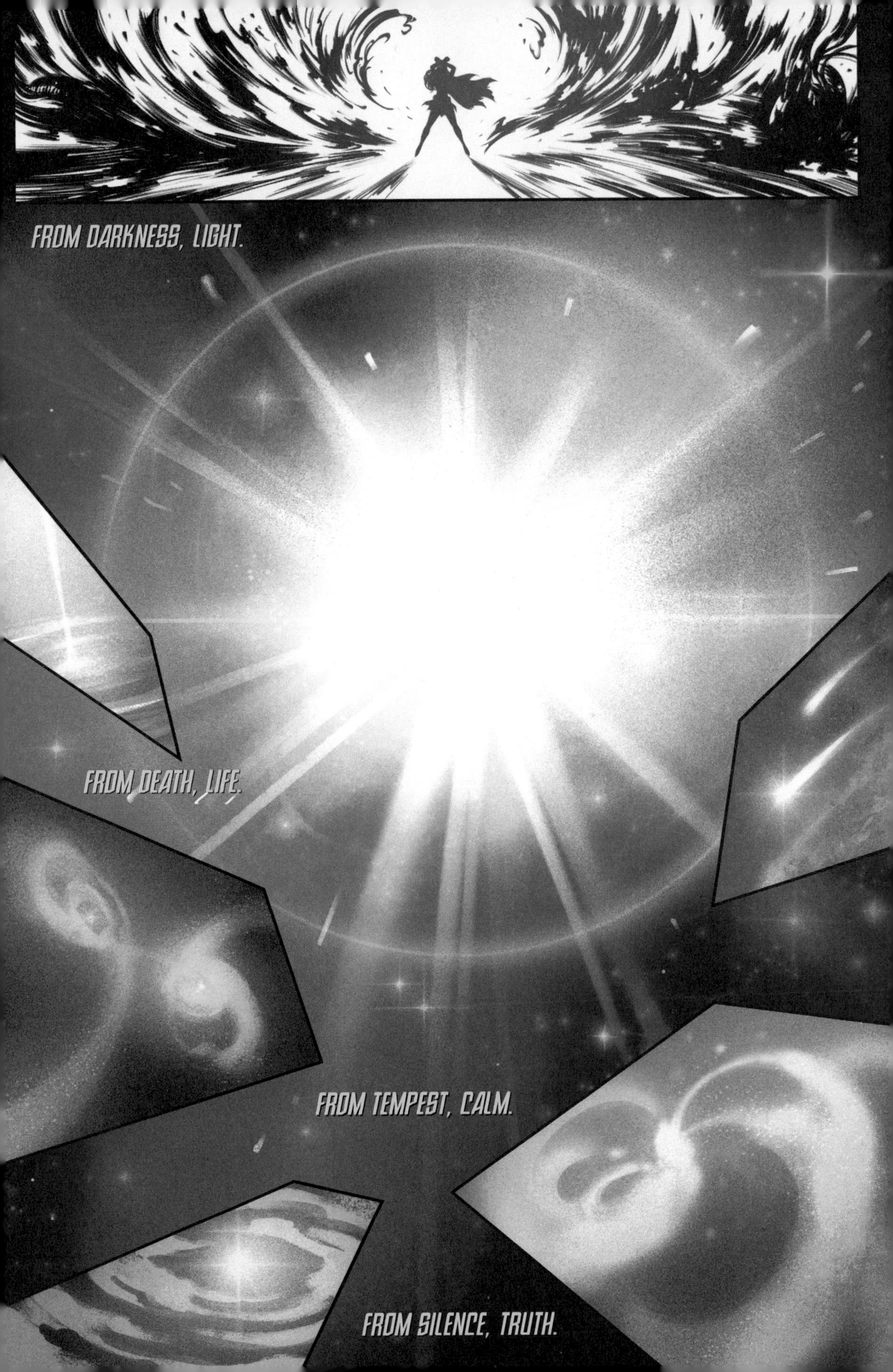
FROM DARKNESS, LIGHT.
FROM DEATH, LIFE.
FROM TEMPEST, CALM.
FROM SILENCE, TRUTH.

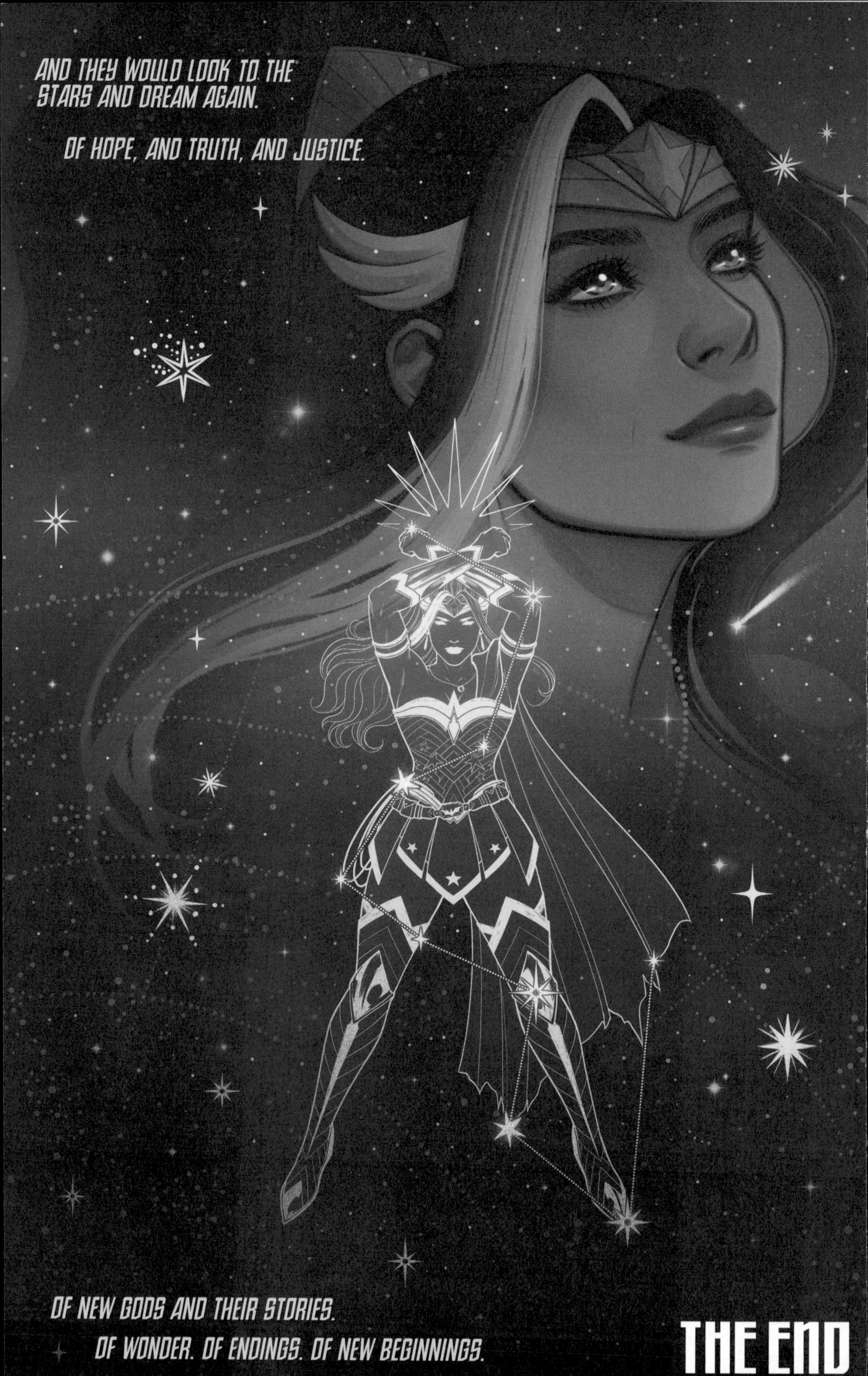
AND THEY WOULD LOOK TO THE STARS AND DREAM AGAIN.
OF HOPE, AND TRUTH, AND JUSTICE.
OF NEW GODS AND THEIR STORIES.
OF WONDER. OF ENDINGS. OF NEW BEGINNINGS.
THE END

Future State: Wonder Woman #1
Variant Cover Art by **JENNY FRISON**

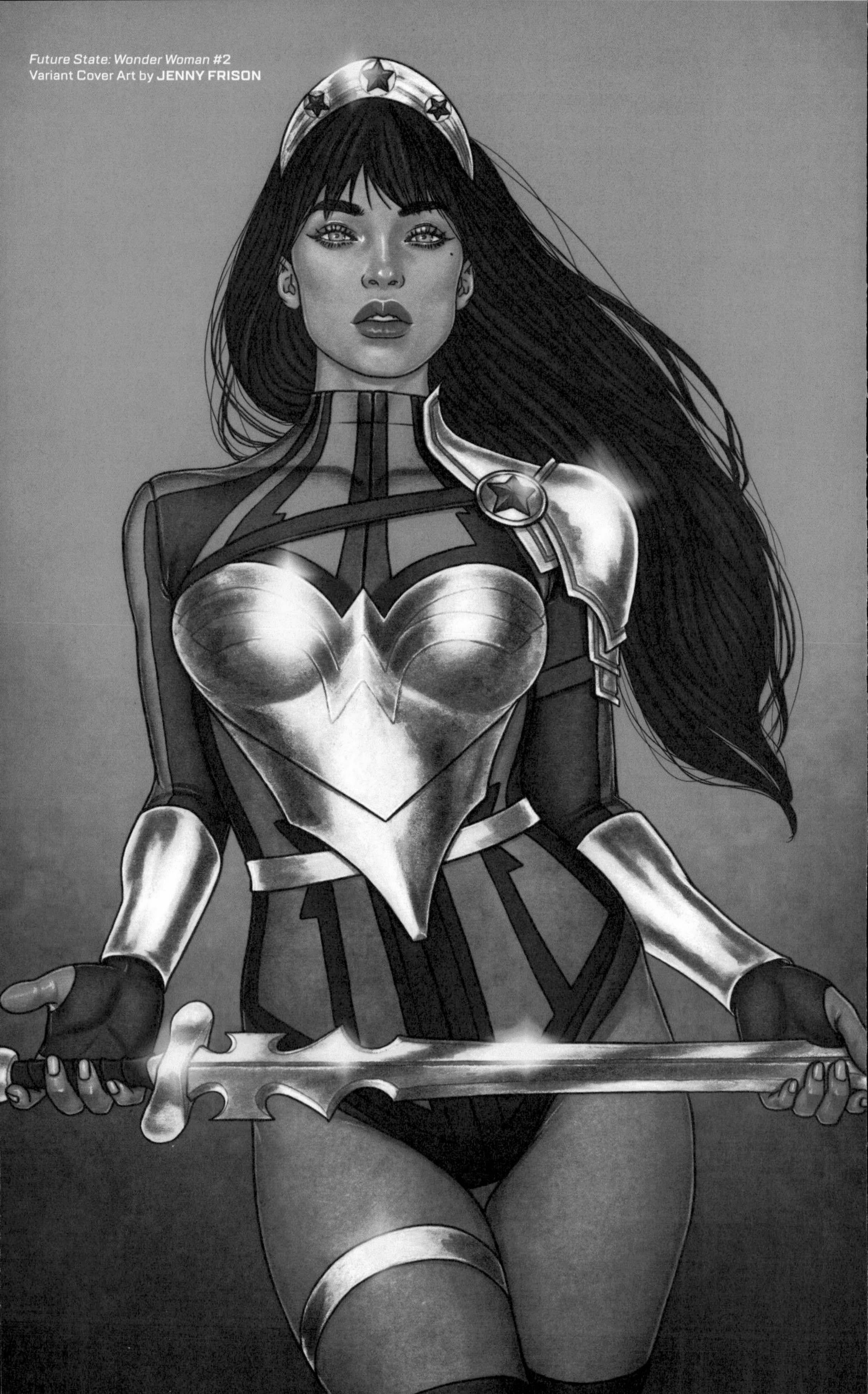

Future State: Wonder Woman #2
Variant Cover Art by **JENNY FRISON**

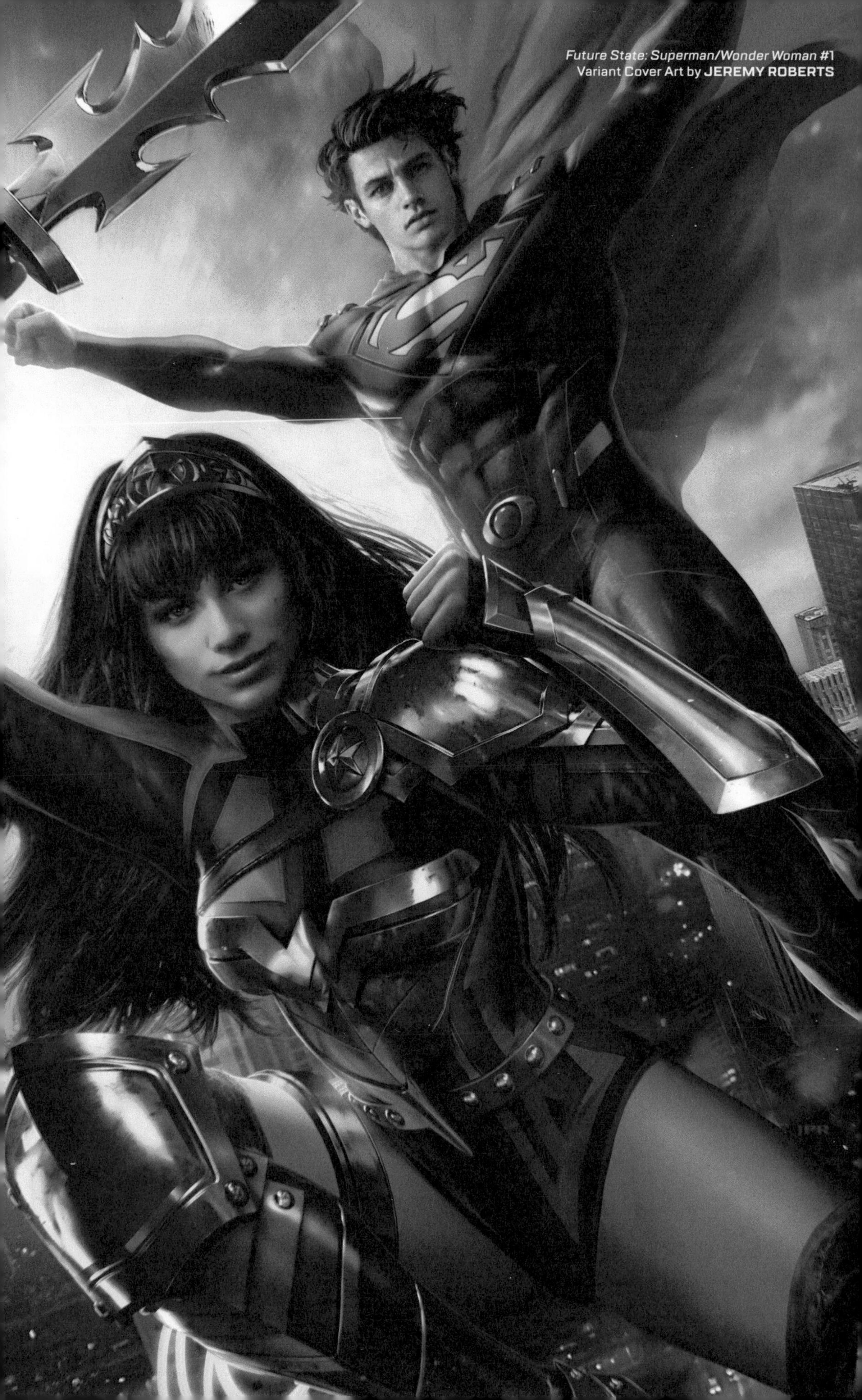
JPR

Future State: Superman/Wonder Woman #1
Variant Cover Art by **JEREMY ROBERTS**

Future State: Superman/Wonder Woman #2
Variant Cover Art by **TERRY DODSON** and **RACHEL DODSON**

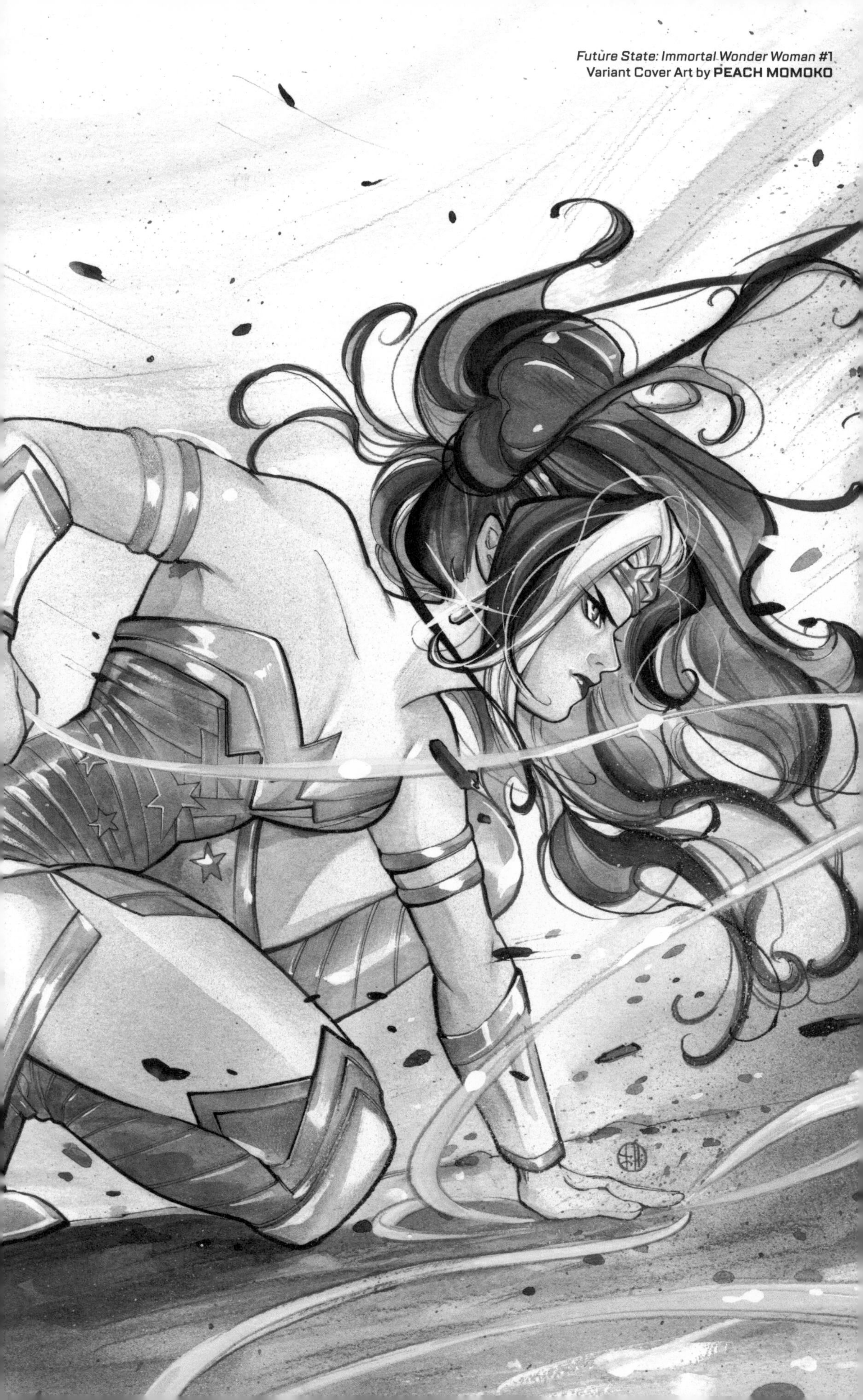

Future State: Immortal Wonder Woman #1
Variant Cover Art by **PEACH MOMOKO**

Future State: Immortal Wonder Woman #2
Variant Cover Art by **BECKY CLOONAN**

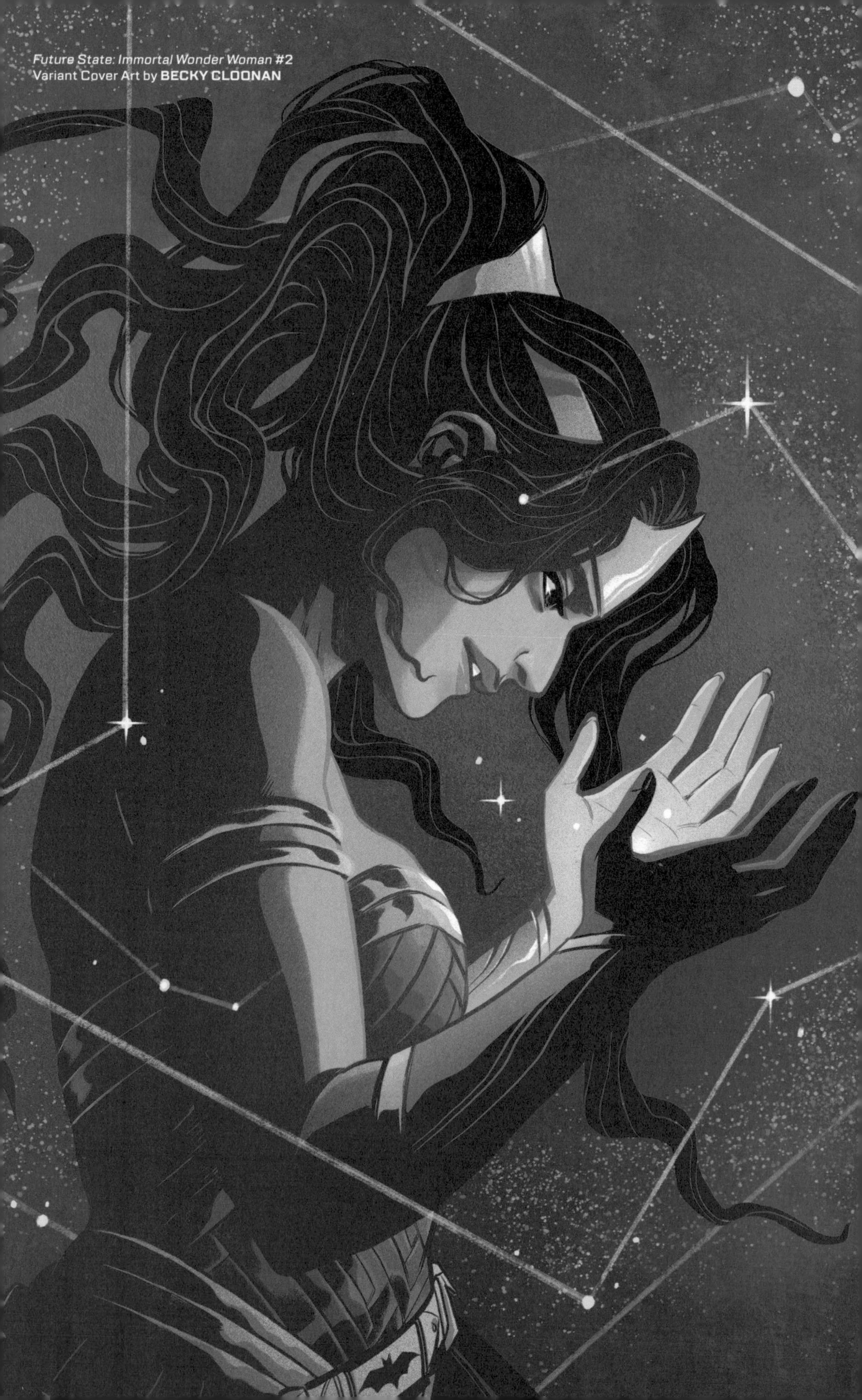

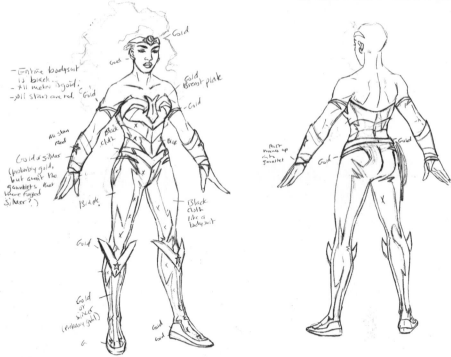

- Entire bodysuit is black.
- All metal is gold.
- All stars are red.

Gold
Gold
Gold breast plate
Gold
Gold
All stars Red
Black cloth
Black
Gold or silver (probably gold, but aren't the gauntlets that were forged silver?)
Blade
Black cloth like a bodysuit
Gold
Gold or silver (probably gold)
G
Gold
Gold

Part mono up into gauntlet
Gold
Gold

Nubia Designs by
ALITHA MARTINEZ

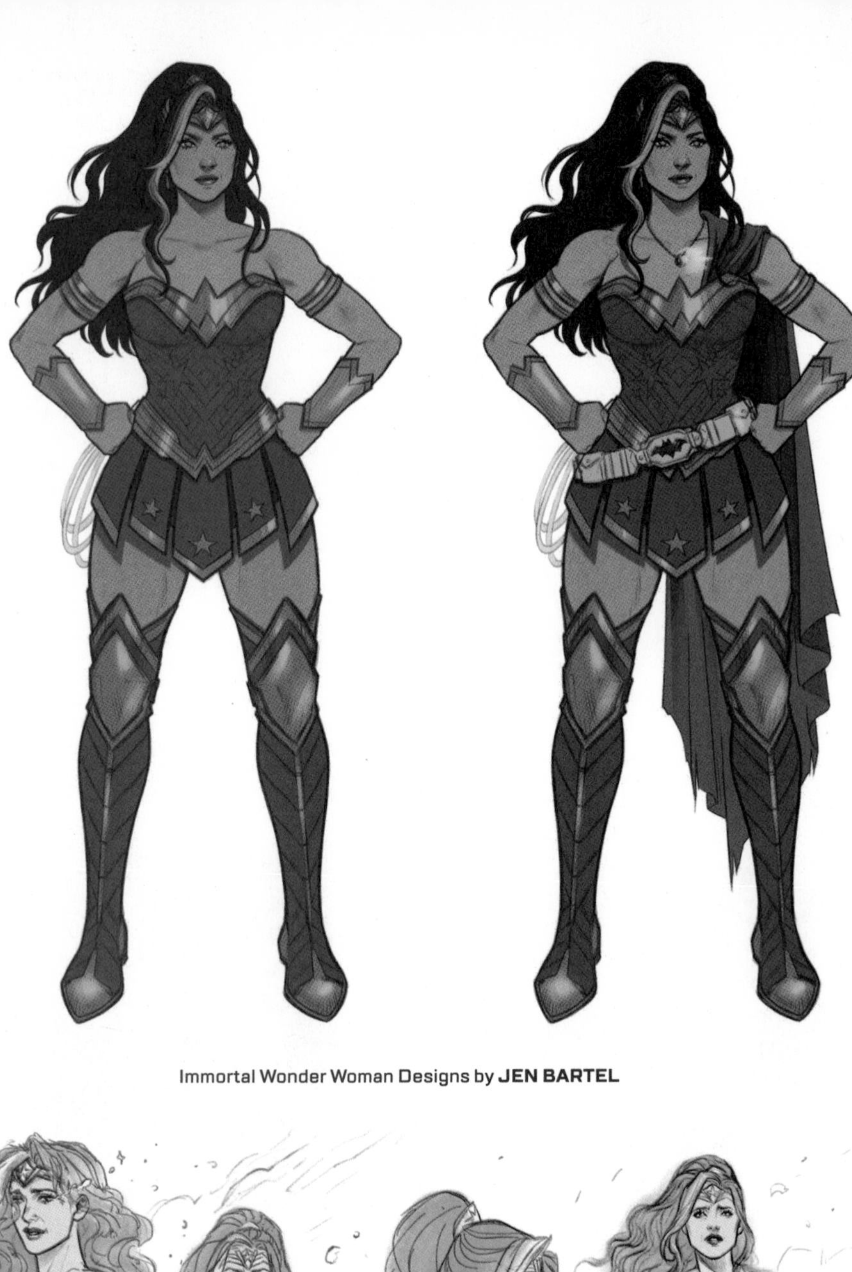

Immortal Wonder Woman Designs by **JEN BARTEL**

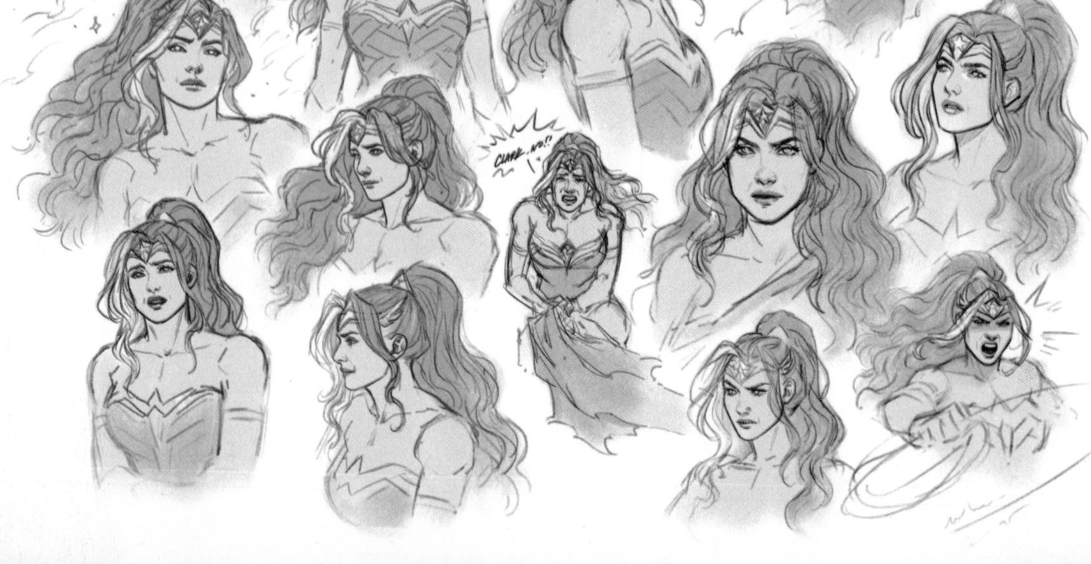
CLARK...NO!?

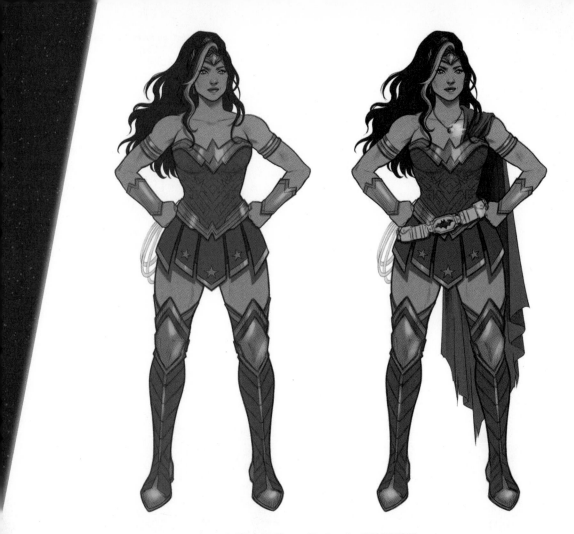

Additional Character Designs by **JEN BARTEL**

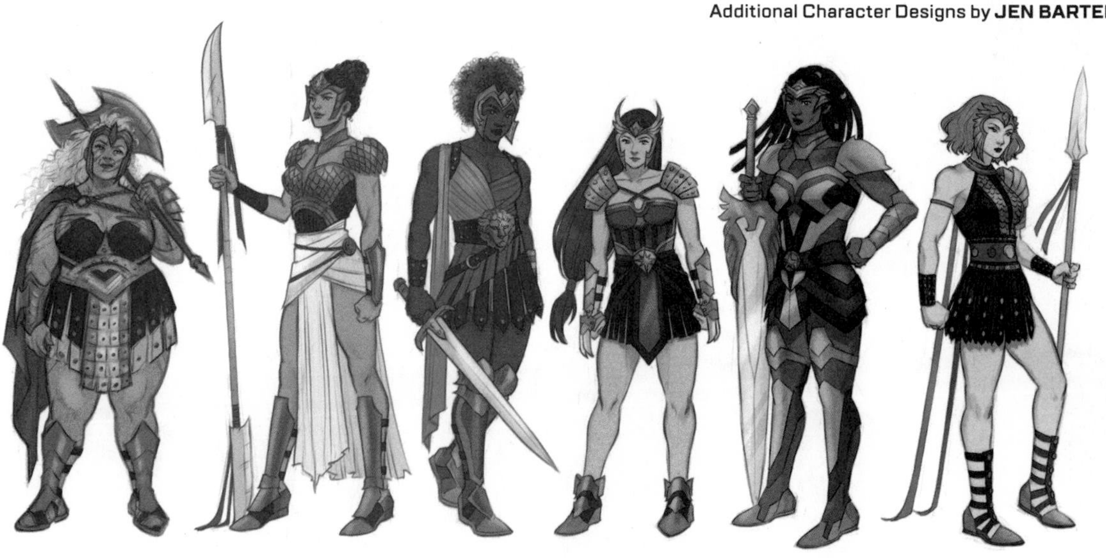

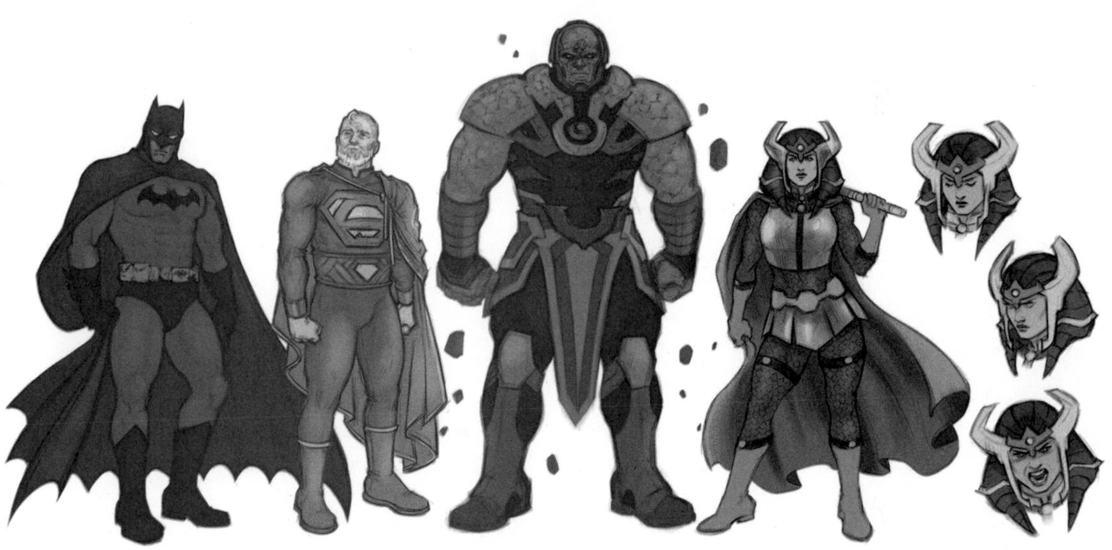

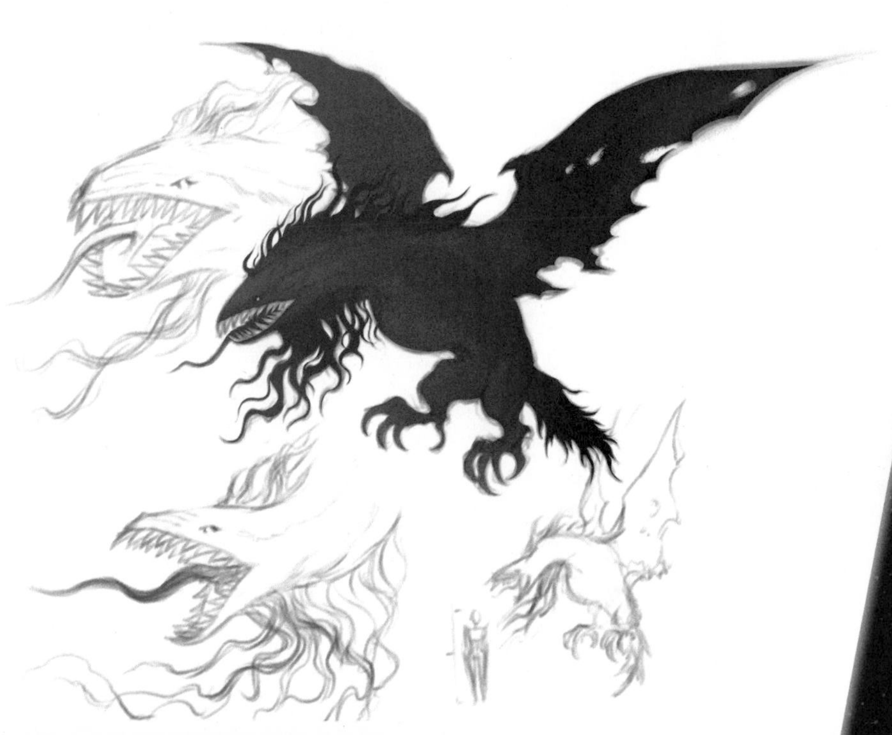

Yara Flor Designs by **JOËLLE JONES**

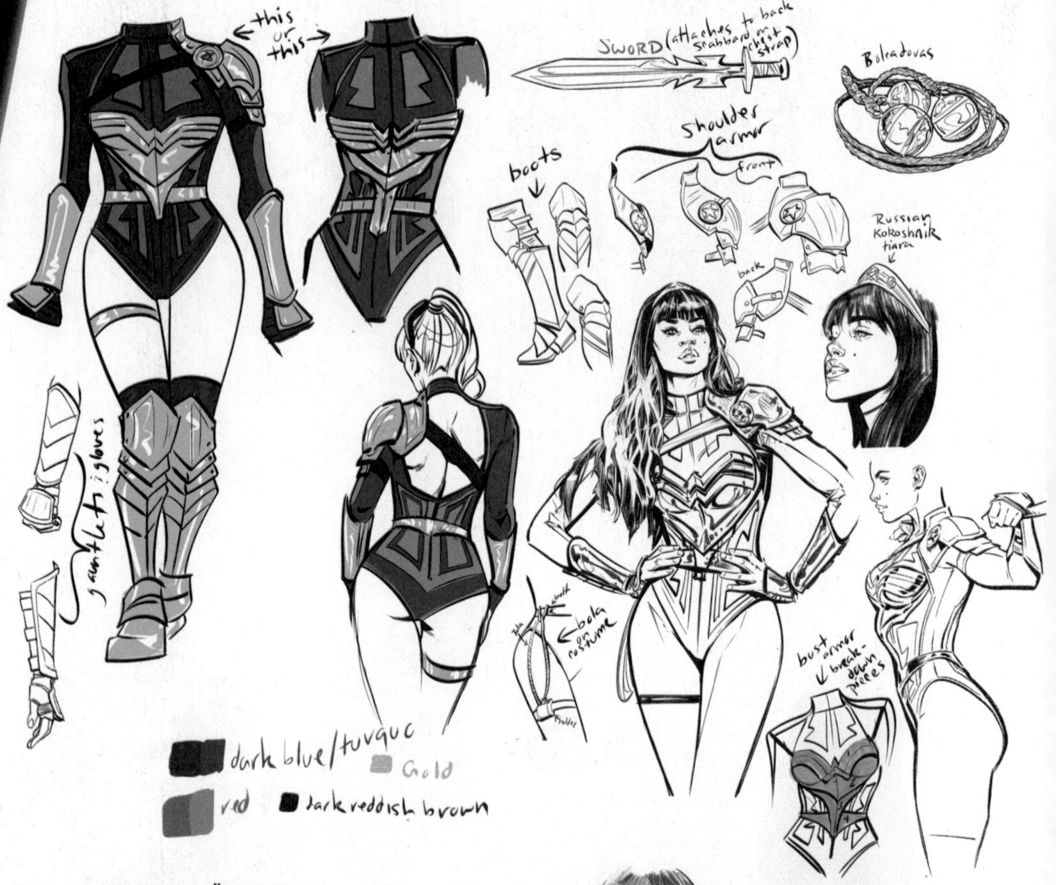
this or this
SWORD (attaches to back scabbard on chest strap)
Boleadoras
shoulder armor
front
back
boots
Russian Koroshnik tiara
gauntlets / gloves
bola on costume
bust armor break-down pieces
dark blue/turquo
Gold
red
dark reddish brown

Caipora Designs by **JOËLLE JONES**

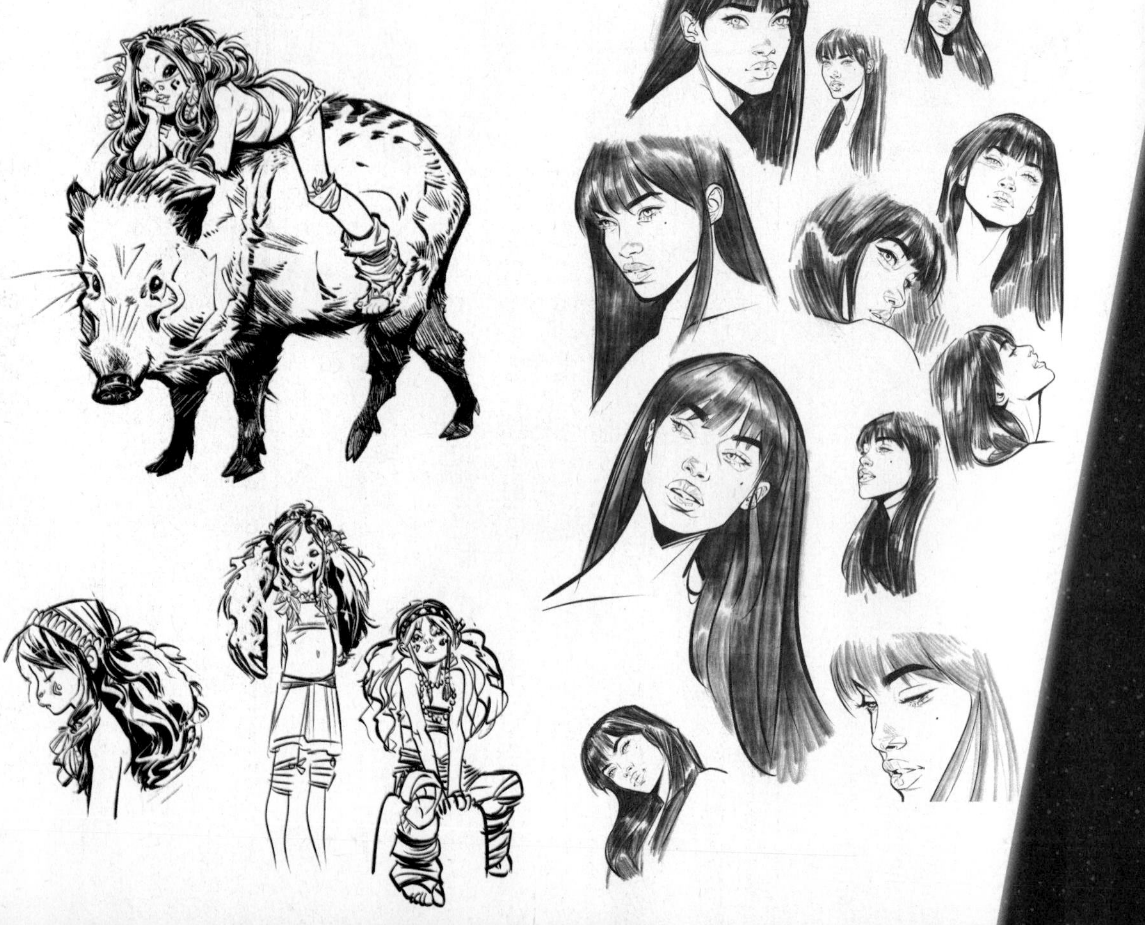